T0385278

STUDIES IN CHRISTIAN HISTORY AND THOUGHT

Edward Irving:

Romantic Theology in Crisis

STUDIES IN CHRISTIAN HISTORY AND THOUGHT

Edward Irving:

Romantic Theology in Crisis

Peter Elliott

First published 2013 by Paternoster

Paternoster is an imprint of Authentic Media
52 Presley Way, Crownhill, Milton Keynes, Bucks, MK8 0ES, UK

www.authenticmedia.co.uk
Authentic Media is a division of Koorong UK, a company limited by guarantee

09 08 07 06 05 04 03 8 7 6 5 4 3 2 1

British Library Cataloguing in Publication Data
A catalogue record for this book is available from the British Library

ISBN 978–1–84227–783-6

Typeset by Peter & Deborah Elliott
Printed and bound in Great Britain
for Paternoster

S

STUDIES IN CHRISTIAN HISTORY AND THOUGHT

Series Preface

This series complements the specialist series of Studies in Evangelical History and Thought and Studies in Baptist History and Thought for which Paternoster is becoming increasingly well known by offering works that cover the wider field of Christian history and thought. It encompasses accounts of Christian witness at various periods, studies of individual Christians and movements, and works which concern the relations of church and society through history, and the history of Christian thought.

The series includes monographs, revised dissertations and theses, and collections of papers by individuals and groups. As well as 'free standing' volumes, works on particular running themes are being commissioned; authors will be engaged for these from around the world and from a variety of Christian traditions.

A high academic standard combined with lively writing will commend the volumes in this series both to scholars and to a wider readership.

STUDIES IN CHRISTIAN HISTORY AND THOUGHT

Table of Contents

Preface

All books are journeys for the author as well as the readers. This book began from my growing fascination with Edward Irving as I lectured in Church History. Here was a man with many characteristics to recommend him: he was noble, a loyal friend, a compassionate pastor and a vibrant and popular preacher. Yet he was, also, surrounded by controversy for his Christology and stance on the charismatic gifts and eventually charged with heresy. As I read about Irving, it became obvious that authors were struggling to understand how someone with Irving's gifts and abilities could end the way he did. None of the answers proposed seemed satisfactory. Eventually, the questions became important enough to me to pursue a PhD on the subject, and that research has become this book.

The journey drew me into Irving's relationship with Romanticism and, especially, his close relationships with Thomas Carlyle and Samuel Taylor Coleridge. These relationships are comprehensively recorded in vibrant primary sources and provide important lenses for viewing Irving and his milieu. Carlyle and Coleridge, both Romantic giants in their own spheres, interacted with Irving's thought extensively and examination of these letters, journals and marginalia reveals much about all three men. Most importantly for the purposes of this book, these sources provide vital information for unravelling some of the long-standing and perplexing questions surrounding Irving, himself.

Acknowledgements

This journey has been enriched by many colleagues and co-travellers. Firstly, my supervisor, Associate Professor Rowan Strong of Murdoch University, who was, also, my supervisor for my Master's degree. Rowan's ability to provide supervision that was both light-hearted and gimlet-eyed as I stumbled through his beloved nineteenth century was immensely encouraging.

I am grateful, also, to Dr. Tim Grass for making available the manuscript of *The Lord's Watchman: Edward Irving* prior to its publication by Paternoster, and to Mrs Barbara Waddington for providing scans of Edward Irving's correspondence.

Along the way, I have been blessed by the generosity of others. In London, I enjoyed the hospitality of Sister Patricia McMahon, a cousin, and her fellow Sisters of Mercy in Tower Hamlets. In Oxford, Richard, Liz and Nat Mortimer graciously lent me their Abingdon home.

Librarians at New College Library in Edinburgh, the British Library and the Bodleian were invariably helpful and efficient. Special thanks to Christopher Hunwick, archivist at Alnwick Castle, Northumberland for allowing free access to the castle archives. To be handling Irving's correspondence in Alnwick Castle in a tower room that was probably the spot where Sir Henry Percy (Harry Hotspur) was born in the mid-fourteenth century (and, coincidentally, above the lawn where a young Harry Potter learnt to fly a broomstick) was a heady privilege indeed. Thanks, also, to His Grace, the Duke of Northumberland, for this opportunity and for permission to use some extracts from the Drummond papers.

Many people along the way have offered encouragement, including staff at Riverview Leadership College, Harvest West Bible College and Vose Seminary (formerly the Baptist Theological College of Western Australia). I would especially like to thank Dr. Michael O'Neil, Dr. Ashley Crane, Dr. Mick Stringer, Dr. Mark Jennings and Robert Andrews in this regard.

Finally, there is my family. My parents, Dorothy and Keith Hill, have been a consistent source of practical help at a time in their lives when they could easily have justified non-involvement. My wife Deborah, yoked to a history-obsessed husband for over a quarter of a century, has demonstrated preternatural patience and support. My sons Joel and Jason, both rapidly leaving childhood behind, seemed to understand not only that I enjoyed this undertaking, but also gradually came to accept that someone my age could still be studying.

All of this demonstrates the truth of John Donne's famous line about no-one being an island. Although Donne wrote this long before the Romantic era, it encapsulates a core Romantic insight about history, as well as the reason for the gratitude I feel towards all those who have contributed to this journey of exploration into the complexities surrounding Edward Irving.

Acknowledgements

Introduction

Edward Irving (1792-1834) was a complex and controversial Church of Scotland minister living at the height of the Romantic period in Britain, so it is little wonder that he has received scholarly attention, a process that has intensified in the last forty years. Faced with Irving's complexity it is, also, understandable that scholars have generally chosen to focus on certain aspects of his career and/or theology; to do otherwise would have been to undertake a daunting multi-volume work. Therefore, some have focused on Irving's Christology, others on his millennialism or his interest in the charismata; still others have attempted biography with less of a theological focus. In some of these works, mention is made that Irving was a Romantic, but this has not been an aspect that has been explored in depth. David Bebbington's 1989 publication first alerted me to the Irving-Romanticism nexus, and piqued my curiosity to explore further.[1]

Both Irving's contemporaries and more recent scholars have noted his strengths, for example, his preaching ability, lofty vision for the Church, and his indefatigable pastoral efforts. The same scholars have, also, identified faults, but as we shall see, they share a suspicion that these faults were not sufficient to explain subsequent events adequately. This book proposes an answer to the question that has haunted Irving scholars, namely, how could someone with such promise end up isolated, relegated and dead at forty-two? I will argue that Irving's Romanticism was a unifying factor informing and creating his theological distinctives and explore ways in which Irving's Romantic convictions precipitated the various crises he faced during his ministerial career.

We begin by surveying the historiography of Romanticism and religion in Britain during the period of Irving's lifetime, drawing primarily from the scholarship of the past forty years. Romanticism proves an elusive beast, but gaining some understanding of it and its potential affinities with religion is essential for understanding Irving. After chapters surveying Irving's life and historiography, chapters four and five offer an extended journey into primary sources. Irving had significant friendships with two giants of nineteenth century British Romanticism: Samuel Taylor Coleridge and Thomas Carlyle. Coleridge made many references to Irving in his notebooks, marginalia and correspondence, and this is the first time these sources have been comprehensively examined for the purpose of establishing the details of the poet-philosopher's relationship with Irving. Coleridge was twenty years

---

[1] D. Bebbington, *Evangelicalism in Modern Britain: a History from the 1730s to the 1980s* (London: Unwin Hyman, 1989), 78ff.

Irving's senior, but they shared a profound commitment to the Christian Church.

The letters of Thomas and Jane Carlyle give us another lens through which to see Irving. This lens has a specifically Scottish tint and is set in the context of a life-long friendship and a romantic triangle, but little sympathy for theological pursuits. Irving's Romanticism emerges more clearly through the affinities and disagreements in these relationships. The Coleridge and Carlyle sources contribute a great deal to our understanding of Irving's personality and Romanticism, and, also, indicate something of the diversity within British Romanticism as a whole.

The sixth chapter examines the comprehensive Romanticism underlying Irving's theological distinctives and the final chapter shows how Irving's dogged pursuit of his Romantic convictions contributed to the ministerial crises of his life. Irving's Romanticism emerges as fundamental and axiomatic to his worldview.

This examination of Irving's Romanticism will not only demonstrate Irving's own motivations but will, also, show that he had a significant impact on Coleridge's theological views and that he was at the forefront of integrating Christian theology within a Romantic worldview.

CHAPTER 1

The Historiography of Romanticism and Religion in England and Scotland, 1789-1834

It has become virtually compulsory for works on Romanticism to begin by acknowledging the difficulty in defining the term, one calling it "a notoriously slippery concept".[1] While the reasons for this will emerge during this historiographical survey, it is worth noting at the outset that despite these difficulties, scholars persevere with the term due to the conviction that despite its elusiveness and complexity, it remains useful for expressing certain significant characteristics of the period between 1785 and 1832. While these years are usually seen as the core Romantic period, the years 1789-1834 have been chosen with reference to the life of Edward Irving: 1789, the year of the French Revolution, is a landmark in the development of Romanticism and Irving was born shortly afterwards; 1834 is the year of Irving's death. The majority of this chapter will focus on England. Developments there, also, affected Scotland, but distinctively Scottish characteristics will be noted at the end of the chapter.

A large part of the problem with defining Romanticism is its complexity: numerous characteristics are described as "romantic" and many contemporaries exhibited some, but not all of these. "Romanticism is problematic," Boyd Hilton wrote (with specific reference to the political and religious diversity amongst the canonical Romantic poets), "partly because it is so capacious."[2] The issue becomes one of taxonomy: too narrow a definition would result in very few "Romantics"; too wide a definition would enlist a diversity that would render the term meaningless. The latter has been seen as a real risk: in the middle of the twentieth century, A.O. Lovejoy argued that Romanticism's very inclusiveness had resulted in the term meaning "nothing".[3] More recently, explicitly affirming Lovejoy's conclusion, M. Brown alleged it is impossible to

---

[1] I. McCalman (ed.), *An Oxford Companion to the Romantic Age: British Culture 1776-1832* (Oxford: Oxford University Press, 1999), 1.

[2] B. Hilton, *A Mad, Bad and Dangerous People? : England, 1783-1846* (Oxford: Oxford University Press, 2006), 487. The canonical Romantic poets are Blake, Wordsworth, Coleridge, Shelley, Byron and Keats.

[3] A.O. Lovejoy, *Essays in the History of Ideas* (Baltimore, ML: Johns Hopkins Press, 1970. Orig. 1948), 232.

define Romanticism.[4] Yet, as noted above, most scholars want to persevere with the term, even if some do so grudgingly, because they recognise that it attempts to describe an important cultural shift which cannot be ignored.[5] Others, less peeved at the term's coquettishness, value its very elusiveness as a key characteristic, as, for example, Søren Kierkegaard: "I must first protest against the notion that romanticism can be enclosed within a concept; for romantic means precisely that it oversteps all bounds."[6] Clearly, taxonomies and definitions must be approached with great care in this case.

Contemporaries realised that a new sensibility had arrived in the early nineteenth century; they, also, recognised immediately the difficulty in defining it. In 1801, Louis Mercier attempted to compile a *Neology*, or *Vocabulary of New Words*. When he came to "romantic", he said a definition should not be attempted – it should be felt![7] A slightly later, but more substantive example of awareness of the Romantic mood was literary critic William Hazlitt's collection of individual portraits which had first been published in the *New Monthly Magazine* under the title 'Spirits of the age'. When issued in a single volume in 1825, the title was altered to *The Spirit of the Age*, implying the existence of a recognisable *zeitgeist* to which those characterised contributed, either positively or negatively. Hazlitt fought desperately against his society's acceptance of Utilitarian principles, which he felt had taken morality and imagination captive.[8] On the positive side, he felt that had Wordsworth (whom Hazlitt praised as an exemplar of the spirit of the age) appeared in any other period, it would have been incapable of recognising his genius.[9] While we may suspect exaggeration on Hazlitt's part, this shows just how distinct Hazlitt felt his own age was from all its predecessors – it was the *only* period with the ability to perceive Wordsworth's gifts. The clear suggestion is that there had been a fundamental shift in culture and perception. Although Hazlitt used the word "romantic" frequently in this work, he did not attempt a formal definition, yet in his treatment of Wordsworth, he does give us some insight into what he saw as distinctive about this new "spirit". To Hazlitt, this spirit was innovative, embracing the revolutionary political views of the day and thereby giving voice to egalitarianism; derived from this was the view that the heart and the imagination can perceive meaning in the apparently trivial.[10]

---

[4] M. Brown, "Romanticism and Enlightenment" in Curran, S. (ed.), *The Cambridge Companion to British Romanticism* (Cambridge: Cambridge University Press, 1993), 25.

[5] B. Lenman, *Integration, Enlightenment, and Industrialization: Scotland 1746-1832* (London: Edward Arnold, 1981), 130-131.

[6] B.M.G. Reardon, *Religion in the Age of Romanticism: Studies in Early Nineteenth-Century Thought* (Cambridge: Cambridge University Press, 1985), 1. Original reference not given.

[7] McCalman, *An Oxford Companion,* 1.

[8] J. Whale, *Imagination under Pressure, 1789-1832: Aesthetics, Politics and Utility* (Cambridge: Cambridge University Press, 2000), 137.

[9] W. Hazlitt, *The Spirit of the Age* (Oxford: Woodstock Books, 1989), 231.

[10] Hazlitt, *The Spirit of the Age*, 233, 236.

Mercier and Hazlitt were by no means isolated in their perception that a substantial change of sensibility and culture had taken place. This was the generation that lived through the American Revolution, the French Revolution, the Napoleonic wars and the beginnings of the Industrial Revolution: the ensuing recalibration of the roles of monarchy and empire, government and the individual was both disorienting and intoxicating. The rapid societal changes experienced during these years were unavoidable and invited reflection: "Never before, John Stuart Mill observed in the *Examiner* in 1831, had the notion of comparing one's own time with earlier epochs been *the* dominant idea of an age. Contemporaries sensed, and often said, that they were part of a second cultural Renaissance."[11]

Having noted both the contemporary conviction that a "new spirit" had arrived during this period and the difficulty in defining Romanticism, the remainder of this chapter will survey the work of recent writers on Romanticism and religion, then draw on this material to draft a working description of Romanticism; in the meantime, we will continue to use this mercurial term, in anticipation that it will gain substance as we progress.

In 1965, Isaiah Berlin gave an influential series of lectures on Romanticism which remained unpublished for thirty years.[12] Although religion was not a major part of Berlin's focus, he acknowledged that the Pietist movement in Germany was really the "root" of Romanticism.[13] In the context of discussing Byron, Berlin saw Romanticism as both an expression of "a terrible unsatisfied desire to soar into infinity" and a challenge to the Enlightenment premise that neat and non-contradictory answers exist to all legitimate questions.[14] Romanticism drew on the Kantian revulsion against authority for its own sake, and his corresponding elevation of the primacy of the will.[15] Romantics did not accept imposed authority, but moulded and created their own vision of what could be.[16] Eschewing neat definitions, Romantics embraced myth and symbol as the only legitimate ways of expressing the inexpressible.[17] Romanticism was inherently subversive of the status quo, eager to shed the current skin in order to become something more.[18] In its rejection of Enlightenment "neatness" and classicism, Romanticism embraced diversity, plurality and complexity.[19] This meant that Romantics admired those who struggled for ideals, whether they could personally agree with them or not: sincerity and authenticity became

---

[11] McCalman, *An Oxford Companion*, 5. The exact reference in the *Examiner* is not given.

[12] The reason for such a delay was that Berlin planned to issue a formal work on the subject; he never achieved this and the lectures were published posthumously in 1999.

[13] I. Berlin, *The Roots of Romanticism* (Princeton: Princeton University Press, 1999), 36.

[14] Berlin, *The Roots of Romanticism*, 15, 21-22.

[15] Berlin, *The Roots of Romanticism*, 77-78.

[16] Berlin, *The Roots of Romanticism*, 116, 119.

[17] Berlin, *The Roots of Romanticism*, 121.

[18] Berlin, *The Roots of Romanticism*, 135.

[19] Berlin, *The Roots of Romanticism*, 138.

virtues.[20] The natural result of all this diversity and idealistic striving was disagreement, which was to be expected. Berlin noted the recurring Romantic theme of "the outcast, the exile, the superman, the man who cannot put up with the existing world because his soul is too large to contain it, because he has ideals which presuppose the necessity for perpetual fervent movement forward, movement which is constantly confined by the stupidity and the unimaginativeness and the flatness of the existing world."[21] While Berlin's focus was not specifically on religious aspects, his profile of Romanticism certainly shows how it can fit comfortably within a Christian context, with its explicit yearning for a greater reality than is offered by this world.

In the early 1970s, one of the most influential recent works on Romanticism appeared: M.H. Abrams's *Natural Supernaturalism*. Although his focus was primarily on the literary aspects of Romanticism, Abrams suggested a thesis about the relationship between Romanticism and religion that became widely accepted. After the customary acknowledgement that Romanticism is a "conventional though ambiguous term", Abrams sketched a general context for the emergence of the movement.[22] He saw that from the 1780s onwards, certain intellectual leaders concluded that Enlightenment-driven analysis had led to a worldview that was reductionistic, mechanistic and alienating.[23] The Romantic response to the perceived inadequacies of the Enlightenment was to reforge religious elements into a secular framework. Abrams saw Romantics taking concepts which had originated theologically (e.g. the relationship between God and humanity) and essentially reworking them to eliminate the divine element. The relationships Romantics focused on were those between subject and object, consciousness and emotion, humanity and nature.[24] The concept of the "sublime" was present, in which Romantics sensed the numinous and were overwhelmed by their own relative insignificance in the universe. This would have previously been seen as expressive of the individual's awareness of God; now it was secularised to be "intellectually acceptable, as well as emotionally pertinent".[25] There was the implication that orthodox Christian theology was no longer "intellectually acceptable" to Romantics.

Whatever shortcomings Abrams's Romantics saw in the Enlightenment, it is obvious from their activities as sketched above, that they were also children of the Enlightenment. Religion became an object of observation and dissection, and (buying into the Enlightenment myth of the detached observer) the Romantic observer had little doubt of his own ability to discern the

---

[20] In this, as Berlin points out, Romanticism is the natural predecessor of existentialism. Berlin, *The Roots of Romanticism*, 139.

[21] Berlin, *The Roots of Romanticism*, 133.

[22] M.H. Abrams, *Natural Supernaturalism: Tradition and Revolution in Romantic Literature* (New York: W.W. Norton & Co., 1971), 12.

[23] Abrams, *Natural Supernaturalism*, 170-171.

[24] Abrams, *Natural Supernaturalism*, 13.

[25] Abrams, *Natural Supernaturalism*, 66.

"intellectually acceptable" and to reconstitute it into a more valid form. Abrams argued that this Romantic reworking either greatly diminished or completely eliminated the role of God (obviously dependent on the individual Romantic's personal convictions): what remained were "man and the world, mind and nature, the ego and the non-ego, the self and the not-self".[26]

There were scholars who saw Romanticism as an abnormal expression of a religious impulse that had been suppressed by rationalism, such as T.E. Hulme, who defined Romanticism as a "mess" of "spilt religion"; Abrams disagreed – at least about motivation, if not result – seeing this tendency as a noble Romantic struggle rather than a weakness.[27] To Abrams, the Romantics grappled to find meaning in their world which was beset by war, rapid industrialisation, urbanisation and social dislocation; in this context "the inherited pieties and integrative myths seemed no longer adequate to hold civilization together".[28] The implication was that religion was supposed to provide cohesion in society and a means of adequately understanding contemporary events; its perceived failure in these areas led to its wide-spread rejection. One response to this increasingly complex world was a determined, if not dejected, solitude, encompassing the internalisation of what had once been communal. The generation which had seen the rise and fall of political revolution turned instead to the more controllable and quietistic revolution of new worlds of the imagination.[29] This fostered a culture of individual diversity: the concept of a single Creator had apparently proved inadequate for the spirit of this new age and had therefore been eclipsed; human *creators* were in the ascendant. Abrams's secularising Romantics used Enlightenment tools to excise what they wanted from their theological heritage, and, travelling light, arrived at a frontier of the imagination beyond which there were few landmarks and where any religious motifs retained were only symbols to new creative ends. What had proved adequate in the old age was inadequate in the new.

Also writing in the 1970s, Bernard Reardon acknowledged, as we have come to expect, that Romanticism "defies precise characterization".[30] He noted the overwhelming impact of the French Revolution on English political and religious thought, and that one of the responses to the Reign of Terror was a re-evaluation of the role of reason. This perception that the excesses of reason resulted in disillusionment led to one of the main interpretations of Romanticism – that it was a reaction against rationalism and formalism.[31]

---

[26] Abrams, *Natural Supernaturalism*, 91.

[27] T.E. Hulme, *Speculations: Essays on Humanism and the Philosophy of Art* (London: Routledge & Kegan Paul, 1971. Orig. 1924), 118; Abrams, *Natural Supernaturalism*, 68.

[28] Abrams, *Natural Supernaturalism*, 292-293.

[29] Abrams, *Natural Supernaturalism*, 338.

[30] B.M.G. Reardon, *Religious Thought in the Victorian Age: a Survey from Coleridge to Gore* (London: Longman, 1980. Orig. 1971), 9.

[31] Reardon, *Victorian Age*, 92.

Whereas Abrams's chief interest was in the Romantic secularisation of the religious impulse, Reardon noted ways in which religious life contained and embraced Romanticism. He saw Friedrich Schleiermacher, for instance, channelling Romanticism and imaginative perception when he wrote, "The feelings, the feelings alone, provide the elements of religion."[32] Reardon saw other Romantics, such as Coleridge, echoing similar sentiments when he insisted that "man's felt need" was what validated Christianity.[33] This inward authentication and validation of religious truth was the corollary of the rejection, or at least marginalisation, of the idea that religion consisted of a formal set of doctrines to which assent was required; in keeping with the anti-authoritarianism of the times, this was now seen as, at best, unnecessary and, at worst, repressive.[34] Romanticism represented a "dissatisfaction with the 'reality' of the surface of things, a reality which in the age of the Enlightenment was too readily taken for the whole".[35] Thus, while Abrams's thesis suggested that Romanticism pointed towards agnostic or atheistic existentialism, Reardon highlighted other possibilities.

Stephen Prickett, publishing in the late 1970s and early 1980s, argued that Romantics opposed the earlier empirical trend which saw the mind as passive; instead, they adapted Kantian concepts to claim that the mind was active in creating perception from the available sense-data. This eliminated the assumed disjunction between the self and the external world.[36] But, instead of following Abrams's suggestion that this creative Romantic imagination was secularising, Prickett argued that Romantics saw humanity as essentially "spiritual", rather than physical and mechanistic.[37] He credited the Methodists with a significant preliminary role in this Romantic reassertion of humanity as spiritual.[38] While poets and philosophers contributed to this renewed spiritual perspective, Prickett insisted that "It is not merely a philosophic or aesthetic truth, but a *religious* one to assert that 'the law of the imagination is a law of fellowship or intercommunion with nature'."[39] In other words, given Romanticism's intense interest in both imagination and nature, any attempt to excise the religious element was misguided and doomed to failure.

---

[32] Reardon, *Victorian Age*, 10. The original source in Schleiermacher is not given.

[33] Reardon, *Victorian Age,* 10. The original source in Coleridge is not given, but the statement dates from the 1820s.

[34] Reardon, *Victorian Age*, 10.

[35] B.M.G. Reardon, "Religion and the Romantic movement", in *Theology*, lxxvi, no. 638. August 1973, 404.

[36] S. Prickett, *Romanticism and Religion: the Tradition of Coleridge and Wordsworth in the Victorian Church* (Cambridge: Cambridge University Press, 1976), 100.

[37] Prickett, *Romanticism*, 132.

[38] S. Prickett, "The religious context" in S. Prickett, (ed.), *The Romantics* (New York: Holmes & Meier, 1981), 129-130.

[39] Prickett, "The religious context", 131. Emphasis original. The quote appears to be from F.D. Maurice, but the source is not given.

Nevertheless, there was a Romantic critique of certain aspects of organised religion that reflected disdain for inherited religious affirmations: "In a peculiar kind of way, Romanticism is rooted in the felt tension between moribund religious institutions and the reaction of *believers* against them."[40] Romantics then, often remained believers; the criticisms they levelled at the Church and Christianity were not so much those of militant iconoclasts, breathing the heady air of an atheistic new age, but of stakeholders identifying faults as a means towards renewal. Yet the ideals the Church fell short of, and against which it was judged by the Romantics, were Christian, not secular. Unlike Abrams, Prickett concluded that Romanticism was "primarily a religious phenomenon".[41] In a much later work, Prickett argued that those Romantics who retained a robust Christian faith did so at a time when the surrounding society had lost the strong sense of a communal religious world-view. The days of a unified collective religious sensibility had passed, and devotion appeared increasingly idiosyncratic.[42] This later work nuanced the earlier one: the impression is that the religious impulse Prickett saw underlying Romanticism was now more diffuse and individualistic.

If we accept Prickett's premise that the Romantic age experienced this sense of loss of a comprehensive, communal religious world-view, when exactly did this loss take place? Prickett seems to describe a lost medievalism, waning from the time of Renaissance humanism, looking decidedly unwell at the Reformation, and given last rites at the Enlightenment, rather than a phenomenon specific to the Romantic period. Given the length of the "illness", it seems unlikely that the Romantic generation was sufficiently devastated at the drawn-out passing of this collective religious culture to feel compelled to pursue idiosyncratic pieties. Prickett ascribed a negative motivation to the Romantic subjectivisation of religious truth, but we have already noted more positive, and far more likely, motivations. However, even if the Romantics pursued their personal religious visions from positive motives, was there anything to prevent their noble pursuit degenerating from idiosyncratic to irrelevant?

Writing at the same time as Prickett's earlier works, and with a particular focus on Scotland, Bruce Lenman took a stance reminiscent of Abrams. After the now-customary acknowledgement of Romanticism as an imprecise but essential term, Lenman argued that it drew from a new liberal and essentially secular view of humanity which was individualistic and emotional.[43] Like Abrams, he saw little place for religion in Romanticism, although it seems that at the beginning of the 1980s, Lenman was one of the few still reflecting the secularising Abrams tradition of the previous decade.

---

[40] Prickett, "The religious context", 121. Emphasis original.

[41] Prickett, "The religious context", 143.

[42] S. Prickett, *Origins of Narrative: the Romantic Appropriation of the Bible* (Cambridge: Cambridge University Press, 1996), 152-153.

[43] Lenman, *Integration, Enlightenment, and Industrialization*, 130-131.

By way of contrast, a few years later, Bernard Reardon saw the foremost distinguishing feature of "the Romantic understanding of Christianity [as] its subjectivization of all religious truth".[44] This subjectivisation arose from the loss of absolute points of reference, and the resulting sense that each individual and event was completely unique.[45] This uniqueness was not seen as artificially insulated from what had preceded it. The Romantic view of history saw each age as significant, with tradition expressing "the truth of permanence in fluidity".[46] From the time of the Renaissance through to Enlightenment writers such as Gibbon, history had often been seen as the chronological conduit through which humanity had arrived at its present enlightened state, and it could be useful as a source of tutelary examples, but little else.[47] If history was regarded primarily as a textbook for practical guidance, it produced a degree of dissociation: reason could view itself as separate from the roiling waters of historical circumstance. The Romantics had moved on from this Enlightenment myth of the detached and passive observer to the point where all observers were seen not only as participants but creators of perception, thus diminishing the subject-object distance. It is logical then, that Romantics felt this attraction to history in which they were both actors and acted-upon, but it is, also, ironic that they would have affection for tradition in an age characterised by discontinuity and revolutionary breaks with the past. In a religious context, this affection tended to focus on the idealisation of either the early Church period or the later middle ages, before the Protestant Reformation. What was there, though, to prevent this subjectivisation from fragmenting into increasingly idiosyncratic, eccentric (if creative), and even irreligious forms, as indicated by Abrams and Lenman? Where was the communal element in the religion of the Romantic age?

In 1989, David Bebbington described Romanticism as "the movement of taste that stressed, against the mechanism and classicism of the Enlightenment, the place of feeling and intuition in human perception, the importance of nature and history for human experience," and described the movement as having "immense potential affinity for religion".[48] He noted that Romanticism influenced all streams of Christianity in Britain: Broad and High Church and Evangelicalism; part of this influence was to heighten expectations of the Second Advent.[49] Bebbington argued that under this new *zeitgeist*, there was nothing unusual in expecting a divine intervention in the midst of everyday life (as opposed to the gradual, cause and effect expectations of the previous age) and focus on the Second Advent was particularly attractive to the spirit of the

---

[44] Reardon, *Religion in the Age of Romanticism*, 10.
[45] Reardon, *Religion,* 6.
[46] Reardon, *Religion*, 11-12.
[47] J. Chandler, "History" in McCalman, *An Oxford Companion*, 355.
[48] D.W. Bebbington, *Evangelicalism in Modern Britain: a History from the 1730s to the 1980s* (London: Unwin Hyman, 1989), 81.
[49] Bebbington, *Evangelicalism in Modern Britain*, 81, 84.

age which chafed under some Enlightenment views.[50] Expectations of the Second Advent became "a symptom of Romanticism".[51] Although Bebbington acknowledged the influence of "the alarming political events of the times" on early nineteenth century religion, he, nevertheless, believed that Romanticism was the most significant influence on Evangelicalism amounting to a "transformation . . . in the years around 1830".[52] The previously-mentioned affinity between Romanticism and religion was a dual-carriageway of influence.

David Simpson, writing in the early 1990s, saw Romanticism as continuing a trend that began with the Protestant Reformation of elevating the individual's desire for spiritual breakthrough above all other concerns.

> In these formulations Romanticism is governed by a sense of the inadequate fit between the real and the apparent, heaven and earth. It is thus governed by struggle (between soul and body, content and form) and by desire (for something always still to come). It imposes not the peace of being or understanding, but the anxiety of becoming and wondering.[53]

In this quote, we can see several factors aligning: there is the "immense potential affinity for religion" noted by Bebbington; the sense of isolation combined with internal and external struggles; and the angst resulting from a less-than-ideal reality.

In the same volume, Marshall Brown claimed that although there is much in Romanticism that can be seen as a reaction against the Enlightenment – for example its emphasis on strong emotion, intuition and imagination; its fascination with the past; its ready embrace of mystery - there was, also, continuity in areas such as tolerance. Brown saw Romanticism as "the fulfilment and awakening of Enlightenment", rather than the repudiation of it.[54]

Robert Ryan placed the Romantics into the wider context of the developing sense of British identity in a time of social turmoil, which he believed was strongly tinged by eschatological hopes and religious debate.[55] What contribution did the Romantics bring to this religious and social turmoil? Ryan believed they were primarily subversive of those religious beliefs that were seen as "coercive and obscurantist" and primarily on a quest to discover and promote religious concepts that were deemed "more psychologically

---

[50] Bebbington, *Evangelicalism in Modern Britain*, 84.
[51] Bebbington, *Evangelicalism in Modern Britain*, 85.
[52] Bebbington, *Evangelicalism in Modern Britain*, 103.
[53] D. Simpson, "Romanticism, Criticism and Theory" in Curran, *The Cambridge Companion*, 9.
[54] M. Brown, "Romanticism and Enlightenment" in Curran, *The Cambridge Companion*, 38.
[55] R.M. Ryan, *The Romantic Reformation: Religious Politics in English Literature*, 1789-1824 (Cambridge: Cambridge University Press, 1997), 3.

wholesome and socially beneficent".[56] Ryan's perception of this religio-cultural mission of Romanticism as "primary" clearly contradicted Abrams's view; Ryan, also, opposed Abrams's perception that the Romantics lapsed into disillusionment and despair, claiming instead that Romantics engaged creatively and effectively in the religious tensions of the times.[57]

Ryan maintained that by the 1820s the religious environment was becoming less volatile, and that Romanticism offered "a spirit of religious spontaneity and innovation" which was inherently unsettling and liberalising in its effects and had wider social ramifications.[58] The religious impulse of Romantics then, was not relegated to daffodil-contemplating dilettantes, but contributed to the social and political milieu of the time; it could even be seen as maintaining a revolutionary flame in an age that was jaded with political revolution. In fact, Ryan claimed that far from being peripheral, this "spirit of religious spontaneity and innovation" was central to British Romanticism. Ryan's view of the centrality of religion to Romanticism was diametrically opposed to that of Abrams's secularised view.

In 1999, David Jasper, also, rejected Abrams's concept of Romantic secular theology as "oversimplified".[59] While acknowledging that Romanticism encompassed a profound sense of the disintegration of received assumptions, including religious assumptions, which encouraged the subjectivising of truth, Jasper asserted that Romanticism offered a vision that looked beyond this disintegration to a time of redemption and harmony.[60] This vision, which in religious terms often inclined towards millennialism, also, included a determined search for community that would transcend the sense of fragmentation and alienation.[61] So if, as we have mentioned earlier, communality was often lost in the fragmented Romantic world, its reapprehension became part of the Romantic struggle. Jasper used the words "vision" and "unity" a number of times, underscoring the centrality of these concepts for Romantic religion. This pursuit of a unifying communal religious vision undermines the force of the Abrams-Lenman argument that Romanticism tended towards a fissiparous individualism.

In a similar vein, Robert Barth saw Romanticism as a unifying quest to mediate between the world of the senses and a transcendent reality - a quest through human experience towards immortality.[62] It is no surprise that

[56] Ryan, *The Romantic Reformation*, 5.
[57] Ryan, *The Romantic Reformation*, 5.
[58] Ryan, *The Romantic Reformation*, 29.
[59] D. Jasper, *The Sacred and Secular Canon in Romanticism: Preserving the Sacred Truths* (London; Macmillan Press, 1999), 114.
[60] Jasper, *The Sacred and Secular Canon*, 11, 20.
[61] Jasper, *The Sacred and Secular Canon*, 125.
[62] J. R. Barth, "Wordsworth's 'Immortality Ode' and Hopkins' 'The leaden echo and the golden echo': in pursuit of transcendence" in J.R. Barth, (ed.), *The Fountain Light: Studies in Romanticism and Religion, in Honor of John L. Mahoney* (New York: Fordham University Press, 2002), 119-120.

Romantics questing towards a transcendent vision wanted to remove any obstructions to epiphany. In response to earlier Enlightenment attacks on the miraculous, influential Romantics argued for the subjective appropriation of the supernatural and the possibility of divine manifestations in humanly intelligible terms.[63]

The moment of transcendence sought by Romantics is often described as awareness of the "sublime." The Romantic sublime was itself elusive, describing objects whose "very sublimity renders indefinite, no less than their indefiniteness renders them sublime,"[64] and it was different from the earlier eighteenth century concept, which had to do with overwhelming forces. For Romantics, the sublime could be *discovered* almost anywhere; one didn't have to passively wait to be overwhelmed by it: "the Romantic sublime is a moment of vision which, by providing an intuition of the absolute grounds of existence, claims to close the gap between subject and object".[65] The emphasis, and the initiative, moved towards the individual. So, even if Jasper's previously mentioned unifying communal vision was a goal of Romanticism, it appears that the way to it was through the individual pursuit of the vision: shared vision was only achieved through individual decision.

In its broadest sense, the millennialist theme in Romanticism mentioned by Jasper was the hope and expectation that the present social and economic discomforts would come to an end, either through political or divine intervention. This was often supplemented by an apocalypticism that fitted comfortably with the revolutionary 1790s, but in the jaded post-revolutionary years, argued John Beer, it was often internalised and the Romantic writers "came to believe that the apocalypse had in one sense already happened – in their own consciousness".[66] Beer continued the trend that we have seen developing in scholars since Abrams – observing greater complexity in the relationship between Romanticism and religion in this period and a subsequent interest in examining the development of individual concepts within this relationship.

In 2003, Jon Mee considered the links between Romanticism and religious enthusiasm. Noting that the term "enthusiasm" had remained suspect in Britain since the religious excesses of the seventeenth century Civil War period, Mee claimed that the Romantics tried to preserve their core value of imaginative and transcendent visions, and at the same time insulate themselves against the

[63] F. Burwick, "Coleridge and De Quincey on miracles" in Barth, *The Fountain Light,* 194.

[64] K. Coburn & M. Christensen, (eds), *The Notebooks of Samuel Taylor Coleridge*, volume 1, (London: Routledge, 1990) 1379.

[65] P. Otto, "Sublime" in McCalman, *An Oxford Companion*, 723.

[66] J. Beer, "Romantic apocalypses" in T. Fulford, (ed.), *Romanticism and Millenarianism* (New York: Palgrave, 2002), 61.

perceived excesses of enthusiasm.[67] The situation was, also, coloured by the cultural concept of "sensibility", which entailed a supra-rational unity based on emotion and sensation; while widespread, it, also, was seen as a risk, in which emotions were "feared as inflationary, [potentially] flooding the market with cheap passions, which threatened to drown real values and stable identities".[68]

Despite the negatives associated with enthusiasm, there was a genuine drive to preserve the older understanding of the term which equated to "poetic inspiration"; there was, also, a particularly English identification of enthusiasm with their own perceived national "propensity toward liberty".[69] The real concern remained, as Mee amusingly puts it, that "this transport of enthusiasm might not come with a return ticket".[70] Some Romantics, such as Coleridge, attempted to rehabilitate the term "enthusiasm" to mean something like "a quiet sense of the nearness of God's being", rather than fanaticism.[71] This attempt to domesticate enthusiasm etymologically speaks powerfully of its value as a concept in the Romantic view of religious life. It was one way of diluting the view that enthusiasm, millennialism and apocalypticism were virtually synonymous and all potentially revolutionary, envisaging and anticipating an ideal world, and pursuing it with various degrees of determination and violence.

In his PhD thesis Mark Patterson specifically linked apocalyptic premillennialism and a Romantic worldview with the Albury circle and *The Morning Watch* journal with which Edward Irving was associated.[72] Patterson's focus was on the premillennialism of the Albury group and its journal, rather than specifically on Irving, but his observation that the "interfusion of the finite and the infinite" was central to Romanticism furthered its potential resonance with religion.[73]

In 2004, Mark Hopkins argued that Romanticism had a pronounced effect on both ethics and theology. Hopkins asserted that Romantics not only internalised and subjectivised religious experience; they did the same with authority. It was this that motivated a re-engagement with theology and ethics and liberal theology was a result.[74] Contrary to some of the other evidence surveyed in this chapter, Hopkins saw an initial period of sharp division between the Enlightenment and Romanticism, which extended to the 1820s for "the elite"

---

[67] J. Mee, *Romanticism, Enthusiasm and Regulation: Poetics and the Policing of Culture in the Romantic Period* (Oxford: OUP, 2003), 5, 13, 36.

[68] Mee, *Romanticism*, 49.

[69] Mee, *Romanticism*, 54, 82.

[70] Mee, *Romanticism*, 54.

[71] Mee, *Romanticism*, 165. Coleridge was adept at coining new words, therefore his attempt to rehabilitate "enthusiasm" indicates the value he placed on the term.

[72] M. Patterson, "Designing the last days: Edward Irving, the Albury circle, and the theology of The Morning Watch" (PhD thesis, King's College, London, 2001), vol. 1, 31.

[73] Patterson, "Designing the last days", vol. 1, 34

[74] M. Hopkins, *Nonconformity's Romantic Generation: Evangelical and Liberal Theologies in Victorian England* (Carlisle: Paternoster Press, 2004), 250.

and to mid-century for popular culture. It was only after this, he argued, that Enlightenment influences returned.[75] While this observation is helpful in its reminder that it takes a period of time for new cultural movements to filter through the population, it proposes a purity of division between Romanticism and Enlightenment that seems unsupported by the evidence to hand; most Romantics continued to demonstrate their Enlightenment inheritance in various ways, and it would be difficult to maintain that even those very few Romantic spirits who openly eschewed all aspects of the Enlightenment were completely unaffected by its cross-currents.

In many ways, from the late eighteenth century until the 1830s, the religious and cultural situation in Scotland increasingly reflected the trends and issues apparent in England, yet some distinctive features need to be noted. The very similarities only served to highlight the issue of Scottish identity, which had been in question ever since the union with England in 1707, at the dawn of the Enlightenment. Having earlier acknowledged the elusiveness of the term, "Romanticism", we now face a similar difficulty with the term "Scottish Enlightenment".[76] As we shall see, however, it is possible that the former may assist in elucidating the latter. M. Fitzpatrick has claimed that "The Scottish Enlightenment was in part an assertion of national identity by a country which had lost its statehood."[77] The reality of the United Kingdom simultaneously joined Scotland to England and reduced it to a subservient role. Romantic themes of alienation and exile fomented naturally in this context.[78] Having been required by union to be more cognisant of events south of the border, the Scots looked even further afield and began to think of themselves as "citizens of the world", with "some knowledge of the continent [becoming] the mark of every cultured gentleman".[79] In addition to this increasingly cosmopolitan outlook, the combination of the Scottish Enlightenment and the agricultural revolution had given Lowland Scotland a dynamic economy and transformed the region "from the periphery to the centre of European cultural and intellectual life".[80]

---

[75] Hopkins, *Nonconformity's Romantic Generation*, 256.

[76] R.B. Sher, *Church and University in the Scottish Enlightenment: the Moderate Literati of Edinburgh* (Princeton, N.J.: Princeton University Press, 1985), 3-19, is a good summary of the issues involved.

[77] M. Fitzpatrick, "Enlightenment" in McCalman, *An Oxford Companion*, 299.

[78] L. Davis, I. Duncan, & J. Sorensen, (eds), *Scotland and the Borders of Romanticism* (Cambridge: Cambridge University Press, 2004), 6.

[79] M. Fitzpatrick, "Enlightenment" in McCalman, *An Oxford Companion*, 299, and A.L. Drummond & J. Bulloch, *The Scottish Church 1688-1843: the Age of the Moderates* (Edinburgh: The Saint Andrew Press, 1973), 84.

[80] L. Upton, "'Our Mother and our Country': the Integration of Religious and National Identity in the Thought of Edward Irving (1792-1834)" in R. Pope, (ed.), *Religion and National Identity: Wales and Scotland c. 1700-2000* (Cardiff: University of Wales Press, 2001), 244.

Nor is this simply the view of recent scholarship; even Voltaire was impressed with Scottish advances.[81]

In the case of Edinburgh, where Irving would attend university, there was an interesting tension between the quality and availability of education. On the one hand, there was a desire to encourage as many as possible to attend, which meant that education was inexpensive, and in many ways highly geared towards the professions.[82] In some ways, this produced a lower quality of graduate, but on the other hand, there was a strong desire to achieve academic distinction which fostered a robust critical engagement in the various disciplines.[83] Edinburgh, therefore, provided an inexpensive education for rural youth that could nevertheless offer a challenging intellectual pathway. This combination of circumstances in Edinburgh was favourable for Irving: his modest rural circumstances did not prohibit his university education and he was exposed to rigorous academic standards which would serve him well in his later controversies.

The relationship between Scotland and England tended to focus the Scottish mind on issues of church and state and political theory. Scottish traditions of humanism and Calvinism gave history an elevated status "as a storehouse of human experience, a record of the workings of providence [with] predictive potential, and a means of inculcating private and public moral virtue".[84] The result of this was "that the legacy of the Scottish Enlightenment was that of a pre-Romantic historical school. In fact, the division between Enlightenment and Romanticism is even more dubious in Scotland than elsewhere in Europe".[85]

This fluidity of boundaries has been noticed by Stafford, who has pointed out diverse yet simultaneous tendencies within Scottish culture. On the one hand, the Scottish bard Ossian (purportedly an ancient Gaelic writer whose work was presented to the eighteenth century by James Macpherson) was the "ultimate ancestor" of the "modern Romantic imagination" with more contemporary expressions in Robert Burns and Walter Scott; on the other, there was, also, a stern, provincial focus on the utilitarian.[86] Stafford goes on to argue that these two apparently opposing strands were creatively combined in Macpherson's reworking of the Ossian poems and early Scottish literary criticism to forge the concept of a passionate and free artistic expression that was also socially useful.[87] Scottish Romanticism then, was partly a unique

---

[81] Voltaire's positive assessment is quoted in Sher, *Church and University*, 3. The original source was Voltaire's review of Kames's *Elements of Criticism* (1762).

[82] L.J.Saunders, *Scottish Democracy 1815-1840: the Social and Intellectual Background* (Edinburgh: Oliver & Boyd, 1950), 307.

[83] Saunders, *Scottish Democracy*, 309.

[84] K. Haakonssen, "Scottish Enlightenment" in McCalman, *An Oxford Companion*, 693.

[85] Haakonssen, "Scottish Enlightenment", 693.

[86] F. Stafford, "Scottish Romanticism and Scotland in Romanticism" in M. Ferber, (ed.), *A Companion to European Romanticism* (Oxford: Blackwell Publishing, 2005), 49-50.

[87] Stafford, "Scottish Romanticism", 52-54.

hybrid of disparate forces, which has led some to overlook it, and argue that Scotland's contribution to Romanticism was minimal or has allowed them to ignore the topic completely. Some recent commentators go further, claiming Scotland demonstrated "an oppressive anti-Romanticism."[88]

Cairns Craig reacted against the "marginalization of Scotland in relation to Romanticism", claiming instead that, "Far from being at the margin of Romanticism...Scottish tradition was to shape profoundly the development of British and Irish Romanticism not only from the 1760s to the 1820s" but to the end of the nineteenth century.[89] Combining the insights of Haakonssen and Craig, we see that Scotland not only drew from continental Europe, it *led* Europe as the place in which the Enlightenment tended to be closest to Romanticism. We have argued earlier in this chapter that Romanticism was a development from, rather than a denial of, the Enlightenment: in Haakonssen's view (and implicitly in Stafford's), Scotland was a pre-eminent expression of this proposition.

The trend in recent scholarship has clearly been away from the Abrams's thesis of the 1970s which saw in Romanticism a wholesale rejection of religion as outmoded, and a resulting secularisation of its transcendent themes. Instead we have seen the emergence of Romanticisms that re-thought religious concepts, took them out of the more traditional and rigid categories, and re-worked them in individualistic ways in active pursuit of visionary illumination that some have argued could become communal. Romanticism, for many, was comprehensively religious; the noteworthy diversity of individuals and movements classified as "Romantic" remains, however.

Michael Ferber has recently suggested a positive approach to the taxonomic dilemma that is Romanticism. He takes the various lists of features proposed by other authors, adds some of his own, and proposes a Venn diagram approach in which the circles representing various expressions of Romanticism exhibit certain features from the list and therefore overlap other circles when features are common. This concept, helpfully, allows for the diversity which has threatened to dilute the term "Romanticism" beyond usefulness, without lurching to the opposite extreme of imposing a draconian list of essential features which would be unhelpfully exclusive.[90] It underlines the reality that whenever we are using the term "Romanticism" in its broadest sense, we are really meaning "Romanticism*s*". This seems particularly appropriate for an age extolling subjectivity, the imagination, and individual pursuit of transcendence. It, also, implies that it is perfectly legitimate to choose from the lengthy list of Romantic characteristics those that are particularly appropriate for the subject at hand; this is not circularity, simply a recognition of the fact that the presence of a certain number of core characteristics will qualify a person or movement as

---

[88] Davis, Duncan & Sorensen, (eds), *Scotland and the Borders of Romanticism*, 5.

[89] C. Craig, "Coleridge, Hume, and the chains of the romantic imagination", in Davis, Duncan & Sorensen, *Scotland and the Borders of Romanticism*, 21, 35.

[90] Ferber, "Introduction", *A Companion to European Romanticism*, 5-7.

Romantic, whereas the absence of certain specific characteristics does not automatically disqualify them. It is, also, important to note that no *one* characteristic can be labelled as "exclusively" Romantic. For example, Romantics were passionate about transcendence, but so were all medieval mystics; it is the aggregate of several characteristics that enable us to confidently identify an individual or movement as Romantic. With this in mind, we will draw from our exploration of the relationship between Romanticism and religion in the context of the period, to hazard (despite the chorus of caveats), if not a definition, at least a working description of Romanticism that will be helpful in our consideration of Edward Irving.

Romanticism saw the powers of reason as limited and emphasised the imagination, feelings, and the pursuit of a transcendent sublime, which was frequently an overtly religious pursuit. Romanticism rejected aphoristic theories about politics and society and adopted an empathetic and organic view of history which placed it, alongside nature, as potentially revelatory. Romanticism elevated individual experience and struggle, often in the context of alienation and exile, as the ideal Romantic persevered towards a noble and idealised goal, usually at great personal cost – the concept of the Romantic hero was born. Romanticism, also, sought to circumvent any authority that stood in the way of its quest for transcendence, and so was implicitly anti-authoritarian. All of these characteristics would be widely accepted as "Romantic core values" that would regularly appear in the overlapping segments of Ferber's Venn diagram concept of comparing Romanticisms. Of course, this description is not intended to be completely comprehensive, but simply to capture some of the key features of the "spirit of the age", which will be particularly helpful as we seek to understand the nature of Irving's Romanticism.

We now turn to one who brought Scottish Romanticism into cosmopolitan London - Edward Irving - native son of Scotland, adopted son of England's capital.

CHAPTER 2

An Overview of Edward Irving's Life

Edward Irving was born on 4 August 1792 in Annan, south-west Scotland. He was the second son to Gavin, a tanner by trade, and Mary (nee Lowther). Edward had a lengthy Protestant heritage: previous generations of Irvings had descended from Huguenots, and the Lowthers had apparently descended from Martin Luther.[1] Eventually surrounded by seven siblings, Edward grew tall, strong and athletic, thriving on outdoor pursuits, especially walking. Annandale combined the brash new prosperity of Lowland Scotland mentioned in the previous chapter with a rich mix of folk myth, religious history and a cosmopolitan awareness.[2]

One of the early influences on Irving was the local schoolmaster, Adam Hope. Thomas Carlyle, a younger contemporary of Irving's in Annan, credited Hope's influence for Irving's life-long "rigorous logic and clear articulation".[3] For many, religious life in Annan had settled into a prosaic comfort, but outside this "was a world of imagination and poetry, never to be dissevered from that border country".[4] Much of this derived from tales of the sacrifices of the Scottish Covenanters, a group of seventeenth century Presbyterians who fought against the imposition of episcopacy. These Scots looked back with pride to their Reformation of 1560 which had been born of struggle against the monarch, and was, therefore, highly suspicious of State interference in ecclesiastical affairs.[5] When James VI of Scotland became James I of England, he quickly decided that episcopacy better suited monarchical security than Presbyterianism, and his attempts to change the worship of the Scottish church provoked anger.[6] His successor, Charles I, demonstrated absolutist tendencies which provoked open rebellion in Scotland in the form of the Covenanters;

---

[1] M. Oliphant, *The Life of Edward Irving* (London: Hurst and Blackett, n.d. 5th edition), 1; A. Dallimore, *The Life of Edward Irving: the Fore-runner of the Charismatic Movement* (Edinburgh: Banner of Truth, 1983), 3.

[2] L. Upton, "'Our Mother and our Country': the Integration of Religious and National Identity in the Thought of Edward Irving (1792-1834)" in R. Pope, (ed), *Religion and National Identity: Wales and Scotland c. 1700-2000* (Cardiff: University of Wales Press, 2001), 244.

[3] T. Carlyle, *Reminiscences* (London: J. M. Dent & Sons, 1932. Orig. 1881), 175.

[4] Oliphant, *Irving*, 5.

[5] D. Stevenson, *The Covenanters: the National Covenant of Scotland* (Stirling: The Saltire Society, 1988), 6-7.

[6] Stevenson, *The Covenanters*, 13-14.

years of bloodshed resulted.[7] There is evidence that the tales of the Covenanters fascinated and terrified the imaginations of the young and had a lasting influence on Irving; Annandale, itself, had its list of such worthies, including James Welwood and John and Sarah Colvin.[8] It is, perhaps, not surprising then, that stirred by these tales and dissatisfied with local religious practice, some sought a more vibrant religious experience by walking six miles to attend a Seceding church in Ecclefechan where the doctrine was little different but the level of passion and commitment was higher;[9] alongside his teacher Adam Hope, the young Edward Irving often joined this pilgrimage.[10]

We have already seen three characteristics in the young Irving that will be referred to frequently as we progress: his abilities with logic, speech, and his level of religious commitment. Irving developed and used these abilities in his adult life and it is worth noting that they were already present in an early form in Annandale, and therefore part of his Scottish heritage. Irving's boyhood in Annan was soon left behind as, at the age of thirteen, he went to Edinburgh University with his brother John; John to study medicine, Edward to prepare for the ministry of the Church of Scotland.[11] It was the usual practice in those days to send boys of this age to university and the lifestyle was not easy as they lived on limited means in a loft room and assumed full responsibility for their studies. There is little surviving information about the influence of his Edinburgh studies on Irving's development, but one glimpse we have concerns his choice of reading material: it included Richard Hooker's *Ecclesiastical Polity*, the *Arabian Nights*, *Don Quixote*, *Paradise Lost* and Ossian.[12] The mixture of theology, quest, romance and cosmic drama reflected by this reading list would follow Irving throughout his adult life.

Hooker pursued a middle path between the Catholics and the Puritans and his work highlighted several themes which can be seen in Irving's later career: his work's main concern was church governance and Hooker argued that authority was commanded by the Bible and by the traditions of the early church, but it had to be based on piety and reason rather than automatic investiture. This was because once invested, authority had to be obeyed even if it were wrong, thus the necessity for it to be informed by right reason through

---

[7] Stevenson, *The Covenanters*, 45.

[8] R. Simpson, *Traditions of the Covenanters* (Edinburgh: Gall & Inglis, n.d.), 207ff.

[9] In the case of Annan, this was further heightened because the local minister had a problem with alcohol. Carlyle, *Reminiscences*, 176. The seceding churches took a stance against ministers being appointed through the patronage system and civil interference in church affairs.

[10] Oliphant, *Irving,* 11-12; Dallimore, *Irving,* 5.

[11] Oliphant, *Irving,* 15. It appears that Irving's university costs were at least partly met by an inheritance from an uncle. Irving, "Diary", fol. 75, quoted in T. Grass, *The Lord's Watchman: Edward Irving* (Milton Keynes: Paternoster, 2011), 8.

[12] Oliphant, *Irving,* 19; Dallimore, *Irving,* 10.

the Holy Spirit.[13] Hooker's views on the relationship between Church and State were highly valued in High Church and Tory quarters in the years following the French Revolution, which were the years of Irving's youth.[14] The Elizabethan Hooker and Milton's epic seventeenth century poetry had their impact on Irving's own writing and speaking style; many of his listeners and readers noted the echoes of an earlier age.[15]

The authorship of the Ossian poems was already controversial in Irving's time. Nevertheless, this collection of, allegedly, ancient Scottish poems became a significant influence on Romanticism, especially on Walter Scott and J.W. von Goethe. The Ossian poems stimulated the early nineteenth century sense of "inadequacy in the face of the sublimity of antiquity".[16] So, the young Irving was already drinking from a distinctly Romantic stream. In later life, he acknowledged the influence of "the poems of Ossian and the minstrelsy of the Border",[17] the latter being a reference to Walter Scott's early popular work of the same name.[18] Scott's work drew significantly on the Romantic traditions of the lowland Scotland of Irving's youth. Scott had influenced Irving, and would, later, be in Irving's congregation on visits to London.[19]

After four years in Edinburgh, Irving graduated with the Master of Arts degree and returned home briefly. The seventeen-year old Edward Irving who returned to Annan had coal-black hair and was an imposing, well-muscled figure over six feet tall.[20] The one flaw in his otherwise handsome features was a squint in one eye. The young Thomas Carlyle owed his first conscious memory of Irving to this time: Carlyle was a pupil in Adam Hope's schoolroom when Irving visited.[21]

Irving's Edinburgh years took him only part-way towards qualifying as a minister in the Church of Scotland. For the next few years, he was required to be a "partial student" in Divinity, pursuing self-directed study, but appearing

---

[13] J.K. Stafford, *Richard Hooker's Doctrine of the Holy Spirit* (Winnipeg: University of Manitoba PhD thesis, 2005), 25, 37, 121, 200.

[14] D. MacCulloch, "Richard Hooker's reputation", *The English Historical Review* 117.473 (Sept 2002): 773(40). Academic OneFile. Gale. Murdoch University Library. 5 Mar. 2008

[15] Oliphant, *Irving*, 19; Dallimore, *Irving*, 40-41.

[16] J. Mee, "Ossianism" in I. McCalman (ed.), *An Oxford Companion to the Romantic Age: British Culture 1776-1832* (Oxford: Oxford University Press, 1999), 630.

[17] E. Irving, "Historical view of the Church of Scotland before the Reformation," in G. Carlyle (ed.), *The Collected Writings of Edward Irving* (London: Alexander Strahan & Co., 1864), vol. 1, 595. Original publication date 1831. Henceforth *CW1*.

[18] Full title: *Minstrelsy of the Scottish Border: consisting of Historical and Romantic ballads, collected in the Southern Counties of Scotland; with a few of modern date, founded upon local tradition.* It was first published in 1802 when Irving was ten.

[19] Dallimore, *Irving*, 33.

[20] Oliphant, *Irving*, 20-21; Dallimore, *Irving*, 11.

[21] Carlyle, *Reminiscences*, 179-180.

periodically for examination.[22] In the meantime, there was, also, the necessity of making a living and Irving became a teacher, like many other hopeful would-be ministers of his day. Irving obtained the position of schoolmaster at Haddington, a town with a long-term Seceder presence.[23] He remained there for two years, during which time he made friends with the Welsh household, and tutored their young daughter Jane. Irving appears to have been a strict, but much-loved teacher; he, eventually, left Haddington to oversee a larger school in Kirkcaldy.[24]

Irving began teaching at Kirkcaldy as a twenty-year old in 1812. During his time there, he completed his Divinity studies, and began two significant relationships. The first was within the Martin household. Dr Martin was the minister at the local Presybterian church and his daughter, Isabella, was one of Irving's pupils.[25] Shortly after she ceased to be Irving's pupil an understanding developed between her and Edward that one day they would be married, pending his secure placement.[26] The second significant relationship was with Thomas Carlyle, who arrived in Kirkcaldy some time after Irving as master of a new (and potentially rival) school. Some fifty years later, Carlyle recalled the scene of their first actual meeting, at which Irving showed no sense of rivalry, but extended the warmest welcome to Carlyle and offered him complete access to his library.[27] Their friendship continued until Irving's death and will be examined in greater detail later.

Irving served as master of Kirkcaldy School for seven years but with his Divinity qualification and licence to preach, he waited with increasing impatience for a call to a church. His attempts to preach in Kirkcaldy had not been well received by the locals who thought his manner too grand.[28] Thus, in 1818, in his twenty-sixth year, Irving resigned his position and moved to Edinburgh where he tutored students and occasionally preached.[29] Irving spent more than a year in Edinburgh and seemingly moved no closer to his dream of a ministerial position. Oliphant points out that Irving's situation was far from exceptional, but rather the norm for ministerial candidates without patronage; Irving spent his spare time writing sermons and contemplating missionary service overseas.[30]

In Edinburgh, however, he renewed the acquaintance of his former pupil, Jane Welsh, now a striking young woman attending finishing school.[31] The

[22] Oliphant, *Irving*, 21.
[23] A.L. Drummond & J. Bulloch, *The Scottish Church 1688-1843: the Age of the Moderates* (Edinburgh: The Saint Andrew Press, 1973), 51.
[24] Oliphant, *Irving*, 21, 28.
[25] Oliphant, *Irving*, 34.
[26] Dallimore, *Irving*, 16.
[27] Carlyle, *Reminiscences*, 186.
[28] Oliphant, *Irving*, 37.
[29] Oliphant, *Irving*, 41; Dallimore, *Irving*, 17.
[30] Oliphant, *Irving*, 42-45.
[31] Oliphant, *Irving*, 43-44.

rekindled friendship soon grew into something stronger, and when Jane completed her schooling and returned to Haddington, it continued through correspondence. There is reason to think that Irving's love for Jane led him to regret his earlier commitment to Isabella Martin, and attempt to be released from it. This request was declined, as Isabella had been waiting expectantly for several years.[32] Irving accepted this, and restricted his relationship with Jane Welsh to a brotherly one.[33] Irving, later, introduced Jane to her future husband, Thomas Carlyle, and the Irving-Carlyle relationship will be explored more fully in chapter five.

At this time, Irving received an invitation that was to be the key to his ministerial career: Dr Andrew Thomson, minister of St George's Edinburgh, invited him to preach, indicating that Dr Thomas Chalmers, "the greatest preacher and most eminent man in the entire Scotch establishment", would be present, and he was in need of an assistant.[34] Irving's hopes soared, he preached in the presence of Chalmers, and waited. When there was no news from Chalmers after several days, an exasperated Irving packed a bag and headed for Ireland, throwing himself into the physical exertion of walking through the north.[35] He had been in Ireland for some time when he checked the Coleraine post office and found that his father had forwarded to him a letter from Chalmers. The letter invited Irving to Glasgow, but was not yet a definite offer of an appointment. Encouraged, but still in suspense, Irving sped to Glasgow where Chalmers formally offered him the position of his assistant at St. John's.[36] Finally, after years of preparation, Irving's goal of a ministry opportunity was within his grasp, yet he still remembered former failures, even in the face of Chalmers's encouragement, admitting, "I will preach to them if you think fit, but if they bear with my preaching, they will be the first people who have borne with it!"[37]

It was October 1819 when twenty-seven year old Irving began work at St. John's.[38] This was at a time when Chalmers was engaged in a bold social experiment in his impoverished parish which would see him, shortly, become

---

[32] L. & E. Hanson, *Necessary Evil: the Life of Jane Welsh Carlyle* (London: Constable, 1952), 27; R. Ashton, *Thomas and Jane Carlyle: Portrait of a Marriage* (London: Chatto & Windus, 2001), 17.

[33] Dallimore, *Irving* , 19. Oliphant is very discreet on this topic. Although Isabella Irving died seven years before Oliphant published, two of their children were still alive. Dallimore argues that Irving was "never actually engaged" (51) to marry Isabella, yet the understanding between them was sufficient that Irving believed it was necessary for him to seek freedom from it before pursuing Jane Welch.

[34] Oliphant, *Irving*, 46-47, 56.

[35] Oliphant, *Irving*, 47-48.

[36] Oliphant, *Irving*, 49-50.

[37] Oliphant, *Irving*, 51.

[38] Oliphant, *Irving*, 51.

"Britain's foremost proponent of the parish ideal."[39] Drawing from Calvinist social principles, Chalmers saw no hard division between Church and State; the goal was that the two would work together for the spiritual and physical well-being of the people in a "godly commonwealth".[40] Influenced by the economist Malthus, Chalmers wanted to encourage the poor to take responsibility for their own well-being and cease being dependent on "poor relief" funding.[41] Chalmers's plan involved the parish taking responsibility for ensuring only the "worthy poor" received relief, which would come from wealthy parishioners.[42] Irving's arrival fitted neatly into this plan and he duly visited hundreds of parishioners in their homes, at a time when poverty and discontent were intense. The French Revolution was still fresh in many memories, and there was a fear that the resentment of Glasgow's poor could, also, become violent.[43] Drawing on his background as the son of an Annandale tanner, Irving instinctively related to the struggling workers of Glasgow's slums: he ate potatoes with them, prayed for them, blessed their children, and distributed whatever cash he possessed.[44]

After Irving had been working with Chalmers for two years, he became restless once again. Although grateful to Chalmers for the opportunity, Irving was now approaching the age of thirty and eager to lead a congregation himself.[45] As Oliphant noted, Irving was in the shadow of his mentor, with the majority preferring the preaching of Chalmers and some actually avoiding church when Irving preached.[46] In addition, Irving could not be ordained until a congregation offered him a position.[47] In his restlessness, he was once again considering the mission field when an invitation arrived from the Caledonian Chapel in London for him to preach for them with a view to becoming their next minister. This invitation, apparently, came about through someone unknown to Irving who had heard of his work with Chalmers and recommended him.[48] The invitation was probably less of a compliment to Irving than a reflection of the dwindling fortunes of the congregation; nevertheless, Irving leapt at the chance and preached for them during December

---

[39] S.J. Brown, *The National Churches of England, Ireland and Scotland 1801-46* (Oxford: Oxford University Press, 2001), 79.
[40] S.J. Brown, *Thomas Chalmers and the Godly Commonwealth in Scotland* (Oxford: Oxford University Press, 1982) xv-xvi.
[41] Brown, *Thomas Chalmers*, 118.
[42] Brown, *Thomas Chalmers*, 119.
[43] Brown, *Thomas Chalmers*, 94; Oliphant, *Irving,* 53-54.
[44] Irving received a legacy of up to £100. He changed this into £1 notes and distributed one each day until it was gone. Oliphant, *Irving,* 60.
[45] Oliphant, *Irving,* 66-67; Dallimore, *Irving,* 27-28.
[46] Oliphant, *Irving,* 60, 67.
[47] Dallimore, *Irving,* 16.
[48] Oliphant, *Irving,* 68. Irving refers to this matter obliquely in his dedication to his publication *The Last Days* in 1828.

1821.[49] The congregation was happy to accept him as their new minister, but for two obstacles which were well-known from the beginning: the requirement that the minister be able to preach in Gaelic and the ability of the congregation to afford his salary. Characteristically, Irving promised to learn Gaelic quickly and absolved the congregation of any financial restriction, but it proved unnecessary; the first requirement was dropped and the finances were obtained.[50]

Full of expectation, Irving returned to Annan to be ordained in the church of his youth, then proceeded to Glasgow to make his official departure from St John's.[51] He arrived in London to assume his new role in July 1822, a month before his thirtieth birthday and seventeen years after he entered the University of Edinburgh with this very goal in mind.[52] The small congregation of fifty gradually began to grow, but one event more than any other expedited this growth. Sir James Mackintosh heard Irving refer in a prayer to a recently orphaned family as being "thrown upon the fatherhood of God".[53] The phrase was memorable, and Mackintosh repeated it to George Canning, the future Prime Minister, who was, also, struck by it. After Canning, himself, heard Irving preach, he told Parliament it was "the most eloquent sermon" he had ever heard.[54] This was during a debate about Church finances and Canning had used Irving as evidence that talented churchmen did not always demand high pay.[55]

Such a lofty recommendation as Canning's encouraged the noble and wealthy to flock to the chapel in Hatton Garden and the street outside became blocked with carriages.[56] The building could seat five hundred, but a year after Irving's arrival, two or three times that many were attempting to gain admittance.[57] Demographically, the congregation was on the spectrum from

---

[49] Oliphant, *Irving*, 68.

[50] Oliphant, *Irving*, 70-72.

[51] Dallimore, *Irving*, 28.

[52] Cameron, incorrectly, has Thomas and Jane Carlyle welcoming Irving to London. The reality was the reverse: the Carlyles' marriage was some years in the future and Thomas had not even visited London at this stage. G.C. Cameron, *The Scots Kirk in London* (Oxford: Becket Publications, 1979), 107.

[53] Oliphant, *Irving*, 79.

[54] Oliphant, *Irving*, 80. Canning (1770-1827) was Prime Minister for only four months in 1827, dying in office.

[55] Oliphant, *Irving*, 79. The Hansard records do not preserve this event; if it did not happen exactly as Oliphant indicates, *something* certainly aroused Parliamentarians' interest in Irving, cf. Grass, *Lord's Watchman*, 53-54.

[56] This was not the first time that a mention in Parliament had gained attention for a religious figure. In 1795, Nathaniel Halhed, member for Lymington, had similarly gained a greater audience for the unconventional Richard Brothers, cf. C. Garrett, *Respectable Folly: Millenarians and the French Revolution in France and England* (Baltimore, ML: John Hopkins University Press, 1975), 191-194.

[57] Dallimore, *Irving*, 32.

middle-class to very wealthy.[58] In the crowd could be found the Dukes of York and Sussex, the Earl of Aberdeen, Lord Liverpool, Zachary Macaulay, William Wilberforce, Charles Lamb, William Hazlitt, Thomas De Quincey, S.T. Coleridge, Dorothy and William Wordsworth, Sir Walter Scott, and William Gladstone and Thomas Macaulay as boys.[59] More surprisingly, the Utilitarian Jeremy Bentham and philosopher William Godwin, neither of whom were friends of the church, were, also, to be seen there.[60] Canning's remark may have instigated a widespread curiosity, but what captured and retained the interest of such a varied and luminous crowd? Perhaps the best way of answering that is by examining the words of William Hazlitt, whose essay on Irving is a sustained examination of the appeal of his preaching from the perspective of a drama critic. According to Hazlitt, the crowds who heard Irving came away delighted and astonished because Irving gave them a combination of theology and dramatic rhetoric and he was unashamed to be controversial. Irving named individuals and criticised their actions and ideas, many of whom appeared eager to hear what he would say about them next![61] Irving kept "the public in awe by insulting all their favourite idols".[62]

Having quickly forged a reputation as London's favourite preacher, Irving began his second year in London with his first major publication, *For the Oracles of God, four Orations, for Judgment to come, an Argument in nine parts*.[63] In the first part of this work, Irving argued for the style of preaching which he had adopted and for which he had found such a receptive audience; in the second, and larger part of the work, he focused on the second coming of Christ.[64] Although the book was widely criticised, it went through three editions in a year.[65] No sooner was it published than Irving headed for

---

[58] J.F.C. Harrison, *Robert Owen and the Owenites in Britain and America: the Quest for the New Moral World* (London: Routledge & Kegan Paul, 1969), 97.

[59] Hanson, *Necessary Evil*, 57; R.A. Davenport, *Albury Apostles: the Story of the Body known as the Catholic Apostolic Church* (London: United Writers, 1970), 54; Dallimore, *Irving*, 33. Dorries listed Jane Austin [sic] as attending Irving's congregation (*Incarnational Christology*, 26). If this were the case, it would indeed have caused a sensation: Jane Austen died in 1817.

[60] A.L. Drummond, *Edward Irving and his Circle, including some consideration of the 'Tongues' Movement in the light of Modern Psychology* (London: James Clarke, 1934), 50. They came to hear if they were to be denounced by Irving; they returned to show that they weren't offended.

[61] W. Hazlitt, *The Spirit of the Age* (Oxford: Woodstock Books, 1989), 83, 84, 89-91. This no doubt explains the presence of Bentham and Godwin in Irving's congregation.

[62] Hazlitt, *The Spirit of the Age*, 91.

[63] Although this is sometimes referred to as Irving's first publication, it was actually Irving's second published work: the first was his farewell address to St John's, which had been published the previous year.

[64] As noted in the previous chapter, varieties of millennialism and apocalypticism were widespread in the years following the French Revolution and the Napoleonic era.

[65] Dallimore, *Irving*, 41.

Kirkaldy, where his eleven-year engagement to Isabella Martin ended with their marriage on 13 October 1823.[66]

One of Irving's earliest acquaintances in London was Basil Montagu, whose home in Bedford Square was a mecca for literati.[67] Montagu was a lawyer specialising in bankruptcy law and married to his third wife by the time he met Irving; Irving called her "noble lady".[68] Included in Montagu's circle were William Hazlitt, Leigh Hunt, Percy Bysshe Shelley, Samuel Taylor Coleridge (a friend of Montagu's since their undergraduate days), Dorothy and William Wordsworth (William had been a houseguest of Montagu's for some time), Charles Lamb, Henry Crabb Robinson, Robert Southey, Samuel Parr, Robert Burns, and William Godwin. It was in Montagu's home that Irving first met Coleridge and their relationship is explored in a subsequent chapter.[69]

In 1824, Irving was asked to preach for the anniversary of the London Missionary Society; no doubt they were hoping that obtaining the city's most famous preacher would help increase their financial support. They were to be sorely disappointed. The building was so crowded that the service began an hour before the appointed time, and an astonished crowd heard Irving proclaim the ideal missionary as one who went with no visible means of support and was answerable to no committee – a Calvary-driven apostle.[70]

In his three and a half hour address, Irving promoted what he saw as the biblical pattern for missions against an overly pragmatic prudence which he believed dishonoured God by valuing worldly wisdom more than courageous faith.[71] The reaction was outrage, which only increased when Irving published his address and dedicated it to Coleridge, whose own religious past was far from orthodox.[72] In July of this year, Isabella and Edward's firstborn son, also called Edward, was born.

Early in 1825, Irving met Hatley Frere, a former lieutenant turned student of biblical prophecy who had decided, largely on the basis of Daniel and Revelation, that most prophecy had already been fulfilled and that Christ's second coming was imminent.[73] This fitted in well with the views Irving had expressed in his first major publication.[74] Irving began writing on the subject,

---

[66] Oliphant, *Irving*, 87. There is some discrepancy about the actual date, but only by a day or two, cf. Grass, *Lord's Watchman*, 82.

[67] Hanson, *Necessary Evil*, 81.

[68] Lester, V.M., 'Montagu, Basil (1770–1851)', *Oxford Dictionary of National Biography*, Oxford University Press, 2004 [http://www.oxforddnb.com/view/article/19003, accessed 6 Dec 2007]. Montagu's first two wives had died in childbirth.

[69] Oliphant, *Irving*, 92.

[70] Oliphant, *Irving*, 96.

[71] Dallimore, *Irving*, 48. During this lengthy address, there were two breaks for hymns.

[72] We will return to this dedication in detail when considering the Irving-Coleridge relationship.

[73] Oliphant, *Irving*, 104. Frere's brother John was friends with Coleridge.

[74] i.e., *For Judgement to Come*, the second part of his 1823 publication.

and *Babylon and Infidelity Foredoomed of God* subsequently appeared in 1826.[75] In the meantime, the Irving household suffered both joy and grief in October 1825 as young Edward died ten days after his sister Margaret was born. Irving's grief at the loss of his fifteen-month old son is expressed, poignantly, in surviving letters and journals, and its impact on his motivation and theology has been variously assessed.[76] At the very least, it further lessened the gloss of what this world could offer, and, no doubt, made the next world more attractive.

During the last months of 1825, Isabella and young Margaret remained in Scotland, while Irving returned to London and began studying Spanish, apparently, as a distraction from his grief.[77] Early in 1826, he came across a Spanish book called *The Coming of the Messiah in Glory and Majesty*, apparently, by Juan Josafat Ben-Ezra, a Jewish convert to Christianity. In fact, the author was a Jesuit priest, named Lacunza.[78] In an astonishing feat, Irving accelerated his Spanish studies, translated the book and had it published, complete with his own two-hundred page preface.[79] It is an indication of Irving's character that, despite his opposition to Catholicism, his discovery of the author's true identity did not dampen his enthusiasm for the project. In the summer of 1826, Irving took some weeks off from his congregation (although returning to preach on the weekends) and he and Isabella spent the weekdays together in a village. Irving's idea of leisure though, was to translate *Ben-Ezra* while Isabella worked as his amanuensis.[80]

As we saw in the previous chapter, millennialism was reasonably common amongst the Romantic generation, so Irving was not unusual in his interest in prophecy in the mid-1820s. The banker and politician, Henry Drummond, held similar views and in late 1826, the first of several conferences on the subject convened at his Albury Park estate. Irving's attendance at the conference delayed publication of *Ben-Ezra* until January of 1827.[81] In Irving's preface to the work, he discussed his expectation that there would be an outpouring of the Spirit in the last days which he saw as a "latter rain".[82] 1827 was, also, the year in which Irving's growing congregation moved into its newly constructed,

[75] E. Irving, *Babylon and Infidelity Foredoomed of God: a Discourse on the Prophecies of Daniel and the Apocalypse, which relate to these latter times, and until the Second Advent* (Glasgow: Chalmers & Collins, 1826), 2 vols.

[76] For an example of its impact in Irving's own words, cf. his preface to *Ben-Ezra*, quoted in Oliphant, *Irving*, 114. We will discuss these varied assessments in the following chapter.

[77] Oliphant, *Irving*, 115, 198.

[78] Oliphant, *Irving*, 199.

[79] Oliphant, *Irving*, 199; Dallimore, *Irving*, 62.

[80] Oliphant, *Irving*, 201.

[81] Oliphant, *Irving*, 206.

[82] E. Irving, *The Coming of Messiah in Glory and Majesty, by Juan Josafat Ben-Ezra, a converted Jew: translated from the Spanish, with a preliminary discourse, by the Rev. Edward Irving, A.M.* (London: L.B. Seeley and Son, 1827), 5-6.

1800-seat church in Regent Square, with Chalmers giving the opening address.[83] Later in the year, Irving gave what is often considered to be his greatest address (and later, publication), in his ordination charge to Rev. Hugh Maclean of Scots Church, London Wall.[84] Even an author not overly enamoured of Irving has described it as a sustained and passionate production from beginning to end, portraying a challenging view of ministry.[85] He, also, began a work on baptism. In the midst of all this achievement though, there was more grief as another child, Mary, was born and lost.[86] Isabella was to spend much of 1828 in ill-health, recuperating at her father's home in Kirkcaldy.[87]

We have seen that Irving's interest in prophecy and the second advent of Christ was shared by many in his day. During 1828, Irving published a theological view which was far more individual and controversial, concerning the nature of Christ. In this year, Irving published three volumes of sermons, the first of which contained six sermons on the Incarnation.[88] All of these sermons had been preached some time previously in his church, without a hint of objection, and had been mentioned in his letters during 1825.[89] Irving's thesis in these sermons, which he was fully convinced was orthodox and borne out by church history, was that Christ fully assumed fallen human nature, rather than Adam's nature before the fall, despite which he never sinned. Irving argued that a Christ who had not assumed human nature as we experience it, had not truly identified with us at all, but had taken on a faux-humanity. Christ identified with our fallen humanity, but remained sinless through the power of the Holy Spirit.[90]

The first objection to Irving's teaching came from a clergyman named Cole who, after hearing Irving preach on this subject, challenged him to clarify his teaching, and then wrote to him about his "awful doctrine".[91] There was no immediate further remonstrance, and Irving visited Edinburgh in the spring where his 6.00am lectures on the Apocalypse packed the largest churches in the city; even Chalmers couldn't get a seat on one occasion.[92] On this trip to the North, Irving met two men who would be significant in his later life. One was McLeod Campbell, the minister of Row, who had rejected the Calvinist

---

[83] Oliphant, *Irving*, 207.

[84] E. Irving, *The Discourse and Charges at the Ordination of the Rev. H.B. McLean at the Scotch Church, London Wall, 15th March* (London: James Nisbet, 1827). Oliphant, *Irving*, 217; Dallimore, *Irving*, 69ff.

[85] Dallimore, *Irving*, 69.

[86] Oliphant, *Irving*, 216. Mary died in December, 1827.

[87] Isabella remained in Kirkcaldy from May to September of 1828. Oliphant, *Irving*, 225, 247-248.

[88] E. Irving, *Sermons, Lectures and Occasional Discourses*, 3 vols., (London: R.B. Seeley & W. Burnside, 1828)

[89] Oliphant, *Irving*, 220.

[90] Irving's preface to *The Doctrine of the Incarnation Opened*, in *CW*, vol. 5, 4-5.

[91] Oliphant, *Irving*, 222.

[92] Oliphant, *Irving*, 228-229.

distinctives of total depravity and divine election; the other was Alexander (Sandy) Scott, who believed that the charismata – the supernatural gifts of the Spirit mentioned in the New Testament - had only been lost to the church due to lack of faith.[93] Irving, later, employed Scott to be his assistant for the work in London. Then tragedy struck while Irving was in Kirkcaldy: the church was overcrowded with people waiting to hear him preach, but as Irving was walking there, he was met with the terrible news that the gallery in the church had collapsed and thirty-five people had been killed.[94]

During 1828, Irving issued three other publications, the chief of which was *The Last Days*,[95] and attended Henry Drummond's annual prophecy convention at Albury. When in early 1829 this Albury circle began issuing a journal called *The Morning Watch*, with Irving as a major contributor, it seemed as if millennialism was becoming Irving's chief theological interest, although his Christology was, also, deeply woven through these articles. In May, Irving headed to Scotland once more, and in Annan, ten thousand people gathered in a field to hear him preach for four hours.[96] Annan empowered Irving to represent it at the General Assembly in Edinburgh; when he arrived, the Assembly debated whether or not he should be allowed to represent Annan, and ultimately, decided against him.[97] He continued preaching at places like Dumfries and Nith, to crowds of approximately ten and thirteen thousand.[98] Not everyone received Irving warmly, however (there were some taunts in Glasgow), but he continued preaching to small groups or large, visiting sick-beds and death-beds, and, eventually, made his way back to London. This whole trip to Scotland was how Irving chose to spend his leisure time, for he was officially on holiday; it, also, shows that his London ministry had won him a considerable reputation in his homeland.

While Irving had been in Scotland, a Baptist polemicist named James Haldane had published a document accusing him of heresy for his views of Christ.[99] Irving regarded Haldane's argument as slight, but the accusation of

---

[93] Dallimore, *Irving,* 87.

[94] Oliphant, *Irving,* 234-235.

[95] E. Irving, *The Last Days: a Discourse on the Evil Character of these our times: proving them to be the 'perilous times' of the 'Last Days'* (London: R.B. Seeley & W. Burnside, 1828)

[96] Oliphant, *Irving*, 261. Irving preached from noon until 5.30pm, with an hour's break in the middle. The size of the crowd indicates something of Irving's fame in the region; Annan's population in the 1790s was only estimated to be 1,000, F. Miller, *Poems from the Carlyle Country* (Glasgow: Jackson son & Co, 1937), 39.

[97] Oliphant, *Irving*, 262-263.

[98] Oliphant, *Irving*, 265. The crowd estimates were undertaken by a surveyor, based on the area of land occupied.

[99] J. Haldane, *A Refutation of the Heretical Doctrine Promulgated by the Rev. Edward Irving, respecting the Person and Atonement of the Lord Jesus Christ* (Edinburgh: W. Oliphant, 1829)

heresy had been made. Back amongst his flock in London, Irving closed 1829 by participating in another Albury conference.

1830 began with the publication of a tract, *The Orthodox and Catholic Doctrine of our Lord's Human Nature*, Irving's first elaboration of his Christology since the publication of his sermons on the incarnation.[100] Oliphant describes this tract as "a controversial reassertion [of his previously expressed Christology], strongly defensive and belligerent".[101] At this time, Hugh Maclean, a colleague of Irving's and, previously, minister at Scots Church, London Wall, had left this position for a church in Ayrshire, and Sandy Scott, Irving's assistant, had, similarly, accepted a position in Scotland. As part of their pre-ordination interviews after arriving in their respective positions, both men indicated views of Christ's humanity similar to Irving's. Their respective churches responded with concern, and Irving's name once more came under scrutiny and suspicion.[102] It was while these events were unfolding that developments of a different nature were occurring in Scotland which were to have a profound impact on the remainder of Irving's life.

A family named Campbell lived on a farm in Fernicarry in the Scottish parish of Rosneath. A daughter of the house, Isabella, who had died in 1827 at the age of twenty, had gained a reputation for holiness. Another daughter, Mary, had recently discussed theology with Sandy Scott: he had tried unsuccessfully to convince her that baptism with the Holy Spirit was a distinct experience from regeneration.[103] Mary, like her sister, was, also, suffering from tuberculosis and was not expected to live long. One evening in March, 1830 "the Holy Ghost came with mighty power upon [Mary] as she lay in her weakness, and constrained her to speak at great length, and with superhuman strength, in an unknown tongue, to the astonishment of all who heard, and to her own great edification and enjoyment in God".[104] A family called Macdonald in Port Glasgow became noted for a healing ministry, including the healing of Mary Campbell, herself.[105]

The news of these remarkable events soon reached London, as Irving and Isabella were watching the sad decline of another young son, Samuel. Although Irving's hopes for Samuel's healing soared on the news from Scotland, the boy died in July 1830.[106] It was too late in the week to find a substitute preacher, so

---

[100] E. Irving, *The Orthodox and Catholic Doctrine of our Lord's Human Nature, tried by the Westminister Confession of Faith, set forth in four parts* (London: Baldwin and Cradock, 1830)

[101] Oliphant, *Irving*, 278.

[102] Dallimore, *Irving*, 96.

[103] Oliphant, *Irving*, 286.

[104] Oliphant, *Irving*, 287. Oliphant is quoting from R.H. Story, *Memoir of the Life of the Rev. Robert Story, late Minister of Rosneath* (London: Macmillan & Co. 1862). No page number is given.

[105] Oliphant, *Irving* 288-289. Mary Campbell was healed on reading a letter from James Macdonald, quoting Psalm 20: "Arise, and stand upright."

[106] Oliphant, *Irving*, 298.

Irving dutifully preached, going straight from the pulpit to throw himself on his son's coffin.[107] Irving, Isabella and their one surviving child, Maggie, retreated to Ireland, and Irving filled the void with preaching engagements.[108]

While the Irvings were in Ireland, a group from London visited the Campbell and Macdonald homes to investigate the manifestations. This group, apparently all Anglicans, consisted of J.B. Cardale, his wife and sister, a doctor Thompson and two others.[109] After spending three weeks in the area, they compiled a favourable report on the genuineness of the gifts.[110] People began to hope and pray that London would soon experience a similar spiritual outpouring, and when a Miss Fancourt was healed there, excitement grew.[111] At this moment of excitement for Irving, other issues became a concern. Hugh Maclean's case was still pending, but Sandy Scott had temporarily withdrawn his case for ordination from the London Presbytery because of the objections against him.[112] The presbytery turned its attention to Irving and his Christology. Irving objected to the presbytery's manner of dealing with him, and that he would be subject to the judgment of six men, with no avenue of appeal. He claimed that as the minister of the National Scotch Church in Regent Square, he was subject to a Scottish Presbytery and could, therefore, not be dealt with by the London Presbytery.[113] Unsurprisingly, the presbytery ruled against him, requiring him to be placed on trial for his doctrine of "the sinful substance of Christ", should he ever attempt to preach in Scotland again.[114] Nevertheless, his congregation stood by him, making a robust declaration against the misconception that they taught or believed Christ actually sinned.[115]

1831 dawned with Irving having rejected, and having been rejected by, the Presbytery of London which he had previously admired. Irving published another work on Christology as his colleagues Campbell, Scott and Maclean faced the Edinburgh General Assembly: Campbell was deposed, Scott lost his

---

[107] Oliphant, *Irving*, 298.
[108] Oliphant, *Irving*, 299.
[109] The Cardales would shortly join Irving's congregation.
[110] Dallimore, *Irving*, 111.
[111] Dallimore, *Irving*, 110-111.
[112] Oliphant, *Irving*, 304.
[113] Oliphant, *Irving*, 305.
[114] Oliphant, *Irving*, 304-306; Dallimore, *Irving*, 113.
[115] The Regent Square congregation's statement in support of Irving was dated 15 December 1830 and is reprinted in *A Brief Statement of the Proceedings of the London Presbytery , in communion with the established Church of Scotland in the case of the Rev. Edward Irving, and of a book, written by him, and entitled "The Orthodox and Catholic Doctrine of our Lord's Human Nature"* (London: Basil Steuart, 1831), 16-17, also in G. Strachan, *The Pentecostal Theology of Edward Irving* (London: Darton, Longman & Todd, 1973), 45.

licence to preach and Maclean was referred to the jurisdiction of his local assembly.[116]

In July, Irving wrote to Robert Story, minister of Rosneath, with the news that two members of his congregation were speaking in tongues and prophesying.[117] Apparently, this had occurred as early as April, and the people were Mrs Cardale and Miss Hall.[118] The three-month gap between the occurrence and Irving's letter is due to Irving demonstrating a characteristic he usually eschewed – prudence. A further four months would elapse before these gifts appeared publicly in the congregation. The reason was that Irving was investigating the manifestation of the gifts before allowing them to become public, permitting them only in private prayer meetings. Oliphant has pointed out that Irving's bias in favour of the gifts hardly made him the most detached of observers, but she is convinced that he, at least, attempted to be so, and "it is evident that he proceeded with a care and caution scarcely to be expected from him".[119]

As time passed, Irving felt pressure to allow the gifts in the public worship services, pressure both from those manifesting the gifts and from his own logic: if he really believed these gifts were from the Holy Spirit, on what basis could he restrict their operation? It was in October 1831 that he took the step of removing this restriction, and he wrote, "Now, observe, I took to myself, according to the commandment of Jesus, the privilege and responsibility of trying the prophets in private, before permitting them to speak in the Church. I then gave the Church an opportunity of fulfilling its duty; for beyond question, it belongeth to every man to try the spirits; it belongeth not to the pastor alone."[120]

Irving's congregation had substantially supported him through his other theological passions, i.e., his millennialism and his emphasis on Christ's full identification with fallen humanity; the arrival of the charismata would prove a different story. Although it was not the only manifestation, it is perhaps not surprising that the focus of attention was on the glossolalia: how to understand it and how to respond to it. For some, the most important aspect was whether the glossolalia was actually *xenolalia*, i.e., a divinely given ability to speak in human languages not normally known to the speaker, with obvious benefits for missions.[121] For others, the outbreak of "the gifts" was nothing more or less

---

[116] E. Irving, *Christ's Holiness in the Flesh, the Form, Fountain head, and Assurance to us of Holiness in Flesh. In three parts.* (Edinburgh: John Lindsay & Co., 1831); Oliphant, *Irving*, 314; Dallimore, *Irving*, 113.
[117] Oliphant, *Irving*, 317.
[118] Dallimore, *Irving*, 112.
[119] Oliphant, *Irving*, 320.
[120] Oliphant, *Irving*, 322. Original reference not given.
[121] This was, also, of great interest in early twentieth century Pentecostalism. For some, this was the only valid purpose of tongues: if it didn't help expedite the last-days missions' outreach, it was of little use.

than chaos. Contemporary accounts, certainly, reveal that some people were alarmed at the proceedings, some were busy investigating them, but all were fascinated. In the wintry November of 1831, evening attendances at the Regent Square church numbered three thousand, and services at 6.30 am still drew one thousand people.[122]

All utterances in tongues were accompanied by the intelligible speech of interpretation, and Irving retained a steering hand (sometimes with difficulty), appointing times in the services for the operation of the gifts.[123] While Oliphant expressed her personal inability to decide whether the tongues were supernatural in origin, she acknowledged that the "mass of testimony" which she reviewed concluded that the glossolalia in Irving's congregation was "something awful and impressive".[124]

As 1831 drew to a close, the Trustees of the Regent Square congregation asked Irving to restrict the operation of the gifts to the morning prayer or mid-week services, and not to allow them in public worship on Sundays. They were confident that this measure would overcome the division of opinion that had arisen in the church.[125] From this, it is apparent that the Trustees did not have a deep-seated theological objection to the concept of charismatic gifts, but were more concerned to prevent schism. Nevertheless, Irving did not accede to their request. On Christmas Eve, Irving wrote a letter to the Trustees that demonstrated his belief that the charismata represented a return to the spiritual power of the early church.

> My dear Brethren, There is nothing which I would not surrender to you, even to my life, except to hinder or retard in any way what I most clearly discern to be the work of God's Holy Spirit, which, with heart and hand, we must all further, as we value the salvation of our immortal souls. I most solemnly warn you all, in the name of the most High God, for no earthly consideration whatever, to gainsay or impede the work of speaking with tongues and prophesying which God had begun amongst us, and which answereth in all respects, both formally and spiritually, to the thing promised in the Scriptures to those who believe; possessed in the primitive Church, and much prayed for by us all. ...[126]

Irving's passionate defence of the gifts is made more remarkable by the fact that he, himself, never actually spoke in tongues or prophesied.

In early 1832, attempts were made to heal this breach between Irving and the Trustees, but without success. In March, the Trustees lodged a complaint against Irving with the London Presbytery and he was ordered to stand trial in

---

[122] Oliphant, *Irving*, 326-327.
[123] Oliphant, *Irving*, 324, 326.
[124] Oliphant, *Irving*, 329.
[125] Oliphant, *Irving*, 336, 339; Dallimore, *Irving,* 144.
[126] Oliphant, *Irving*, 340. Letter dated December 24, 1831.

April.[127] A year before, Irving had stood before this Presbytery with his Trustees defending him; now they were his accusers. As there was nothing in the regulations of the Church of Scotland formally prohibiting exercise of charismatic gifts, the charges brought against Irving were essentially that he had allowed public worship to be interrupted by people who were not Church of Scotland ministers, some of whom were women.[128] Oliphant described the trial as "irrelevant, confused, and partial".[129] Irving defended his actions at length, along lines broadly similar to those indicated in his Christmas Eve letter, quoted above. Eventually, the Presbytery handed down its ruling that Irving had "rendered himself unfit to remain the minister of the national Scotch Church . . . and ought to be removed therefrom, in pursuance of the conditions of the trust-deed of the said church".[130] Irving had hoped to officiate at one last communion service, but found the gates of the church locked against him the following Sunday.[131] Approximately eight hundred people followed Irving and gathered to worship in a large room at Gray's Inn Road.[132] This new location proved unsuitable, and, although Irving complemented it with outdoor preaching, the congregation soon moved to a large gallery in Newman Street, and became known for some time as "The Church in Newman Street".[133] In this new location, argues Oliphant, the prophets in the church became more directive in their utterances.[134]

Towards the end of this eventful year of 1832, the Presbytery of Annan wrote to Irving asking him to confirm his authorship of three of his works; their intention was to bring him to trial over his teaching on Christ's assumption of fallen human nature. This trial took place in Annan on 13 March 1833 and Irving was formally charged with "printing, publishing, and disseminating heresies and heretical doctrines, particularly the doctrine of the fallen state and sinfulness of our Lord's human nature".[135] Two thousand people were gathered for the trial, which was conducted by Annandale men; the only evidence deemed necessary against Irving were his books *The Orthodox and Catholic Doctrine of our Lord's Human Nature*, *The Day of Pentecost* and one article from *The Morning Watch*.[136] After some hours' deliberation, including Irving's passionate defence of his teaching, he was pronounced guilty of heresy, but not before one further dramatic development.

---

[127] Oliphant, *Irving*, 355ff.
[128] Oliphant, *Irving*, 355-356.
[129] Oliphant, *Irving*, 357.
[130] Oliphant, *Irving*, 366-367.
[131] Oliphant, *Irving*, 368.
[132] Oliphant, *Irving*, 369; Dallimore, *Irving*, 146.
[133] Dallimore, *Irving*, 147.
[134] Oliphant, *Irving*, 379-380.
[135] Oliphant, *Irving*, 391.
[136] Oliphant, *Irving*, 391-392.

It was evening as proceedings were drawing to a close and the church was lit by only one candle. As the Presbytery was about to pronounce sentence, the senior member raised his voice in prayer, and a louder voice came from the gloom, "Arise, depart! Arise, depart! Flee ye out, flee ye out of her! Ye cannot pray! How can ye pray? How can ye pray to Christ whom ye deny? Ye cannot pray. Depart, depart! Flee, flee!" It was Dow of Irongray, one of Irving's supporters. Dow's voice caused some confusion in the gloom and as he and Irving (and perhaps others) rose to go, Irving exclaimed, "Stand forth! Stand forth! What! Will ye not obey the voice of the Holy Ghost? As many as will obey the voice of the Holy Ghost, let them depart".[137] The Presbytery was left to pass sentence on the absent defendant. The effect of the sentence of heresy on Irving can be imagined: it had been uttered in the town of his birth, in the church where he had been baptised and ordained. His association with the Church of Scotland had ended. Dallimore argues that although Irving outwardly appeared to bear up under the deposition, his spirit was crushed and his life lost meaning.[138]

On Irving's return to London, his status soon changed in the Newman Street Church. Although we will consider these changes in greater detail in a later chapter, what can be said here is that in the new church the senior authorities became those with the title of apostle or prophet, all of whom manifested some of the charismata. Because he didn't manifest any charismata, Irving was ineligible to fulfil one of these senior roles, and was appointed "angel" (pastor) of the congregation by the apostle J.B. Cardale.[139] For this reason, the Newman Street Church, which later evolved into the Catholic Apostolic Church, has never considered Irving to be its founder, and objects to the sobriquet "Irvingite".[140] In the midst of this apparent demotion, the Irvings lost yet another infant, Ebenezer.[141]

As the new church increasingly organised itself, *The Morning Watch* periodical folded for this very reason: the participants in both ventures were essentially the same people and the new organisation was seen as a greater realisation and outworking of the journal's purpose in drawing attention to prophetic fulfilment.[142] As 1833 drew to a close, we see Irving accommodating himself to the realities of life in the Newman Street Church, and continually expecting an outpouring of God's Spirit in his life.[143] Nevertheless, his role in the new context appeared to limit the previously wide-ranging impact of Irving's ministry.

---

137 Oliphant, *Irving*, 395.
138 Dallimore, *Irving*, 150.
139 Oliphant, *Irving*, 402.
140 C.G. Flegg, *"Gathered under Apostles": a study of the Catholic Apostolic Church* (Oxford: Clarendon, 1992), 63.
141 Dallimore, *Irving*, 153. Ebenezer died in April, 1833.
142 Oliphant, *Irving*, 400-401.
143 Oliphant, *Irving*, 404.

In January of 1834, Irving undertook a short visit to Edinburgh, returning in poor health.[144] Cardale and Drummond (both now apostles) then went to Edinburgh to follow up on initiatives undertaken by Irving. In their absence from London, one of the other prophets, Edward Taplin, issued a statement "in the Spirit" concerning the appointment of some evangelists and Irving immediately complied. On their return, Cardale and Drummond rebuked both Taplin and Irving, declaring the appointment of evangelists at Taplin's instigation to be a delusion. Taplin withdrew in anger for some months; Irving, humbled, confessed his "error" before the congregation.[145]

Towards the middle of the year, Irving's friends and relatives were beginning to express their concern over his situation: he didn't relax enough; his manner was uncharacteristically lethargic. There is no better description of the deterioration in Irving than Carlyle's, who hadn't seen Irving for two years until May of 1834 when he chanced upon him in Kensington Gardens:

> we were proceeding towards Chelsea in the middle of a bright May day, when I noticed, well down in Kensington-Gardens, a dark male figure sitting between two white female ones under a tree; male figure, which abruptly rose and stalked towards me; whom, seeing it was Irving, I hastily disengaged myself, and stept out to meet. It was indeed Irving; but how changed in the two years and two months since I had last seen him! In look he was almost friendlier than ever; but he had suddenly become an old man. His head, which I had left raven-black, was grown grey, on the temples almost snow-white; the face was hollow, wrinkly, collapsed; the figure, still perfectly erect, seemed to have lost all its elasticity and strength. ... He admitted his weak health, but treated it as temporary, it seemed of small account to him... His tone was not despondent; but it was low, pensive, full of silent sorrow. Once, perhaps twice, I got a small bit of Annandale laugh from him, strangely genuine, though so lamed and overclouded; this was to me the most affecting thing of all, and still is when I recall it.[146]

In September, one of the Newman Street prophets declared that God had a work for Irving to do in Glasgow.[147] Irving headed out alone, circling through Wales, intending to finish the journey by ship. Nevertheless his health continued to decline, and his regular letters home reveal overwhelming fatigue and fever. At the end of six weeks, he asked Isabella to join him in Liverpool, where she found him looking much worse than when she last saw him.[148] They journeyed to Glasgow together, but Irving's ill-health continued and he died on

---

[144] Oliphant, *Irving*, 405-407.
[145] Oliphant, *Irving*, 407; Dallimore, *Irving*, 163.
[146] Carlyle, *Reminiscences*, 302-303.
[147] Oliphant, *Irving*, 408.
[148] Dallimore, *Irving*, 167.

7 December, 1834. He was buried in the crypt of Glasgow Cathedral, with the number of mourners at his funeral being described as "vast".[149]

[149] Dallimore, *Irving*, 169.

CHAPTER 3

A Historiography of Edward Irving

As the previous chapter has shown, Edward Irving was a significant figure in Scottish and English church life in the first third of the nineteenth century. His relatively short life and ministry embraced several (overlapping) phases and convictions including: his reputation as an outstanding preacher; an interest in prophecy resulting in a premillennial stance; a controversial Christology; and an acceptance of charismata that anticipated the Pentecostalism of the early twentieth century. Irving's theological development made him an object of controversy both during his lifetime and in the years since, resulting in a variety of interpretations of his character and career.

Irving's first major biographer was Margaret Oliphant, whose two-volume work, *The Life of Edward Irving*, appeared in 1862.[1] It went through several subsequent editions in the nineteenth century; we will be using the fifth edition which, although it is undated, was probably published around 1870.[2] This edition has been chosen because the preface states it was a careful revision of earlier editions. Oliphant had the triple advantages of having known Irving personally, easy access to many of his contemporaries, and access to family correspondence. However, Oliphant's closeness to Isabella Irving and her surviving children, also, affected her neutrality in some ways.[3]

Only a few pages into Oliphant's work, she gave an early indication that she interpreted Irving as exhibiting a tension between scepticism and extreme belief, and in transition from the former to the latter as he aged: "The main quality in himself [Irving] which struck observers was – in strong and strange contradiction to the extreme devotion of *belief* manifested in his latter years – the critical and almost sceptical tendency of his mind, impatient of superficial 'received truths,' and eager for proof and demonstration of everything."[4]

---

[1] Oliphant's work quickly eclipsed in popularity the couple of biographies that had preceded hers.

[2] In B. Flikkema's 1997 bibliography of Irving sources, there seems to be confusion over the dates of the various editions of Oliphant's work, which is not surprising since some of these are undated. He says the 4th, 5th and 6th editions were published in 1865, 1870 and 1862, respectively. Obviously, the 6th edition could not be earlier than the 4th and 5th.

[3] Isabella had, however, died several years before Oliphant's first edition was printed.

[4] M. Oliphant, *The Life of Edward Irving* (London: Hurst and Blackett, n.d. 5th edition), 24. Emphasis original.

This "strong and strange contradiction" between Irving as passionate believer and critical intellect echoes through Oliphant's work and remains an enigma that she (and others) tried to resolve, with limited success. She indicated that Irving's critical faculties were later eclipsed by his theological passions, but it is an interpretation that she wrestled with throughout her work, and never seemed completely at ease with. Her observations, though, are completely in keeping with our previous comments about Romanticism: it did not generally refute the rationalism of the previous age, but it perceived its limitations and wanted to transcend it. Oliphant's observation did not make an explicit connection with the wider Romantic context, and, therefore, this interpretive possibility eluded her.

When Irving entered the world of Thomas Chalmers, Oliphant compared the two men, characterising the former as a "poet-enthusiast" and the latter as "statesman and philosopher". Despite concluding that Chalmers had a greater intellectual capacity than Irving, Oliphant was convinced that Chalmers never really understood Irving's "instinctive comprehensions and graces".[5] Others were less complimentary about Chalmers's intellect, claiming, "The great orator had but the smallest capacity for abstract thought" and that he was "not a thinker of the first rank".[6] If there is some truth in this latter observation, it would only have deepened the gulf between Irving and Chalmers. Certainly Chalmers's early biographer and son-in-law described Irving's intellect as "vigorous".[7] It is possible Oliphant was allowing later events to colour this reading somewhat, but she painted a picture of Irving in the eyes of Chalmers as an enthusiast, credulous and potentially unsteady. This was modified by her repeated emphasis that Chalmers didn't understand Irving. Nevertheless, it is clear that Chalmers was concerned about Irving's future direction, because when he later visited Irving, a month after the latter's induction into his new London role, he journalled: "that he [Irving] is prospering in his new situation . . . I hope that he will not hurt his usefulness by any kind of eccentricity or imprudence."[8] Here Chalmers offered another lens through which to interpret Irving: eccentricity and imprudence, and, certainly, some would see Irving's later career in this way. Yet, these terms also may simply be expressive of the difference in age and temperament between the two men.

Once Irving was established in London – and through the circle around Basil Montagu he met many notable Londoners - he became exposed to several key theological influences, including, chronologically, Coleridge's view of the

---

[5] Oliphant, *Irving*, 61-62.

[6] W.G. Berry, *Scotland's Struggles for Religious Liberty* (London: National Council of Evangelical Free Churches, 1904), 99; A.L. Drummond & J. Bulloch, *The Scottish Church 1688-1843: the Age of the Moderates* (Edinburgh: The Saint Andrew Press, 1973), 162.

[7] W. Hanna, *Memoirs of Thomas Chalmers* (Edinburgh: Thomas Constable, 1854), vol. 1, 567.

[8] Oliphant, *Irving*, 79.

church, Hatley Frere's interpretation of prophecy, Henry Drummond's Albury conferences and the outbreak of charismata. Oliphant has raised the issue of Irving's credulity: was Irving merely susceptible to every new idea that crossed his path? Oliphant herself provided evidence to the contrary. Although portraying Irving's attitude to Coleridge as one of "reverential respect", a little later we see Irving writing in his journal for 29 October 1825: "There are no philosophers now-a-days, because they are all ambitious of power or eminence. Even Basil Montagu is desirous of power, - that is, his own will; and Coleridge is desirous of power, - that is, the good-will of others, or the idolatry of himself."[9] Irving, certainly, admired Coleridge, but it was not uncritical admiration.

Irving's new church in Regent Square opened in early 1827 and Oliphant believed this was a turning point:

> If fashion had crazed him with her momentary adulation, here was the critical point at which fashions and he parted; the beginning of a disenchantment which, next to personal betrayal, is perhaps the hardest experience in the world. This has been accepted by many – and asserted by one who knew him thoroughly, and from whose judgment I know not how to presume to differ – as the secret cause of all the darker shadows and perplexing singularities of his later life. I am as little able to cope with Mr Carlyle in philosophic insight as I am in personal knowledge.[10]

There are two problems with this passage. Oliphant has posited an "If-then" argument: *if* fashion had crazed Irving momentarily, *then* here is the beginning of disenchantment. This inclines the reader to accept both the protasis and the apodosis, yet the protasis has by no means been established. Oliphant provided no evidence of a starry-eyed Irving dazzled by new-found fame in London and therefore set forth a hollow argument. The second problem is her overly deferential attitude to Carlyle and information obtained from him.[11] Carlyle's later *Reminiscences* show that his personal knowledge of Irving was sporadic after Irving moved to London. Intriguingly, though, on the very next page following the above extract, Oliphant wrote: "I can find no evidence whatever, except in what he himself says in the dedication of his Sermons to Mr Basil Montagu, of even a tendency on Irving's part to be carried away by that brilliant social stream." Oliphant's case is inconsistent and unpersuasive.

So Irving wasn't "crazed by fashion" and Oliphant was driven by the weight of evidence to conclude that the interpretation of Irving that she had advanced on the previous page, invoking Carlyle's name in its favour, ultimately had little support. This demonstrates both Oliphant's essential fairness in trying to assess the evidence, as well as her genuine struggle in trying to interpret

---

[9] Oliphant, *Irving*, 92, 129.
[10] Oliphant, *Irving*, 211.
[11] Oliphant, *Irving*, 211.

Irving's character. And if Irving hadn't been unduly affected by his popularity, how valid is the interpretation that its departure was "the beginning of a disenchantment"? In fact, Oliphant's work goes on to demonstrate that Irving's popularity did not decline from 1827 (as the above quote implies) but increased for several more years.[12] If Irving suffered any "disenchantment" at this point, it would have to be for some other reason; those proffered by Oliphant simply didn't exist in 1827.

Later, in describing the final meeting between Irving and Chalmers in October 1830, Oliphant indicated another interpretation of Irving: that he "abrogated reason".[13] If we ask when this alleged abrogation of reason occurred, we once more see Oliphant struggling to maintain this interpretation in light of the evidence. In fact, in the concluding section of her biography, she wrote that Irving died: "without, so far as his last writings leave any trace, either decadence of intellect or lowering of thought".[14] Oliphant's biography retained a great influence and later writers often elaborated on some of her more negative observations without noticing the internal contradictions in her work. A recent Oliphant scholar who has noticed this tension is Elisabeth Jay. She argued that Oliphant's status as the "authorised biographer" led her to sympathise with Irving as "romantic hero", and her scepticism about supernatural religion surfaced when she portrayed him as the "sacrificial victim" of the Catholic Apostolic Church.[15] A century after Oliphant wrote, her influence could still be seen in one writer (whose main focus was Coleridge) who described Irving as "not primarily a thinker" and as "laps[ing] into extreme emotionalism."[16]

The next major nineteenth century interpreter was Irving's life-long friend, Thomas Carlyle; their relationship will be examined in detail in chapter five. Carlyle's *Reminiscences* contain his memories of Irving and six others, including the poets Southey and Wordsworth. The section on Irving is the largest in the book, although as Carlyle himself noticed, it often seems to be more about Carlyle than Irving. We have mentioned above that Carlyle saw little of Irving during the London years: nothing during the first two years in London; nothing from 1827-1831 and almost nothing in the last two years of Irving's life. There was, however, a ten-month period from 1824-25 during which he saw a lot of Irving and noted that Irving was enthused with the

---

[12] In 1831, the church services at the new building were described as full to "overflowing" (Oliphant, *Irving*, 312).

[13] Oliphant, *Irving*, 294. Emphasis mine. This meeting took place several months before the occurrence of tongues in Irving's congregation.

[14] Oliphant, *Irving*, 427-428.

[15] E. Jay, *Mrs Oliphant: a Fiction to herself. A Literary Life* (Oxford: Clarendon Press, 1995), 253. Jay argues that Oliphant continues to explore this nexus between sympathy and suspicion of religious activity in a later work, *The Minister's Wife* (1869).

[16] J.D. Boulger, *Coleridge as Religious Thinker* (New Haven: Yale University Press, 1961), 46.

possibility that God was using him to restore vitality to Christianity. No adherent of Irving's theology, Carlyle still noted that "The force and weight of what he urged was undeniable, the potent faculty at work, like that of Samson heavily striding along with the Gates of Gaza on his shoulders."[17] Carlyle claimed that Irving maintained this conviction to the end of his life, and combined with credulity on Irving's part, it explained his later "extravagances" and "aberrations".[18] Carlyle was theologically far more remote from Irving than was Chalmers, and there is evidence that Carlyle's dismissal of Irving's religious hopes was almost a reflex action: an interest in prophecy is regarded, as by definition, an "aberration", yet in the same meeting Carlyle described Irving as "wise and shrewd" when talking on non-religious matters.[19] Carlyle has raised credulity once more as a possible key to understanding Irving's character, but at no point does Carlyle imply that Irving "abrogated reason"; the furthest he goes is to say that some of those around him (and Carlyle does believe that some of these were hysterical) "puddled" his thinking.[20] At any rate, we see in Carlyle's description a potent image of Irving as Samson, convinced that he has a noble and God-given role to restore vital Christianity to the world, unwilling to settle for anything less than this Ideal and committed to this cause until his death. It is an image that resonates strongly with the concept of the Romantic hero.

Both Oliphant and Carlyle made the assumption that something must have gone "terribly wrong" for someone of Irving's abilities to end up as he did, and explaining the disparity between Irving's abilities and his sad relegation and early death has vexed Irving scholars ever since. As two major nineteenth century interpreters of Irving, both of whom knew him personally, the only significant possible interpretation of Irving's "decline" that Oliphant and Carlyle have in common that is not contradicted by other internal evidence is the possibility of credulity - implicitly theological credulity – although, neither of them engaged in a theological assessment.

There were other nineteenth century interpreters, some of whom, like Robert Story, had personal knowledge of Irving. Story's view was that Irving's "lofty mind [was] wasting itself on . . . vague uncertainties" and his "pure and heroic spirit" was "worn out in the feverish excitement of a restless and bewildering supernaturalism".[21] Tulloch acknowledged Irving as, in some respects, an "unrivalled" genius, especially in the area of preaching and the spiritual life, but ranked him low in the area of ideas and critical thought.[22] Tulloch's Irving

[17] T. Carlyle, *Reminiscences* (London: J. M. Dent & Sons, 1932. Orig. 1881), 254.
[18] Carlyle, *Reminiscences*, 254.
[19] Carlyle, *Reminiscences*, 293.
[20] Carlyle, *Reminiscences*, 298.
[21] R.H. Story, *Memoir of the Life of the Rev. Robert Story, late Minister of Rosneath, Dunbartonshire* (Cambridge: Macmillan, 1862), 227.
[22] J. Tulloch, *Movements of Religious Thought in Britain during the Nineteenth Century* (Leicester: Leicester University Press, 1971. Orig. 1885), 156.

was overly emotional, readily influenced by transcendent ideas, and unwilling to change any conviction once adopted.[23]

As the twentieth century dawned, all those with personal knowledge of Irving had joined him in the dust, and, therefore, the next generation of Irving interpreters lacked their direct assistance. The title of J.C. Root's 1912 publication, *Edward Irving: Man, Preacher, Prophet*, clearly indicated the direction of the author's interpretation, which was further clarified in the foreword in which she characterised Irving as someone who was prepared to put aside prejudice and pursue truth at all costs.[24] Like her nineteenth century predecessors, Jean Root provided no bibliography, gave little by way of exact references, and her treatment was more biographical than theological. As with a number of authors, she noted the impact on Irving of the loss of his infant son, Edward, arguing that it lifted Irving above selfishness to a place of greater consecration.[25] This interpretation will contrast with a later writer's assessment of this incident.

Root dated Irving's interest in a possible renewal of the spiritual gifts to the first Albury meeting of 1826, and the dual influences of Rev. J. Haldane Stewart who was praying for an outpouring of the Holy Spirit in his congregation, and Henry Drummond, who had decided against a cessationist position on the gifts, concluding that their absence was due to the lack of faith of the Church.[26] She saw Irving's subsequent assessment of the gifts that manifested in his congregation as suitably cautious and prudent, but acknowledged that there was an alternative view that Irving lost "his mental balance and that an epidemic of religious madness held high carnival in the Regent Square church".[27] Root claimed that there are, fortunately, several "dispassionate" descriptions available of these events and, as an example, quoted at length from Henry Drummond who, while possibly fulfilling part of the dictionary definition of dispassionate, was hardly completely impartial on the issue of spiritual gifts.[28] Unfortunately, Root did not give adequate consideration to the voices of Irving's critics, and in fact, summarily dismissed them; the result is a biased picture of Irving that veers uncomfortably towards hagiography.

The second major twentieth century treatment of Irving was A.L. Drummond's 1934 publication, *Edward Irving and his Circle*. Drummond, also, discussed Irving in a posthumously-published work; we will consider the

---

[23] Tulloch, *Movements of Religious Thought*, 157.

[24] J.C. Root, *Edward Irving: Man, Preacher, Prophet* (Boston: Sherman, French & Co., 1912). The foreword is only one page, and has no page number. Root was from a New England liberal perspective.

[25] Root, *Irving*, 41.

[26] Root, *Irving*, 78.

[27] Root, *Irving*, 91-92.

[28] Root, *Irving*, 92ff.

two together here.[29] Early in the first book, Drummond provided a short quote from one of Irving's letters to Carlyle which gives insight into the young minister's personality: "Dr. Chalmers, though a most entire original by himself, is surrounded with a very prosaical sort of persons, who please me something by their zeal to carry into effect his philosophical schemes, and vex me much by their idolatry of him."[30] Apart from indicating that Irving was unlikely to be satisfied with a "prosaic" Christianity, this quote demonstrates both Irving's discernment and his innate lack of propensity to hero-worship: Chalmers was the foremost Scottish churchman of his generation, and at this point Irving had only been his assistant for five months. Even at this early stage, Irving was not cowed by a person's reputation, and seems an unlikely candidate to adopt a stance of "idolatrous" credulity towards anyone. This evidence qualifies the view of Chalmers's biographer who claimed Irving's attitude to Chalmers was one of "veneration".[31]

Still early in his book, Drummond made a comprehensive assessment of Irving's character. He claimed Irving was overly subjective and disregarded mature Christian advice, claiming "to advance in the apprehension of truth, but it was neither a clear rational development nor a simple religious experience. He gradually identified himself so closely with the Lord's purposes that he either ignored opposition or denounced it as the work of knaves or fools."[32] Drummond saw elements of reason and experience in Irving, with an overarching pursuit of truth, but he could not easily classify him. In the context of Drummond's book, his judgement on Irving seems somewhat premature. At this point in the biography, Irving was at the peak of his popularity and Drummond has provided no evidence as yet for his assertions. However, we will summarise this list of Irving's alleged flaws and assess whether the evidence is forthcoming in the remainder of the volume. Essentially, the flaws Drummond saw in Irving were: his disregard for the judgement of mature Christians; a confused subjectivism in his pursuit of truth; and an inflated view of his own mission which resulted in a dismissal of all contrary views. These perceived flaws, clearly, align with Romantic characteristics, specifically, its anti-authoritarianism and its confidence in individual ability to pursue transcendent truths.

Drummond added to his interpretation of Irving by criticising both his education and intellectual abilities. Irving imperfectly apprehended Coleridge and Irving's "partial" studies as a theological student did not give him the

---

[29] Drummond & Bulloch, *The Scottish Church*, 200-208.

[30] A.L. Drummond, *Edward Irving and his Circle, including some consideration of the 'Tongues' Movement in the light of Modern Psychology* (London: James Clarke, 1934), 34. The letter is dated 14 March 1820, but Drummond does not refer to his source for it. A.L. Drummond is no relation to Henry Drummond.

[31] S.J. Brown, *Thomas Chalmers and the Godly Commonwealth in Scotland* (Oxford: Oxford University Press), 1982, 139.

[32] Drummond, *Edward Irving and his Circle,* 55.

grounding he would have received from a "regular Divinity course".[33] Yet, a few pages later, Drummond modified this slightly, claiming Irving's "erudition was certainly above the average of his time in Scotland though he had little 'exact scholarship'".[34] And a little later, Drummond referred to Irving's *Ordination Charge* to Hugh McLean as "without peer in theological literature".[35] Would it be possible for someone with a second-rate theological education to write peerless theology? It appears Drummond was struggling to find a consistent interpretation of Irving in this field, the danger being, of course, if he ceded too much ground to Irving the theologian early on, it would be harder to discount his later theological developments. The praise Drummond gave to Irving's *Ordination Charge* was diluted by his comment on Irving's statement that Catholicism was a superstition to be resisted: "We see here the growth of that fanaticism which was ultimately to darken his life by driving out the spirit of enlightenment."[36] Drummond's Irving would end his life as an unenlightened fanatic. Yet Drummond overlooked the historical context of the debate about Catholic emancipation; Irving's anti-Catholicism was by no means idiosyncratic, but expressive of a resurgent view in the 1820s.[37]

Through most of his book, Drummond maintained that Irving was impulsive and illogical.[38] When it came to the eventual manifestation of the gifts in Regent Square and Irving's attempt to assess them, Drummond claimed that Irving's critical faculty was lacking, he had an obvious bias in favour of the gifts, and that while he had the ability to detect a complete fraud, he could do little else.

> But he could scarcely differentiate between the genuinely inspired and those weak-willed, suggestible people who are so often the passive victims of revival mania. To differentiate between true and false candidates would be beyond the power even of one who combined intense psychic power, psychological insight, and spiritual intuition. It would require the power of reading men's souls which only One Man has ever possessed. Irving's faith was simple and absolute: he had neither historic sense nor knowledge of the

---

[33] Drummond, *Edward Irving and his Circle*, 66, 69. Even if the first allegation had substance, it would only have the effect of putting Irving amongst a large group of intelligent men (including Chalmers) who acknowledged their difficulty in understanding Coleridge's philosophy. Yet Chalmers felt there was a bond of understanding between Coleridge and Irving that he could not share, Dallimore, *Irving*, 46.

[34] Drummond, *Edward Irving and his Circle*, 69.

[35] Drummond, *Edward Irving and his Circle*, 71.

[36] Drummond, *Edward Irving and his Circle*, 71.

[37] B. Hilton, *A Mad, Bad, & Dangerous People? England 1783-1846* (Oxford: Clarendon, 2006), 238, 380.

[38] Drummond, *Edward Irving and his Circle*,131.

> maze of motives and cross-currents which are found in men's minds and hearts.[39]

This is internally inconsistent: having granted that only Jesus Christ can read men's souls, Drummond lamented that Edward Irving lacked this ability! It is a cheap shot to set the standard impossibly high and then criticise someone for not achieving it. Drummond's closing sentence above also needs to be challenged. Irving's published writings attest to his wide reading in the Church Fathers and the theology of the Reformers; his attempt to restore a vision of Christianity which he felt had been lost over the centuries does not imply he lacked historic sense. Secondly, all writers agree that Irving was indefatigable in visiting parishioners both in the slums of Glasgow and in his London churches; surely when this is seen alongside his access to the wealthy and powerful in London, it is evident that Irving had well above average access to the "knowledge of the maze of motives and cross-currents" of the human heart. Paradoxically, towards the conclusion of his book, Drummond argued that the unparalleled variety of Irving's acquaintances (he names Carlyle, Coleridge, Chalmers, the Welshes, as well as the reality of the Glasgow slums) would have been a counter-balance against any possible fanaticism.[40]

As Drummond's book draws to a close, there is a sense of struggle as he tried to reconcile his chosen position of Irving as fanatic with the evidence. He wrote of Irving's humility as he accepted a subordinate role in the nascent Catholic Apostolic Church, yet on the very next page claimed Irving was becoming increasingly absolutist in his judgements.[41] And after having disparaged Irving's intellect and education earlier in his book, in his closing pages Drummond wrote of Irving, "One thinks of the glorious eclecticism of an intellect that ranged freely through mathematics and foreign languages, poetry and history. One envies a personality so much at home in the most diverse company and yet not lonely in solitude."[42] In the end, despite Drummond's best efforts, the flaws he assigned to Irving earlier in the book remain largely unsubstantiated. Nor did he make any significant progress in understanding Irving during the next thirty years, as his posthumous work indicates. Although mentioning Irving's "profound insights" and, generally, criticising the degree to which the Westminster Confession had become the Church of Scotland's authority, Drummond partly justified the Church's condemnation of Irving because of "obscurity or ambiguity" in his teaching.[43] He, also, made the colourful allegation that Mary Campbell of Gairloch was Irving's "evil

---

[39] Drummond, *Edward Irving and his Circle*, 155-156.
[40] Drummond, *Edward Irving and his Circle*, 272.
[41] Drummond, *Edward Irving and his Circle*, 272, 273.
[42] Drummond, *Edward Irving and his Circle*, 273.
[43] Drummond & Bulloch, *The Scottish Church, 1688-1843*, 208, 207.

genius".[44] This unsubstantiated allegation (which Drummond built on to, haphazardly, name Campbell as the foundation of modern Pentecostalism) continued the assumption that Irving's involvement with the charismata led to his undoing.[45] This probably influenced an author who published just after Drummond and referred to the charismata as "psychopathic contagions from Scotland", although just how much attention should be paid to an author who claimed Irving served under Dr *James* Chalmers in Scotland is debatable.[46] Other authors, referring briefly to Irving in following years, found it all too easy to glean convenient adjectives from Oliphant and Drummond and dismiss him as "fanatical" or "credulous".[47] Yet, for those, like Drummond, who examined Irving at length, such a dismissal was too facile. There is a note of wistful lament as Drummond concluded his 1934 work: "There must have been some fatal flaw in [Irving's] personality that undid the good of all his gifts."[48] "Must have been" conveys the tacit admission that, ultimately, the interpretations Drummond offered were inconsistent and unsatisfactory, even to himself. Irving had eluded him.

H.C. Whitley's 1953 PhD thesis was condensed and published two years later as *Blinded Eagle*, its title indicating his interpretation of Irving. Yet this condensed version of the thesis is highly frustrating, hinting at views that are not fully elaborated. Early in the book, Whitley tended to blame Irving's wife Isabella's absences for Irving's decline: "At his darkest hour she was not with him, and she failed to influence him at a time when restraint might have saved him from his later tragic mistakes."[49] What these "tragic mistakes" were is not clearly established; neither is the reason for Whitley's confidence in Isabella's ability to divert Irving from them. There were hints that Whitley regarded Drummond as having a negative effect on Irving, calling their friendship "one of the enigmas of the whole Irving story. Was he in fact Irving's evil genius? Only a complete account of Albury happenings and the publication of many private papers of the Catholic Apostolic Church could answer that question."[50] Twenty years before, A.L. Drummond had suggested Mary Campbell was Irving's "evil genius"; now Whitley suggests Henry Drummond in that role. Obviously, both interpreters felt Irving's life needed somebody to fill this role! But both comments were gratuitous: Whitley (and Drummond) nowhere

---

[44] Drummond & Bulloch, *The Scottish Church, 1688-1843*, 205-206. For Campbell's role in the Gairloch manifestations see pages 48-50 and 265.
[45] Drummond & Bulloch, *The Scottish Church, 1688-1843*, 206.
[46] P. Butler, "Irvingism as an Analogue of the Oxford Movement", *Church History*, vol. 6, no. 2, June 1937, 101-102.
[47] E.g., L. & E. Hanson, who used both adjectives in *Necessary Evil: the Life of Jane Welsh Carlyle* (London: Constable, 1952), 9, 81, 164.
[48] Drummond, *Edward Irving and his Circle*, 274.
[49] H.C. Whitley, *Blinded Eagle: an Introduction to the Life and Teaching of Edward Irving* (Chicago: A.R. Allenson, 1955), 15. Due to the inaccessibility of the original thesis, scholars tend to refer to this publication.
[50] Whitley, *Blinded Eagle*, 41.

established why an "evil genius" was necessary in his understanding of subsequent events or why Henry Drummond was the most likely candidate, and if, as he indicated, the friendship was an "enigma", then there was scant justification for lurid speculation.

Whitley believed that part of the key to understanding the "enigma" of Irving was to see him in a conflict between "prophetic inspiration" and "clear philosophic thought" which would often lead him to "overleap the limits of reason."[51] Once again, this indicates not only issues faced by Edward Irving, but something of the tension of the age between the heritage of the Enlightenment and the new Romantic spirit. If Irving wanted to leap beyond the limits of reason, it was a desire shared by many of his contemporaries who perceived those limits as reductionist, and felt a duty to go beyond them. Whitley, also, praised Irving's gifts as a writer, speaker and described his mind as "incisive".[52] So with these gifts and abilities in full flight, how could Irving's downfall be explained? Whitley gave another hint, and now it seems as if the "tragic mistakes" he mentioned earlier have reduced to one: "Only once in later years was he to falter and lose his way, when the drama of the 'tongues' promised him disaster in his own church."[53] Yet, Whitley did not make it clear exactly *how* Irving faltered, nor what he *should* have done. Whitley was, clearly, an admirer of Irving's, and he anticipated a time when Irving's reputation as a great Scottish theologian would be vindicated.[54] He saw Irving as a reformer who suffered the rejection most reformers experience,[55] and, although he stopped short of describing Irving as a prophet, the picture he painted in the closing pages is very close to this, even though he doesn't actually use the word.

The book can be seen in two halves: in the first, Whitley discussed Irving's "tragic mistakes" and proposed Drummond as an evil background figure (neither of which is given substance); by the second half, Irving simply "falters" and loses his way once, a failure which is eclipsed by the final claim that Irving was a significant theologian, an unfairly rejected reformer of nearly prophetic status. While Whitley's gratuitous cul-de-sacs are frustrating (and his repeated use of the word "enigma" possibly revealing), his book in some ways echoed Oliphant's: both writers end up with an overwhelmingly positive appreciation of Irving, but seem at a loss to know how to interpret the events of his life. If Irving *had* clearly made a series of tragic mistakes, or if Drummond's activities *could* be established as nefarious, this would make the task of interpretation so much easier. None of this is demonstrated and Whitley's work remains unconvincing; nevertheless it was a preliminary

---

[51] Whitley, *Blinded Eagle*, 102-3.
[52] Whitley, *Blinded Eagle*, 102-3.
[53] Whitley, *Blinded Eagle*, 103.
[54] Whitley, *Blinded Eagle*, 106. As we shall see, much of the recent work on Irving's theology tends to fulfil Whitley's hope.
[55] Whitley, *Blinded Eagle*, 105.

attempt to rehabilitate Irving's reputation as a theologian: it was a path others were shortly to follow.

In 1973, Gordon Strachan published *The Pentecostal Theology of Edward Irving*. It was the first major work on Irving since Whitley's and represented a watershed in Irving studies as it began a new trend of focusing closely on Irving's theological contributions; most previous writers had attempted biographies which had been forced to address issues of theology in a tangential manner. As the back cover made clear, the author was very conscious of the expanding "pentecostal revival" and the newly arrived "charismatic renewal". The transdenominational charismatic movement gave a new perspective and credibility to those who had aligned with Pentecostal phenomena in the past, and Irving was a beneficiary of this appreciative retrospection. Strachan's focus was almost exclusively on Irving the theologian, and within that primarily his Christology and the charismata; his millennial interests were almost ignored.

Early in his book, Strachan highlighted Irving's theological abilities, claiming that "the centrality of a coherent theological system" underpinned the revival of charismata in Irving's ministry.[56] While some have maintained that the outbreak of tongues in the congregation was wildly hysterical and opposed by many,[57] Strachan marshalled evidence to the contrary and noted that the overwhelming majority of the congregation followed Irving after his expulsion from Regent's Square.[58] Strachan saw Irving's contemporaries polarised into two groups: one group represented Irving as a noble man who was going out of his mind, in charge of a deluded group of hysterics; the other camp supported Irving, sometimes reluctantly, but felt that he was theologically consistent and innocent of the charges brought against him.[59] Strachan's sympathies were clearly with the second group. Like Oliphant, he could see no reason for doubting Irving's sanity and lucidity, arguing that to the end of Irving's life he expounded a theological system "which can now be clearly understood as cogent and coherent in the light of the theology and experience of the twentieth century Pentecostal movement".[60] This is a double-edged sword: is this an admission that Irving's theological writings *can't* be seen as cogent and coherent without the posthumous arrival of Pentecostalism? As an admirer of Irving's theology, Strachan would not want to push the issue this far. but he does feel that Irving's relative isolation amongst his fellow ministers on this issue was the main restraint holding back the full acclamation of his many

---

[56] G. Strachan, *The Pentecostal Theology of Edward Irving* (London: Dartman, Longman & Todd, 1973), 15.
[57] Carlyle was one who described the tongues as hysterical, *Reminiscences*, 298. Dallimore talks about the "many beloved people" Irving left behind at Regent Square, *The Life of Edward Irving: the Fore-runner of the Charismatic Movement* (Edinburgh: Banner of Truth, 1983), 146.
[58] Strachan, *Pentecostal Theology*, 17.
[59] Strachan, *Pentecostal Theology*, 17.
[60] Strachan, *Pentecostal Theology*, 21.

admirers. So Strachan's argument would appear to be that the Pentecostal and charismatic movements belatedly purchased a respectful hearing for Irving's theology.

One of the disadvantages of Strachan's treatment is the way it almost completely divorced Irving, the theologian, from Irving, the man: with biographical and historical detail largely absent, Irving appears as a de-contextualised theological proponent, rather than a person. It is only as a theologian that he is assessed and when Strachan concluded that "Irving today can be understood as the first Reformed-Pentecostal theologian,"[61] the assessment is a positive one. The issue of possible theological credulity that lingered from Oliphant's and Carlyle's writings is not on the horizon here – Strachan's admiration for Irving's theological acumen simply excludes it – and whereas Oliphant and Carlyle offered no theological assessment to support their stance, Strachan offered this exclusively.

Strachan presented the first comprehensive theological assessment of Irving in recent decades and in doing so he undermined the one remaining interpretation of Irving's decline offered by both Oliphant and Carlyle, but, because his focus is not on the social and cultural influences surrounding Irving, he offered little of substance in its place. When we look for clues as to why Strachan believed Irving's ministry ended the way it did, we find only an image of Irving isolated from support because he was a pioneer of proto-Pentecostalism, at least seventy years ahead of his time. While this may well be part of the picture, given Strachan's theological focus it would have been difficult for him to discover anything outside of this.

Publishing in 1978, Massey University History Professor W.H. Oliver's chosen focus was on "prophets and millennialists" and Irving was one of a number considered in this work. Early on, Oliver indicated his view that Irving's millennial views began as he knelt at the deathbed of Edward Jr, forged from his conviction that he would one day see his son again, raised from death on the earth.[62] Oliver has identified a key tragedy that had a profound effect on Irving's life; as we noted in the previous chapter, Irving's grief over the loss of his first-born son was immense, and probably never left him. Oliphant believed that "no other event of [Irving's] life penetrated so profoundly the depths of his spirit".[63] Has Oliver identified the well-spring of Irving's millennialism? Later in the book, he argued his case:

> One should begin at the point where, by his own account, he began to perceive the full significance of prophecy; by the corpse of his infant son.

---

[61] Strachan, *Pentecostal Theology*, 21.

[62] W.H. Oliver, *Prophets and Millennialists: the uses of Biblical Prophecy in England from the 1790s to the 1840s* (Auckland: Auckland University Press, 1978), 24. Emphasis original.

[63] Oliphant, *Irving*, 114-115.

> His own words serve the situation best. This loss was a great grief; his beliefs about death and the last things took shape as
> "a meditation ... with which the Lord did comfort my solitary and sorrowful hours, when that sweet child, who was dear in life and dear also in death, lay near me in shrouded beauty, the daintiest morsel that death did ever feed upon. That was the blessed aera when, to me, the light of this blessed morning star broke through the clouds in which the church is presently shrouded up. I prayed God to avenge me of death. I have sought diligently ever since to fight against Satan, the Prince of darkness. The Lord hath given me no mean success, blessed be his name. And while I live I will fight against death that so bereft me. And I will conquer him when we come to mortal battle; and I will reign with him under my feet; because I have made the Lord my refuge, and the Holy One my habitation."
> This passage identifies the personal crisis which made Irving a millennialist.[64]

There are two main problems with Oliver's contention. The first is that the quote from Irving which Oliver supplied as evidence focuses on the believer's struggle with death and ultimate victory in Christ, not on millennialism per se. The second problem is with chronology. Edward Jr died in October 1825, so if it was this tragedy that "made Irving a millennialist", we would not expect to find him holding millennial views before this date. However, only two pages after the above quote, Oliver acknowledged that the death of Edward Jr only *reinforced* conclusions that Irving had already arrived at when he published *Argument for Judgment to come* in 1823, two years before his son's death.[65] Oliver has, therefore, undercut his own previously identified "fundamental motivation" for Irving's millennialism. We may readily agree that grief at the loss of his son would have intensified Irving's millennialism; we cannot agree that the loss initiated it.

In addition to misinterpreting the source of Irving's millennialism, Oliver was, also, inconsistent in how he interpreted Irving's character. At the beginning of his chapter on Irving and Drummond, he writes, "Much about [Irving] is second-hand, derivative, credulous, shallow, conceited and inflated, and yet he contrived to fall only narrowly short of greatness . . . He is a bizarre figure in the London of the 1820s: a scrappily educated Scot accidentally placed in a London pulpit, there to achieve an unexpected eminence."[66] Oliver supplied no references to support these conclusions about Irving, and a glance at the footnotes to the chapter shows that although he drew extensively from Irving's own works, where secondary sources were concerned, he made only minimal use of Drummond and Oliphant. Had he used Oliphant more

---

[64] Oliver, *Prophets and Millennialists*, 100-101. The quote from Irving is from the Introduction to *The Coming of the Messiah*, clxxii.
[65] Oliver, *Prophets and Millennialists*, 102.
[66] Oliver, *Prophets and Millennialists*, 99.

extensively or turned to more recent available sources such as Strachan, Christensen, or even Whitley, he would have realised that a new appreciation of Irving's ability as a theologian was underway. Was Irving "scrappily educated"? From another source we discover that he spent four years at the University of Edinburgh, "received the Master of Arts degree, earned prizes and won the special commendation of two of his professors, Sir John Leslie and Professor Christison. His academic record was a worthy one."[67] One writer publishing just a few years after Oliver ranked Irving amongst Scotland's "greatest theologians".[68] It would seem that Oliver's educational standards were set unreasonably high.

Oliver acknowledged that Irving's interests and concerns were shared by many of his contemporaries. These included the rejection of Catholic emancipation and popular democracy and fascination with prophecy and the charismata, all collectively and anachronistically labelled aberrations by Oliver. "Aberration" is a pejorative term, and while these issues may have appeared as such to a scholar of the second half of the twentieth century, Oliver himself supplied the evidence that they did not appear as aberrations in Irving's day.[69] So Irving was a man of his time; Oliver distinguished him from his fellows because of the "extravagance" of his responses.[70] Credulity was alleged in the issue of tongues and healing, yet we established in the previous chapter that Irving evidenced some caution in regards to accepting these gifts. This point had been further emphasised in an article that appeared between Strachan's publication and Oliver's. Larry Christensen argued that because Irving himself never exercised any of the charismatic gifts, he was led to accept them based on theological reflection and observation over a period of time.[71] Of course, if Oliver's position was that the possibility of such charismata should *never* be considered, then any degree of receptivity could hardly be seen as other than credulity. Of greater interest is the extravagant extremism Oliver saw in Irving. Irving's passionate commitment to his beliefs exceeded that of many of his contemporaries who shared similar beliefs. What deeply-held convictions led to this depth of commitment?

In the conclusion to his work, Oliver argued that in the early nineteenth century, people with widely differing religious and political views, nonetheless, had their worldviews shaped by biblical prophecy. In this context, he grouped Irving together with Joseph Priestly, John Henry Newman and Robert Owen, describing them all as intellectually respectable.[72] Having previously described

---

[67] Dallimore, *Irving*, 10-11.

[68] Brown, *Thomas Chalmers*, 213.

[69] See also J.F.C. Harrison, *The Second Coming: Popular Millenarianism 1780-1850* (London: Routledge & Kegan Paul Ltd, 1979), 3.

[70] Oliver, *Prophets and Millennialists*, 100.

[71] L. Christenson, "Pentecostalism's forgotten forerunner" in Synan, V., (ed.), *Aspects of Pentecostal-Charismatic Origins* (Plainfield, NJ: Logos International, 1975), 19.

[72] Oliver, *Prophets and Millennialists*, 239.

Irving as "second-hand, derivative, credulous, shallow, conceited and inflated", Oliver's promotion of him to "intellectual respectability" was an act of parting largesse that is transparently inconsistent. However, Oliver's work helpfully established the widespread following that various types of millennialism and prophetical subjects gained during this period, and that to maintain such an interest was by no means eccentric. Writing in the 1970s, Oliver was in the era when Abrams's theory of Romanticism as secularisation held sway: perhaps this is why he nowhere mentioned the term in connection with Irving. This exclusion means, of course, that he could not consider the possibility that Romanticism may have been the underlying fuel for the depth of Irving's passion.

In 1982, J.J. Nantomah published an ambitiously titled PhD thesis. Following Strachan's lead, Nantomah took Irving seriously as a theologian; unlike Strachan, Nantomah noted the relevance of both Romanticism and Irving's relationship with Coleridge.[73] He clearly implied that he saw Irving as a Romantic hero, and that the role of Romantic hero had a cost.[74] As Nantomah's focus was on Irving's Christology, not the links between Irving and Romanticism, he did not take this further, but we will explore this in greater depth in the course of this book.

It is likely that Strachan's description of Irving as "the first Reformed-Pentecostal theologian" instigated a work from an author for whom those two adjectives preferably do not occur in the same sentence, let alone joined with a hyphen. Arnold Dallimore's *The Life of Edward Irving: the Fore-runner of the Charismatic Movement* appeared in 1983, and showed indications that it was provoked by Strachan's admiration for Irving as a theologian. From the third sentence of his introduction, Dallimore signalled that his interest in Irving was sparked by the contemporary Pentecostal and charismatic movements, and as he was writing from within the Reformed tradition, he saw these movements as erroneous.[75] Dallimore's work is divided into two parts: The Upward Moving Career 1792-1828 and The Downward Course 1829-1834. Clearly, Dallimore regarded 1828-9 as the beginning of Irving's decline. Dallimore described Irving at the age of twenty-seven as governed by impulse, idealism and imagination, rather than logic and reason.[76] It is a comment that echoed Whitley's earlier observation about Irving's "prophetic inspiration" dominating his reason. Yet at this stage in his book, all Dallimore had shown is a young

[73] We will explore Nantomah's comments on Irving's relationship with Coleridge in a later chapter.

[74] J.J. Nantomah, *Jesus the God-man: the Doctrine of the Incarnation in Edward Irving in the light of the teaching of the Church Fathers and its relevance for a Twentieth century African Context* (University of Aberdeen, PhD thesis, 1982), 33.

[75] "That is, during his last five years his doctrinal position was virtually that of the Pentecostal body of today." On the following page, Dallimore makes his disagreement with Irving's position clear: Dallimore, *Irving*, ix-x.

[76] Dallimore, *Irving*, 23-24.

man who has steadily pursued his studies, been circumspect in his relationships with women, and resolutely pursued his goal of ministry, despite frustrating delay. While Dallimore's assertion moved him towards Oliphant's "abrogation of reason" stance, he had shown little supporting evidence at this point in his book; instead Irving was emerging as a man of principle and determination.

Dallimore alleged that Irving's generosity of character blunted his perception so that he was more open to accept ideas that would appeal to his imagination.[77] He, later, implied that Irving was undiscerning and rather credulous, at least where Coleridge was concerned.[78] Yet, again, though, Dallimore failed to present any evidence to convince the reader of his case. Dallimore, also, echoed one of Whitley's unsubstantiated assertions, lamenting Irving's choice of Isabella as a wife because she lacked the strength and wisdom the restrain his "impulsive behaviour".[79]

Dallimore said that the 1824-1828 period was dominated by Irving's focus on prophecy; after this, he became absorbed with things charismatic and here we have the key to why Dallimore began Irving's "Downward Course" in 1829 – in his view, dalliance with the charismatic was the key to Irving's decline.[80]

In discussing the outbreak of tongues in Irving's congregation, Dallimore devoted an entire chapter to Robert Baxter, a member of Irving's congregation who was initially an enthusiastic supporter of the charismata, later concluded they were delusional, and then remained troubled about this conclusion for many years.[81] While Baxter's view is valuable as a contemporary and intimate of Irving, Dallimore was unbalanced in not giving equal billing to those whose conclusions were the opposite, including, for example, the Trustees' continued willingness to allow tongues in the prayer service, which clearly indicates that despite all the division over the issue, they were far from convinced that the charismata were delusional or satanic. Dallimore adopted some of the earlier possible interpretations of Irving - irrational, credulous, deluded – without summoning sufficient evidence to support them. In the end, Dallimore was simply using Irving to serve the purpose of being an anti-charismatic object lesson, that is: charismatics end up in a ministry back-water and dead at the age of forty-two. This reductionist polemic is intellectually dishonest and unfair to Irving, who deserves a less constrained interpretation.

Also published in the same year as Dallimore's book was another biography of Irving with a completely different approach. *Edward Irving: the Forgotten Giant* was written by William Merricks, an author within the Pentecostal tradition.[82] While Merricks interacted in a limited way with recent authors such

---

[77] Dallimore, *Irving*, 24.
[78] Dallimore, *Irving*, 46-47.
[79] Dallimore, *Irving*, 55.
[80] Dallimore, *Irving*, 61.
[81] Dallimore, *Irving*, 129ff.
[82] W.S. Merricks, *Edward Irving: the Forgotten Giant* (East Peoria, ILL: Scribe's Chamber Publications, 1983), xiii.

as Strachan and Christenson, the bulk of his book consists of lengthy quotes from primary documents. This, no doubt, provides a service to the general reader for whom access to the works of Irving or Oliphant is very difficult, but it makes the book more a compilation than an original contribution. Merricks gave very little historical context, did not mention Romanticism, and made only fleeting reference to important figures like Coleridge.[83]

Early on, Merricks gave a hint as to how he would interpret Irving's decline: "Irving would also rise to greatness but wither into obscurity at the hands of little men."[84] Irving was misinterpreted and unfairly treated, but contributed little to this process personally apart from, perhaps, choosing some terminology which may have lent itself to misinterpretation. When Merricks praised Irving's analytical approach to the arrival of the charismata as cautious yet decisive, it carried less weight than if he had more carefully assessed the arguments of those accusing Irving of imprudence and headstrong enthusiasm. While Merricks's personal commitment to Pentecostalism gave him an obviously favourable bias toward Irving and led to one or two eccentricities within the text, he, nonetheless, took pains to cover areas where his personal interests were less served and, on balance, treated Irving more fairly than Dallimore's portrayal.[85] Irving emerges from Merricks's work as a prudent, dedicated and idealistic pastor-preacher, but overall, Merrick added little to the existing range of views on Irving and his motivations.

In 1987, D.W. Dorries's PhD thesis focused on Irving's Christology. As part of his biographical section Dorries looked at the relationship between Irving and the leadership of the nascent Catholic Apostolic Church. He rejected the view that Irving was isolated and demoted by a new and scheming charismatic hierarchy, a view he attributed to Oliphant, and we have just seen echoed in Merricks.[86] Dorries concluded that the tension between Irving and the emerging leadership had been overstated, and although we will look at this relationship in greater detail later, one aspect is worth focusing on here – his conclusion that Irving's personality was in fact too dominant in the beginning of the new church.[87] As evidence for this, Dorries writes,

---

[83] Ironically, Merricks's work (despite its recent date) is as rare as many of the nineteenth century works, presumably because of a limited print run. Merricks, *Irving*, 60.

[84] Merricks, *Irving*, 28.

[85] An example of the eccentricity is Merricks's interest in relating Irving to the contemporary United Pentecostal Church, a sect which has itself been considered heretical for its essentially modalistic view of the Trinity, *Irving*, 117ff.

[86] D.W. Dorries, *Nineteenth Century British Christological Controversy, centring upon Edward Irving's Doctrine of Christ's Human Nature* (Aberdeen: University of Aberdeen, 1987), 65-66.

[87] Dorries, *Nineteenth Century British Christological Controversy*, 66.

Looking back over his ministry, Irving expressed to his congregation his one regret. He was convinced that he had assumed a place of stature among them that should have been reserved only for Christ. Irving wrote,

> "Understand, dearly beloved, that such a fullness of the Spirit as our God proposeth to give to His Church in London can only stand under the headship, government, and administration of the Lord Jesus. No Apostle, Prophet, Evangelist, nor Pastor, no Angel of any church, no man nor creature, hath more than a measure of the Spirit, nor can occupy nor administer more than a measure or proportion of the Spirit. To Jesus alone pertaineth the fullness, and to the Church over which He ruleth. ...But we were beguiled to think that the full measure of the tabernacle of the Lord would be given to that church over which I preside as Angel; which was no less than the exalting of the Angel of the Church into the place of Christ. I tremble when I think of the awfully perilous place into which I was thrust. ...and this exaltation of the Angel of the Church to sit head over the fullness of the Spirit, was truly the making of the calf to worship it, instead of worshipping Him who sitteth between the cherubim."[88]

In his later years, Irving used the word "angel" as a synonym for minister/pastor.[89] Does this quote really give solid evidence that Irving had assumed too much power? Firstly, the mistake which Irving was confessing was the belief that "the full measure of the tabernacle of the Lord would be given to that church over which I preside as Angel". In other words, that the Newman Street Church would be pre-eminent amongst the seven churches they were in the process of establishing. This was not just Irving's mistake alone, but one his phrase – "we were beguiled" – implied was shared by most of the leadership. In other words, it seems less like an assumption of personal power by Irving and more like an open acknowledgement of a corporate mistake as the new leadership thought through their developing ecclesiology. Secondly, Irving did not "assume" this place, as Dorries alleged; "I tremble when I think of the awfully perilous place into which I was thrust." He was passive in this; it was not something he sought. In short, Dorries's view of Irving's assumption of power cannot be supported by this quote alone. While this quote was Dorries's main evidence for his view, he, also, provided some shorter quotes which, without the support of the main quote, are not overly convincing. Irving's self-recriminations and admissions of failure in these quotes could easily be interpreted as the utterings of a tender conscience and a humble heart.

Shortly after Dorries, Kenneth Hylson-Smith published a work on Church of England evangelicals. As would be expected in a work with this focus, mention of Irving was slight, but it contained an unfortunate misquotation which threw

---

[88] Dorries, *Nineteenth Century British Christological Controversy,* 67. The quote from Irving is referenced to W. Wilks, *Edward Irving, an Ecclesiastical and Literary Biography* (London: W. Freeman, 1854), 281-282.

[89] This was based on Irving's understanding of the angels of the churches in Revelation.

doubt on Irving's sincerity. According to Hylson-Smith, Thomas de Quincey described Irving as "by many degrees the greatest actor of our times".[90] Judging from the footnote, Hylson-Smith's source was a secondary work, rather than de Quincey, himself. What de Quincey actually wrote was that Irving was "unquestionably, by many, many degrees, the greatest *orator* of our times".[91] While the natural association of ideas between acting and oratory probably explains the mistake, it is sad that Hylson-Smith's error inadvertently enlisted de Quincey as one of the few voices attacking Irving's sincerity.

British systematic theologian Colin Gunton was another writer whose work substantially contributed to the rehabilitation of Irving's theological image. In a 1989 collection of essays honouring Karl Barth, Gunton praised Irving as having a "surer instinct" than Barth in dealing with the doctrine of election in the context of pneumatology.[92] Considering Barth's standing in modern theology, this is no small praise for Irving. In another work, Gunton favourably compared Irving to both Coleridge and Augustine who, he felt, were both representatives of a Western tradition that was "deficient" in its incarnational theology.[93] Irving's journey from heretic to near equivalence with both Barth and Augustine is the Protestant equivalent of canonisation.

From 1990 onwards, a number of theses and articles on Irving appeared. Most of these continued in the tradition of Nantomah and Dorries, focusing in-depth on various aspects of Irving's distinctive theology. Yet, they, also, contained interpretations of Irving's personality, motivation and the historical context. Graham McFarlane commented on the relationship between Irving and Coleridge, and while this is the subject of a later chapter, one comment is worth noting here: "The influence of Coleridge upon Irving was a strong but distilled one, for Irving took nothing from Coleridge unless it would serve his own ends."[94] Out of context, this sentence may sound as if Irving was arrogant and manipulative, but this is certainly not the direction in which McFarlane took it. His intention was simply to express that Irving was not a mindless disciple, a Scottish sponge soaking up the wisdom of the Sage, but intelligent and discerning, quite prepared to disagree when necessary with one of the greatest minds of his day.

In 1993 an article by Sheridan Gilley focused attention on Irving's millennialism. In this article, Gilley explored tensions between Irving's beliefs and the evangelicalism of his day. Gilley described Irving as a holy man with a

---

[90] K. Hylson-Smith, *Evangelicals in the Church of England, 1734-1984* (Edinburgh: T & T Clark, 1988), 95.

[91] T. De Quincey, *Literary Reminiscences from the Autobiography of an English Opium-eater*, vol. 2 (Boston: Ticknor, Reed, and Fields, 1854), 236.

[92] C. Gunton, "The triune God and the freedom of the creature" in S.W. Sykes (ed.), *Karl Barth: Centenary Essays* (Cambridge: Cambridge University Press, 1989), 64.

[93] C. Gunton, *The Promise of Trinitarian Theology* (Edinburgh: T & T Clark, 2004), 98.

[94] G. McFarlane, *Christology and the Spirit in the Teaching of Edward Irving* (London: King's College, PhD, 1990), 206.

common touch,[95] an "'otherworldly' Christian who ultimately wanted to withdraw from a world he despaired of reforming".[96] Thus Irving was unwilling to compromise with an evangelicalism that he saw as increasingly mirroring the surrounding cultural values of respectability, prudence, and utilitarianism.[97] Gilley contrasted Irving's pessimistic premillennialism with the optimistic postmillennialism of his evangelical contemporary, William Wilberforce, who had a "holy worldliness", and a far more sanguine view of the possibilities for world transformation through human effort under God's grace.[98]

Gilley claimed that Irving's main influence in his own day was his millennialism, with the effect of converting evangelicals to his premillennial views.[99] While Gilley elaborated on Irving's millennialism and its sources, he did not really substantiate his case thoroughly. There was no evaluation, for instance, of the contemporary influence of Irving's millennialism as opposed to, say, his Christological views. In light of the controversies and publicity surrounding Irving's teaching on the humanity of Christ and the charismata, Gilley would need to make a strenuous case that Irving's millennialism was more influential, which is an avenue he has not pursued. In addition, just because numerous people held millennial views similar to Irving's doesn't mean that Irving himself was the source of these views. As Oliver and others have shown, millennialism was present in nineteenth century England in many different forms; it appears that, in the absence of supporting evidence, Gilley may have overstated Irving's individual influence in this area. Of interest though, is another assessment Gilley makes of Irving's character: he saw Irving as easily influenced, describing his personality as "plastic".[100] In this context, he was referring to Hatley Frere's influence on Irving's prophetic views. While there is no doubt that Frere influenced Irving's view of prophecy, we have already seen evidence that this view of a malleable Irving is a misinterpretation; he was quite capable of rejecting any idea that did not fit with his convictions, no matter how strong or influential the source.

In an historical work focusing on Swiss and British evangelicals, Timothy Stunt described Irving's personality as impetuous and extroverted.[101] Stunt dismissed the view of Irving as a dreamer surrounded by eccentrics, noting that beneath Irving's surface conservatism there lay the heart of a radical whose mission was to liberate the Church from Reformed scholasticism in pursuit of a

---

[95] S. Gilley, "Edward Irving; prophet of the millennium" in J. Garnett & C. Matthew (eds), *Revival and Religion since 1700: Essays for John Walsh* (London: The Hambledon Press, 1993), 98.
[96] Gilley, "Edward Irving; prophet of the millennium", 98.
[97] Gilley, "Edward Irving; prophet of the millennium", 97.
[98] Gilley, "Edward Irving; prophet of the millennium", 98.
[99] Gilley, "Edward Irving; prophet of the millennium", 103, 108.
[100] Gilley, "Edward Irving; prophet of the millennium", 106.
[101] T.C.F. Stunt, *From Awakening to Secession: Radical Evangelicals in Switzerland and Britain 1815-35* (Edinburgh: T & T Clark, 2000), 128.

warm, experiential faith. The same Irving who could oppose Catholic emancipation, was, nevertheless, capable of perceiving the devotional value of Catholic mysticism over against an arid Reformed rationalism.[102]

Stunt saw the Romantic influence as a motivating factor on Irving. This allowed him to picture Irving as active rather than being led by others; those who have not perceived the importance of Irving's underlying Romanticism have tended to see Irving as passive, easily manipulated and overly credulous. Stunt has perceived a key element in a comprehensive understanding of Irving, one which has often been missed even by writers whose works, unlike Stunt's, have had Irving as their entire focus. Irving's ability to perceive value in certain aspects of Catholicism demonstrates that although he shared the anti-Catholic prejudice of many of his contemporaries, for him it was not a mindless and irrational prejudice, but one based on a theological reflection through which can still be seen something of the generosity of spirit for which he was so well known.

In 2001, Mark Patterson noted the attempts of recent scholarship to restore Irving's theological reputation, but argued that most of these had ignored Irving's premillennialism, which Patterson believed to be "the single most determining influence upon [Irving's] thought".[103] Yet, Patterson proceeded to acknowledge that his thesis was not primarily a study of Edward Irving, but of *The Morning Watch* journal, which was issued by the Albury group during the early 1830s.[104] And, herein, lies a significant flaw in Patterson's argument: by restricting his focus to the theology of *The Morning Watch* (a journal which by definition focused on prophecy and millennialism) Patterson, unsurprisingly, found Irving's dominant interest to be prophecy and millennialism! This conclusion could only have been justified if Patterson had read widely in other Irving sources, which he clearly admits he has not done: "no attempt is made to compare or contrast [Irving's] writings in *The Morning Watch* with his collected works".[105] Patterson then footnotes this by saying "This would actually be of little value, as Irving's collected works tend to edit out aspects of his premillennialism." It appears that it didn't occur to Patterson that by ignoring the general absence of premillennialism in Irving's collected works he is actually tilting the argument his own way, and is thereby basing his claim that premillennialism was the "centre and determining structure" of Irving's thought on very shaky ground.

Patterson was, at least, consistent in this methodological error throughout his thesis. Towards the end of the second volume he wrote:

---

[102] Stunt, *From Awakening to Secession*, 133-134.

[103] M. Patterson, "Designing the Last Days: Edward Irving, the Albury circle, and the Theology of the Morning Watch" (PhD thesis, King's College, London, 2001), vol. 1, 18.

[104] Patterson, "Designing the Last Days", vol. 1, 22.

[105] Patterson, "Designing the Last Days", vol. 1, 22.

> Irving's writing in *The Morning Watch* reveal that he was, above and before anything else, a pretribulational-premillennial theologian. This cannot be overstated. From his meeting with Hatley Frere in 1825 until his death in December 1834, Irving's every thought and writing was shaped under the aegis of his imminent Adventism and premillennial convictions. This fact, obvious in *The Morning Watch*, is easily missed in Irving's other writings, especially perhaps, his collected works, and has led to several errors in the study of Irving and his theology.[106]

Patterson believed it was an "error" not to emphasise something that Irving's collected works themselves minimise, but correct to proclaim it as Irving's dominant thought on the strength of contributions to one journal and calculated avoidance of Irving's other writings. Patterson's point that Irving's millennialism needed fuller investigation could have been made without such a cloistered approach.

Patterson made little attempt to investigate Irving other than as a millennialist, so, when he came to make a closing assessment of Irving's personality it is not surprising that he found a contradictory enigma.

> Beyond the doctrine and theology is the very complex person of Edward Irving. Through his writings in *The Morning Watch*, he exists as an enigma, a paradox of conflicting characteristics, impossible in the end to reconcile. Here Irving is revealed as a gentle pastor, careful theologian, and viperous prophet of the last day's [sic] wrath. Through the journal one finds in Irving deep wells of reasoned intellect and irrational passion, and the evidence that he drew liberally from both.[107]

It should come as little surprise that Patterson, despite his claim to know what Irving was "above and before anything else", should, having chosen such a narrow lens through which to contemplate Irving, ultimately find himself in the company of those who conclude Irving was an "enigma".

In 2003, D.T. Lee, despite having a theological focus in his thesis, made the salutary observation that Irving would have seen himself more as a pastor than a theologian.[108] It is worth recalling that Irving's ministry as a pastor gave him an awareness of the full gamut of human experience from great wealth and power to poverty and misery.[109] This made him much more than an "armchair theologian" and tends to undermine the interpretation of those who see him as a distracted enthusiast. In the context of exploring Irving's relationship with

---

[106] Patterson, "Designing the Last Days", vol. 2, 228-229.
[107] Patterson, "Designing the Last Days, vol. 2, 231.
[108] D.Y.T. Lee, "The Humanity of Christ and the Church in the teaching of Edward Irving" (Brunel, PhD, 2003), 10.
[109] Lee, "The Humanity of Christ", 14.

Coleridge, Lee asserted that Irving remained a critical and original thinker in his own right.[110]

Earlier in this chapter we noted that the two major nineteenth century interpreters of Irving who both knew him personally – Oliphant and Carlyle – were left with only one shared possible interpretation of Irving's decline: theological credulity. Yet, we, also, noted that neither of these two authors engaged in a theological assessment. We can now see that the trend in recent scholarship has been in the opposite direction: Lee echoed the increasing chorus of recent authors who had decided that Irving was neither credulous, nor derivative, but that he made an original contribution to nineteenth century theology that resonates to the present day. Lee ended by disagreeing with Patterson's conclusion that Irving's millennialism was his governing thought, believing that his Christology was central, and that Irving's appropriation of Christ's humanity was influenced by Romanticsm.[111] Lee, also, made the comment that "an accurate picture of Irving the theologian is elusive".[112] This is an accurate summation of the various attempts to grapple with and understand the complexities of a man whose abilities and achievements were in stark contrast to the opposition he faced and his arguably unnecessary early death.

In this chapter, we have surveyed a number of different approaches to Irving, some primarily biographical, others primarily theological. The most recent assessment of Irving is *The Lord's Watchman: Edward Irving*, which attempts both biography and theological assessment. Like other authors before him, Tim Grass noted that Irving was affected by Romanticism.[113] However, the authors we have surveyed do not identify Irving's Romanticism as a core value that fundamentally affected not only his theological views, but every aspect of his worldview and his sense of destiny and identity. We have noted that several scholars, having considered Irving's rise and decline, his personality and motivations, have simply concluded that he was an "enigma". Our argument here is that further light can be shed on this enigma and that all of Irving's theological distinctives – his Christology, ecclesiology, eschatology and pneumatology - were fundamentally informed by his underlying Romanticism. Irving's Romanticism flowed deeply under the more obvious controversies of his life and offers the most comprehensive explanation for his worldview, motivation, and also for the subsequent conflicts in his ministerial career.

---

[110] Lee, "The Humanity of Christ", 46.
[111] Lee, "The Humanity of Christ", 186.
[112] Lee, "The Humanity of Christ", 11.
[113] T. Grass, *The Lord's Watchman: Edward Irving* (Milton Keynes: Paternoster, 2011), 300. This book is essential reading for all those with an interest in Irving.

CHAPTER 4

Irving and Coleridge

This chapter examines the relationship between Irving and Coleridge by drawing significantly on Coleridge's own writings. This has not been comprehensively attempted before. When Margaret Oliphant described their relationship only a few decades after their deaths in 1834, she was able to say with accuracy, "Scarcely any record remains of the intercourse which existed between Irving and Coleridge."[1] Thanks to the efforts of the late Kathleen Coburn and her editorial colleagues, this is no longer the case. The Bollingen edition of Coleridge's works and Griggs's edition of his letters enable us to see numerous references to Irving throughout Coleridge's notebooks, marginalia and correspondence. This chapter explores, chronologically, this largely untapped and rich vein of material to shed light on the developing relationship between the preacher and the poet-philosopher. Christopher Burden is one writer who has used this material, but his focus was much broader than the Coleridge-Irving relationship.[2] One of the benefits of my approach will be access to Coleridge's perspective on Irving's personality: did Coleridge see Irving as credulous, superficial, or any of the other adjectives proposed by Irving interpreters? Also, Coleridge retains a lofty position in the Romantic pantheon: this survey will enable us to see Irving's Romanticism in the light of Coleridge's and, thereby, provide a valuable insight as to where their respective Romanticisms aligned and differed.

Determining the exact date when Irving and Coleridge first met is problematic. Oliphant does not attempt to date the meeting exactly, but by discussing it after Irving and Isabella's October 1823 marriage, she gave the impression it occurred later that year. On the other hand, she, also, affirmed that the preacher and the poet met through Basil Montagu, whom she described as one of Irving's earliest acquaintances in London, which may allow for an earlier date.[3] Drummond claimed that Irving and Coleridge met shortly after Irving's arrival in London, which would imply possibly July or August 1822.[4] Even the editors of the Bollingen collection seem uncertain on this issue. In the

---

[1] M. Oliphant, *The Life of Edward Irving* (London: Hurst and Blackett, n.d. 5th edn), 92.

[2] C. Burdon, *The Apocalypse in England: Revelation Unravelling, 1700-1834* (Basingstoke, Hampshire: Palgrave Macmillan, 1997), 152-160.

[3] Oliphant, *Irving,* 91-92.

[4] A.L. Drummond, *Edward Irving and his Circle, including some consideration of the 'Tongues' Movement in the light of Modern Psychology* (London: James Clarke, 1934), 65. As we saw in chapter 2, Irving began his London ministry in July 1822.

chronological table at the beginning of one volume, Edward Irving's first visit to Coleridge is listed at the end of 1822, and while no exact date is given, its placement in the chronology implies that it occurred in the last few days of the year.[5] Yet, in the chronological table of another volume in the series, it appears that the meeting took place in July 1823.[6] So, we have a range of possibilities extending from Irving's July 1822 arrival in London through to December 1823.

Evidence from Coleridge's own correspondence, unavailable to both Oliphant and Drummond, allows us to date this meeting more exactly. Firstly, there is no trace of Irving in Coleridge's writings throughout 1822, which would make it likely their meeting occurred later. When we turn to Coleridge's 1823 correspondence, we find the following passage in a letter dated 7 July 1823, "I have been many times in town within the last 3 or 4 weeks; but with one exception when I was driven in and back by Mr Gillman to hear the present Idol of the World of Fashion, the Revd. Mr Irving, the super-Ciceronian, ultra-Demosthenic Pulpiteer of the Scotch Chapel in Cross Street, Hatton Garden, I have been always at the West End of the Town..."[7] This is the first mention of Irving in Coleridge's correspondence, and although not conclusive, Coleridge's phrasing gives the impression that he has not yet met Irving personally; he appeared to know Irving only as a preacher. This situation soon changed, however, for the very next letter in the volume is dated simply "July 1823" and contains, by way of an excuse, "In consequence of having been thus employed in town, and of being obliged on my return to meet Mr Irving at the Table of a Friend, I have not had the time..."[8] The internal evidence, therefore, points to the first meeting between Irving and Coleridge taking place somewhere during the last three weeks of July 1823; we will shortly be able to narrow it down a little further. Before doing so however, because Coleridge was significantly older than Irving, it is necessary to outline Coleridge's life prior to their initial meeting.

Samuel Taylor Coleridge was twenty years Irving's senior, having been born in Devon in 1772. At the time of their July 1823 meeting, Coleridge already had a chequered and peripatetic career behind him. The last-born of Reverend John Coleridge's thirteen children, the young Coleridge (like the young Irving) devoured the *Arabian Nights*.[9] His father's early death propelled the nine-year

---

[5] C. Woodring (ed.), *Table Talk* volume 1 (London & Princeton: Routledge, & Princeton University Press, 1990), xxxiii. The visit is placed after an event occurring on December 29, 1822.

[6] J. Beer (ed.), *Aids to Reflection* (London & Princeton: Routledge & Princeton University Press, 1993. Orig. May 1825), xxxvii.

[7] Letter to Charlotte Brent (no. 1338) in E.L. Griggs (ed), *The Collected Letters of Samuel Taylor Coleridge*, vol. v, 1820-1825 (Oxford: Clarendon, 1971) 280. Henceforth *CLSTC*.

[8] Letter to C.A. Tulk, (no. 1339) *CLSTC*, vol. v, 284.

[9] R. Ashton, *The Life of Samuel Taylor Coleridge: a Critical Biography* (Oxford: Blackwell Publishers, 1996), 14.

old future poet to London as a student at Christ's Hospital, then a boarding school which, also, catered for the poor,[10] where he was drawn to Platonic philosophy, excelled at languages and in 1798 was selected for the University Exhibitions, thereby, entering Jesus College, Cambridge, in 1791.[11] Coleridge's university career began promisingly enough, but late in 1793 he left Cambridge in haste. Various reasons have been proposed for his rapid departure, including debt and an unhappy love affair.[12] Regardless of the reason, Coleridge enlisted in a company of dragoons where he remained for some months before returning, chastened and admonished, to Jesus College in April 1794.[13]

After Coleridge met the future poet Robert Southey in Oxford, the two developed a scheme called Pantisocracy, intending to establish a small utopian community in America where goods would be held in common and the cultivation of subsistence crops would allow ample time for leisure and education.[14] At this time, Coleridge's religious views could be described as Unitarian.[15] Plans were made to relocate to America, and because couples were desired for the new settlement, Coleridge speedily became engaged to Sara Fricker, a move probably facilitated by Southey's prior engagement to Sara's sister.[16]

In December 1794, Coleridge left Cambridge without taking his degree, claiming his allegiance to Pantisocracy as the reason.[17] Intriguingly, he did not join Southey and the Pantisocrats at Bristol, but went to London to stay with his school-friend, Charles Lamb. He wrote neither to Southey nor to Sara Fricker, although the former eventually tracked him down and took him to Bristol. It seemed Coleridge's enthusiasm for Pantisocracy (and perhaps, also, for Fricker) was already waning.[18] Eventually, Southey abandoned the scheme, causing a quarrel between the two men which was not reconciled for some months.[19] Despite these events, Coleridge and Sara married in October 1795.[20] Even at this early stage in his life, Coleridge was showing the tendencies to procrastination and lack of perseverance that would exasperate his friends and provide ammunition for his enemies in the years to come, keeping financial

---

[10] J.D. Campbell, *Samuel Taylor Coleridge: a Narrative of the Events of his Life* (London: Macmillan & Co., 1894), 8.

[11] T.E. Jones, *The Broad Church: a Biography of a Movement* (Lanham, ML: Lexington Books, 2003), 13.

[12] Campbell, *Coleridge*, 26.

[13] Campbell, *Coleridge*, 29.

[14] Campbell, *Coleridge*, 33.

[15] Ashton, *Coleridge*, 85; Campbell, *Coleridge*, 33.

[16] Ashton, *Coleridge*, 54; Campbell, *Coleridge*, 35.

[17] Campbell, *Coleridge*, 41.

[18] Campbell, *Coleridge*, 42.

[19] Ashton, *Coleridge*, 72; Campbell, *Coleridge*, 46.

[20] Southey secretly married Edith Fricker the following month, making the two poets brothers-in-law.

supporters waiting for promised projects while getting distracted by new ones.[21] One such distraction was the short-lived magazine, *The Watchman*. It was during the ten-issue life of this magazine that Coleridge's first volume of poetry, *Poems on various subjects*, was published in April 1796.[22]

When Sara gave birth to a son, Hartley, Coleridge fancied combining the roles of poet and farmer and the family settled at Nether Stowey, near Bridgwater in Somerset, close to his friend, Thomas Poole.[23] In these days, Coleridge was not idle, preparing a second edition of his *Poems*, writing a play and preaching regularly in Unitarian chapels. It was during this time, also, that Coleridge met William Wordsworth and his sister, Dorothy, who were inspired enough by his company to take a cottage in the district.[24] The Coleridges remained in this rural setting through 1797 and 1798, and it was here he wrote his best-known poems – the *Ancient Mariner*, *Christabel* (partly) and *Kubla Khan* – but money was a perennial problem. Coleridge considered a paid position as a Unitarian minister in Shrewsbury, but money worries were greatly eased when Thomas and Josiah Wedgwood, sons of the founder of the great pottery, offered Coleridge a life-long annuity of £150.[25] 1798 ended with the birth of another son to the Coleridges, and a trip by Wordsworth and Coleridge to Germany, just as their joint effort *Lyrical Ballads* was published.

Coleridge spent the first half of 1799 in Germany learning the language, during which time he, belatedly, received the news that his infant second son had died. Shortly after his return, he visited the Wordsworths and a tour of the Lake District ensued, with the Wordsworths deciding to settle in Grasmere. This trip was noteworthy for other reasons: the Wordsworths had been staying with the Hutchinson family, and William was later to marry Mary Hutchinson, while Coleridge was to fall in love with her sister Sara.[26] While in the north, Coleridge received an offer of work at a London newspaper which he immediately accepted, but only pursued for about three months, until February 1800.[27] At the end of this period, Sara and Hartley, who had joined him in London, left for her mother's home, and Coleridge spent some weeks with Lamb, where he concentrated on translating Schiller's *Wallenstein*, which was

---

[21] Campbell, *Coleridge,* 51.
[22] *The Watchman* was issued every eight days, so its total span was less than three months. The *Poems* was the project which the long-suffering Cottle finally brought to fruition. Ashton, *Coleridge*, 83.
[23] Campbell, *Coleridge,* 62-63.
[24] Campbell, *Coleridge*, 72.
[25] Ashton, *Coleridge*, 118; Campbell, *Coleridge,* 83.
[26] Campbell, *Coleridge,* 105. Much has been made of the relationship between Coleridge and Sara Hutchinson and although several writers argue that the relationship was consummated, John Worthen has argued effectively that it was not, cf. "In bed with Sara Hutchinson", *The Cambridge Quarterly*, Vol. 28, 3, 1999, 232-248. There was a surfeit of Saras: Coleridge married one, fell in love with another, and his daughter was a third.
[27] Campbell, *Coleridge,* 105-110.

published with little commercial success.[28] Unable to find a house back in Stowey, the Coleridges moved to the Lake District to be near the Wordsworths, and the second half of 1800 was a social, but unproductive time for the poet, although Sara produced another son, Derwent.

1801 began with a confusing flurry of different schemes, which seemed to come to nothing. Coleridge was afflicted with a variety of ailments, including gout, swelling of joints, and stomach and head pains.[29] In discussing his complaints with others, he, also, admitted his reliance on brandy and laudanum in dealing with them. Coleridge made another attempt at newspaper work in London before ending up with the Wordsworths in Grasmere in early 1802, and staying at nearby Greta Hall.[30] The poet arrived there at a low ebb, concerned about his opium addiction and the increasing estrangement from his wife.[31] During this period, Coleridge wrote *Dejection: an Ode* and heard (via the Wordsworths) that he had become a father once more, this child being a daughter. Southey and his wife had just lost an infant daughter, and they moved to Greta Hall so the two sisters could be together; the Southeys were to remain there for decades, providing a presence and stability for Coleridge's family that the poet, himself, did not.

During 1803 Coleridge lived a nomadic lifestyle, staying with various friends and struggling with his opium addiction before sailing to Malta in early 1804.[32] Here he remained (apart from a diversion to Sicily), obtained some work as the result of the sudden death of the Public Secretary and, finally, returned to England in mid-1806, having been away for two years.[33] On landing at Portsmouth, he transferred to London and moved in with Lamb again; it was a month before he wrote to his wife and a letter from Wordsworth indicates Coleridge's aversion to living with her. A separation was eventually negotiated.[34]

Coleridge spent most of 1807 between Bristol and Poole's home in Stowey, and if little was coming from his pen at this time, it became clear from his notebooks and correspondence that his religious opinions had changed, and that he was now firmly Trinitarian.[35] At the end of the year and into 1808 Coleridge was in London, writing and delivering lectures; by this time his abuse of

---

[28] Campbell, *Coleridge*, 110-111.
[29] Campbell, *Coleridge*, 122.
[30] Campbell, *Coleridge*, 129.
[31] Campbell, *Coleridge*, 130.
[32] Campbell, *Coleridge,* 136-144.
[33] Campbell, *Coleridge*, 150.
[34] Campbell, *Coleridge*, 154, 159. The letter from Wordsworth was addressed to Sir George Beaumont. The original source of this letter was W. Knight, *The Life of William Wordsworth*, vol. 2, 74
[35] M.A. Perkins, "Religious thinker", in L. Newlyn, *The Cambridge Companion to Coleridge* (Cambridge: Cambridge University Press, 2002), 189; Campbell, *Coleridge,* 165.

laudanum was widely known amongst all his associates.[36] Later in 1808 Coleridge relocated to the Wordsworths' home, where he spent most of the next eighteen months involved with his periodical *The Friend*,[37] before moving to London to stay with Basil Montagu. Unwise words from Montagu opened a rift between Wordsworth and Coleridge which lasted for two years and Coleridge left Montagu's home to stay with the Morgans of Hammersmith.[38] This would prove to be one of Coleridge's long-term residences, lasting from 1810 to 1816. During this period, Coleridge wrote newspaper editorials, delivered a series of lectures on poetic principles based on Shakespeare and Milton, and oversaw the production of his play *Remorse* at Drury Lane.[39] At this time, the recently-mended rift between Wordsworth and Coleridge reopened via correspondence, resulting in Coleridge permanently avoiding the region that contained not only the Wordsworths, but, also, his wife and children.[40]

During late 1813 and into 1816, Coleridge oscillated between London, Bristol and Calne in Wiltshire, often in company with the Morgan family, lecturing and writing about Christianity and aesthetic principles.[41] Throughout this time, Coleridge made no attempt to contact his family or Southey, until his son, Hartley, visited briefly on vacation from Oxford in 1815.[42] Nonetheless, further poetry and his *Biographia Literaria* came from these years. By mid-1816, Coleridge had taken up his last long-term residence, with the Gillmans in Highgate. He arrived there forty-four years of age, poor in both health and finances, and alienated from many of his friends as well as his wife and three children.[43] Under Gillman's supervision, Coleridge's use of opium and wine moderated, and he pursued a variety of literary projects, but with a great deal of disorganisation. In London, Coleridge made new friends, kept some old ones like Lamb and even, at the end of 1817, received Wordsworth and a significant rapprochement was made.[44] In 1820 his sons, Derwent and Hartley, visited him in London, singing the praises of their sister Sara, now a young woman; Coleridge had not seen her for seven years.[45] Shortly after this visit, Hartley lost his Fellowship at Oriel for drunkenness, and Coleridge, after failing to get the decision reversed, blamed himself for passing on this disposition to his son. Hartley came to London where he lived in Basil Montagu's household (this rift having been healed).[46] It was January 1823 when the two Sara Coleridges

---

[36] Campbell, *Coleridge,* 169.
[37] Campbell, *Coleridge,* 170-176.
[38] Campbell, *Coleridge,* 180.
[39] Campbell, *Coleridge,* 180-181, 188-190.
[40] Campbell, *Coleridge,* 196-197.
[41] Ashton, *Coleridge*, 288; Campbell, *Coleridge,* 207, 209.
[42] Campbell, *Coleridge,* 214.
[43] Ashton, *Coleridge*, 297; Campbell, *Coleridge,* 219-220.
[44] Campbell, *Coleridge,* 234-236.
[45] Campbell, *Coleridge,* 243.
[46] Campbell, *Coleridge,* 245.

arrived in London and the poet saw his daughter for the first time in nine years.[47]

As we have seen, it was shortly after this that Irving and Coleridge first met, when they were aged, respectively, thirty-one and fifty-one. Irving was then a young man with lofty hopes, on the verge of marriage and acclaimed as London's greatest preacher; Coleridge was middle-aged with his greatest poems already written, alienated by choice from his wife and children and even his staunchest friends expected his future contribution to be limited by his opium addiction. Therefore, Irving did not meet the youthful poet with a head full of revolutionary Pantisocratic schemes, nor did he meet the potential Unitarian preacher: he met the mature Coleridge who had returned to Anglicanism and Trinitarianism. Although their differences were more obvious than their similarities, their great common ground was their Christian faith, combined with a high view of the role of the church in God's purposes. Coleridge opposed the utilitarian expediency produced by the Enlightenment with the positive restraint of selfless Christian love and emphasised "the internal evidence of the spirit and the function of the will in deciding religious truths".[48] Coleridge was on a quest to "fuse the intellectual, volitional, and emotional elements in religious experience into one harmonious whole".[49] It was a quest that would resonate strongly with Irving's own Romantic sensibilities.

A glance at the interpretations of Coleridge's religious pilgrimage reveals a breath-taking variety: some authors downplay his Christian convictions or dismiss them as the opium-induced softening of a great mind;[50] some seriously question his orthodoxy or at least his consistency;[51] still others celebrate him as the single most significant figure in the later rise of what has become known as the Broad Church movement.[52] Of course, these interpretations are often heavily flavoured by the perspective of the interpreter. A significant contingent is interested in Coleridge the poet; their focus is primarily on the first half of his life when he produced his best poetry. They, therefore, have to produce an explanation as to why his poetry declined in his later years. If the interpreter is unsympathetic with Coleridge's religious views (as is often the case), then the poetic decline is frequently attributed to the combination of opium and a latter-

---

[47] Ashton, *Coleridge*, 347.

[48] R. Hole, *Pulpit, Politics and Public Order in England 1760-1832* (Cambridge: Cambridge University Press, 1989), 182; J.D. Boulger, *Coleridge as Religious Thinker* (New Haven: Yale University Press, 1961), 47.

[49] Boulger, *Coleridge as Religious Thinker*, 92.

[50] E.g. Richard Holmes's two otherwise comprehensive biographies of Coleridge tend to downplay religious aspects.

[51] A. Dallimore, *The Life of Edward Irving: the Fore-runner of the Charismatic Movement* (Edinburgh: Banner of Truth, 1983), 49: "Nothing whatsoever in Coleridge's actions or writings qualified him to be addressed as an orthodox Christian."

[52] Jones's *The Broad Church* collates opinions acknowledging Coleridge's seminal role in the thought of this movement.

life repose in Christian conservatism. A similar stance is sometimes taken by those with an interest in Coleridge as both poet and philosopher, if they are not prepared to take his Christianity seriously. If the interpreter is concerned to maintain certain Evangelical or Calvinist bastions, Coleridge will not be seen as a religious conservative at all, but as a purveyor of dangerous heterodoxies.[53] Depending on one's perspective, then, Coleridge could be located anywhere on the religious spectrum from tediously conservative to dangerously radical. All of these hermeneutic lenses not only tend to distort Coleridge by attempting to over-simplify him (although if this tendency is forgivable anywhere, Coleridge must be the place!) but, also, by minimising the duration and intensity of the intellectual struggle he undertook to arrive at his mature Christian faith. Both Coleridge and Irving exemplified the Romantic principle of struggle in a noble cause, just as both have been variously assessed as either religious conservatives or radicals.

Earlier in this chapter we saw Coleridge's first description of Irving was as "the super-Ciceronian, ultra-Demosthenic Pulpiteer". While some have seen this as a straight-forward compliment, another possible interpretation is that Coleridge saw Irving's oratory as exaggerated, an impression only strengthened by the following comment in his notebook, also dated from the month of first contact, July 1823: "Mr Irving's error. <To use> Declamation (high & passionate Rhetoric not introduced & pioneered by calm and clear Logic) is (borrowing the simile tho' with change in the application) from the witty-wise, tho' not always wisely witty, Fuller) 'to knock a nail into a board without wimbling a hole for it, which then either not enters, or turns crooked, or splits the wood it pierceth'."[54] The Bollingen version of the notebooks added the following editorial comment on this entry: "[Irving's] *fervid Regard* was to become an embarrassment . . . by Feb 1826, Coleridge had become highly critical [of Irving]."[55] Introducing such a note at this point is anachronistic: Irving and Coleridge had barely met (if at all), so there had been no chance for Irving to develop any attitude towards Coleridge, "fervid regard" or otherwise. Whether Irving ever demonstrated this attitude towards Coleridge, and to what degree Coleridge was embarrassed by, or critical of, Irving, will emerge as we progress. What *is* clear from these early comments is that Coleridge believed Irving's sermons needed less rhetoric and more logic.

In earlier chapters we noted the influence of Scottish Romanticism on the youthful Irving, as well as the Romantic flavour of his personal reading. Before examining how Irving's Romantic theology developed through his association

[53] Dallimore, *Irving*, 46-47, 77.

[54] K. Coburn & M. Christensen (eds), *The Notebooks of Samuel Taylor Coleridge*, vol. 4, 1819-1826 (London: Routledge, 1990), July 1823, 4963. The published notebooks do not have page numbers, only using the dates of the entries and the sequential numbers assigned by the editors as references. Henceforth, *NSTC*.

[55] *NSTC*, Volume 4, 4963. "fervid Regard" is a quote from Coleridge to which we will shortly return.

with Coleridge, we need to assess his position prior to meeting the poet-philosopher. In his farewell sermon to the congregation at St John's, Glasgow, preached more than a year before meeting Coleridge, Irving called for those with a ministerial vocation to "stand aloof from the unholy influences under which the Church hath fallen", naming, specifically, "power and patronage", "ecclesiastical intrigue" and the desire to stoop to "popular taste". Rather, they should imitate the poverty and dedication of the early disciples, looking solely to the providence of God to meet their needs. The future glory of the church depended on a ready supply of such apostolic ministers.[56] "Such a seed would make the Church once more to be glorious," he believed.

> One such youth trained amidst nature's extremities, and hope's obdurate fastnesses his soul fed not on patron's hopes nor favour's smiles, but upon the stern resolves, and heavenward enjoyments of an apostle's toilsome calling that youth, I say, were worth a hundred, and a hundred such were worth a host, to revive and quicken this our land the land, the only land, of a free plebeian church, which never pined till she began to be patronised.[57]

This summoned a new generation to arise, but it is clear that Irving was, also, romanticising his own journey as the obscure but dedicated youth on a valiant quest towards an apostolic ministry that, without the aid of worldly power and influence, would, nevertheless, transform the church to a higher level of glory. This journey would proceed by shunning the accustomed paths that had only served to lower the church from its apostolic standard. Although Irving strived to keep his pronouns plural, by the end of the passage we have "seed" in the singular, and "one such youth"; Irving idealised his thirty-year journey to this point, and established an ambitious agenda for his future. While the Romantic theme of individual questing is obvious in this farewell sermon at St John's, Irving's goal was far more expansive than personal spiritual rejuvenation through contact with the sublime; it was nothing less than a transformation of the church and society by revival, a quickening of the land. This wider transformation, however, began in the gallant questing of brave hearts.

Later in the same sermon we find these concepts developed further:

> There is a tide in public favour, which some ride on prosperously, which others work against and weather amain. Those who take it fair at the outset, and will have the patience to observe its veerings, and to shift and hold their course accordingly, shall fetch their port with prosperous and easy sail; those again, who are careless of ease, and court danger in a noble cause, confiding also in their patient endurance, and the protection of Heaven, launch fearlessly into the wide and open deep, resolved to explore all they can

[56] G. Carlyle (ed.), *The Collected Writings of Edward Irving* (London: Alexander Strahan & Co., 1865), vol. 3, 347-348. Henceforth *CW3*.

[57] *CW3*, 348.

> reach, and to benefit all they explore, shall chance to have hard encounters, and reach safely through perils and dangers. But while they risk much, they discover much; they come to know the extremities of fate, and grow familiar with the gracious interpositions of Heaven. So it is with the preachers of the gospel.[58]

Here, Irving began (whether consciously or not) by recalling Brutus's speech to Cassius:

> There is a tide in the affairs of men.
> Which, taken at the flood, leads on to fortune;
> Omitted, all the voyage of their life
> Is bound in shallows and in miseries.
> On such a full sea are we now afloat,
> And we must take the current when it serves,
> Or lose our ventures.[59]

Yet Irving's activism made Brutus passive by comparison; Irving was far from idly gazing at tide-charts awaiting an opportune moment, but was pursuing adventure; in fact, Irving used the word "adventure" five times in the passage from which the above extract is taken (also, "danger" and "explore" three times each). Irving was eschewing the well-trodden paths because he was after a greater prize – the "gracious interpositions of Heaven", the perspective of a "holy and heavenly mind" from which to do "battle" against everything that stood in the way of his expansive view of religious life.[60] What was the goal of this noble spiritual battle? It seems to consist of several parts: firstly, to challenge the entrenched cultural "idolatries" that were supplanting God in the hearts of Irving's contemporaries; secondly, to oppose corruption and indolence in the Church; and, thirdly, on a positive note, to enlarge the scope of religion.

> The multitude of preachers will plod the beaten track, and weary you with the same succession of objects and views, constantly presenting the same aspect of things to the same faculties of the mind, and if you would have the relief of freshness and novelty, no less necessary for the entertainment of the spiritual than of the natural eye if you would have religion made as broad as thought and experience, then you must not discourage, but bear patiently with, and hear to an end, any one who takes his natural liberty to expatiate over all the applications of the Word of God to the wants of men, bringing him to no bar of favourite preachers, but to the bar of your own religious feelings and experience alone.[61]

---

[58] *CW3*, 350.
[59] W. Shakespeare, *Julius Caesar*, Act 4, scene 3, 218-224.
[60] *CW3*, 351.
[61] *CW3*, 350-352.

Irving urged his hearers to make their own "religious feelings and experience" the measure by which they judged preachers, although, in context, this is clearly subject to the written Word. This is a remarkable speech from a thirty-year old preacher who had only experienced three years in ministry. He was clearly demonstrating Romantic characteristics: an advocacy of the benefits of abandoning customary paths; a central role for feelings and experience; an incipient anti-authoritarianism.

Irving sounds very Coleridgean here, echoing concepts we noted earlier, for example, Coleridge's conviction that deep thinking had to be accompanied by deep feeling, and that religious meaning had to embrace the subjectivity of the consciousness of individuals.[62] Irving's description of the perspective of such adventurers as "a holy and heavenly mind", also, echoed Coleridge's concept of the higher reason, which he valued above the "understanding", which could not go beyond the evidence of the senses. The fascinating point here is that these sentiments came from the Irving of Glasgow, not the Irving of London; he had not yet met Coleridge, nor had he come under any other strong neo-Platonic influences. These sentiments, then, illustrate the depth of Irving's innate Scottish Romanticism and the way in which he applied this to an adventurous approach to ministry. It is, perhaps, appropriate to note, at this point, that Irving's ready embrace of adventure and danger was shared by others from his hometown of Annan. For instance, Irving's school friend, Hugh Clapperton, left home as a teenager for an adventurous life at sea: after travelling through Gibraltar, India, Mauritius, America, Canada, and through the Sahara, he died of dysentery in Nigeria.[63] His last letter to England before his death in 1827 was to his childhood friend, Edward Irving.[64] In addition, Irving's own older brother John, a doctor, died in obscure circumstances in India, in the service of the East India Company.[65] Adventure and danger, it seems, came fairly readily to the young men of the Scottish border region of Annandale, and these close examples must have influenced Irving's framing of his own desired future.

Irving published once more before coming under the influence of Coleridge. *Oracles* was written in the first part of 1823, and its dedication to Thomas Chalmers was dated July of that year, the month of the first meeting between Irving and Coleridge. Part of the purpose of this new work was to demonstrate

---

[62] B.M.G. Reardon, *Religious Thought in the Victorian age: a Survey from Coleridge to Gore* (London: Longman, 1980), 64, 72.

[63] Christopher Fyfe, 'Clapperton, Hugh (1788–1827)', *Oxford Dictionary of National Biography*, Oxford University Press, Sept 2004; online edn, Jan 2008. [http://www.oxforddnb.com/view/article/5433, accessed 14 Aug 2008]

[64] Oliphant, *Irving*, 14. Oliphant indicates the two had met again as successful young men in London in the 1820s, but gives no details. It was probably in June 1825, when, according to the ODNB, Clapperton returned briefly to England.

[65] Oliphant, *Irving*, 3.

what Irving believed was needed: new modes of communicating truth.[66] In the early pages of the work, Irving was concerned with sectarianism. "The Christian public," he wrote, "are prone to preoccupy themselves with the admiration of those opinions by which they stand distinguished as a church or sect from other Christians; and instead of being quite unfettered to receive the whole council of the divinity, they are prepared to welcome it, no farther than as it bears upon, and stands with opinions which they already favour."[67] Yet again, Irving sounds astonishingly Coleridgean, this time echoing one of Coleridge's best-known aphorisms from the yet-to-be published *Aids to Reflection*: "He, who begins by loving Christianity better than Truth, will proceed by loving his own Sect or Church better than Christianity, and end in loving himself better than all."[68] Irving went on to allege that in an effort to be "orthodox and evangelical", people pursued controversy with abstractions until "cold intellect" had replaced religious passion.[69] Here, again we see an essential similarity between Irving and Coleridge: the shared dislike for sectarianism and the observation that too many Christians (and often especially the evangelicals) were idolatrously worshipping their own opinions rather than God. Once again, this is Irving writing *before* coming under Coleridge's influence; the synchronicity between the outlooks of the two Romantics is significant.

Later, in *Orations*, Irving argued that much contemporary Christianity ignored the affections of the heart, echoing Coleridge's previously-noted concern for a Christianity that involved the emotions as well as the intellect.

> Who can bear the logical and metaphysical aspect with which Religion looks out from the temples of this land, playing about the head, but starving the well-springs of the heart, and drying up the fertile streams of a holy and charitable life! An accurate, systematic form is the last perfection of knowledge; and a systematic thinker is the perfection of an educated man.
>
> Therefore, it is high intolerance of the far greater number, whose heart and whose affections may be their master faculty, to present nothing but intellectual food, or that chiefly: and moreover, it is a religious spoliation of the heavenly wisdom, which hath a strain fitted to every mood; and it is an unfeeling, unfaithful, dealing between God and the creatures whom he hath been at such charges to save.[70]

---

[66] *For the Oracles of God, four Orations, for Judgment to come, an Argument in nine parts* (London: T. Hamilton, 1823), v-vi. We will be quoting primarily from the 1825 edition, which omits the date from the dedication.

[67] E. Irving, *For the Oracles of God, four Orations, for Judgment to come, an Argument in nine parts* (New York: S. Marks, 1825. Orig. 1823), 20.

[68] Aphorism XXV in J. Beer (ed), *Aids to Reflection*, (Princeton: Princeton University Press, 1993), 107.

[69] Irving, *Oracles*, 21.

[70] Irving, *Oracles*, 45.

Little wonder then, considering his alignment with Coleridge's thought, that when, just after publishing this work, Irving first met Coleridge, he quickly came to admire him, for, in Coleridge, he found not only a concern for the role of the feelings in religion, but, also, a thinker who, if not consistently systematic in his published works, certainly idealised relatedness and integration in his thought.[71]

Also, in *Orations*, Irving addressed himself to the issue of pursuing a life of "heavenly enterprise", defined as a determined pursuit of scriptural guidance which would transcend the slavery of the customs and habits of the age.[72] The enemies of this venture included weakness of will, cultural pressures, and dominating but negative passions.[73] Then he issued a rallying call.

> Some there are blessed with such weak passions and strong reason as to steer without foreign help; but though such may be found to succeed, instead of being admired for their noble independence by the crowd who cling to ancient and present customs, they will generally be stigmatized as self-conceited, or persecuted as innovators, so that disturbance from without, if not from within, shall invade every one who, shaking loose of religious or customary restraints, adventures for himself.
>
> Yet such adventurers should all men become. What to us are the established rules of life, that they should blindly overrule us? Must we be bound in thraldom, to fill and do no more than fill, the narrow bounds of the condition we are born into? Is there nought noble, nought heroical, to be undertaken and achieved? Must the budding desires of our youthful nature be held in check by the narrow prescriptions of an age and an authority we despise; and the labour of a life end in nothing but contemptible drudgery, to keep our tabernacle in being? - Adventurers above your sphere I would have you all to become; brave designs, not antiquated customs, should move your life. A path heroical you should trace out, and follow to glory and immortality.[74]

Once again, the word "adventure" predominates, and Irving's pronouns were in the plural, but this was clearly another manifesto for his own future ministry, the heavenly enterprise he had aligned himself with a few pages before. He had now been in London a year and his popularity had soared; it must have seemed to him that almost anything was possible. Here, we see that independence was valued as noble and innovation praised above the restraint of custom. Youth was called to heroism and adventure; glory awaited those who sloughed off

---

[71] D.Y.T. Lee, "The Humanity of Christ", 33. Coleridge had a long-term plan to outline his philosophical system in his *Magnum Opus*, which, unsurprisingly, he didn't complete.

[72] Irving, *Oracles*, 71.

[73] Irving, *Oracles*, 73-74.

[74] Irving, *Oracles*, 74.

restrictive authorities and customs. This is a theme that was seen frequently in his writings, whether it was applied to individual believers or corporately.[75] Irving was using the language of revolution with gusto because, as a child of the 1790s, he was not, like Coleridge's generation, disillusioned by having lived through the French Revolution. Coleridge did not annotate a copy of *Orations*, so we have no direct evidence whether his new Anglican orthodoxy was offended by Irving's obvious aspiration to be a Romantic religious revolutionary. The above passage shows that, like most Romantics, Irving valued the role of reason, yet clearly realised its limitations and insufficiencies.

> The enemy hath written Reason on his recruiting standard; and we would also write Reason upon the Christian standard, not only for the purpose of defeating his malicious aspersions, but for the justification of the truth, which we conceive to be this - That our religion doth not denounce the rational or intellectual man, but addeth thereto the spiritual man, and that the latter flourishes the more nobly under the fostering hand of the former.[76]

Reason, itself, was not enough, yet reason offered an essential and nurturing context for the spiritual perspective.

As noted in chapter two, *Oracles* was widely criticised and the next comment of Coleridge's refers to this publication. In a postscript to a letter to his brother, dated 23 July 1823, he wrote:

> Irving (the Scotch Preacher so blackguarded in the John Bull of last Sunday), certainly the greatest *Orator*, I ever heard (N.B. I make & mean the same distinction between Oratory & Eloquence as between the Mouth + Windpipe & the Brain + Heart), is, however, a man of great simplicity, of overflowing affections and enthusiastically in earnest, & I have reason to believe, deeply regrets his conjunction of Southey with Byron – as far as the *men* (& not the Poems) are in question.[77]

There is more confirmation here that Coleridge thought Irving's preaching at this point lacked substance, but there is, also, the beginning of a genuine appreciation of Irving, the man, especially his sincerity and enthusiasm. In fact, it appears that this letter allows us to further narrow the likely date range of the first Coleridge-Irving meeting to between 7 and 23 July 1823, because it seems that the meeting had now taken place and Coleridge had discussed with Irving his views of Southey and Byron published in the second part of *Oracles*. It is impossible to believe Coleridge could have written the above lines without

---

[75] For example, Irving, *Oracles,* 254; E. Irving, *The Last Days* (London: James Nisbet & Co., 1831), xxxi, xl; *CW2*, 138.

[76] Irving, *Oracles*, 300.

[77] Letter to Edward Coleridge (no. 1340) in *CLSTC*, vol. v, 1820-1825 (Oxford: Clarendon, 1971), 286-287. This refers to *Oracles*, 119, 303.

having had a personal meeting with Irving. Having established a narrow range for the date of their first meeting, this, also, puts some parameters on Coleridge's influence on Irving's theological development. David Dorries has argued, convincingly, that Irving's view that Christ took fallen human nature but remained sinless through the power of the Holy Spirit was essentially in place from the time of his earliest extant sermons of 1822.[78] This 1822 date precedes the actual controversy over the doctrine by more than five years, and Irving's initial meeting with Coleridge by a year. Therefore, Coleridge can neither be blamed nor credited for being a major formative influence on Irving's distinctive Christology.

The acquaintance between the two men quickly developed into a friendship: a September 1823 letter of Coleridge's depicts a relationship in which the two men discussed books, and when a sought-after volume proved difficult to obtain in London, Irving undertook to obtain it for Coleridge through his contacts in Scotland.[79]

A couple of months later, Coleridge explored the difference between the True and the Good in his notebook. He argued (similarly to his Aphorism XXV, quoted earlier) that some of those who claim to be defending the Truth are, in fact, only opposing those who oppose them and not really seeking Truth at all. They demonise opposition views and, thus, become enemies of Truth. This hypocrisy needed to be exposed.

> Well would it become an Irvine (sic) to lay bare to contempt and indignation the maxims, sanctioned even by Divines & Moralists (woeful misnomers!) – keep to *this* – it is the safest side – and you think it true, you know now - & why should you disturb your mind? And if it should be otherwise, yet while you think it true, it is true for *you* &c. – and therefore take no means of ascertaining the one of the other! – Gracious Heaven! – What means the Parable of the Talents? Or are not Reason, the Understanding, the Affections, *Talents* entrusted to us?[80]

Coleridge's opinion of Irving, the preacher, was improving: he no longer saw Irving simply as an overly-passionate orator, but as a potential ally and prophet, able to discern and expose self-serving pseudo-intellectualism.

In May 1824, Irving made his controversial address to the London Missionary Society mentioned in chapter two, publishing it shortly afterwards. It was his first significant publication since *Oracles* and since meeting Coleridge, to whom it was dedicated. This dedication is reproduced below in

---

[78] D. Dorries, *Edward Irving's Incarnational Christology* (Fairfax, VA: Xulon Press, 2002), 82. Irving destroyed his 1819-1822 sermons preached at St John's Glasgow, with the exception of his farewell sermon, which was published.

[79] Letter to J.A. Hessey dated 9 September 1823 (no. 1350) in *CLSTC*, vol. v, 301.

[80] *NSTC*, vol. 4, Oct/Nov 1823, 5052. Coleridge misspelled Irving's name fairly regularly.

full as it is the most comprehensive view we have of how Irving saw his relationship with Coleridge.

> My dear and honoured Friend, - Unknown as you are in the true character of your mind or your heart to the greater part of your countrymen, and misrepresented as your works have been by those who have the ear of the vulgar, it will seem wonderful to many that I should make choice of you from the circle of my friends, to dedicate to you these beginnings of my thoughts upon the most important subject of these or any times; and when I state the reason to be, that you have been more profitable to my faith in orthodox doctrine, to my spiritual understanding of the Word of God, and to my right conception of the Christian Church, than any or all the men with whom I have entertained friendship and conversation, it will, perhaps, still more astonish the mind and stagger the belief of those who have adopted, as once I did myself, the misrepresentations which are purchased for a hire and vended for a price, concerning your character and works. ... I have partaken so much high intellectual enjoyment from being admitted into the close and familiar intercourse with which you have honoured me; and your many conversations concerning the revelations of the Christian faith have been so profitable to me in every sense, as a student and preacher of the gospel; as a spiritual man and a Christian pastor; and your high intelligence and great learning have at all times so kindly stooped to my ignorance and inexperience, that not merely with the affection of friend to friend, and the honour due from youth to experienced age, but with the gratitude of a disciple to a wise and generous teacher, of an anxious inquirer to the good man who hath helped him in the way of truth, I do presume to offer you the first fruits of my mind since it received a new impulse towards truth, and a new insight into its depths from listening to your discourse. Accept them in good part, and be assured that, however insignificant in themselves, they are the offering of a heart which loves your heart, and of a mind which looks up with reverence to your mind.[81]

This generous and deferential dedication contrasts Irving's view of Coleridge with what Irving believed to be the prevailing view of the poet. Coleridge was not "unknown", but his true character was, and Irving was using his new-found popularity to set the record straight, admitting that he had, himself, once shared the misconceptions about Coleridge's character. When many considered Coleridge at best heterodox, Irving not only trumpeted his orthodoxy, but willingly portrayed himself as Coleridge's pupil. By clear implication, Irving claimed to have learnt more about scripture and the Church through a year of

---

[81] E. Irving, *For Missionaries after the Apostolical School: a Series of Orations, in four parts* (London: Hamilton, Adams & Co, 1825. Orig. 1824), vii-ix.

regular meetings with Coleridge than in three years' full-time ministry with Chalmers.[82]

An obvious question raised by this dedication is whether Irving would have gained any material advantage from it. This question can be answered in the negative. In fact, Irving could hardly have chosen a more controversial way to introduce the printed version of a sermon that had already alienated him from large sections of London's evangelical community. Acknowledgement of an intellectual debt to Samuel Taylor Coleridge whose Unitarian background, Pantisocratic socialist experiments, marital separation and opium addiction were relatively common knowledge, was hardly likely to lead to a rapprochement with piqued religious conservatives. Could Irving have been naïve enough not to know this? The answer comes from the pen of Charles Lamb, Coleridge's old school friend, in a letter from March 1825:

> While I can write, let me abjure you to have no doubts of Irving. ...Irving has prefixed a dedication (of a Missionary Subject, 1st part) to Coleridge, the most beautiful, cordial and sincere. He there acknowledges his obligation to S.T.C. for his knowledge of Gospel truths, the nature of a Christian Church, etc., to the talk of S.T.C. (at whose Gamaliel feet he sits weekly)[?more] than to that of all the men living. This from him, The great dandled and petted Sectarian – to a religious character so equivocal in the world's Eye as that of S.T.C., so foreign to the Kirk's estimate. Can this man be a quack? The language is as affecting as the Spirit of the Dedication. Some friend [Mrs. Basil Montagu] told him, 'This dedication will do you no Good,' i.e. not in the world's repute, or with your own People. 'That is a reason for doing it,' quoth Irving. I am thoroughly pleased with him. He is firm, outspeaking, intrepid – and docile as a pupil of Pythagoras. You must like him.[83]

Lamb leaves it open for us to consider Irving rash, but certainly not naïve. In a few words, Lamb has painted a portrait of Irving that demonstrates an intriguing and unlikely combination of characteristics: he was enjoying the world's favour – "dandled and petted" – yet, he was more than happy to risk this status by acknowledging his debt to Coleridge; he was firm and outspoken in his opinions, yet, he remained teachable. Lamb has, also, made explicit what is soon implicit in Coleridge's correspondence: Irving and Coleridge were in weekly contact by early 1825, if not before.

Lamb highlighted the other main issue arising from Irving's Dedication – credulity or impressionability. To what degree did Irving uncritically accept Coleridge's opinions? Firstly, it should be noted that Coleridge had a tendency

---

[82] Grass sees Coleridge's influence in Irving's idealistic view of missionary activity, *Lord's Watchman* (Milton Keynes: Paternoster, 2011), 93ff.

[83] Letter to Bernard Barton, quoted in E.V. Lucas, *The Life of Charles Lamb*, 1818-1834 (London: Methuen, 1905), vol. 2, 129.

to monologue even in the most gifted and spirited company, so relative silence was common in the poet's loquacious presence. Many made the pilgrimage to the Gillmans' to absorb Coleridge's famous monologues, which were often seen as a work of art in themselves. As one observer wrote, "Coleridge's monologue is perhaps better even than his writing: for it is as profound, as nobly and precisely expressed; while it exhibits more of the union of poetry and philosophy than any of his books either in verse or prose, and is perhaps more fresh and flowing, and a little more adapted to ordinary comprehension."[84] Certainly, those critical of Irving have levelled the accusation that he was merely a passive and overawed recipient of what he perceived as the older poet's wisdom.[85] In chapter three we noted that Irving has been labelled as theologically credulous by some interpreters who didn't, themselves, attempt an assessment of his theology.[86] Often, those wanting to dismiss Irving barely even considered the possibility that Coleridge may have learnt something from him, and it must be admitted that Irving's deferential Dedication gives impetus to this view, succinctly expressed by Drummond: "It has sometimes been suggested that the Sage received from the Caledonian divine as much as he imparted. The fact is, that far from anticipating Coleridge's teaching, Irving embraced it with the enthusiasm and imperfect apprehension of a late learner."[87] One of the few writers to have examined the Coleridge-Irving relationship with reference to Coleridge's notebooks, letters and marginalia, is, also, one of the very few to acknowledge that Irving influenced Coleridge in any way whatsoever. Christopher Burdon's book has a much broader focus – on English interpretations of the Apocalypse - but he has still perceived that Irving's interest in the book of Revelation stimulated Coleridge to a closer study of the text of scripture.[88] Our focus on Coleridge's writings will indicate that Irving's influence was more extensive than this and that Irving's Dedication should, certainly, not be taken completely on face-value to mean that he made no intellectual contribution to the relationship.

As we turn to Coleridge's correspondence of this period, we see the relationship developing as the following extracts from letters dated May to June 1824 reveal.

> Of one thing I am certain, that I did not pay you so ill a compliment as to imagine that you would not think an evening passed with so interesting and highly gifted [a] Man as Irvine [Irving], and so acute and effective a

[84] John Sterling writing to Trench, 16 May 1828 in M. Trench (ed.), *Richard Chenevix Trench, Archbishop: Letters and Memorials*, vol. 1, 8, quoted in Jones, *The Broad Church*, 28.
[85] E.g. Dallimore, *Irving*, 46.
[86] Chapter 3, page 46.
[87] Drummond, *Edward Irving and his Circle,* 66.
[88] Burdon, *Apocalypse in England*, 160.

> Reasoner as my excellent Friend Montague a sufficient compensation for a bad dinner, or rather for a bad apology for a dinner.[89]

> I know, *you* need no additional inducement; but yet I *should* like you very much to be here one of the Evenings which Basil Montague and Mr Irving spend with us – Whether the friendly Sympathies and Collisions between Mr I. and myself act as exciting causes, I cannot say; but I am not the only person who thinks Mr Irving more delightful still at these times than even in the pulpit.[90]

> Dear Sir
> On Thursday Evening (10 June) Mr Irving with Mr Basil Montagu and two or three 'female Intelligences' will, we expect, light up the hours from 5 to 10, in our Drawing-Room [91]

Coleridge was quite capable of expressing adverse opinions of the character and views of others. Here, in his private correspondence with friends, he was able to write in a frank and unguarded manner and he describes Irving as "interesting" and "highly gifted". It, also, appears that Coleridge's impressions of Irving, the preacher, continue to improve, for here his pulpit manner is "delightful". More revealing are the "friendly Sympathies and Collisions" which occurred in Coleridge's discussions with Irving: this phrase shows clearly that Irving was not playing the role of mindless sycophant to Coleridge's sage, but was able to publicly disagree with him and earn Coleridge's respect in the process – the collisions were potentially "exciting". Coleridge's monologue was neither uninterrupted nor unchallenged when Irving was present, and in his own correspondence, Irving revealed his ability to perceive flaws in Coleridge: "There are no philosophers now-a-days, because they are all ambitious of power or eminence...Coleridge is desirous of power, - that is, the good-will of others, or the idolatry of himself."[92] Each man admired the other; each could see flaws in the other. Coleridge's appreciation of Irving only seemed to increase throughout his 1825 correspondence: Irving "has a vigorous & (what is always pleasant) a *growing* mind: and his character is *manly* throughout"[93]; he has "fewer prejudices, national or sectarian" than almost anyone else Coleridge has met.[94] To Coleridge, "manliness" meant an opposition to dogmatism, to be "fully aware of the mysteries of the human condition, [avoiding] intellectual cowardice and spiritual blindness".[95] This,

---

[89] Letter to Henry Taylor (no. 1397), dated 18 May 1824 in *CLSTC*, vol. 5, 362-363.
[90] Letter to Mrs Charles Aders (no. 1403), dated 3 June 1824 in *CLSTC*, vol. 5, 368.
[91] Letter to Henry Taylor (no. 1405), dated 8 June 1824 in *CLSTC*, vol. 5, 369.
[92] Letter to Isabella Irving, dated 29 October 1825, in Oliphant, *Irving*, 129.
[93] Letter to Daniel Stuart (no. 1473), dated 8? July 1825 in *CLSTC*, vol. 5, 474.
[94] Letter to J. Blanco White (no. 1474), dated 12 July 1825 in *CLSTC*, vol. 5, 476.
[95] R. Holmes, *Coleridge: Darker Reflections* (London: Harper, 2005), 539.

then, was Coleridge's estimation of Irving, and he wrote with a sense of satisfaction to his nephew that he had arranged for him to meet with Irving and Charles Lamb.[96]

Irving met Coleridge at a time when he could benefit from Coleridge's mature Christian thought. This was a Coleridge whose Christian Romanticism convinced him that the Enlightenment's view of humanity ignored some of the most fundamental experiences, including the poetic imagination, the sublime, and revelation, and who was pursuing a reconciliation between finite and infinite.[97] In 1825, Coleridge published his first major work since meeting Irving, *Aids to Reflection*. The genesis of this book was Coleridge's admiration for the seventeenth century Archbishop Leighton and his concept of pursuing truth through insight and experience, rather than speculation.[98] Coleridge felt that Leighton and some of his contemporaries had far greater insight into the human condition than the "mechanical" outlook of the eighteenth century;[99] but the final product was much broader than a paean to Leighton. It, also, included Coleridge's first public assessment of Irving. At one point, Coleridge was discussing infant baptism, and he began and ended the passage as follows:

> P.S. A mighty Wrestler in the cause of Spiritual Religion and *Gospel* morality, in whom more than in any other Contemporary I seem to see the Spirit of LUTHER revived, expressed to me his doubts whether we have a right to deny that an infant is capable of a spiritual influence. To such a man I could not feel justified in returning an answer *ex tempore*, or without having first submitted my convictions to a fresh revisal. I owe him, however, a deliberate answer; and take this opportunity of discharging the debt. [Coleridge continues for some time on the subject of infant baptism.] But *you*, honored IRVING, are as little disposed, as myself, to favour such doctrine!
>
> Friend pure of heart and fervent! we have learnt
> A different lore! We may not thus profane
> The Idea and Name of Him whose absolute Will
> Is Reason – Truth Supreme! – Essential Order![100]

---

[96] Letter to Edward Coleridge (no. 1500), dated 8 December 1825 in *CLSTC*, vol. 5, 521.
[97] M.A. Perkins, "Religious thinker" in L. Newlyn (ed), *The Cambridge Companion to Coleridge* (Cambridge: Cambridge University Press, 2002), 191; Holmes, *Coleridge: Darker Reflections*, 462.
[98] Ashton, *Coleridge*, 347.
[99] Perkins, "Religious thinker", 195.
[100] S.T. Coleridge, Aphorisms on Spiritual Religion B, Aphorism XXIV in J. Beer (ed.), *Aids to Reflection*, 378.

Coleridge may be accused of many things, but careless use of words is seldom one of them. After a friendship of less than two years, Coleridge saw Irving as Luther *redivivus*, a spiritual giant in mid-1820s English Protestantism. Coleridge could hardly have expressed his admiration of Irving more enthusiastically. At this point it is appropriate to return to the editorial comment cited earlier, that "[Irving's] *fervid Regard* was to become an embarrassment . . . by Feb 1826, Coleridge had become highly critical [of Irving]."[101] While "fervid regard" could easily become embarrassing, let us consider Coleridge's actual use of the term in context. In a notebook entry for 1825-26, he discussed his life's work and how important it was to him to help people share his understanding of Reason as the source of ideas, then, "I shall have deserved the Character which the fervid Regard of my friend, Irving, has claimed for me, and fulfilled the high Calling, which he invokes me to believe myself to have received."[102] There is no sense here that Coleridge was embarrassed by Irving's fervid regard, rather, that he believed it was something he needed to live up to, which is further implicit testimony to his regard for the Scottish preacher. It is worth noting that Coleridge, approvingly, described Irving as "fervent" in the passage quoted above from *Aids to Reflection*; his usage of "fervent" and "fervid" did not seem to carry any connotations of febrility or instability.[103] Other contemporaries used the same adjective of Irving in a clearly approving way as a synonym for "passionate".[104] So, contrary to the assertion of the Bollingen editors, there is, certainly, no indication at this point that Coleridge was embarrassed by Irving in any way.

If the Bollingen editors were incorrect about this point, was their nominated date of February 1826 of *any* significance in the Irving-Coleridge relationship? We noted, in chapter two, that Irving met Hatley Frere in early 1825, which intensified his interest in prophecy and led to him publishing, in 1826, *Babylon and infidelity foredoomed of God*. Correspondence from February 1826 shows that Coleridge had doubts about this new direction.

> I confess, I do not at all understand our Friend's late excursions into the prophecies of a sealed Book, of which no satisfactory proof has yet been given whether they have already been or still remain to be fulfilled. Cocceius, the best & most spiritual of all our learned Commentators interprets [the] Chapter on the Millennium as of events already past. But as I do not understand, I do not judge – but am willing to believe, that as preached by Mr Irving, it will be to edification – tho' for myself, I am not ashamed to say, that a single Chapter of St Paul's Epistles or St John's

[101] *NSTC*, vol. 4, 4963.
[102] *NSTC*, vol. 4, 5293.
[103] Coleridge also approvingly described others as "fervid", e.g. James Gillman. Holmes, *Coleridge: Darker Reflections*, 431.
[104] For example, C.K. Paul, *Biographical Sketches* (London: Kegan Paul, Trench & Co., 1883), 4.

> Gospel is of more value to me, in light & in life, in love & in Comfort, than the Books of the Apocalypse, Daniel, & Zachariah, all together. In fact, I scarcely know what to make even of the second Coming of our Lord.[105]

Here Coleridge was unconvinced that Irving's new interest would lead to much of substance, yet his respect for Irving remained strong and he was convinced that whatever Irving touched would be to the edification of his congregation. Only a week later, Coleridge commented further on the situation, noting that Irving had been "lately very much with Hatley Frere ... a pious and well-meaning but gloomy & enthusiastic Calvinist, and quite swallowed up in the quicksands of conjectural prophecy". Coleridge's concern was that Irving had mistaken Frere's solemnity and earnestness for truth, had exhausted himself by preaching lengthy sermons on eschatology, and was "going wrong".[106] Coleridge sounded a note of warning, telling Irving "that with the great activity and inventiveness of intellect, which I possessed in common with him, I should have been wrecked, had it not pleased the Almighty that it should meet with a Counter-check in my rooted aversion to the *Arbitrary*, and my solicitude to bring back all my positions to their *Premises* – to understand distinctly what I set off from".[107]

This is an extension of the previous comment, with an added note of concern: Coleridge was worried about Irving's health. The quote is remarkable for Coleridge equating Irving's intellect with his own; Coleridge recognised a kindred spirit in Irving and his concern was clearly that Irving's intellect would be wasted on trifles. However, a February notebook entry refers to Coleridge being "impelled" to the study of the book of Revelation "solely by the rumours, that had reached me, of my friend, Edward Irving's, Aberrations (for such, I fear, they are) into the Cloud-land of Prophecies of The approaching fulfilment of certain Prophecies, his long Orations on the Millennium, the expulsion of the Gentiles from the Church analogous to that of the Jews, the collection of Gentile False-Believers in Armageddon ... – But these studies were against my inclinations & cravings."[108] Although he used the term "aberration" here, it seems that the Bollingen editors overstated the case in saying that, by February 1826, Coleridge had become embarrassed and highly critical of Irving. There is no indication whatsoever of any embarrassment on Coleridge's part, and although Coleridge could be described as critical (or at least wary) of Irving's particular interest in prophecy and the millennium, he was certainly not highly critical of Irving as a person.

---

[105] Letter to Basil Montagu (no. 1518), dated 1 February 1826 in *CLSTC*, vol. 5, 549. Johannes Cocceius (1603-1669) was a Dutch theologian who emphasised covenant or federal theology.
[106] Letter to Edward Coleridge (no. 1521), dated 8 February 1826 in *CLSTC*, vol. 5, 557.
[107] Ibid.
[108] *NSTC*, vol. 4, February 1826, 5323.

As Coleridge's first major work since meeting Irving, *Aids to Reflection* offers an opportunity to see Coleridge's mid-1820s thought that so inspired Irving. Coleridge maintained that fundamental religious truth could be discovered if the "spirit of sectarianism" was eschewed and a process of free thought and evaluation followed.[109] Although other religions contained elements of truth, foundational truth was in the universal Church and the knowledge of God.[110] Openness to other opinions did not imply that they were all equally valid, however, and Coleridge reacted against both the remote God of the Deists and the mechanistic God of extreme Calvinism, arguing that both views emphasised certain divine attributes while ignoring others.[111] One has to proceed carefully when commenting on Coleridge and Calvinism: despite a number of anti-Calvinist sentiments in his works, Coleridge retained a hearty respect for its moderate forms. He admired Archbishop Leighton's Calvinism, and his own view, which he described as "pure Lutheranism", has been described by others as a modified Calvinism.[112] To Coleridge, Christianity was something that the rational man could accept, but more importantly, it was a self-testifying truth that had to be experienced in life: deep thinking had to be accompanied by deep feeling.[113] Coleridge was impatient with the idea that rational proofs could somehow argue people into a Christian faith, being convinced that people came to faith through appreciation of the power of Christianity to meet human need.[114] Developing the Kantian concept that reason takes us beyond the senses, Coleridge's contribution meant that all subsequent discussion of religious meaning had to embrace the subjectivity of the consciousness of individuals.[115] Although one commentator has noted that with *Aids to Reflection* Coleridge was so far ahead of his contemporaries that many of them simply ignored it, this Romantic focus on individual consciousness and feeling resonated with Irving's own inclination to venture beyond the accepted and inherited norms in order to discover a more vital, personal Christianity.[116] Coleridge was, also, pessimistic about future possibilities, and it is likely that this had its own subtle impact on the

---

[109] C.R. Sanders, *Coleridge and the Broad Church Movement* (New York: Octagon Books, 1972), 74.
[110] Sanders, *Coleridge and the Broad Church Movement*, 77.
[111] Sanders, *Coleridge and the Broad Church Movement*, 78.
[112] H.N. Coleridge (ed.), *The Literary Remains of Samuel Taylor Coleridge*, vol. 3 (London: William Pickering, 1838), 303-304; J.R. Barth, *Coleridge and Christian Doctrine* (New York: Fordham University Press, 1987) 156.
[113] B.M.G. Reardon, *Religious Thought in the Victorian Age: a Survey from Coleridge to Gore* (London: Longman, 1980. Orig. 1971), 64.
[114] Reardon, *Religious Thought in the Victorian Age,* 66-67.
[115] G. Green, *Imagining God: Theology and the Religious Imagination* (Grand Rapids, MI: Eerdmans, 1998), 20; Reardon, *Religious Thought in the Victorian Age,* 72.
[116] Reardon, *Religious Thought in the Victorian Age,* 64.

development of Irving's millennialism.[117] These, then, were some of the ideas which Irving would have discussed with Coleridge in the mid-1820s, which would have contributed to the enthusiasm of Irving's dedication.

Understandably, Coleridge read the book dedicated to him, and between May 1825 and 1827 Coleridge annotated his copy of Irving's *For Missionaries after the Apostolical School*, annotations contemporaneous with Coleridge's 1826 concern about Irving's excursion into prophecy. Coleridge describes "the two most uncommon things in the World [as] the Love of the Good, *as* good, and the Love of the True *as* Truth" and goes on to say, "The former rare excellence I could confidently attribute to my Friend, Edward Irving; but not with equal confidence, or so unexceptionally, the latter", the reason being that Irving's conviction that Revelation 20 pictures a future millennium excluded other interpretations from his consideration. Nevertheless, Coleridge continues, "I say this with less suspicion of any counterwarp in my own mind, that (only cutting all connection with Daniel and the Apocalypse) I am inclined to think in the main with him & Lacunza respecting the Second Coming of our Lord."[118]

Coleridge's opinion of Irving remained high: the fault he found here was that Irving's millennialism was affecting his interpretation of the book of Revelation. Nonetheless, notwithstanding Coleridge's aversion to Irving's use of Daniel and Revelation, the final sentence was an acknowledgement that Coleridge had been won over by Irving's argument on the Second Coming. Earlier in this chapter, we noted that on 1 February 1826 Coleridge wrote, "I scarcely know what to make even of the second Coming of our Lord."[119] Now, at some point in 1827 – the year in which Irving published his translation of Lacunza – Coleridge had accepted Irving's theological position on the *parousia*. This distinct movement in Coleridge's theology was clearly due to Irving's influence, and is conclusive evidence that the intellectual traffic between them definitely flowed in both directions. It, also, further highlights the inaccuracy of the Bollingen editors' comments: a Coleridge who was being convinced of the truth of Irving's eschatology was certainly not "embarrassed" by and "highly critical" of Irving.

A notebook entry of 13 April 1827 shows Coleridge praising the improvement in Irving's literary style since he published his *Orations*, comparing his "spirit" to that of "our best Writers", but with his own individual style. Coleridge read Irving's translation of Lacunza with "wonder", regretting how little thought he had personally given to the Second Coming previously,

---

[117] Grass notes that Irving's earliest millennial thought was of the optimistic post-variety, but that after meeting Coleridge, it moves to the more pessimistic premillennialism, *Lord's Watchman*, 100.

[118] H.J. Jackson & G. Whalley (eds), *The Collected Works of Samuel Taylor Coleridge, Marginalia* (London & Princeton: Routledge & Princeton University Press, 1992), 3.9.

[119] Letter to Basil Montagu (no. 1518), dated 1 February 1826 in *CLSTC*, vol. 5, 549.

but, also, expressing the wish that Irving's theology be grounded on less "disputed" scriptural texts.[120]

In the same month, Coleridge, also, wrote, "One other inference I draw – viz. that the rationalized *mind* is more precise & appropriate than the rational Understanding – and that Mr I. may safely assert that even the mind of unregenerated or unspiritualized Man even in it's [sic] most rationalized state is incapable of any direct discernment of spiritual Verities."[121] This is a significant alignment of the thought of Coleridge and Irving in an area where Romanticism and theology have mutual interests. Like all Romantics, Coleridge was limiting the scope and potential of reason alone, yet he was, also, making a far bolder claim: direct discernment of spiritual truth is beyond its reach. The resulting chasm between the abilities of unaided reason (or, in Coleridgean terminology, the understanding, which is limited to sense evidence) and the perception of spiritual truth pointed to the emptiness of philosophy and metaphysics apart from faith. Faith had a vital role in supplementing reason. This resonated clearly with Irving's own Romantic quest to pursue and share a vital Christian spirituality with his contemporaries, a faith that far exceeded what he saw as the sensual expediency of contemporary church culture.

Around this time, Coleridge confessed some of his self-doubt in his notebook. Although he felt he was getting some of his best insights, he wondered if he was deluding himself. Although surely, he argued, if his faculties were in a state of decline, his friends would advise him of this fact? "Yet my Friends, have not professed to observe any such declension," he writes, and proceeds to list the names of six or seven of his closest and most trusted friends, including Edward Irving.[122] Then, lamenting his own complacency and sinfulness, Coleridge wrote, "And this I do feel so deeply, that I am often and often forced to cry for help against the opposite temptation of what Mr Irving calls 'atheistic Self-contempt' paralysing the Hope, that should lay hold of the Promises."[123] By now it should be abundantly evident that Coleridge was not in any way dismissive of Edward Irving: not only has he praised Irving's intellect and writing, seen him as a nineteenth century Luther and adopted his theology of the Second Coming, he listed him amongst his closest friends, trusting Irving's opinion on his own creative faculties! If higher praise were possible, it is difficult to conceive it.

From the middle of 1827 Coleridge seemed to qualify his position on the Second Coming. We have already seen Coleridge's acknowledgement that he had moved towards Irving's position, and in April his notebook records, "Doubtless, of transcendent importance is the Question respecting the second

---

[120] *NSTC*, vol. 4, 13 April 1827, 5486.
[121] *NSTC*, vol. 4, April 1827, 5495. Emphasis original.
[122] *NSTC*, vol. 4, April 1827, 5498.
[123] *NSTC*, vol. 4, April 1827, 5498.

personal coming of the Son of Man."[124] Yet later that year, he met John Sterling[125], a poet who became an admirer and recorded some of Coleridge's conversation.

> I care not for [Irving's] opinions, - as to them I differ from him entirely, - but I shall always say Mr. Irving is a noble creature. It is unfortunate that he thinks these views of his about the second coming of Christ of such importance as to induce him to discuss them in the pulpit while so many of his congregation must be hungering for the mere common bread of life. Yet the book he has translated is a most powerful piece of reasoning – except where they rely upon a part of Daniel - & the Revelations. It is there Mr. Irving fails. It is clear from certain passages in the Gospels & in St. Paul – that the Apostles interpreted the ancient prophecies as foreshadowing a second advent of Christ in the body upon earth. It is for Mr. Irving's opponents to shew reason for dissenting from the Apostles on this point.[126]

If we assume that John Sterling recorded this conversation accurately, then Coleridge was being, at least, inconsistent and possibly exaggerating (perhaps both):[127] having begun with the declaration that he differed from Irving's opinions "entirely", Coleridge proceeded to agree with them substantially, apart from the previously mentioned aversion to his use of Daniel and Revelation, and, in fact, to challenge Irving's opponents to find reason for disagreeing with him! It may be unwise to overlook the possible effects of opium on this conversation. Nevertheless, the above quotation does indicate that Coleridge apparently downgraded the importance of the Second Coming from "transcendent" to secondary, at least in the context of suitable material for preaching. I believe these apparent inconsistencies are very revealing about Coleridge's political and theological journey, pointing us towards a deeper understanding of why Coleridge, although deeply appreciative and supportive of Irving in many ways, nevertheless, disagreed with him in at least two significant areas.

In chapter one, we noted that enthusiasm, millennialism and apocalypticism were almost synonymous terms for the generation that lived through the French Revolution. All these terms were potentially revolutionary because they envisaged and anticipated an ideal world, and pursued it with various degrees

---

[124] *NSTC*, vol. 4, April 1827, 5497.

[125] Sterling's acquaintances included John Stuart Mill, F.D. Maurice, Alfred Tennyson and Thomas Carlyle.

[126] C. Woodring (ed.), *Table Talk* vol. 1 (London & Princeton: Routledge, & Princeton University Press, 1990), Appendix N, 400.

[127] Coleridge's internal inconsistencies have been frequently commented on, eg. J.C. McKusick, reviewing D. Vallins, *Coleridge and the Psychology of Romanticism: Feeling and Thought* (New York: St Martin's Press, 2000) in *Studies in Romanticism*, Winter, 2002.

of determination and violence. Born in 1772, Coleridge was part of this generation, whereas Irving, twenty years his junior, was not. Like his friend, Wordsworth, Coleridge had been excited by the early promise of revolution in France (which found expression in his Pantisocratic phase of the mid 1790s). In fact, his 1794 poem, *Religious Musings*, contains apocalyptic imagery, borrowed from the book of Revelation, to describe the new heaven and new earth that will follow the French Revolution.[128] It is highly ironic then, that Coleridge later criticised Irving for using the book of Revelation to support *his* millennialism.[129] Like other contemporaries, Coleridge became disillusioned when bloodshed and autocracy resulted from revolution (although he hoped it was but a temporary over-reaction to the previous despotism), but, finally, recanted in the face of French violence against Switzerland.[130] This is expressed in his 1798 poem, *France: an ode*:

> Forgive me, Freedom! O forgive those dreams
> . . . forgive me, that I cherished
> One thought that ever blessed your cruel foes! ...
> O France, that mockest Heaven, adulterous, blind,
> And patriot only in pernicious toils![131]

Therefore, by the time Coleridge and Irving met, the poet's recantation of his youthful revolutionary sympathies had been in place for a quarter of a century, and the corollary of that was a distrust of any millennial or apocalyptic convictions.[132] Curiously, however, Coleridge focused on, and attempted to rehabilitate, the term "enthusiasm".[133] In other contexts, Coleridge was adept at inventing new terminology; therefore, it is intriguing that he chose to rehabilitate a loaded term like enthusiasm. When Coleridge was revising his essays from *The Friend* for an 1818 edition, he attempted to associate the more negative connotations with "fanaticism", and reserve enthusiasm to indicate "a quiet sense of the nearness of God's being, that is, for exactly the kind of religious experience that it had traditionally been seen as so scandalously

---

[128] Ashton, *Coleridge*, 84.

[129] Coleridge's mid-life reservations about revolutionary leanings were shared by many, but, in tension with this and unlike most of his contemporaries, he was, also, immersed in German Idealism, which carried its own revolutionary possibilities. For the tension between the two, see T.M. Gouldstone, *The Rise and Decline of Anglican Idealism in the Nineteenth Century* (Basingstoke, Hampshire: Palgrave Macmillan, 2005), 25-26.

[130] Barth comments on this disillusionment in *Coleridge and Christian Doctrine*, 8-9.

[131] S.T. Coleridge, "France: an ode", lines 64, 70-71, 78-79 in E.H. Coleridge (ed.), *The Poems of Samuel Taylor Coleridge* (London: Oxford University Press, 1960) 246.

[132] Coleridge was criticised, especially by Hazlitt, for reneging on the revolutionary principles of his youth, eg. Ashton, *Coleridge*, 299.

[133] J. Mee, *Romanticism, Enthusiasm and Regulation: Poetics and the Policing of Culture in the Romantic Period* (Oxford: OUP, 2003), 164.

exceeding".[134] Coleridge's etymological attempt to domesticate enthusiasm speaks powerfully to the value he placed on the concept in the religious life, and his desire to preserve this context, in the face of the contemporary view that enthusiasm, millennialism and apocalypticism all envisaged and anticipated an ideal world, and either awaited or pursued it with various degrees of determination. Whether religious or political in nature, these movements were all potentially revolutionary. In the years following the French Revolution, Coleridge increasingly distanced himself from the more radical elements in this mixture. Coleridge saw the kinship between religious enthusiasm and Romantic transcendence and was determined both to preserve it and to limit its extreme variants.

Irving's doctrine of the Second Coming was closely allied with his premillennialism, and although we have seen that Coleridge was convinced by the former, we can now understand why he would instinctively struggle to distance himself from the latter. In the same marginal note in which we have already seen Coleridge's approval of Irving's view of the Second Coming, we, also, saw his conviction that Irving's view of Revelation 20, as describing a future millennium, was mistaken.[135] This is a clear indication that the difference in eschatology between Coleridge and Irving was mainly over the issue of millennialism. This is further supported in a letter from Coleridge to Mrs Basil Montagu (which, also, makes clear that Irving was still a regular and welcome guest at Highgate) in which he aligns himself with the "Anti-millenarian Plea".[136] The idea that the Second Coming of Christ would usher in a millennial period in which all existing social ills would cease, especially the conviction that such an event was *imminent*, caused Coleridge concern about its effects on the lives and morality of its adherents.

> One of the strongest *cui bono* arguments in favor of my good Friend, Irving's Aberraçion – What is man without Hope? and Hope needs an embodiment, & a specific Object to give it *objective* influence – The religious and moral fervor of the Christian Church scarcely survived the expectation of the *crastine* coming of our Lord![137]

So, although Coleridge could see some positive benefits arising from the belief that the Second Coming was imminent, he still saw it as an aberration, and one that, historically and socially, had been unhelpful. No doubt Coleridge's use of the Spanish form of "aberration" reflects Irving's identification with the views of the Spanish Jesuit Lacunza. The term "aberration" usually refers to a

---

[134] Mee, *Romanticism, Enthusiasm and Regulation*, 165.

[135] Coleridge's marginal notes on Irving's *Missionaries after the Apostolical School* in Jackson & Whalley, *Marginalia* volume III, 9.

[136] Letter to Mrs Basil Montagu (no. 1584), dated 1 May 1827 in *CLSTC*, vol. 5, 676.

[137] *NSTC*, vol. 4, 25 October 1827, 5622. *Cui bono* means "who benefits?"; *crastine* is an obsolete word meaning "the day after tomorrow".

deviation from what is regarded as normal, and while Coleridge regards Irving's emphasis on the imminence of the Second Coming/millennium this way, we should recall the point made in a previous chapter that millennial and apocalyptic views were widely held in this period. The Coleridge of the mid-1820s had personally retreated from his early 1790s hopes that the French Revolution was the dawn of a secular millennium, and therefore regarded Irving's millennial hopes as a deviation, even though various millennialist views were widely-held amongst contemporaries.

From April 12 until the end of December 1827, Coleridge made marginal notes in his copy of Lacunza, which Irving had not only translated but supplied with his own two-hundred page preface. In some additional pages stuck in the front of the book Coleridge wrote that he believed Irving's teaching on the Second Coming to be completely orthodox and "probable", but he disagreed with Irving's teaching on the millennium (which Coleridge saw as starting with the reign of Constantine) and his continued use of Daniel and Revelation.[138] Coleridge objected most strongly to Irving's close juxtaposition of the *parousia* with the "Apocalyptic Millennium". Yet, although Coleridge disagreed with Irving in this area, he read Irving's preface with an open heart and occasional self-rebuke. Coleridge was "shamed" by reading it for he acknowledged that, although he had "long entertained" the orthodox view of the Holy Spirit, he had "lacked courage to make known & promulgate the same".[139]

Only shortly afterwards in Irving's preface, Coleridge noted a desire to align himself with Irving and share his faith.

> Now so far in all the deep & concerning Points which Mr Irving has most ably maintained against the current dogmata of both Churches, his own & ours, in all the great moments of his Warfare; I am his fellow combatant & prepared to fight under his banner. Up to this stone he & I are one. Shall we differ then respecting our Lord's Kingly office? Scarcely I trust. – Or of Christ's 2nd coming to possess his Kingdom? I have no foreboding of dissent on this either. It is the personal coming, to the coming of Jesus, & the erection of an earthly monarchy, an imperial Theocracy, under Jesus, as the visible head & Sovereign, that my fear points. Fears that I shall find myself called on to withstand him to attack his positions & despoil him of his Faith? O no! no! no! but that I may not be able to partake of it! There will be no [? Unitency/ uniting/ resistency], but a yearning & a predisposition. If reason does not hold me back, my Will will project me at all events Daniel & the Apocalypse shall not part us
> 12 April 1827 [140]

[138] Jackson & Whalley, *Marginalia* 3.416-417.
[139] Jackson & Whalley, *Marginalia* 3.427-428. This refers to cv of Irving's preface.
[140] Jackson & Whalley, *Marginalia* 3.430. This refers to cxiii of Irving's preface.

In this powerful imagery, Coleridge presented himself as a soldier fighting under Irving's banner, giving further substance to the influence the preacher had on the poet. Coleridge did not merely agree with Irving, but was prepared to fight alongside him in a battle against the current teaching of both the Church of Scotland and the Church of England. Coleridge's desire to agree with Irving on all points is noticeable, yet he still cannot agree on the establishment of an earthly millennial kingdom following the Second Coming. The dispute about Irving's use of Daniel and Revelation remains, but is now seen as less significant to Coleridge than his warm approval of Irving's overall direction.

In succeeding Lacunza marginalia, all written at some point between April and December 1827, Coleridge evinced some concern about whether Irving, "in the onrush of his eloquence", had sufficiently clarified whether he meant some things to be taken in a literal or a spiritual sense.[141] He, also, quarreled with Irving's use of terminology (especially, reason and understanding) when it did not line up with his own usage,[142] and thought Irving's kind nature prevented him from a more rigorous editing of Lacunza's prolixity.[143] And then, despite the depth of Coleridge's opposition to Irving's view of the millennium, we find an astonishing passage to the contrary.

> In short, the longer I think and the more I reflect on the subject, the more scriptural does the Belief of Christ's reign on the Earth appear to me – and I cannot help auguring, that the millenarian tenet stripped of all its rabbinical figments will not be overthrown, if it ever be overthrown, without an earthquake Shaking of sundry other now universally received opinions respecting the 1st Century of the Xtn Church, and a strange revolution in the minds of the educated Classes as to the rank and character of the Hebrew Oracles! Nay, this doctrine blown abroad from the awakening Trumpet of my friend's eloquence & thus brought into general discussion with all its mighty Satillitium of Scripture Proofs and strong Arguments from the analogy of Faith (like the production of a missing Bone in a Mammoth Skeleton – proved by its fitting and filling the evident vacancy) – the forcible vindication, I say, of this Doctrine may be one of the means of accelerating that reign of Infidelity, the coming of which as the precursor of the Messiah King forms so prominent a part of the Doctrines. 'When the Son of Man cometh, shall he find Faith in the Earth? I say unto you, Nay!' - But likewise the more shaken I am in my hitherto contempt & rejection of the Doctrine & the stronger I feel its attractive force drawing me towards my

---

141 Jackson & Whalley, *Marginalia* 3.430. This refers to cxxvi of Irving's preface.

142 Jackson & Whalley, *Marginalia* 3.435, referring to clxi of the preface. As previously noted, Coleridge tended to use "understanding" for reasoning based on sense evidence, and "reason" for a higher faculty that included the conscience.

143 Jackson & Whalley, *Marginalia* 3.451. This is referring to Coleridge's comments in the preliminary pages of volume 2 of Lacunza.

> friend's Belief – the more lively does my conviction become, that the Apocalypse is the most formidable Obstacle in his way, and that the greatest service, that could possibly be rendered to the Millenarian Scheme, would be to reduce this book to the same rank with Hermes, and Esdras.[144]

This shows the development in Coleridge's thought as a result of having read at least a substantial amount of Irving's Lacunza. He has moved from the position of being completely dismissive of the concept of a future millennium to not only accepting it, but believing it rests on very solid evidence indeed. He remained consistent in his rejection of the book of Revelation as supporting evidence, but believed the doctrine was supportable without any evidence from this source. This quote shows that, not only did Edward Irving win Coleridge over to his doctrine of the Second Coming, but, also, to pre-millennialism. It will be remembered that while Coleridge initially admitted to no fixed opinion on the issue of the Second Coming, his anti-millennial convictions were deep and firmly held: for Coleridge to completely change his mind through reading Irving's preface to, and translation of Lacunza, is a powerful demonstration of the Scottish preacher's ability to influence the Highgate sage.

Coleridge's new (or renewed) support for millennialism did not hamper his ability to criticise "the very worst tenets of popery" he found in the Jesuit writer[145] but still he admitted "a more convincing Chain of Reasoning I have never read" and Irving/Lacunza "generally commands my Belief, and always my Respect."[146] His final marginal note confirms his essential agreement with the main thrust of the argument.[147]

By 1828 Irving's congregation had moved into the new Regent Square Church, he was a regular attender at the Albury conferences mentioned in chapter two, and later in the year he first published his distinctive views on Christology.[148] In many ways, he was at the peak of his ministerial career. It was, also, a year in which Coleridge's health rallied and he oversaw the three-volume edition of his poetry, and in the summer spent some weeks travelling through the Netherlands and the Rhineland with Wordsworth and his daughter, Dora. With Coleridge more nomadic than usual there was less contact between the two men, which is reflected in Coleridge's correspondence. The sole 1828 reference to Irving is in a letter to George Dyer in June, in which Coleridge is

---

144 Jackson & Whalley, *Marginalia* 3.452. This is referring to Coleridge's comments in the preliminary pages of volume 2 of Lacunza.

145 Jackson & Whalley, *Marginalia* 3.457. This is referring to Coleridge's comments on pages 20-21 of volume 2 of Lacunza.

146 Jackson & Whalley, *Marginalia* 3.464. This is referring to Coleridge's comments on page 59 of volume 2 of Lacunza.

147 Jackson & Whalley, *Marginalia* 3.481. This is referring to Coleridge's comments in the end pages of volume 2 of Lacunza.

148 E. Irving, *Sermons, Lectures and Occasional Discourses*, 3 vols., (London: R.B. Seeley & W. Burnside, 1828)

seen to be reassuring Dyer of his friendship by a comparison with Irving: "My dear long-known and long-loved Friend! Be assured that neither Mr Irving nor any other person, high or low, gentle or simple, stands higher in my Esteem or bears a name endeared to me by more interesting recollections and associations than Yourself."[149] Coleridge was here using Irving as the template by which his affections to others could be measured.

This paucity of Irving references during most of 1828 changed at the end of the year as Coleridge extensively annotated his copy of Irving's *Sermons* between November/December 1828 (shortly after its publication) and February 1829. One of the earliest notes complimented Irving's "high heart and vehement intellect"[150], but a little later, Coleridge expressed concern about Irving's understanding of the Trinity:

> I trust, the time will come, when Mr Irving will have contemplated the Trinity in the light of the Absolute ONE, for so only can the mind be secure against the risk of Tritheism by the too exclusive attention to the Distinctities under the unhappy translation of hypostasis by Person, and of thus introducing diversity of Attributes where only the eternal Proprieties of Form, <Subsistency,> and essential Relations dare be affirmed.[151]

As can be seen from this quotation, Coleridge objected to the use of the term "Person" when discussing the Trinity as opening the possibility of tritheism, but Irving was not the only one to feel the brunt of Coleridge's disapproval about this, as the term had been part of Trinitarian discussions for centuries.[152] Yet Coleridge followed this cautionary comment by the assertion that he thought those opposing Irving's Christology were mistaken,[153] and then by a passage in which he gave his impression of Irving's theological position as partly Calvinist.

> I cannot help – notwithstanding the unfeigned and earnest respect, in which I hold Mr Irving, I yet cannot help at times comparing him in my fancy to a Hornet or Dragon-fly who having been caught and bound in the strongly-woven Spider-web of Calvinism had at length by vigorous efforts liberated himself, left the Web, rent and ruined but alas! Carried off with him a

[149] Letter to George Dyer, (no. 1628), dated 6 June 1828 in *CLSTC*, volume 5, 746.

[150] Jackson & Whalley, *Marginalia* 3.11. This refers to volume 1, page 1 of *Sermons*. According to the OED, the contemporary meaning of vehement was "extremely strong, ardent, passionate."

[151] Jackson & Whalley, *Marginalia* 3.17.

[152] *NSTC*, vol. 5, 1827-1834, 6157 reads, "Coleridge's argument is that the use of the term 'person' tends to give a misleading, perhaps overly anthropomorphic, idea of the nature of the Trinity. He raised this objection to some of the pronouncements of authors whose views he otherwise admired, for instance Jakob Böhme and Edward Irving."

[153] Jackson & Whalley, *Marginalia* 3.18. Refers to vii-viii of the preface to volume 1.

> portion of the Threads & viscous bonds that impede the free action of his Wings, and render his flight unsteady and bewildered – now soaring by his native vigor, now sinking by the weight of his still adhering bondage. – He writes like a fugitive from modern Calvinism, who has freed the chain from the Staple-ring, but not his ancles from the Chain.[154]

This passage is revealing for Coleridge's view of Calvinism: his spider-web and prison metaphors clearly show he saw Calvinism (or at least the "modern" version of it) as the enemy of freedom. This passage, also, gives us a Romantic image of an Irving who is struggling to rise above the confines of the Scottish Calvinist environment which was his by birth, training and daily experience. Irving's pursuit of truth led him beyond the accepted conventions of his context, earning the respect of Coleridge who, nonetheless, saw him as still partly encumbered and inhibited. Coleridge was as admiring of Irving's struggle as he was frustrated by the remaining inhibition.

As Coleridge proceeded with his annotations, he described Irving's writing as "sound and scholarly; soberly grounded & happily built up"[155] and that "both the selection and the exposition of the Texts here cited do, as I have acknowledged, evince the hand of a Master: and the whole passage is in my friend's happiest manner", although Coleridge retained all his customary reservations about the use of Daniel.[156] Coleridge lamented – not for the first time – that Irving didn't express himself in Coleridgean terminology, believing that if he did so, he would be better understood.[157] This is quite ironic, as few people complained that Irving was difficult to understand, but more than a few levelled this charge against Coleridge![158] There is further irony when Coleridge says that he was personally not much concerned with Irving's doctrine of Christ assuming fallen human nature, then criticised Irving for not sticking closely enough to the text of scripture.

> But surely I cannot be wrong in wishing that he would either enunciate his doctrines in the words of Scripture, or attach a less terrific importance & in a less angry and imperious tone, to statements & assertions in words of his

---

[154] Jackson & Whalley, *Marginalia* 3.26-27, referring to *Sermons*, vol. 1, 19-25. Mumpsimus means "a traditional notion obstinately adhered to".

[155] Jackson & Whalley, *Marginalia* 3.32, referring to *Sermons*, vol. 1, 74.

[156] Jackson & Whalley, *Marginalia* 3.32, referring to *Sermons*, vol. 1, 74.

[157] Jackson & Whalley, *Marginalia* 3.32, referring to *Sermons*, vol. 1, 35-36, referring to Sermons, vol. 1, 80-81. "The Principle here introduced would, I am persuaded, have been more generally understood, if my Friend had enunciated the same in my own words – viz. Religion is distinguished from Philosophy on the one hand, and from History on the other, by being both in one – All its Facts are intelligential Truths, all its Truths are Historical Facts. – The two equally indispensable Factors of a Religion are Ideas and Facts manifesting ideas. Corollary. A Religion not revealed, or a Natural Religion, is a contradiction in terms."

[158] Ashton, *Coleridge*, 252, 301. Coleridge was, himself, aware of this, 391.

> own finding, that are no where directly asserted or declared in Scripture, and which so many both learned and pious Divines have not considered deducible therefrom. But alas! There are too many of these heat-pimples and fever-spots on the fair and manly face of my Friend's Elocution.[159]

It was Coleridge's expressed belief that ideas could only really be communicated by means of symbol and that religion "consists of ideas . . . that can only be spiritually discerned, and to the expression of which words are necessarily inadequate, and must be used by accommodation".[160] In addition, Coleridge was the first English writer to use the term "bibliolatry" to pejoratively describe an attitude that appeared to place the scriptural text on a level with God himself.[161] It is, therefore, strange that Coleridge upbraided Irving for not using the language of scripture to defend what he believed to be an important doctrine validly inferred from scripture, especially when Coleridge had previously accused Irving of being too literalistic in his approach to scripture. Coleridge did not see Irving's distinctive Christology as particularly significant when (as we saw in chapters two and three, and will see again in chapter six) it caused such a commotion elsewhere. The explanation for this is no doubt to be found in the passage quoted earlier in which Coleridge discussed his view of Calvinism and salvation; his distance from much contemporary evangelical Calvinist soteriology meant that not as much was at stake for him with this issue, which was certainly not adiaphora for others.

A little later in his marginal notes, Coleridge did become alarmed by Irving's Christology, but his objections were different from Irving's other opponents, as can be seen in the following passage which once again picks up the issue of tritheism.

> The glaring Tritheism – what do I say? The palpable Tri-angelism, the Holy Ghost being clearly the superior Person, the least confined and crippled of the three, and to all intents and purposes the true and only effective Agent in our Redemption – the strange enunciations of fancies the most startling without a single expression of the Sacred Writers to warrant, or that could even be supposed to have suggested them – and above all the continued attribution to the transitory material Body of Jesus, from which he in so many ways endeavored to wean & withdraw the still sensual minds of the disciples, all the powers, attributes, and functions of the mystical and

---

[159] Jackson & Whalley, *Marginalia* 3.36-37, referring to *Sermons*, vol. 1, 35, referring to *Sermons*, vol. 1, 139.

[160] S.T. Coleridge, in J. Engell & W.J. Bate (eds), *Biographia Literaria*, vol. 1 (Princeton: Princeton University Press), 156, quoted in Jones, *The Broad Church*, 35; S.T. Coleridge in H.N. Coleridge (ed.), *The Literary Remains of Samuel Taylor Coleridge* (London: Pickering, 1839), vol. 4, 63, quoted in Jones, *The Broad Church*, 36. Coleridge adapted the word from a German term used by Lessing.

[161] Jones, *The Broad Church*, 36.

> spiritual Flesh and Blood of the Word that had become Man, constituting the proper *Humanity* (not combining with it as with an element already existing previously to the combination) the Flesh and Blood that nourish to life everlasting, the supersensual Body which *is* Life, and whereto we must be assimilated, assimilated to the divine food as the food inferior to ourselves is assimilated to our Bodies, or we *cannot* live![162]

Coleridge's previous concern about the risk of tritheism has here blossomed into overt alarm because he thought that Irving had made too much of the role of the Holy Spirit. In addition, he clearly believed Irving had overemphasised the physical rather than the spiritual nature of Christ's humanity. Coleridge's concerns differed from the majority of Irving's opponents, who saw Irving's assertion that Christ fully assumed fallen human nature as equivalent to saying Christ actually *sinned.* Yet in Coleridge's reaction against this portrayal of Christ's sacrifice there appears to be something more than just a critique of Irving's position, and this becomes clearer as we progress. When Irving wrote, "Whence it follows, that, whatever [Christ] suffered, and, which is far more, whatever he forewent of infinite glory and blessedness in order to suffer, is all to be placed to the account of mankind, and not to his own account,"[163] Coleridge retorted, "And yet this is the Man who … talks with contempt of 'the Debtor and Creditor Scheme' of Redemption!! Mr I. *alarms* me with his shouldering mob of Inconsistencies! Calvinism & Popery stand like Mule & Ass with their heads in contrary directions: and here Mr I. ties them together by the Tails & then sets them a kicking!"[164] Here we see a vivid echo of Coleridge's previous comment that Irving had broken free from, but in some ways was still restrained by, the "spider-web" of contemporary Calvinism. Coleridge's reaction against Irving here is largely determined by his opposition to the penal substitution theory of atonement and his frustration that Irving has distanced himself from it to some degree, but apparently not as consistently as Coleridge would like.

Shortly afterwards, when Irving wrote of the whole future human race being identified with Adam in his fall from grace and with Christ in redemption,[165] Coleridge's response was equally dismissive: "Surely, Mr I. must have been dreaming, must have written under Somnambulism! I can call to mind no book from which he could have taken it – unless he has met with some old volume

---

[162] Jackson & Whalley, *Marginalia* 3.41-43, referring to *Sermons*, vol. 1, xxxiv (140)-lviii (140). This pagination requires explanation: the three volumes of *Sermons* were printed with consecutive pagination, but after volume 1 had been set and printed, two further sermons were added, with the final page number of the previous section (140) added, and Roman numerals for the pages of the new section.

[163] Irving, *Sermons*, vol.1, liv, 140.

[164] Jackson & Whalley, *Marginalia* 3.47.

[165] Jackson & Whalley, *Marginalia* 3.47, referring to volume 1, lv, 140.

written by some obscure Follower of Jacob Behmen."[166] Yet it appears Coleridge was being disingenuous here for Irving was not espousing an esoteric idiosyncrasy, but an established doctrine from within the Reformed tradition.[167]

Coleridge later approved of a passage on the Trinity, because Irving seemed to be emphasising the unity, rather than the distinctions, within the divine being,[168] but then reacted strongly against Irving's teaching that after Calvary, Christ descended into Hell, a doctrine which, though hard to defend from the scriptures used, was of ancient origin and, therefore, certainly not peculiar to Irving.[169]

Dallimore has alleged that Coleridge never completely overcame a lingering Unitarianism and continued to believe that Christ was "something less than divine".[170] Dallimore, in fact, refused to accord the description of Christian to Coleridge at all.[171] He then implied that Irving caught "Coleridge's confusion", which fed into his own Christology.[172] In the light of Coleridge's objections to Irving's theology seen on previous pages, this makes little sense: if Irving was simply mirroring Coleridge's own opinions, why would Coleridge express concern over perceived tritheism in Irving? If Coleridge's Christ was less than divine, why would he object to Irving emphasising Christ's humanity? In fact, Coleridge interpreters have argued the opposite view from Dallimore, that is, that although Coleridge viewed Christ as fully human, he ignored his particularity, seeing the Incarnation more as a symbolic representation of God as humanity's redeemer.[173] Also, that, if anything, Coleridge "edged away" from the human nature of Christ, towards the symbolic Neoplatonic Logos, the efficacious sign of God's work in humanity.[174] In the light of their differences in this area, there seems little ground for crediting (or blaming) Coleridge for the development of Irving's Christology (which Irving always insisted he had learned in his native Scotland anyway).

Near the close of the first volume, Irving wrote about the persecution believers could expect. "While from the enlightened and philosophical (falsely

---

[166] Jackson & Whalley, *Marginalia* 3.47.

[167] In fact, the view stretches back as far as Augustine's *A Treatise on the Merits and Forgiveness of Sins, and the Baptism of Infants*, 1.8-11. Calvin argues this view in chapter 1 of book 2 of the *Institutes*.

[168] Jackson & Whalley, *Marginalia* volume III, 52, referring to volume 1, cx, 140.

[169] Jackson & Whalley, *Marginalia* 3.55-56, referring to volume 1, 200-204. The scriptures Irving used were 1 Peter 3:18-20; 4:6 and Ephesians 4:9. The Apostles' Creed has, also, contributed to this interpretation.

[170] Dallimore, *Irving*, 46.

[171] Dallimore, *Irving*, 49. Merricks is another author who, likewise, fails to acknowledge Coleridge's later Trinitarianism, *Irving*, 60.

[172] Dallimore, *Irving*, 47.

[173] D. Pym, *The Religious Thought of Samuel Taylor Coleridge* (Gerrards Cross: Colin Smythe, 1978), 70-71.

[174] Boulger, *Coleridge as Religious Thinker*, 181, 214; Barth, *Coleridge and Christian Doctrine*, 148.

so called) Sadducees – that is, our liberal and benevolent disbelievers in all the mysteries of our holy religion – you must expect the uttermost scorn and derision, as men of disordered minds and dangerous opinions . . . But we must first drink of his cup, and be baptized with his baptism, in order to enter into his kingdom."[175] To which Coleridge retorted, "I grieve to say it, but for every single contemptuous Sentence published against Mr Irving, I would undertake to produce ten out of his own publications applied to others. And how can it be, that wise men should not be disgusted, to hear him boasting of his persecutions, & his cup of martyrdom, while he lives in the riot of popularity in his own World!"[176] Coleridge was here criticising Irving for being unduly sensitive to criticism, while being more than capable of handing out criticism to others. However, Irving had written in the second person and the first person plural, not the first person singular and did not, therefore, exaggerate his own persecutions above those of any other believer. No doubt Irving saw himself in this picture, but he, also, saw all other faithful believers in this context as well. It would seem that Coleridge protested too much: Irving is not here "boasting" of his personal "persecutions", but proclaiming the common lot of Christians; therefore even though on this occasion Coleridge expressed "disgust" for Irving, he had little reason for such an epithet.

Coleridge spent more time on the first volume of *Sermons* than on the other two. His final annotation was really a reflection on the whole volume.

> This concluding Paragraph – o what affectionate regrets does it awake in my heart, while it reminds me of my friend's saner days, when he was well content to know no more of Christ's History than the Gospels had preserved for him! and to unfold the plain meaning of the Evangelists Chapter-wise, instead of deducing meanings, say rather fancies, of his own from simple words or sentences, these too often mistranslated, and in more than one instance of suspicious Authenticity.[177]

Was Coleridge really doubting Irving's sanity? I believe not. His main grievance was that Irving was looking beyond the "plain meaning" of the scriptural text, and we have already noted the irony in Coleridge making this sort of objection. This is further heightened as Coleridge continued in a similar vein. Coleridge believed that Creation was the "first Act of Redemption", because God must have anticipated the Fall.

> But this was not stuff for the Pulpit: & on this account, tho' I fully believe not with his own consciousness, my friend always turned short off from my discourse on the Chaos, and the antecedents therein implied & presupposed, as so many hypertheological praeterscriptural Sky-scrapers, the mere puff

---

[175] *Sermons*, volume 1, 206.
[176] Jackson & Whalley, *Marginalia* 3.56-57, referring to volume 1, 206.
[177] Jackson & Whalley, *Marginalia* 3.58, referring to volume 1, 211.

> and pride of the Vessel, which he was only too willing to suppose above his comprehension because he saw no motive and felt no impulse to make the attempt. From this one source all his errors & they have been most grievous errors, may be traced & have, in fact, been derived. Hence his ignorance respecting the Absolute, the abysmal Ground of the Trinity – his consequent utter misapprehension of the Trinity itself, neither apprehending aright the unity or the distinctities ...I begin to fear that I ought to regret my intercourse with Mr I. on his own account. For if he had never been tempted out of the popular way of thinking, & guided wholly & exclusively by his honest feelings & the letter of Scripture, treating each subject as an integer, standing on its own grounds, and exerting its appropriate influences within its own sphere, disregarding its connections with other truths, otherwise than as one among others, and thus regarding Theology as a bag of Coins, each of which had a value for itself & might be put out to interest on its own account – he might by his Zeal and exalted disinterestedness and extraordinary eloquence have been the Benefactor of Thousands and Ten Thousands – giving them the medicines, to each what the disease needed, without troubling either the Patients or himself with any SYSTEM of rational Pathology grounded on more general principles of Physiology; and at all events would have avoided the offensive Errors into which a supposed System has seduced him.[178]

Although Coleridge could see his own influence on Irving, he could not see that the very thing Irving thought Coleridge guilty of – building "hypertheological praeterscriptural Sky-scrapers" – was exactly the same charge that Coleridge now brought against Irving! Furthermore, although Coleridge believed Irving misunderstood the nature of the Trinity, this is a charge that has subsequently been levelled more frequently against Coleridge than Irving.[179] Nevertheless, Coleridge had identified another key difference between the two men: Irving was primarily a preacher and a pastor, and regularly thought in these terms, rather than the more abstract philosophical approach that was Coleridge's natural realm. So, yet again, in this quote we see Coleridge's frustration that Irving simply refused to think in the same way he did: Irving was not the systematiser that Coleridge aspired (erratically) to be himself. The substance of the "offensive errors" into which Irving had supposedly fallen was, it seems, to have been somewhat influenced by Coleridge, but not completely. There is something unfairly procrustean in Coleridge's approach to Irving here, and one suspects that Irving would have treated Coleridge somewhat more generously, and not railed against him for failing to see through the eyes of a preacher-pastor.

---

[178] Jackson & Whalley, *Marginalia* 3.66-67, referring to volume 2, 354-66. Fomes = kindling wood or tinder.

[179] Eg. Dallimore, *Irving*, 46-47; D.L. Edwards, *Christian England, vol. 3: from the 18th century to the First World War* (London: Collins, 1985), 147.

There is one more annotation in which Coleridge once again thought that Irving was reading his own "fancies" into the text;[180] but then, as Irving unfolded the idea that until we have some understanding of God's dealings with the Church through history we will never understand or bear his dealings with us as individuals, Coleridge made his final annotation to the final volume of *Sermons*, with a noteworthy passage of self-reflection:

> If I know my own heart, I have every disposition to give the due weight to the arguments for the practical importance, or rather the indispensableness, of a lively watchful Attention to the political events of the World as successive fulfilments of this or that supposed Prediction of the same, now in this now in that text of this, or that, or third, 4th or 5th Prophet. – When an error in the Writings of a Man, whom I respect, flashes upon me, my first thought is to look about & into my own state of opinions, in order to discover if I can, whether it is <not> some Contrary error or defect in myself that has made me so quick in seeing the moat in my Brother's Eye. And truly in this instance, I think, that something of the kind has had place. My position, insulated as it were, & all my habits <both> of study and of life, have drawn my attention too exclusively to the invisible Church, to the communion of the Individual with the Spirit of Truth, in short, to Christianity as a Spiritual Light and at the same time an indwelling Energy from above. I have felt too little respecting the visible Church. – But still, while I earnestly ask for grace to fill up this chasm in my Christian Duties, I find myself wholly unable to reconcile my friend's Doctrines either with the to me palpable sense of the Scriptures, on which he grounds his Anticipations, or with our Lord's solemn declaration, that His Kingdom was not to be of this World . . . My own system of Convictions on this point my honoured Friend will find given at large in my, "Aids toward determining the right *Idea* of the Constitution in Church, and State, with the essential Characters of the three Churches, the national, the Christian, and the Church of Anti-christ" – and will therefore have the opportunity of Ascertaining, wherein & how far my Convictions differ from his.[181]

This comment was written in February 1829. Here is a note of regret on Coleridge's part that his own errors and prejudices have led him to judge Irving too harshly. There is, also, the tacit admission that he may be able to learn something from the pastor-preacher's focus on the visible church after all. Yet again, we see that Irving was able to influence Coleridge, despite flashes of florid opposition. There is a further dissonance here: earlier, we noted that by December 1827, when Coleridge finished annotating his copy of Irving's translation of Lacunza, he had, despite initial opposition, been won over to Irving's millennial views. And yet, here, just over a year later, he seems to have

[180] Jackson & Whalley, *Marginalia* 3.70, referring to volume 3, 1097.
[181] Jackson & Whalley, *Marginalia* 3.71-72, referring to volume 3, 1192-1198.

changed his mind once more. While this is a possibility; it may well have been an inconsistency; certainly the Bollingen editors indicated that Coleridge's conversion to millennialism through Irving-Lacunza was a lasting one.[182] We need, also, to bear in mind Coleridge's ongoing struggle with opium, which would hardly have helped him maintain complete consistency in his viewpoints. Regardless, Irving remained Coleridge's "honoured friend" into 1829.

During 1829, Coleridge was much occupied with the last significant work published during his lifetime, *On the Constitution of Church and State*. Considering Coleridge's February 1829 annotation to Irving's *Sermons*, quoted above, it is logical to assume that Irving's work gave some impetus to *Church and State*, because it deals with the visible church, the very subject Coleridge felt convicted of neglecting while reading *Sermons*. There is a February/March 1829 entry in Coleridge's notebook about his influence on Irving's opinion of the relation of Jesus to the Logos, and one from the middle of the year in which he asks Irving for his interpretation of a difficult scriptural text which is discussed in the Greek.[183] Clearly, whatever Coleridge's concerns about Irving's inclination to read his own fancies into scripture, he still respected Irving's exegetical abilities. *Church and State* was published at the end of 1829, with a second edition brought out early in 1830. As Coleridge's last publication, it was also his last chance to comment publicly on Edward Irving, and he did so, beginning with points of difference.

> Widely differing from my valued and affectionately respected friend, the Rev. Edward Irving, in his *interpretations* of the Apocalypse and the Book of Daniel, and no less in his *estimation* of the latter, and while I honour his courage, as a Christian minister, almost as much as I admire his eloquence as a writer, yet protesting against his somewhat too adventurous speculations on the Persons of the Trinity and the Body of our Lord ...[184]

This was as close as Coleridge came to condemning Irving's Christology, as "somewhat too adventurous". This is, perhaps, not surprising, considering Coleridge's own declared preference for the fourth Gospel from which he had derived so much of his Logos-based philosophy, rather than the genealogically and infancy account-heavy Synoptics which emphasised Jesus' humanity. Coleridge proceeded to take "great delight" in listing points with which he agreed with Irving, including the view that the Council of Trent had "ossified"

---

[182] *NSTC*, vol. 5, 1827-1834, 6099.

[183] *NSTC*, vol. 5, 1827-1834, Feb-March 1829, 5979; *NSTC*, vol. 5, 1827-1834, Summer 1829, 6061. The verse in question was Galatians 6:17.

[184] J. Colmer (ed.), *On the Constitution of the Church and State* (London & Princeton: Routledge & Princeton University Press, 1976), 140-141.

medieval errors into authoritative dogma, and that the Protestant church in England in the early nineteenth century was in a sad state of decline.[185]

> And now, as the conclusion of this long note, let me be permitted to add a word or two of Edward Irving himself. That he possess my unqualified esteem as a man, is only saying, that I know him, and am neither blinded by envy nor bigotry. But my name has been brought into connexion with his, on points that regard his public ministry; and he himself has publicly distinguished me as his friend on public grounds; and in proof of my confidence in his regard, I have not the least apprehension of forfeiting it by a frank declaration of what I think. Well, then! I have no faith in his prophesyings; small sympathy with his fulminations; and in certain peculiarities of his *theological* system, as distinct from his religious principles, I cannot see my way. But I hold withal, and not the less firmly for these discrepancies in our moods and judgments, that EDWARD IRVING possesses more of the spirit and purpose of the first Reformers, that he has more of the Head and Heart, the Life, the Unction, and the genial power of MARTIN LUTHER, than any man now alive; yea, than any man of this and the last century. I see in EDWARD IRVING a minister of Christ after the order of Paul; and if the points, in which I think him either erroneous, or excessive and *out of bounds*, have been at any time a subject of serious regret with me, this regret has arisen principally or altogether from the apprehension of their narrowing the sphere of his influence, from the too great probability that they may furnish occasion or pretext for withholding or withdrawing many from those momentous truths, which the age especially needs, and for the enforcement of which he hath been so highly and especially gifted! Finally, my friend's intellect is too instinct with life, too *potential* to remain stationary; and assuming, as every satisfied believer must be supposed to do, the truth of my own views, I look forward with confident hope to a time when his soul shall have perfected her victory over the dead letter of the senses and its apparitions in the sensuous understanding; when the Halycon [sic] IDEAS shall have alit on the surging sea of his conceptions,
>
> Which then shall quite forget to rave,
> While Birds of Calm sit brooding on the charmed wave
>
> MILTON[186]

This outstanding passage was Coleridge's last public word on his friendship with Irving which had, at the time of publication, extended for five and a half years. After describing Protestant England as in decline, and implying that it needed another great Reformer, Coleridge placed his faith in Irving as

---

[185] Colmer, *Church and State*, 141.

[186] Colmer, *Church and State*, 140-144. The verse is from Milton's *On the Morning of Christ's Nativity*, lines 67-8.

supplying the need. Irving's faults alarmed Coleridge chiefly because he saw them as potential limitations to Irving's influence. While Coleridge disagreed with some points of Irving's theology and his "prophesyings", and thought him sometimes excessive, these concerns were dominated by the overarching respect and esteem he had for the preacher. It is important to note that Coleridge wrote these words before any charismatic manifestations had occurred within Irving's congregation: even the second edition of *Church and State* in January 1830 preceded the earliest London charismata by more than a year.[187] Therefore, the "prophesyings" in question most probably relate to Irving's interest in the Albury conferences and his regular *Morning Watch* contributions on the fulfilment of prophecy throughout 1829.

As 1830 began, Coleridge entered his final period of decline, seldom leaving his room.[188] Apart from rare occasions when he was able to venture forth, he remained at Highgate and his social interaction gradually diminished. 1830 was, also, significant for Irving, but for very different reasons: as chapter two detailed, it began with the publication of a staunch defence of his Christology; he and Isabella lost another infant son and went to Ireland to grieve; the Cardale-led group from London investigated and reported on the Scottish charismata; and he was arraigned by the London presbytery for his unorthodox Christology. The long-standing institution of Thursday evenings at Highgate ended in 1829 due to Coleridge's increasing frailty, and weekly contact with Irving ended with them.[189] From this point onwards, Coleridge's references to Irving diminish, but do not entirely vanish.

In a recorded instance of Coleridge's "table talk" from May 1830, he, once again, criticised Irving's trinitarianism, as well as the issue of the moment – Irving's belief about Christ's human nature.

> Irving's notion is Tritheism – nay rather Tri-Daemonism. His opinion about the sinfulness of the Humanity of Jesus is absurd – and frenzied. Body is not Carcase. How can there be a sinful Carcase? Irving caught many things from me, but would never attend to any thing which he thought he could not use in the pulpit. I told him the consequence would be that he would fall into grievous errors. Sometimes he has five pages together of the purest eloquence, and then an outbreak of almost madman's babble.[190]

---

[187] As established in chapter 2, it appears charismata first appeared in Irving's congregation in April 1831.

[188] Ashton, *Coleridge*, 397. Holmes says that Coleridge was frequently confined to his bedroom from 1829 onwards, *Coleridge: Darker Reflections*, 554. In fact, in Holmes's massive, two-volume biography totalling more than 1,000 pages, the last 11 years of Coleridge's life (1823-34), which encompass his entire association with Irving, are only allocated 26 pages.

[189] *CLSTC*, vol. 5, 1820-1825, xxxix.

[190] C. Woodring (ed.), *Table Talk* vol. 1 (London & Princeton: Routledge, & Princeton University Press, 1990), 127-128. This was from 9 May 1830.

There is nothing substantially new here: we have previously noted Coleridge's objections to Irving's doctrine of Christ's humanity, his irritation with Irving's focus on pulpit-pragmatics, and his concern that in emphasising distinctions rather than unity Irving was heading towards tritheism (a concern apparently shared by no-one else). Of much greater interest at this point is whether in May 1830 Coleridge was actually doubting Irving's sanity. At this point, it is relevant to refer to another footnote of the Bollingen editors. When Coleridge was annotating his copy of Richard Baxter's *Reliquiae Baxterianae* in the mid-1820s, he referred to the "honor and happiness of [his] familiar acquaintance with the Revd Edward Irving" but the editor's footnote says that around 1826, Coleridge "began to doubt Irving's integrity of purpose, and then to question his sanity".[191] We have already demonstrated the inaccuracy of a previous footnote's assertion that Coleridge was embarrassed by and "highly critical" of Irving. The material we have surveyed has given ample evidence that despite some theological differences, at least up to this point in their relationship – May 1830 - Coleridge never doubted Irving's integrity. But we have to examine Coleridge's view of Irving's sanity in the light of the above quote about "almost madman's babble". Earlier we noted that Coleridge's comment about looking back to Irving's "saner days" simply equated to, in context, "less speculative with regard to the text of scripture". In other words, "saner" equated to "less fanciful". We do not know for certain which of Irving's books Coleridge was referring to here, but it is perhaps not a coincidence that some of his terminology, that is, "grievous error" and "purest eloquence", are remarkably similar to "grievous error" and "extraordinary eloquence" which he used in a previously quoted annotation to volume two of Irving's *Sermons*.[192] Coleridge's concern in this context was that Irving was overemphasising the distinctions within the Trinity. If this is, indeed, the passage he has in mind, then disparaging it as "almost madman's babble" was simply hyperbole, and certainly, not an attempt at a formal diagnosis of Irving's mental state. It is important to realise that Coleridge uttered the words quoted above from *Table Talk* barely four months after *Church and State* published his overwhelmingly positive assessment, continuing the theme of Irving as Luther *redidivus*. It would be risky indeed, to judge Coleridge's view of Irving's mental state on the basis of an exaggeration in conversation, rather than by the carefully-crafted published tribute of January 1830, yet it appears that this is what the editor of *Marginalia* volume one has done. This risk is further heightened in light of Coleridge's opium use and his generally-recognised tendency to explosive outbursts in these later years.[193]

On May 31, 1830, Thomas Chalmers visited Coleridge with his wife and daughter. Coleridge wrote later that day that "The main topic of our Discourse

---

[191] G. Whalley (ed.), *Marginalia,* vol. 1 (London: Routledge & Kegan Paul Ltd, 1980), 309. The footnote extends to 310.

[192] Jackson & Whalley, *Marginalia* 3.66-67, referring to volume 2, 354-66.

[193] Ashton, *Coleridge*, 387.

was Mr. Irving and his unlucky phantasms".[194] This meeting was, also, recorded by Chalmers, who noted that Coleridge poured out an "eloquent tribute" in Irving's regard, "mourning pathetically that such a man should be so throwing himself away".[195] What were these phantasms on which Coleridge felt Irving was wasting himself? The most likely answer was the charismatic outpouring of tongues, prophecy and miraculous healing which had begun in Port Glasgow in March 1830, news of which had soon reached London and the Regent Square congregation. In fact, only two days after this visit between Chalmers and Coleridge, as Chalmers was about to return to Scotland, Irving wrote to him about the condition of the church in their native country, and mentioned the news from Port Glasgow had brought him a sense of spiritual conviction and reproof.[196]

There is a brief reference to Irving and three others visiting Coleridge in early June 1830 (due to the state of his health, Coleridge was exhausted afterwards), but only two other references to Irving for the remainder of the year.[197] The first of these is from November and the context was Coleridge writing about "the four states": man, the beast, fallen man, the fiend. Then he added, "Corollary I. In the diversity of the last from the preceding, or of the fourth from the third state lies the ground of the Mystery, a partial & confused view of which has unhappily so bewildered & mystified the highly gifted but undisciplined and *idealess* mind of my still respected friend, the Revd. Edward Irving."[198] While "idealess" may initially seem the equivalent of unintelligent, it is clear that this is not the case from the immediate context, for if Coleridge had meant it thus, how could he have called Irving "highly gifted" and "respected" in the same sentence? In fact, Coleridge had his own specific definition of the term "idea", which, clearly, reveals a Platonic influence: "By an *idea*, I mean, (in this instance) that conception of a thing, which is not abstracted from any particular state, form, or mode, in which the thing may happen to exist at this or at that time; not yet generalized from any number or succession of such forms or modes; but which is given by the knowledge of *its ultimate aim*."[199] In Coleridgean terms then, to be "idealess" was to base one's conceptions more on particulars than ultimates; it was to live in the realm of the sense-based understanding, rather than the higher reason. This, then, was the accusation Coleridge levelled against Irving in November 1830. It is, also,

---

[194] Letter to J.H. Green (no. 1692), dated 31 May 1830 in *CLSTC*, vol. 6, 1826-1834 (Oxford: Clarendon, 1971), 839.

[195] W. Hanna, *Memoirs of the Life and Writings of Thomas Chalmers*, vol. 3 (Edinburgh: Thomas Constable, 1851), 262. Although this meeting, clearly, took place without Irving present, Irving did accompany Chalmers on a visit to Coleridge around this date, Oliphant, *Irving*, 291.

[196] Letter dated 2 June 1830, quoted in Oliphant, *Irving*, 292-293. This was prior to the visit of Cardale and the investigating group.

[197] *NSTC*, vol. 5, 1827-1834, 4 June 1830, 6327.

[198] *NSTC*, vol. 5, 1827-1834, November 1830, 6527.

[199] Colmer, *Church and State*, 12. Italics original.

worth noting that one of the most frequent charges Coleridge levelled against his age was that it was "idealess".[200] Irving had a lot of company, and, clearly, Coleridge was not slighting his intelligence.

The final 1830 reference to Irving was in December, referring to Coleridge's view that Irving relied too much on Revelation and Daniel.[201] This is, also, Coleridge's last direct mention of Irving in any of his writings; there is nothing more in the notebooks, correspondence or any of the marginalia. Yet Coleridge lived until July 1834, dying less than five months before Irving, and continued writing for all of this time: why was there no further mention of Irving for the last three and a half years of Coleridge's life? We have already noted that Coleridge's ill-health limited his social life from 1829 onwards, so this was undoubtedly a factor.[202] These last years were, also, hectic for Irving. As we saw in chapter two, for Irving 1831 began with his rejection by the London presbytery over his Christology (he responded with another publication); the charismata began to be experienced by members of his congregation in April of that year; he allowed their operation in public worship in October; and before the end of the year, the Trustees were moving to restrict the charismata. 1832 saw the removal of Irving from the ministry of the Church of Scotland and his ejection from the Regent Square building, his exodus with hundreds of followers to Gray's Inn Road and then to Newman Street, and the initial movement against him by the Presbytery of Annan. 1833 saw his trial in Annan, the sentence of heresy, and adjustment to his new role in the Newman Street church; it, also, marked the beginning of his physical decline. Irving began 1834 with a trip to Edinburgh, and, with his own health failing, was far less outgoing than in former years. Thus, Coleridge's ill-health combined with the tumultuous developments in Irving's ministerial career from the beginning of 1831 until Coleridge's death in July 1834 to ensure that the two men saw much less of each other. But, was this the only reason why there were no more entries about Irving in Coleridge's notebooks and correspondence? Perhaps not.

We have seen from the conversation with Chalmers that Coleridge did not share Irving's enthusiasm for the supernatural manifestations at Port Glasgow, therefore, it is fair to assume Coleridge would have been even less enthused when similar events occurred in Irving's own congregation in 1831. This chapter has shown that Coleridge commented extensively on Irving and his writings, so it is very strange that he wrote nothing whatsoever about him after December 1830, even though he maintained both his notebooks and his correspondence until his death. We do, however, have one further glimpse of Irving in Coleridge's conversation during October 1832. Richard Trench, future Church of Ireland Archbishop of Dublin, visited Coleridge who spoke of "poor dear Mr. Irving" and said it made "his heart break every time he [thought] of

---

200 *NSTC*, vol. 5, 1827-1834 (London: Routledge, 2002), editors' note 6527.

201 *NSTC*, vol. 5, 1827-1834, December 1830, 6572.

202 During 1830, Coleridge was so ill on several occasions he thought he was about to die. Ashton, *Coleridge*, 393.

him".[203] This remark shows that Irving retained his place in Coleridge's affections even if the contact was infrequent. Nevertheless, this is still vague: was Coleridge's heartbreak because he felt Irving was pursuing "phantasms", or because he felt that the moves against him for heresy were unjust, or both? The evidence remains inconclusive, but, based on the material surveyed in this chapter, it is likely that Coleridge would have been grieved by both.

In this chapter we have established that Irving's Romanticism was in place prior to his initial 1823 meeting with Coleridge; in other words, Coleridge did not "make" Irving a Romantic. Secondly, we have endeavoured to see Irving through Coleridge's published writings, as well as his notebooks, correspondence and marginalia. This has helped to shed further light on Irving's developing Romantic theology, as well as tensions between the two men, and the preacher's influence on the poet-philosopher. We have confirmed that, contrary to near-universal opinion, the intellectual traffic between the men flowed in both directions. We have noted that Irving's distinctive Christology was substantially in place before his first meeting with Coleridge, and that the latter's concern about an over-emphasis on Christ's humanity in Irving, also, argues for little subsequent Coleridgean influence in this area.

In addition, Coleridge, apparently, did not approve of the charismata in Irving's congregation (although, admittedly, this observation is based on inference), so we can hardly expect him to have overtly contributed to the development of Irving's later pneumatology. Also, Coleridge initially disagreed about, but ended by agreeing with Irving's millennialism. Superficially, then, it would appear that in the three areas of Irving's greatest theological distinctiveness – Christology, the charismata, and millennialism – Coleridge had very little influence on him at all. Finally, we have established that Irving processed his theology through a thoroughly Romantic filter before he ever met Coleridge. Nevertheless, one scholar has asserted that Coleridge influenced Irving "more than any other contemporary".[204] It appears then, that this influence must lie *beneath* the distinctive surface topography of Irving's Romantic theology.

Two recent scholars who focused on Irving's Christology agree that Coleridge's emphasis on the primacy of the will influenced Irving's doctrine of the incarnation: revealing God's will was the very purpose of the incarnation.[205] Lee argued that Irving took Coleridge's principle of the polarity of the Logos to "open a new vision of conceptualising the humanity of Christ," claiming this has not been noticed by other interpreters.[206] However, the reason it may not

---

[203] Trench, *Richard Chenevix Trench,* 123. Trench recorded this in a letter dated 10 October, 1832.

[204] G. McFarlane, "Christology and the Spirit in the teaching of Edward Irving" (London: King's College. PhD., 1990), 206.

[205] G. McFarlane, *Christ and the Spirit: the Doctrine of the Incarnation according to Edward Irving* (Carlisle: Paternoster, 1996), 57; Lee, "The Humanity of Christ", 26.

[206] Lee, "The Humanity of Christ", 26.

have been noted by others is that it is claiming too much. While Irving may have taken some impetus from Coleridge in this regard, it is too much to assert that he obtained a "new vision" from Coleridge's principle; we have already seen that Irving's Christological vision was substantially in place before he met Coleridge.

Specifically, it has been claimed that Irving followed Coleridge in identifying the Father as self-originating Will.[207] Despite Coleridge's concerns that Irving's understanding of the Trinity veered towards tritheism, it is perhaps in this area that he most influenced Irving. Certainly, this was the opinion of at least one of Irving's contemporaries, and has been more recently expressed by Drummond and Lee.[208] However, Lee perceptively modified this by noting that, although Irving's debt to Coleridge's Trinitarian thought was "great", Irving took nothing from Coleridge's philosophical thought without first applying a scriptural filter.[209] Lee confirmed McFarlane's earlier opinion: "The influence of Coleridge upon Irving was a strong but distilled one, for Irving took nothing from Coleridge unless it would serve his own ends."[210] The result was that Irving did not simply imitate Coleridge, but was "a creative and innovative thinker in his own right".[211] This sheds further light on Coleridge's previously noted irritation that Irving followed him in some things, but not all.

Since his death, Coleridge has come to be seen as a giant of the Romantic era, and while many have lamented the impact of opium on his productivity, the apparently cavalier way in which he treated his wife and children, and his dependence on the generosity of others, few have questioned the extent of his influence on his contemporaries and later generations. Coleridge was a polymath whose interests and publications ranged through poetry, German philosophy, classical literature, contemporary politics and Christianity. Faced with the complexity of Coleridge, commentators understandably have often chosen to focus on one or two aspects, rather than attempt to address all of them, and his relationship with Irving has been a casualty of this. One of Coleridge's recent biographers noted that he was unable to maintain friendships with other men without quarrelling with them (that with Wordsworth being the most famous in a list that, also, includes Basil Montagu, Charles Lamb and Robert Southey).[212] On closer examination, this seems to apply more accurately to Coleridge's friendships with men his own age; in his later life, as another biographer has noted, Coleridge gathered around him a group of "substitute

[207] McFarlane, *Christ and the Spirit*, 59.

[208] This was the opinion of Bryan Procter (pen name: Barry Cornwall), a member of the Montagu circle. Drummond, *Edward Irving and his Circle*, 68. Lee, "The humanity of Christ", 31.

[209] Lee, "The Humanity of Christ", 31.

[210] McFarlane, *Christology and the Spirit*, 206.

[211] Lee, "The Humanity of Christ", 33.

[212] Ashton, *Coleridge*, 75.

sons", younger men who admired him and valued his counsel.[213] Irving seems to align more with this latter group, because although we have seen that Coleridge disagreed with certain of Irving's ideas, phraseology and theological conceptions, there is no evidence that he quarrelled with Irving the man. Recent biographers of Coleridge have either ignored or barely mentioned his relationship with Irving: Norman Fruman falls into the former category; Richard Holmes and Rosemary Ashton the latter.[214] These glancing references to Irving imply that he was only a peripheral figure in Coleridge's life, and, certainly, never hint at the possibility that Irving may have influenced Coleridge in any way. This chapter has demonstrated the extent of Irving's influence, from the pen of Coleridge himself. Certainly Coleridge's friendship with Irving was neither as lengthy nor as convoluted as his relationships with Lamb, Southey and Wordsworth, but theologically, at least, Irving had a greater influence than the three literati. Future biographers of Coleridge will need to address the significance of Edward Irving with more than a cursory footnote.

The Edward Irving we see through the filter of Samuel Taylor Coleridge is a complex figure. Coleridge consistently saw Irving as noble, courageous and with the heart of a great Protestant Reformer, a reincarnated Luther in Regency Britain. Coleridge was influenced by Irving's theological understandings in three main areas: the Second Coming; the millennium (against his own initial conviction); and the visible church. Yet, Coleridge had little sympathy for Irving the pastor-preacher, accused him of interpreting scripture both too literally and too fancifully, and felt he came too close to tritheism; he, also, had no sympathy with the charismata. While Coleridge, certainly, influenced Irving's thought, this influence was more focused than many have thought, and certainly never absorbed uncritically. The Christian Romanticism both men shared formed the context for their friendship and while Coleridge enthusiastically rallied to Irving's banner in many ways, he was wary of Irving's conception of the Trinity, and even more concerned about the charismata. By the time Irving and Coleridge met, Coleridge's youthful schemes and adventures (Pantisocracy, Malta) were far behind him; Irving met the middle-aged and increasingly sedentary Coleridge. One contemporary described Coleridge as "indisposed to action" and "too content with things as they were".[215] Coleridge's adventures at this point were those of ideas and the Spirit and the Fourth Gospel, while Irving was living in the Synoptics and Acts: God had invaded the world as a human baby and was continuing to do so as

---

[213] Holmes, R., *Coleridge: Darker Reflections*, 495, 524. It was actually amongst this younger generation that Coleridge's literary reputation began to be re-assessed more favourably, 508-509.

[214] N. Fruman, *Coleridge, the Damaged Archangel* (London: Allen & Unwin, 1972); Holmes, *Coleridge: Darker Reflections*; Ashton, *Coleridge.*

[215] R.W. Armour & R.F. Howes, *Coleridge the Talker* (New York & London: Johnson Reprint Corporation, 1969), 267, quoting Leigh Hunt.

risen Lord. Irving was Prometheus, determined to bring heavenly fire to earth, and then set earth on fire with heaven.

For his part, regardless of his respect for Coleridge, Irving never subjected his adventurous Romantic agenda to that of the Sage of Highgate: admiration never became subjugation. This chapter has demonstrated that Coleridge's influence on Irving was not as dominant as it has often been described, whereas, Irving's influence on Coleridge, on the other hand, was far more extensive than previously supposed. Their Christian Romanticisms resonated in several areas, but Irving's Romanticism was infused with a degree of revolutionary change at individual and corporate levels that Coleridge had shed in the 1790s.

CHAPTER 5

Irving and the Carlyles

As detailed in chapter two, the relationship between Edward Irving and Thomas and Jane Welsh Carlyle became complex after simple beginnings. Just as many authors have inaccurately caricatured the Coleridge-Irving relationship as guru-devotee, so, also, the Irving-Carlyle relationship has often been trivialised.[1] Irving and Carlyle grew up in the same area of Scotland and the young Jane Welsh was Edward's pupil. Years later, Edward fell in love with Jane, but was unable to honourably extract himself from his engagement to Isabella Martin. Edward subsequently introduced Thomas to Jane and was, thereby, indirectly responsible for instigating not only their marriage, but one of the nineteenth century's most remarkable correspondences. We are dealing here with a major literary phenomenon, both in terms of quality and quantity. Jane Carlyle has been lauded as the foremost woman letter writer of the nineteenth century and second, overall, behind John Keats.[2] With more than ten thousand letters discovered, the Duke University edition of the correspondence between Thomas and Jane Carlyle, their family and friends, is projected to fill more than fifty volumes.[3] This project is the most comprehensive publication of the Carlyle letters, which have appeared in several earlier, and much shorter, collections. The first seven of these volumes cover the period up to Irving's death, and contain about four hundred references to him. As was the case with the Coleridge notebooks, correspondence and marginalia, there has been no previous attempt to evaluate comprehensively the image of Irving that emerges from this correspondence.[4]

---

[1] For example by Thomas Kirby in "Carlyle and Irving", *Journal of English Literary History*, vol. 13, no. 1, March 1946, 59-63. Kirby superficially uses Irving as a character referee for Carlyle.

[2] J. Gross, *Wall Street Journal*, 2 September 2006, quoted in *The Carlyle Letters Online* [*CLO*]. 2007. <http://carlyleletters.org>. Date viewed: 21 July 2009

[3] Thirty-six volumes have already been published; another fifteen are projected. The printed versions have been consulted for the first seven volumes up to Irving's death; later references have been obtained from the online version. This edition contains hundreds of previously unpublished letters.

[4] L. & E. Hanson, *Necessary Evil: the Life of Jane Welsh Carlyle* (London: Constable, 1952) uses a number of the Irving references in the Carlyles' correspondence, but the focus is Jane, not the Carlyle-Irving relationship.

The Carlyles' contribution to our understanding of Irving is quite different from Coleridge's. We will make no claim that Irving exerted a significant influence on Carlyle's theological opinions, nor vice versa, even though both men attempted to do so. Although Carlyle read at least a couple of Irving's works, and occasionally heard him preach, he did not engage with Irving's ideas with the same degree of seriousness as did Coleridge; the reasons for this lack of engagement will emerge as we progress. For our purposes, the value of the Carlyle correspondence is that both Thomas and Jane knew Irving as a young man in his Scottish context, and then maintained a relationship with him through sporadic mutual visits and their eventual relocation to London. Their lengthy relationship with Irving and lack of sympathy with his theological interests will give a unique perspective on his personality. In addition, Thomas's own beliefs and writings bore Romantic characteristics, which will enable us to further examine the nature of Irving's own Romanticism from a distinctly Scottish perspective. Irving, then, featured large in the thought and writing of two of the nineteenth century's greatest Romantic writers and thinkers – Coleridge, the "Sage of Highgate", and Carlyle, the "Sage of Chelsea". We have the advantage of seeing Irving through both these lenses.

Our method will be to follow the correspondence chronologically, focusing on the first seven volumes which take us to Irving's death. Occasionally, this will be supplemented with material from Carlyle's lengthy late-life tribute to Irving in his *Reminiscences*, written thirty years after Irving's death. At the end of the chapter, we will assess what light the Carlyle evidence sheds on Irving's Romanticism.

In chapter two we noted that Carlyle, three years Irving's junior, first remembered seeing Irving as a schoolboy in Annan when Irving had just returned from university in Edinburgh, but their real association began in Kirkcaldy, some years later, after Carlyle, himself, had studied at the University of Edinburgh.[5] Irving had taken up a position as schoolmaster in Kirkcaldy in 1812, and Carlyle arrived in late 1816 to head a rival school in the town. Irving begins to appear in Carlyle's correspondence in mid-1817, but the first substantial entry is from the following year. Carlyle mentioned to a friend that Irving was "worthy" and, with Irving's time in Kirkcaldy due to expire, gloomily compared Irving's future and brighter prospects in the pulpit with the potential for his own literary pursuits. The letter reveals Carlyle's sense of self-pity and pessimism, which were to be life-long character traits.[6] In drawing his comparison, he used a Latin phrase which was also revealing. The Latin translates as "For indeed truly he alone seems to me to be alive and to enjoy life

---

[5] Chapter 2, page 22.

[6] Thomas Carlyle to James Johnston, 30 April 1818, in C.R. Sanders (ed.), *The Collected Letters of Thomas and Jane Welsh Carlyle*, vol. 1, 1812-1821 (Durham, N.C.: Duke University Press, 1970), 125. Henceforth, *CL1*. Johnston was a friend from Edinburgh University.

who seeks fame absorbed in the pursuit of some excellent work or good art."[7] This sentence, written by the twenty-three year old Carlyle, could be taken as his life-motto, for his sense of self-worth proved intimately connected to the state of his literary production. It, also, establishes an important context for Carlyle's view of Irving in the years ahead, as their respective fortunes waxed and waned. Fame came to Irving when he was still a young man; it came to Carlyle only in his middle years. Irving's relatively early fame in his chosen field, therefore, posed something of a challenge to Carlyle, as we shall see.

Subsequent references through 1818 and into 1819 show the two Annandale friends discussing issues as diverse as chemistry and the "moral sublime", and generally enjoying each other's company.[8] The fledgling Annandale Romantics held a common view of the ministers in Edinburgh as "narrow, ignorant and barren".[9] Here is early evidence that even before his experience in Glasgow, Irving found available ministerial models uninspiring and would be seeking to move beyond these established models in his own career. Another revealing entry came as Irving received news that, subject to a month's probation, he would be working as Thomas Chalmers's assistant in Glasgow. "You will rejoice with me that Irving, has in so honourable a way, obtained admittance to the career, whither his principles and feelings have long been exclusively directed. He has a fair field: and if (somewhat contrary to my hopes) his fervid genius do not prompt him to extravagancies, from which more stupid and less honest preachers are exempted, his success, I doubt not, will be brilliant."[10] Apart from revealing his high estimation of Irving's abilities, it is intriguing that Carlyle describes Irving as "fervid", a term which we previously saw Coleridge apply to Irving in an approving manner. Carlyle seems to use the term to point to a tendency to extravagance in Irving, a theme which will recur. At this point, Carlyle had already travelled from the Church of Scotland orthodoxy of their shared Annandale childhood. By the time he was in his late teens and studying at the University of Edinburgh, Carlyle already knew that he had moved beyond the confines of his parents' beliefs and the possibility of a career in Christian ministry.[11] As will become clear, Carlyle's preference was to liberate Irving's "genius" so it could be exercised in a more worthy field than churchmanship.

---

[7] *verum enim vero is demum mihi vivere atque frui anima videtur qui aliquot negation intentus praclari facinoris, aut artis bonae famam quaerit*. Sallust, *Cataline*, II, 9, translated by *CL1* editors.

[8] Thomas Carlyle to Robert Mitchell, 27 November 1818, *CL1*, 149; Thomas Carlyle to Margaret A. Carlyle (his mother), 17 December 1818, *CL1*, 152.

[9] T. Carlyle, *Reminiscences* (London: J. M. Dent & Sons, 1932. Orig. 1881), 194.

[10] Thomas Carlyle to John Fergusson, 25 September 1819, *CL1*, 197.

[11] F. Kaplan, *Thomas Carlyle: a Biography* (Cambridge: Cambridge University Press, 1983), 40.

In the middle of 1820 Carlyle visited Irving in Glasgow. He wrote that exuberance, enthusiasm and benevolence characterised Irving in his new setting and he expected great things from him.[12] In this passage, Carlyle used a quote from Virgil which seems more prophetic than immediately appropriate: "he strips bare his great limbs and great-boned arms and stands, huge, in the midst of the place of combat".[13] Irving was not really in any great combat during his three years at Glasgow, where his two main frustrations were that some of the parishioners disliked his preaching, and he had an increasing desire for his own parish. The great combats of Irving's life were still years ahead of him, so the quote is most probably expressive both of Irving's physique and his passion for ministry. Although Carlyle himself stood six feet tall, Irving was at least two inches taller; Carlyle was lanky, Irving robust.[14]

In May 1821, Irving was visiting Edinburgh for the meeting of the General Assembly of the Church of Scotland, and he suggested to Carlyle that they travel to Haddington, East Lothian, to visit the recently widowed Grace Welsh and her daughter, Jane.[15] Shortly afterwards, Carlyle, briefly, described the event. "The excellent Irving delights in making all about him happy: a miserable creature in his neighbourhood is to him like a disease of his own. He came here lately to try his hand upon me . . . how sick I was, what work he had to overcome my taciturnity, and then how captious and sophistical I grew, and withal how happy."[16] Here, in Carlyle's own words, is a succinct description of the differences in their personalities: Irving was happy and outgoing, concerned with the needs of others; Carlyle was taciturn and querulous, almost morbidly focused on his own health. In retrospect, Carlyle recognised how much he needed the proximity of someone like Irving as a counter-balance to his own pessimism. The brief mention of happiness at the end of the quote is perhaps Carlyle's obscure acknowledgement of the effect of meeting the nineteen-year old Jane Welsh. By the time Irving introduced Carlyle to Jane his own short-lived and very discreet romance with her was over. As we noted in chapter two, Irving sought to be released from his engagement to Isabella Martin, but when this was denied in late 1820, he and Jane realised their relationship could progress no further.[17] However, Carlyle knew nothing of this, which needs to be kept in mind as we examine subsequent correspondence.

Early in 1822, after Irving had preached at the Caledonian Chapel in London with a view to becoming their minister, Carlyle wrote to his mother (to whom he always wrote respectfully on religious matters) that Irving had "produced a

---

[12] Thomas Carlyle to John Fergusson, 5 August 1820, *CL1,* 269-270.

[13] *Magnos membrorum artus, magna ossa lacertosque; Exuit: atque ingens media consistit arenâ*. Aeneid, V, 422-23. Translation by *CL1* editors.

[14] Estimates of Irving's height vary from 6' 2'' to 6' 4" (185-190cm).

[15] Kaplan, *Carlyle*, 70.

[16] Thomas Carlyle to William Graham, 12 June 1821, *CL1,* 365. Graham was from Ecclefechan and knew both Carlyle and Irving.

[17] Kaplan, *Carlyle*, 74.

great impression" and would "earn a vast renown for himself and do much good among the religious inhabitants of the Metropolis. There are not ten men living that deserve it better."[18] Once established in London, Irving busied himself to find opportunities for his friend, soon obtaining for Carlyle a private tutorship worth £200 a-year.[19] From this point, Jane's correspondence, also, begins to contain references to Irving. "Mr. Irving is making a *horrible* noise in London, where he has got a church – He tells me, in his last, that his head is quite turned with the admiration he has received – and really I believe him."[20] Clearly, Irving was still writing to Jane, despite the change in their relationship. The contrast between Carlyle's and Jane's views of Irving continued in subsequent correspondence: Thomas predominantly seeing Irving as noble and deserving success; Jane, having had to relinquish the man she loved (as we shall see later), was one moment sarcastic about Irving and the next complaining that he doesn't write to her. "What is become of Edward Irving? I have not heard from him these six weeks his silence is quite unaccountable."[21] This comment shows not only that Jane expected to hear from Irving very frequently despite the end of their romance, but, also, that, in relative isolation and nursing her ailing mother, she felt a need for continued contact from her former beau at a time when her relationship with Carlyle was still in its infancy.

If Jane was still in need of regular contact from Irving at this time, Thomas was, also, dependent on him not only for metropolitan job opportunities, but for encouragement. Carlyle had written to Irving asking him for a frank appraisal of his personality and Irving's undated reply survives, expressing concern that sarcasm, contempt and unconstructive doubt were warring against the more positive elements of Carlyle's character; that others would misunderstand him; and that his progress through life would be restricted as a result. Irving, also, noted that Carlyle was not really a man of action, a point explicitly echoed by one of Carlyle's recent biographers.[22] Many of these characteristics identified by Irving would become life-long traits in Carlyle. For our purposes, this exchange is significant for two reasons. There is the implied compliment to Irving. In our previous chapter we noted that Coleridge, twenty years Irving's senior, esteemed Irving's opinion on the possible decline of his mental faculties; here, the younger, twenty-seven year old Carlyle also invited Irving's probing assessment of his personality. This is highly revealing because of Carlyle's lifelong, aggressive sense of independence in his thought and

---

[18] Thomas Carlyle to Margaret A. Carlyle, 12 January 1822, in C.R. Sanders (ed.), *The Collected Letters of Thomas and Jane Welsh Carlyle*, vol. 2, 1822-1823 (Durham, N.C.: Duke University Press, 1970), 6. Henceforth *CL2*.
[19] Thomas Carlyle to John Fergusson, 11 February 1822, *CL2*, 35.
[20] Jane Welsh to Eliza Stodart, 20 February 1822, *CL2*, 50.
[21] Jane Welsh to Thomas Carlyle, 1 July 1822, *CL2*, 144.
[22] Although Irving's reply is undated, it was placed among letters for March 1822. Edward Irving to Thomas Carlyle, March 1822?, *CL2*, 62-64. Kaplan, *Carlyle*, 274.

writing.[23] For Carlyle to make this request of Irving (knowing that Irving would be diplomatic, but hardly reticent) demonstrated a deep sense of trust and respect; he would not have made himself so vulnerable otherwise. Therefore, both Jane and Carlyle remained dependent, in their own ways, upon Irving's emotional support. This exchange is, also, significant because it shows how Irving saw Carlyle, and, therefore, provides us with the lens through which Irving would assess Carlyle's later warnings and concerns. Of great concern to Irving was that Carlyle acknowledged no "authority of any kind",[24] by which Irving would have most likely meant scriptural and ecclesiastical authority: that Carlyle was indeed a nomad between possible loci of authority (including experience, secular humanism and a prophetic elite) will be confirmed later in this chapter.

At this point, it is appropriate to highlight how Carlyle's religious outlook differed from Irving's, and in this effort we are directly encouraged by Carlyle, himself. In his 1846 book *Heroes*, Carlyle wrote that "It is well said, in every sense, that a man's religion is the chief fact with regard to him." He made it clear that he was not talking about merely an outward profession, but the heart's conviction. This, Carlyle argued, was the place to start: determine a person's belief and you determine the person's nature and likely actions.[25] Yet, Carlyle's religious understanding has proven relatively elusive, being described by one recent writer as "either bewilderingly inconsistent or designedly vague".[26] Another has pointed out that, although Carlyle was a central figure in nineteenth century religion versus secularisation debates, his religious position has been variously interpreted as "a counter-modern reassertion of Protestantism, a modern post-Christian pantheism, or post-religious secularism".[27] Elusive indeed, and Carlyle's Romanticism contributed to this complexity.

One general observation worth noting in Carlyle's general religious outlook can be made under the heading of "devotion". Carlyle was quite capable of enthusiastic devotion, as his book *Heroes* makes clear, but, on reflection, it becomes obvious that Carlyle found it much easier to be devoted to either the long-dead or the far-removed. Rightly or wrongly, distance gave dignity, whereas Carlyle's contempt tended to increase with proximity, a tendency noted by Tulloch.[28] This tendency has been seen on several occasions in this

---

[23] B. Willey, *Nineteenth Century Studies: Coleridge to Matthew Arnold* (London: Chatto & Windus, 1955), 104.

[24] Edward Irving to Thomas Carlyle, March 1822?, *CL2*, 63.

[25] T. Carlyle, *On Heroes, Hero-worship, and the Heroic in History* (New York: Wiley & Putnam, 1846), 2.

[26] J. Nicol, *Thomas Carlyle* (Charleston, SC: Bibliolife, 2008), 207.

[27] T. Hogan, "The religion of Thomas Carlyle" in L. Woodhead (ed.), *Reinventing Christianity: Nineteenth Century Contexts* (Aldershot: Ashgate, 2001), 149.

[28] J. Tulloch, *Movements of Religious Thought in Britain during the Nineteenth Century* (Leicester: Leicester University Press, 1971. Orig. 1885), 174.

chapter, yet notably, Irving was frequently the exception to this rule. Nevertheless, this bias meant that Carlyle's comments on contemporary religious events and personalities were frequently jaundiced. Carlyle experienced a spiritual breakthrough of sorts in 1826 – not a Christian conversion, but a moment of illumination in which he felt he had broken through to a new freedom, helped, in Tulloch's view, by relative good health and rustic pleasures.[29] Carlyle's confidante and early biographer, James Anthony Froude, characterised him as "a Calvinist without the theology".[30] What lies beneath the surface of this oxymoron? Carlyle seldom wrote explicitly on the topic of his religious beliefs but Froude pieced it together. Like Irving and Coleridge, Carlyle rejected materialism and believed in God; unlike them, he looked not to external revelation or scripture for authority but to experience.[31] The existence of intellect and conscience could only derive from a Being of intellect and conscience.[32] To Carlyle, the universe and all phenomena were miraculous and inexplicable, therefore to label certain incidents as miraculous was meaningless.[33] All historical religions, including Christianity, had attempted to express eternal spiritual truths, but often distorted this expression by their own baggage.[34] The phenomenon of the universe with humanity at its centre was true Revelation.[35] One result of Carlyle's designation of experience as authoritative was that history, literature, and the documents of collective experience, thereby, also, became authoritative, like a Bible.[36] He revered Christ while substantially rejecting his native Presbyterianism (although often describing it with fond nostalgia), saw history as God's revelation and had an increasing belief in Providence.[37] We see here that Carlyle was quite capable of completely severing religious teachers and prophets from the content of their message. Figures from the past could be revered at the same time as their key doctrines were seen as passé. Humanity was in the process of "becoming": those who had contributed to this process in the past were worthy of reverence, but their continued relevance (in terms of dogma) was limited.[38] The Church was a relic of the past, and should be recognised as such, "with melancholy reverence and respect."[39] Although there are obvious differences in their views here, Irving, also, saw history as

---

[29] Tulloch, *Movements*, 180-183.
[30] J. Clubbe (ed.), *Froude's Life of Carlyle* (London: John Murray, 1979), 219, 220.
[31] Clubbe (ed.), *Froude's Life of Carlyle*, 220.
[32] Clubbe (ed.), *Froude's Life of Carlyle*, 222.
[33] Clubbe (ed.), *Froude's Life of Carlyle*, 220.
[34] Clubbe (ed.), *Froude's Life of Carlyle*, 220-221.
[35] Tulloch, *Movements*, 199.
[36] B. Swaim, "'Our own Periodical Pulpit': Thomas Carlyle's sermons", *Christianity and Literature*, vol. 52, no. 2, winter 2003, 145; Clubbe, *Froude's Carlyle*, 224.
[37] Nicol, *Carlyle*, 208, 211, 212.
[38] Tulloch, *Movements*, 200.
[39] Willey, *Nineteenth Century Studies*, 111.

"prophetic".[40] Carlyle's universe was a spiritual construct which would deliver justice and salvation through individual work and struggle, which rendered ecclesiastical institutions largely unnecessary.[41] This individualism has led one writer to describe Carlyle's "religion" as an "ethical existentialism".[42] Those foremost in the struggle to ascertain and communicate meaning were the authors and critics like Carlyle himself, who virtually assumed a prophetic role.[43] In Carlyle's system, humanity was at the centre, and divinity became vague and certainly impersonal.[44]

Carlyle and Irving, therefore, shared a conviction about the existence of God as well as a rejection of unadulterated materialism, Utilitarianism, and expediency. Yet, whereas Irving was committed to the revitalisation of contemporary Christianity despite its flaws, Carlyle believed formal religion by definition hampered the apprehension of spiritual truth. Although Carlyle retained a belief in God, his was a more amorphous God than Irving's and a key issue was the mediation of divine authority, which we shall examine later. Carlyle's religious position explains why, unlike Coleridge, he didn't engage directly with much of Irving's theology: he simply didn't have the same degree of interest in Christian orthodoxy. Irving's knowledge of Carlyle's position meant he would automatically have had reservations about any of Carlyle's comments about doctrine or ecclesiology, while sharing the Romantic values of struggle, the revelatory nature of history and anti-institutionalism.

As 1822 progressed, we learn from Carlyle's letters that Irving had visited Jane at Haddington; that there was a mixed reception to Irving's farewell address at Glasgow; and, later, that Irving was "making an immense figure in London".[45] At the end of the year, Carlyle wrote to his brother that Irving was "cleaving the hearts of the Londoners in twain" in a flurry of religious activity that was earning him wide approval.[46] Irving was "preaching and speculating and acting so as to gain universal notoriety and very general approbation. Long may he enjoy it!" Carlyle's stated preference was for "shunning [the] clamorous approval of the many-headed monster as well as avoiding its censure, and determined if ever I be marked out never so slightly from the common herd, to be so by another set of judges".[47] There are elements of jealousy, resentment and snobbish disdain in this, as Carlyle implied that Irving's high activity level was motivated by the desire for widespread acclaim.

---

[40] Irving, "Preliminary Discourse" to *Ben-Ezra*, vol. 1, lxix.
[41] Kaplan, *Carlyle*, 114, 49.
[42] Kaplan, *Carlyle*, 375.
[43] Swaim, "'Our own Periodical Pulpit': Thomas Carlyle's Sermons", 149.
[44] Tulloch, *Movements* ,207.
[45] Thomas Carlyle to Jane Welsh, 13 July 1822, *CL2*, 148. Irving had written to Carlyle with an update on Jane's health. Thomas Carlyle to William Graham, 30 October 1822, *CL2*, 192. Thomas Carlyle to Jane Welsh, 18 November 1822, *CL2*, 210.
[46] Thomas Carlyle to Alexander Carlyle, 20 December 1822, *CL2*, 237.
[47] Thomas Carlyle to Alexander Carlyle, 20 December 1822, *CL2*, 237.

This was at a time when Carlyle's own fortunes were not progressing to his liking. Earlier in the year his visit to Jane Welsh and her mother in Haddington had been a "painful disaster" and he was no longer welcome there (although correspondence continued), and, shortly before writing the above lines to his brother, he gloomily condemned his own accomplishments as "meagre".[48] At the end of 1822, Thomas Carlyle was frustrated both in his career and in his relationship with Jane Welsh; by contrast, Irving had quickly become the most celebrated preacher in London and was engaged to Isabella Martin. It would have taken a buoyant optimism to overlook this contrast, but this was not a weapon Carlyle had at his disposal.

Jane continued to wrestle with her own feelings about Irving in her correspondence with Carlyle. She described a letter her mother received from Irving as a "grotesque performance", and satirised his writing style as "absurd".[49] We previously noted Jane's agitation in the absence of correspondence from Irving; now the arrival of his letter addressed to her mother precipitated a torrent of sarcasm. The editors noted that although there was an element of pretension in Irving's letter it "hardly deserve[d] such scorn", and that Jane both quoted Irving's letter inaccurately and exaggerated its style.[50] It would appear the only thing Irving had done to incite Jane's wrath was to end their engagement due to his inability to obtain release from his previous commitment to Isabella Martin, and even this appears to have been a mutual decision, as will be seen shortly. Carlyle, of course, had no idea what prompted this torrent of bitterness from Jane. His reply attempted to defend Irving: "What a wicked creature you are to make me laugh so at poor Irving! Do I not know him for one of the best men breathing, and that he loves us both as if he were our brother?", while simultaneously criticising Irving's taste and ostentation, and admitting he had his moments of absurdity.[51]

Carlyle had to attempt a balancing act: he did not want to alienate Jane, which he well knew from personal experience (as well as from how she was writing about Irving) was a distinct possibility. The editorial footnote describes Carlyle's comment about Irving's taste in context as "curiously unfair".[52] Carlyle's praise and defence of Irving was certainly qualified. He admits that he envied Irving for the "favour . . . he gets from all". In his own way, Carlyle was acknowledging that Irving's personality was much more likely to win accolades than his own, thereby implicitly agreeing with Irving's own previously-mentioned concern that Carlyle's sarcasm and contempt were unlikely to smooth his way in the world. Nonetheless, Carlyle's reply was clearly an attempt to deepen the rapport he had with Jane, and if the price he had to pay was damning his friend with faint praise he was prepared to do it. This dynamic

---

[48] Kaplan, *Carlyle*, 80-81, 84.
[49] Jane Welsh to Thomas Carlyle, 8 January 1823, *CL2*, 264.
[50] *CL2*, 264.
[51] Thomas Carlyle to Jane Welsh, 12 January 1823, *CL2*, 268.
[52] *CL2*, 268 footnote.

continues through much of the subsequent correspondence between Jane and Carlyle.

In following months, despite Carlyle occasionally accusing Irving of laziness (for his infrequent correspondence),[53] Irving maintained his congregational responsibilities, was preparing to publish *Orations*, and still managed to seek opportunities for Carlyle's financial benefit.[54] When Irving wrote to Carlyle about Jane he described her as his "beloved pupil", but was careful to clarify that he loved her "like a Brother".[55] For her part, Jane referred to Irving facetiously as "the Hero of Hatton Garden" for his declared preference for riding on top of coaches in fine weather,[56] and then placed the words "love" and "Irving" in close proximity in a letter to Carlyle:

> fewer people love me than one might imagine – *You* do – my mother does – Mr Irving does and *one* or *two* more that shall be nameless – but depend on it love is by no means the general sentiment I inspire – '*speaking of Swine*' what is become of our gigantic Friend? Where is his book? I wrote to him some *months* ago; but he has vouchsafed me no reply – he has not a head for these London flatteries – I would write him again – a letter of *admonition* – yea verily – a letter of admonition to the '*great centre of attraction*'! [great underscored twice] to the *Spanish Adonis*! to the reverend Edward Irving himself! if I were sure of his address – do you opine he is still in Grosvenor Street? – It is all over with him if he forgets his earliest and best Friends –[57]

No sooner had she acknowledged Irving's love (and, perhaps, because she has done so), than Jane vented her spleen once more with the cutting "speaking of swine", for which there is no obvious referent. Irving had earned this epithet for failing to write to Jane for a period of months. Her description of him as "Spanish Adonis" related to his overall good looks: apart from his height and athletic build, Irving had jet-black hair, a swarthy complexion and was generally acknowledged to be very handsome, apart from his squint. In referring to Irving as a "great centre of attraction", Jane was quoting from contemporary accounts of the impact he was having in London.

Jane's Spanish Adonis was about to slip through her fingers. She already knew that his future lay with Isabella Martin, but whether she knew when she wrote this letter in July that they had actually set an October date for the wedding is uncertain. Certainly Carlyle, when he replied to her letter two weeks later, thought that he was breaking the news to her; but Carlyle's focus was not

---

[53] Eg. Thomas Carlyle to James Johnston, 18 February 1823, *CL2*, 288; Thomas Carlyle to William Graham, 24 April 1823, *CL2*, 342.

[54] Thomas Carlyle to Jane Welsh, 4 March 1823, *CL2*, 300. Irving had spoken to the *London Magazine* about Carlyle writing for them.

[55] Thomas Carlyle to Jane Welsh, 18 February 1823, *CL2*, 292.

[56] Jane Welsh to Thomas Carlyle, 15 July 1823, *CL2*, 397.

[57] Jane Welsh to Thomas Carlyle, 21 July 1823, *CL2*, 404.

so much on Irving's impending nuptials as on his fame and its effects. He felt that Irving should have gained fame more slowly, and that being a "season's wonder" brought with it the potential for disaster. Irving's "path is steadfast and manly," Carlyle wrote, "in general only when he has to encounter opposition and misfortune", yet he acknowledged that Irving was happy in his role and equal to the task.[58]

From Carlyle's perspective, Irving had experienced little or no struggle to date, rocketing from Annandale through Glasgow to London and swift fame; at this point he had no knowledge that Irving had already experienced the disappointment of romantic hope with Jane Welsh. In contrast, Carlyle was working on a translation of Goethe's *Wilhelm Meister* while earning his living in the tutorship which Irving had obtained for him.[59] He remained in relative obscurity, obliged to Irving's fame for his own livelihood. Thus, although Carlyle expressed his admiration of Irving, there was, also, an undercurrent of obligation and melancholy envy as he wrote to Jane: "When shall you and I make an onslaught upon the empire of Dulness and bring back *spolia optima* to dedicate to one another? Some day yet, I swear it!"[60] All of these undercurrents combined so that, collectively, Jane and Carlyle were dealing with a mixture of envy, bitterness and regret where Irving was concerned.

Intriguingly, when Jane replied to Carlyle, she made absolutely no mention of Irving's engagement to Isabella, but, writing from Templand, above the date on the letter, she indicated her place of writing was "Hell".[61] Now it is possible that Jane used this expression because she felt the pain of caring for her mother in isolation at Templand, but it is more probably an expression of her anguish at Irving's impending marriage and the final end to her hopes. Jane spent many years in "isolation" caring for her mother, so it seems more than coincidence that she chose to describe her location as "Hell" only once – at the time she heard of Irving's forthcoming wedding.

Carlyle's first impression of Irving's *Orations* was that it was "rather dull"; but in writing to his mother, he gave contradictory impressions, noting its "strong talent . . . true eloquence, and vigorous thought" before deciding that as a whole, it was a "monster", and then saying that his "true opinion" was "a favourable one; but some thousand degrees below his [Irving's] own".[62] There is obvious inconsistency in these comments: how could he have a favourable impression of a monster? His conclusion on the subject was "I love Irving, and am his debtor for many kind feelings and acts. He is one of the best men breathing: but I will not give his vanity one inch of swing in my company; he

---

[58] Thomas Carlyle to Jane Welsh, 10 August 1823, *CL2*, 413-415.
[59] Kaplan, *Carlyle*, 78, 84-86.
[60] Thomas Carlyle to Jane Welsh, 10 August 1823, *CL2*, 413-415. *Spolia optima* = rich spoils.
[61] Jane Welsh to Thomas Carlyle, 19 August 1823, *CL2*, 416.
[62] Thomas Carlyle to John A. Carlyle, 2 September 1823, *CL2*, 425; Thomas Carlyle to Margaret A. Carlyle, 28 September 1823, *CL2*, 440-441.

may get the fashionable women and the multitude of young men whom no one knoweth to praise and flatter – not I one iota beyond his genuine merits."[63] Whatever additional motives may have been lurking beneath the surface, Carlyle partly saw his role in the friendship as deflator of Irving's vanity. Carlyle's comments were general ones: Irving's chosen material held little interest for him, so he did not invest himself in more specific comments.

On receiving an offer of London hospitality from Irving, Jane wrote ecstatically to Carlyle. The letter began: "I am almost out of my wits with joy – I think, in my life, I was never so glad before – Such a future is before us! I cannot wait for your letter any longer – my happiness is incomplete while you do not partake it – You and I are going to London! You and I!" She goes on to admit she did Irving an injustice in thinking he had forgotten his friends, and asks Carlyle whether she will like Isabella.[64] The shrill euphoria of this letter is all the more noticeable when we recall that less than three months previously Jane called Irving a "swine". What is particularly significant is that Jane wrote this letter just one day after Irving's marriage to Isabella. Now with hopes of a life with her Spanish Adonis permanently dashed, Jane feverishly transferred the intensity of her affections to Carlyle and an alternate future.

Although Irving was beset by vanity and affectation, Carlyle wrote to his brother, yet he remained warm-hearted and generous, offering hospitality which Carlyle refused because it savoured of patronage.[65]

> [Irving] himself is the same man as ever, only his mind seems churned into a foam by the late agitations and is yielding a plentiful scum of vanities and harmless affectations . . . [He talks] abundantly a flood of things, the body of which is nonsense, but intermingled with sparkles of curious thinking, and tinctured with his usual flow of warm-hearted generosity and honest affection . . . He is a kind good man with many great qualities, but with absurdities of almost equal magnitude. He meditates things in which he must evidently fail; but being what he is, he must always retain a high place in the estimation of a certain portion of the public. He and his beloved are returning to Annan in a week or two, where they purpose to make some stay. I shall always wish him well: as men go, I know of no one like him.[66]

Yet again, Carlyle comments on Irving's vanity and affectation, but the striking thing about this letter is the way in which Carlyle, habitually contemptuous of the weaknesses and faults of others in his chosen role as society's critic, seems inevitably drawn to Irving, despite criticising him.[67] Just when it sounds as if

---

[63] Thomas Carlyle to Margaret A. Carlyle, 28 September 1823, *CL2*, 441.

[64] Jane Welsh to Thomas Carlyle, 14 October 1823, *CL2*, 450-451.

[65] Thomas Carlyle to John A. Carlyle, 20 October 1823, *CL2*, 456.

[66] Thomas Carlyle to John A. Carlyle, 20 October 1823, *CL2*, 456.

[67] From his youth, Carlyle was seen as a sarcastic misanthrope: Kaplan, *Carlyle*, 38, 47. Also, Swaim, "'Our own Periodical Pulpit': Thomas Carlyle's Sermons", 141.

Carlyle is annoyed with Irving and about to avoid him he comes out with a genuine appreciation of some aspect of Irving's character, ending on a note of Irving's uniqueness, admitting that he does not know Irving's equal.

Carlyle explained his distinction between popularity and fame, and his conviction that Irving's chosen occupation limited him to the former and placed the latter beyond his reach. "The fame of a genuine man of letters is like the radiance of another star added to the galaxy of intellect to shine there for many ages; the popularity of a pulpit orator is like a tar-barrel set up in the middle of the street to blaze with a fierce but very tarnished flame, for a few hours, and then go out in a cloud of sparkles and thick smoke offensive to the lungs and noses of the whole neighbourhood."[68] Earlier, we noted that Carlyle wished that Irving had chosen another profession; here we have further insight on the subject. It is clear that to Carlyle a ministerial career was by definition inferior to a literary career; one could result at best in fleeting popularity, the other in lasting fame. In Carlyle's view, history was the true reflection of value: only those activities and accomplishments that are remembered long after the event have true value.[69] Carlyle must have been aware of the irony in his imagery: the preacher (whose focus was on heavenly things) was actually trapped in the transitory and the mundane, whereas literary success achieved a heavenly permanence. Now it could certainly be argued that this was either "sour grapes", or self-justification, or both on Carlyle's part, given that Irving's career had soared and Carlyle's career had not. However, the essence of the statement is consistent with sentiments expressed throughout Carlyle's life: whatever acclaim Irving was receiving was shallow and hollow, because the job, itself, was not worth doing.[70] The quote shows clearly the centrality of lasting fame to Carlyle's value system in 1823 (although he was later to express more doubts about it); it is doubtful if it was ever so central to Irving.[71] In this letter, vanity and affectation recur as charges against Irving, alongside "absurdity". Unfortunately, Carlyle did not enlarge on the nature of these absurdities, although it is worth noting that he, also, described Coleridge as "very great but rather mystical, sometimes absurd".[72] This implies that Carlyle did not inevitably equate "absurd" with "foolish", and an examination of his

---

[68] Thomas Carlyle to Jane Welsh, 22 October 1823, *CL2*, 459-461.

[69] "The fame of a genuine man of letters is like the radiance of another star added to the galaxy of intellect to shine there for *many ages*," Carlyle wrote to Jane Welsh, 22 October 1823, *CL2*, 461. My emphasis. He contrasted this with the fleeting fame of a preacher such as Irving.

[70] Carlyle reflected on the fleeting nature of Irving's fame just after the latter's death, Thomas Carlyle to David Hope, 24 December 1834 , C.R. Sanders (ed.), *The Collected Letters of Thomas and Jane Welsh Carlyle,* vol. 7: October 1833 – December 1834 (Durham, N.C.: Duke University Press, 1977), 347.

[71] For example, Thomas Carlyle to Jean Carlyle Aitken, 25 December 1847, *CL22*, 178-181, *The Carlyle Letters online* [CLO], 2007, http://carlyleletters.org>. Date viewed: 17 July 2009.

[72] Thomas Carlyle to John A. Carlyle, 11 November 1823, *CL2*, 468.

correspondence indicates that he, also, used it to mean "exaggerated"[73] and "inaccurate",[74] a usage that fits well with the vanity/affectation language he so frequently used of Irving.

Jane's frustration at the loss of Irving, the delay of his promised offer of hospitality, combined with rumours, boiled over when she wrote to Carlyle in November 1823. Complaining once again that she hadn't heard from Irving, she wrote, "Do you know they are giving out that I am dreadfully disappointed at his marriage!!! and that he has used me very ill – *me* ill! was there ever any thing so insufferable? but it is his own blame he talked of me so absurdly – He has been telling all people that I was 'the Love of his intellect & that the woman he has married was the Love of his youth' [-] confound his intellect I shall never hear the last of it".[75] Of course, she was protesting too much, for she had not yet revealed to Carlyle that she reciprocated Irving's love; but, certainly, Irving was being less than discreet, and the implied slight to Isabella's intellect would hardly have contributed towards his own domestic bliss. The nickname "the Orator" that Jane used of Irving in this letter became a favourite nickname for him within the Carlyle circle.[76] There is no indication that Carlyle drew any conclusions from Irving's indiscretion: he possibly concluded the "intellectual love" referred to was a description of their previous teacher-student relationship overlaid with Irvingesque exaggeration.

As 1824 began Carlyle added to his list of self-contradictory comments on Irving's *Orations* when he described it to his brother as containing some first-rate material but suffering from a lack of polish.[77] Jane railed against Irving from Haddington, firstly, for giving her advice[78] and, later, for saying nothing at all, especially about her proposed visit to London.

> Not a word from the Orator! …I will not go now, not a footlength though he was to write to me on his knees (which there is no great probability of his doing)[.] But no matter the Orator's self is the principal loser by this transaction; he has lost a *friend* – I merely a few weeks amusement – moreover it is possible for me to get to London some other time; but it is absolutely impossible for him ever to recover that place in my affections

---

[73] Thomas Carlyle to Arthur Hugh Clough, 29 December 1852, *CL27*, 380-382, *The Carlyle Letters online* [CLO], 2007, http://carlyleletters.org>. Date viewed: 2 October 2008.

[74] Thomas Carlyle to Thomas Woolner, 2 March 1856, *CL31*, 40-41, *The Carlyle Letters online* [CLO], 2007, http://carlyleletters.org>. Date viewed: 2 October 2008.

[75] Jane Welsh to Thomas Carlyle, 26 November 1823, *CL2*, 481.

[76] For other examples of this, see Thomas Carlyle to Jane Welsh, 12 October 1823, *CL2*, 449; Thomas Carlyle to Jane Welsh, 29 November 1823, *CL2*, 483; Thomas Carlyle to Jane Welsh, 23 June 1824, C.R. Sanders (ed.), *The Collected Letters of Thomas and Jane Welsh Carlyle*, vol. 3, 1824-1825 (Durham, N.C.: Duke University Press, 1970), 84. Henceforth, *CL3*.

[77] Thomas Carlyle to Alexander Carlyle, 13 January 1824,), *CL3*, 13.

[78] Jane Welsh to Thomas Carlyle, 29 February 1824, *CL3*, 37.

> which he has forfeited. I could not have believed it! Nobody but Edward Irving's self could have made me believe him so fickle and heartless.[79]

This shows both Jane's volatility, self-centredness, and the depth of her lingering affection for Irving. When Jane wrote this letter Isabella was six months pregnant with Edward Jr, but Jane could not conceive that Irving's attention might legitimately focus elsewhere than herself.

By mid-1824, Carlyle had been paid for his translation of *Wilhelm Meister*, and he wrote to Jane in his usual vein of attempting both to agree with her and placate her where Irving was concerned. Irving's head had been turned by fashion and he was too absorbed in his own affairs, Carlyle admitted, but his heart remained good and his talent was real, even if he seldom wrote to those he cared for most. Carlyle assured Jane that much of a recent letter he had received from Irving had been devoted to her.[80] Carlyle's continuing ignorance of the nature of the relationship between Jane and Irving allowed him the unconscious irony of assuring Jane of Irving's continuing love for her in this letter.

Shortly afterwards, Jane heard from Irving that Carlyle planned to visit him in London: having been denied the visit herself, she was less than pleased that Carlyle was to take her place.

> I had a letter from that stupendous ass the Orator telling me such nonsensical things, and among the rest, that he is full of joy because Thomas Carlyle is to be with him this month! Can he mean you? this month! and twenty days of it are already past and gone! The man must have been delirious when he wrote such an impossible story. You can never, never mean to be in London this month! You promised to be here before you went, in words that it would be impiety to doubt[.] I have looked forward to your coming for weeks: You cannot dream of disappointing me![81]

Was Jane's tone of rebuke simply, as she implied, due to the fact that she had not been advised of Carlyle's change of plan and, therefore, would be unable to see him as she had hoped? Or, was her frustrated love for Irving fuelling her ire? At this point it is useful to consider an undated letter Irving wrote to Jane. "My dear Isabella has succeeded in healing the wounds of my heart . . . but I am hardly yet in a condition to expose them. My former calmness and piety are returning. I feel growing in grace and holiness; and before another year I shall be worthy in the eye of my own conscience to receive you into my house and

---

[79] Jane Welsh to Thomas Carlyle, 29 April 1824, *CL3*, 65.

[80] Thomas Carlyle to Jane Welsh, 19 May 1824, *CL3*, 66-68. Carlyle wrote that one third of Irving's letters had been about Jane.

[81] Jane Welsh to Thomas Carlyle, 20 May 1824, *CL3*, 69.

under my care, which till then I shall hardly be."[82] Froude has placed this letter immediately after Irving's marriage, yet this seems unlikely considering we have seen that just before his wedding Irving made the offer of hospitality to Jane that so excited her. The internal evidence of the letter, also, argues this because Isabella has had some time to heal Irving's heart-wounds. It is more probable that this letter was not written immediately after the wedding, but came later, and was quite possibly the letter referred to above, to which Jane was reacting so strongly in May 1824.

Either way, Jane's rebuke had little effect on Carlyle's plans. When Carlyle arrived in London for the first time in June 1824 he immediately wrote to his mother that he had been cordially received by the Irvings.[83] Irving delightedly introduced Carlyle to his circle, including the Stracheys, the Montagus and Coleridge.[84] The social whirl meant it was nearly two weeks after arriving in London before Carlyle wrote to Jane, and a fortnight in Irving's presence had clearly made a favourable impression. The Irvings had been very hospitable, and Carlyle wrote that the Orator's "practical warmth of heart" was once again triumphing over his focus on his "supernatural" rise to prominence. Carlyle assured Jane that the Irving who talked of her visiting London "next Summer" still loved her, and he was far too worthy a man to shun.[85] Carlyle expressed similar sentiments to his brother the following day, adding that Irving seemed less ebullient and in weaker health, and although his popularity was not as "furious" as it had been, it was still "great".[86]

In these letters, Carlyle's Irving appeared to improve with proximity: Irving seemed less vain and extravagant at close range. Of course, the Irvings' hospitality may simply have evoked a generous response from Carlyle, or perhaps Carlyle was less jealous of Irving's fame as he was personally gaining entrée to London society through it. Another clue soon emerged in a letter to his mother: "Irving & I are grown very intimate again, and have had great talking-matches about many things. He speaks in glorious language of the wonderful things I am to accomplish here; but my own views are much more moderate."[87] Here, we see another explanation for the charges of vanity and extravagance that Carlyle had previously brought against Irving: when Irving voiced his expectations for his own ministry Carlyle thought him vain; when Irving's high expectations focused on Carlyle's career, Carlyle thought them

---

[82] Edward Irving to Jane Welsh, quoted in J.A. Froude, *Thomas Carlyle: a History of the First Forty Years of his Life, 1795-1835*, vol. 1 (London: Longmans, Green, & Co., 1882), 190.

[83] Thomas Carlyle to Margaret A. Carlyle, 10 June 1824, *CL3*, 80-81.

[84] Kaplan, *Carlyle*, 92-94. For the importance of this visit to Carlyle, see G.J. Calder, "Carlyle and 'Irving's London Circle': Some Unpublished Letters by Thomas Carlyle and Mrs. Edward Strachey" in *Proceedings of the Modern Language Association*, vol. 69, No. 5 (Dec., 1954), 1135-1149.

[85] Thomas Carlyle to Jane Welsh, 23 June 1824, *CL3*, 84.

[86] Thomas Carlyle to John A. Carlyle, 24 June 1824, *CL3*, 90.

[87] Thomas Carlyle to Margaret A. Carlyle, 6 July 1824, *CL3,* 105.

immoderate. Irving was a thorough-going optimist, expecting great things from life, not just for himself but, also, for his friends. When this was viewed through the narrow lens of Irving's personal expectations, it could certainly look like vanity; viewed more broadly it transformed into a hopeful and helpful magnanimity.

Jane noted the difference in Carlyle's mood from his correspondence. "You cannot think how well I liked your last letter – it had more the aspect of hope and happiness than any I ever received from you – My heart is softened towards that vexatious Orator by what you say of him; I will answer his letter tomorrow so please the fates – He has got a little son it seems – have you heard if it has discovered genius yet?"[88] Jane's heart may have been softening, but she was facetious rather than happy about the arrival of Irving's son. Interestingly, though, Jane notes that Carlyle's letter was far more optimistic than any she had previously received from him; it could not be coincidence that this occurred just after he had spent some weeks with the perpetually-hopeful Irving.

Carlyle's letters to Jane during the next two months continued to plead Irving's cause to her, in hope of reconciliation between the two.[89] Then, in one of Jane's letters, there is a revealing passage. Over the years, Jane had enjoyed the attentions of a number of suitors, and although Kaplan believes that by mid-1824 Jane was completely committed to a future with Carlyle,[90] in September she wrote flirtatiously about a Captain James Baillie, priding herself on rejecting a man considered a good catch by others. "Now, dont [sic] you think I deserved to fall seriously in love with him, as a punishment for my sauciness? I believe nothing but his want of genius could have saved me – for in the month we have lived together I have found him more and more amiable every day. He is as generous and affectionate in his nature as the Orator, and more delicate and tender."[91] In this passage, Jane moves effortlessly from consideration of Baillie as a potential suitor to a comparison with Irving! If Carlyle had thought to compare this passage with Jane's previous heated denunciations of Irving, he surely would have come close to guessing the truth.

In October 1824, Carlyle spent some weeks holidaying in Dover with the Irvings and Kitty Kirkpatrick, a cousin of the Stracheys. In this setting, Carlyle and Irving discussed wide-ranging topics while strolling and smoking cigars. What Irving considered "the perfection of Christian elevation" was just vanity to Carlyle, but it is clear that their disagreements took place without the slightest ill-nature. Carlyle claimed that Irving began to see that there was "really nothing supernatural in the former hurly-burly, but that he must content himself with patient well-doing and liberal tho' not immoderate success; not taking the world by one fierce onslaught, but by patient and continued sapping

---

[88] Jane Welsh to Thomas Carlyle, 11 August 1824, *CL3*, 131-132.
[89] 12 August 1824 & 2 September 1824, *CL3*, 136, 147-148.
[90] Kaplan, *Carlyle*, 89.
[91] Jane Welsh to Thomas Carlyle, 17 September 1824, *CL3*, 150.

and mining as others do".[92] He remained convinced of Irving's abilities. The same letter showed Irving, the doting father, and Carlyle, the scornful observer, ridiculing Irving for describing his son as "he" rather than "it"! Irving found in fatherhood yet another outlet for his boundless enthusiasm; an outlet with which Carlyle was not to be troubled. Carlyle's assertion that Irving now saw nothing "supernatural" in his meteoric rise to popularity in London should not be interpreted as Irving's denial of God's involvement in these events, merely an acceptance that God's ways might be more circuitous than they, hitherto, seemed. Both men appeared to benefit from proximity to each other: Carlyle gained a little of Irving's optimism and Irving enjoyed the intellectual challenge Carlyle provided. Carlyle's letter indicates he looked for any evidence that Irving might be moving towards his opinions, and it may be assumed that Irving was similarly alert, although neither man was to gain much ground.

Yet, writing to Jane the very next day Carlyle chose to highlight Irving's flaws more than in the letter to his father. Still convinced that Irving's "pinnacles of Christian sentiment" were nothing more than speculative "pinnacles of human vanity", Carlyle spent much effort parodying Irving, the doting father.[93] It is hard not to suspect that an element of jealousy lurked behind this mockery of Irving's great joy: not only had Irving risen to fame in London, he had, also, achieved marriage and fatherhood; Carlyle was slipping further behind. That Jane shared Carlyle's dislike of children was confirmed in her subsequent letter in which she referred to them as "nasty little beasts".[94]

Later in the same letter, Carlyle expressed a wish that could only have caused Jane further pain. "I hope that he [Irving] will prove as true a friend as you anticipate. In one point, I shall be his debtor deeply, if he do as he proposes: do make him carry you to London, and the south! It is a project that promises abundantly, and seems so easy of execution . . . Nor . . . must you cut the poor Orator: he confidently expects you, he loves you, and his fellowship will do you good."[95] The juxtaposition of the words "propose" and "love" and the imagery of Irving carrying Jane in his arms must have had an impact! Jane's response was matter-of-fact and pessimistic but perceptive. "The Orator, you say, expects me. I am willing to b[e]lieve he does. But the Orator has only *one* voice in the matter; his wife has the other; and his wife I have obliged too deeply to hope for kindness from her. Depend upon it – the Orator's good intentions towards me will evaporate next season as they did the last – When the time for my visit arrives, his house will still be 'unfit for the accommodation of a Lady'."[96] Carlyle was aware that Irving had earlier expressed his love for Jane, but he was still unaware of how enthusiastically

[92] Thomas Carlyle to James Carlyle, the elder, 4 October 1824, *CL3*, 166.
[93] Thomas Carlyle to Jane Welsh, 5 October 1824, *CL3*, 172.
[94] Jane Welsh to Thomas Carlyle, 14 October 1824, *CL3*, 178.
[95] Thomas Carlyle to Jane Welsh, 5 October 1824, *CL3*, 173.
[96] Jane Welsh to Thomas Carlyle, 14 October 1824, *CL3*, 175-176.

Jane had reciprocated his love. Carlyle would have taken Jane's comment as a reference to Isabella's awareness of Irving's previously-declared love for Jane.

Jane may have been realistic in assessing her chance of obtaining an invitation from the Irvings, but she was surprised by the next development. "What do you think, the Orator *has* invited me! I was surprised, indeed terrified at sight of a letter from him, the day before I left Dumfriesshire. My imagination instantly decided that nothing but your illness or something as urgent could have induced him to com[m]it letter-writing; and I broke the seal and read 'My Well-beloved Friend & Pupil' in the utmost trepidation."[97] Jane's breathlessness as she opened the letter is apparent, and we can speculate that perhaps it was not only fear for Carlyle's health that made her heart beat faster as she broke the seal. Having been presented with the invitation she wanted, Jane's pride found a reason to refuse: the offer was too conditional -"if" she came to London. She did not appear to consider the possibility that Isabella might not be negatively disposed towards her. While Jane was struggling over the Irvings' offer of hospitality in London, Carlyle made a fortnight's trip to Paris during October 1824. On his return, Carlyle wrote to his mother describing how the Irvings helped him find lodging close by (they had, themselves, taken a lodger so had no room) and that he intended to visit them frequently, despite the irritation of Edward Jr.[98] Carlyle continued to write about Irving more positively to others than to Jane. To his brother he presented Irving as "valiant" and hopeful, with a positive future ahead of him.[99] The possibility of Jane staying with the Irvings surfaced again during November and December, but it was not to be.[100]

At a point when Jane's visit to London was still a possibility in December 1824, Carlyle shared some information with her that revealed more about himself than Irving. After reassuring Jane that Irving was not dissembling but simply reporting the facts when he said his house wasn't very "suitable" for a lady, Carlyle simultaneously encouraged Jane to come to London and limited her expectations.

> On the whole, I fear I am selfish in wishing you so much to come. As a town London is not worth looking at above a week; and I know scarcely one or two of Irving's friends whom you are likely to take pleasure in, or draw advantage from. There is no truly intellectual person in his list; scarcely, indeed, in London. For my part, at least, I must say that I have fallen in with none: any thing resembling a 'great man,' a man exercised with sublime thoughts and emotions, able even to participate in such, and throw any light

---

[97] Jane Welsh to Thomas Carlyle, 10 November 1824, *CL3*, 190.

[98] Thomas Carlyle to Margaret A. Carlyle, 12 November 1824, *CL3*, 194-196.

[99] Thomas Carlyle to John A. Carlyle, 30 November 1824, *CL3*, 211.

[100] Thomas Carlyle to Jane Welsh, 15 November 1824, *CL3*, 201-202; Jane Welsh to Thomas Carlyle, 18 November 1824, *CL3*, 203; Thomas Carlyle to Jane Welsh, 4 December 1824, *CL3*, 215.

> on them, is a treasure I have yet to meet with. Nevertheless, it has much in it, this monster of a city, that will amuse you and awaken you to new thoughts; and with all its imperfections it is London, the London every one delights to see or to have seen.[101]

There is an unmistakable condescension and arrogance in all of this. Carlyle cast a jaundiced eye not only on London itself but, breathtakingly, the intellectual capability not only of Irving's circle (including Coleridge), but the entire city! Although his biographer noted that Carlyle was homesick at this stage and idealising a return to the Scottish countryside, this is hardly sufficient justification for his sweeping dismissal of London and its intellectual life.[102] Jane swiftly upbraided him in her reply. "There is no intellectual person you say on the Orator's list! Why, what has befallen his acquaintance? Where are all the eminent personages, the very salt of the earth whom you and he told me of? . . . Discontented mortal that you are! if like me you had lived all your days in a little provincial town, you would know better how to appreciate such good company."[103] Jane rebuked Carlyle for inconsistency and discontent, rather than arrogance, perhaps because she thought she had already pushed the limits. She continued to say that she didn't expect Isabella to thank her for returning her "faithless lover" to her.[104]

Carlyle's December comments, also, addressed his Romanticism. It was a natural feature of Romanticism to esteem wild, isolated and untamed places, all of which Scotland had in abundance. For much of the first half of his long life, Carlyle was regularly drawn back from the economic and social benefits of urban life to the isolation of rural Scotland. For all the stories of Irving's love of long country walks, his Romanticism readily transplanted to the city life of Glasgow and then London; Carlyle's did so much less readily.

Carlyle's proximity to Irving in London continued to deepen the bond between them.

> Irving advises me to stay in London; partly with a friendly feeling, partly with a half selfish one, for he would fain keep me near him. Among all his followers there is none whose intercourse can satisfy him; any other than him it would go far to disgust. Great part of them are blockheads, a few are fools; there is no rightly intellectual man among them. Then he speculates and speculates; and would rather have one contradict him rationally, at least now and then he would... He advises me not knowing what he says. He himself has the nerves of a buffalo; and forgets that I have not. His philosophy with me is like a gill of ditch-water thrown into the crater of Mount Aetna; a million gallons of it would avail me nothing. I receive his

---

[101] Thomas Carlyle to Jane Welsh, 4 December 1824, *CL3*, 215-216.
[102] Kaplan, *Carlyle*, 107.
[103] Jane Welsh to Thomas Carlyle, 19 December 1824, *CL3*, 228-229.
[104] Jane Welsh to Thomas Carlyle, 19 December 1824, *CL3*, 229.

> nostrums with a smile: he at length despairs of ever seeing me converted. On the whole, however, he is among the best fellows in London; by far the best that I have met with.[105]

Carlyle here continued his rant against the London intellectual world (this letter was written before he received Jane's, quoted above), specifically, Irving's congregation (now numbering more than one thousand), yet he exempted Irving, himself, from this, exalting him above Coleridge and all the others he has met in London. Although it is likely that these comments were expressive of both men's delight at their shared "Annandale lads in big city" experience, it is apparent that Carlyle saw himself as a necessary corrective to Irving's "speculations", while Irving saw himself as pivotal in Carlyle's (re)conversion to Christian orthodoxy. If Carlyle was correct, Irving enjoyed the rational contradictions that Carlyle provided, which brings to mind Coleridge's description of his own discussions with Irving as exhibiting "friendly collisions". This ability of Irving's not only to tolerate but enjoy Carlyle's attempts to deflate his theology speaks volumes of his open-mindedness and his tolerance of contradiction, especially considering the disparity of their public profiles at this point. It is, also, likely that in the glimpses we get of these lively exchanges we are seeing something of a personification of the tensions within Scottish Romanticism, itself, highlighted in chapter one, that is, the tension between the elements of social usefulness and artistic expression.

In an intriguing comment, Carlyle described Irving to his brother as "the best man I have met in England. But here as I told him lately he has no home; he is a 'missionary' rather than a pastor."[106] The strangely prophetic thing about this comment is that it conjures an image of Irving as a stranger in a strange land, proclaiming a message to a dubious reception; while this can be seen as applicable to Irving's later years, at the time he had a massive audience, was the most popular preacher in London, and took his pastoral duties very seriously indeed. Carlyle distorted Irving into a Romantic character, exiled and alone, one that suited Carlyle's frustrations at his own lack of advancement, rather than accurately portraying Irving's current situation.

In January 1825, Carlyle had marriage on his mind and was idealising a rural retreat with his bride. Jane was horrified: her goal was engagement with the wider world, not trading seclusion with her mother for seclusion with a husband.[107] Contemplating his impending departure from London, Carlyle wrote to Jane regretting that this would remove him from Irving, yet noting that "fortune" had already placed them on different paths. He went on to describe Irving as "a good man; tho' he cannot speak or act one hour without cant, he really means to be sincere".[108] This is an oxymoron: "cant" normally meant

---

[105] Thomas Carlyle to Jane Welsh, 20 December 1824, *CL3*, 232-233.
[106] Thomas Carlyle to Alexander Carlyle, 8 January 1825, *CL3*, 243.
[107] Kaplan, *Carlyle*, 108-110.
[108] Thomas Carlyle to Jane Welsh, 31 January 1825, *CL3*, 272.

insincere speech, and if Irving was striving for sincerity (as Carlyle admits) he could hardly be accused of it. What this reveals is Carlyle's own bias and his inherent lack of sympathy for his friend's position: if he, himself, spoke as Irving did, it *would* have been cant; it was hard for Carlyle to conceive that someone could speak as Irving did and be completely genuine. It is, also, worth noting that "Carlyle was obsessed by the idea that the language of English theologians was permeated by 'cant', and it was eminently distasteful to him to adopt as his own any traditional formula which they employed".[109] Carlyle was revealing a Romantic disdain for inherited belief systems and, clearly, any allegation of Carlyle's that Irving was guilty of cant should not be taken as a slight on Irving's sincerity. That Carlyle did, in fact, have faith in Irving's integrity was made clear in one of the last letters he wrote before leaving London, when he noted that Irving "has a true heart with all its errors" and once again added prophetically that Irving would profit from adversity.[110]

Carlyle's imminent departure lessened the attraction of a London visit for Jane who wrote to Carlyle that "I love [Irving] *still*, after all he has done, and all that he has *not* done, - and I shall love him to the last – *in memory*", but then added that she no longer admired or trusted Irving, and was in fact disgusted with him.[111] Again, we see a potent and contradictory mixture of emotions here, and a casual reader of these comments would undoubtedly have questions about Irving's integrity. What had Irving done to merit Jane's distrust and disgust? From Carlyle's relative ignorance at this point, nothing other than issue an invitation to Jane to stay with them in London, which Jane herself declined. Carlyle's reply encouraged Jane's affection for Irving and repeated what he had written to his brother about the salutary nature of affliction on Irving: disappointment would lessen vanity and inconsistency and bring out the best in him.[112] Carlyle left London with a copy of Irving's newly-printed *Missionaries after the Apostolical School* in his possession.

In February, Carlyle, in pursuit of improved health, headed via Birmingham to Hoddam Hill, a farm his father and brother had taken on the Ecclefechan to Annan Road.[113] This was the beginning of a lengthy absence from London, and, therefore, also, the temporary end of direct contact with Irving. Essentially, Carlyle spent the next six years away from London, not returning until 1831. Carlyle lived for a year at Hoddam Hill, visiting Jane and she him, during which time their marriage became a certainty.[114] With Carlyle in Scotland, his

---

[109] H.L. Stewart, "Carlyle's Conception of Religion", *The American Journal of Theology*, vol. 21, no. 1, January 1917, 45.

[110] Thomas Carlyle to John A. Carlyle, 10 February 1825, *CL3*, 279. In fact, Carlyle's letters frequently refer to Irving's integrity and innate goodness.

[111] Jane Welsh to Thomas Carlyle, 14 February 1825, *CL3*, 282.

[112] Thomas Carlyle to Jane Welsh, 28 February 1825, *CL3*, 288-289.

[113] D.A. Wilson, *Carlyle till Marriage: 1795-1826* (London: Kegan Paul, Trench, Trubner & Co., 1923), 381.

[114] Kaplan, *Carlyle*, 113.

references to Irving naturally became less vital and reduced either to seeking information about Irving or passing on second-hand news.

Some months after his arrival at Hoddam Hill, Carlyle wrote a fateful letter to Anna Montagu, urging her to initiate a correspondence with Jane Welsh.[115] Anna Montagu wrote speedily, and from Jane's reply she deduced not only that Jane was still in love with Irving, but that Irving still loved Jane. Entirely unaware of Carlyle's ignorance of most of this, Anna Montagu became the means of his enlightenment when she shared these observations with him.[116] "I feared to be the means of stirring an old flame the embers of which are still glowing on both sides," she wrote of the love between Jane and Irving; it had only been Irving's "duty" to marry Isabella Martin that had kept them apart. Nevertheless, Anna perceptively concluded that the differences between Jane and Irving meant that they would not have been happy together.[117] The effect of this revelation on Carlyle can be imagined: Irving had not only eclipsed him by rapidly becoming London's most celebrated preacher, a published author, husband and father; it appeared that the woman Carlyle wanted to marry preferred Irving.

Jane's motives in writing thus to Anna Montagu are worth considering. Jane knew that the correspondence was instigated at Carlyle's suggestion and, therefore anything she wrote to Anna Montagu could find its way back to Carlyle. In writing with candour then, she was clearly taking a risk: was she desperate enough for a sympathetic listener to take this risk, or was she secretly hoping that Anna would tell Carlyle and relieve her of that responsibility? Either way, she achieved both. Anna was equally candid with her advice, telling Jane that she was not at liberty to talk of being engaged to Carlyle when her heart was still captive to Edward Irving. She forced Jane to consider what would happen if Irving suddenly found himself single again: would her heart race or would she be unaffected? Only in the latter case should she consider herself free to marry Carlyle.[118]

Finally, Jane wrote the inevitable letter to Carlyle. She acknowledged that she had deceived him by pretending that she did not care for Irving, whom she had "passionately loved". Although she knew Irving was engaged to Isabella at the time, she felt she had partly atoned for this by insisting he preserve honour and marry Isabella. Nevertheless, Jane acknowledged that she had "concealed and disguised the truth", only revealing it when forced to do so through Anna Montagu's intervention, and threw herself on Carlyle's mercy.[119] It is doubtful that Jane would have been able to avoid her own hypocrisy: having assailed Irving's character and integrity (with little or no reason) in many letters to

---

[115] Thomas Carlyle to Anna D.B. Montagu, 20 May 1825, *CL3*, 327ff.
[116] Anna D.B. Montagu to Thomas Carlyle, 30 May 1825, *CL3*, 341 footnote.
[117] Anna D.B. Montagu to Thomas Carlyle, 30 May 1825, *CL3*, 341 footnote.
[118] Anna D.B. Montagu to Jane Welsh, 3 July 1825, *CL3*, 355 footnote.
[119] Jane Welsh to Thomas Carlyle, 24 July 1825, *CL3*, 356-357.

Carlyle, she now had to acknowledge her own duplicity to the man she was planning to marry.

Although Jane referred to her love for Irving in the past tense, she nowhere openly declared that she had stopped loving him. Such a declaration would have been entirely appropriate given her confession and plea for mercy from Carlyle, but it is noticeably absent. Its absence is particularly revealing in the context of Anna Montagu's caveat mentioned above, that is, not to proceed with her relationship with Carlyle unless she could think of Irving with detachment. Carlyle's reply was philosophical and loving; he could certainly afford to be, for the woman he loved was seeking his forgiveness.[120] His offer of forgiveness meant he had gained the moral high ground and Jane was indebted to him. Whether or not Carlyle noticed that Jane hadn't made her current feelings about Irving completely clear, Carlyle's first biographer believed he never completely realised the depth of Jane's love for Irving, despite her confession.[121] Perhaps such a realisation would have simply cost him too much. At another level, these developments potentially threatened the continuity of friendship between Carlyle and Irving: would Carlyle's ego be able to survive Irving's presence? As it turned out, the friendship continued unabated, no doubt benefiting from some myopic stoicism on Carlyle's part.

At this time, Irving's young son, Edward Jr. died at Isabella's family home in Kirkcaldy. Irving took advantage of being in Scotland to visit Carlyle at Hoddam Hill, which Carlyle later reported to Jane.[122] Revealingly, Jane's first concern in her reply, before expressing sadness at Irving's loss, was that he had been in Scotland without visiting her: "So Edward Irving is gone! gone without seeing me!"[123] From this point onwards, with her marriage rapidly approaching, Jane's references to Irving unsurprisingly became fewer. Yet in Margaret Oliphant's autobiography there is evidence that Jane's affection for Irving did not dull with the passing of the years. When Oliphant first met Jane in 1860/61, Irving had been dead for nearly three decades, yet when Jane knew Oliphant was writing Irving's biography, she went out of her way to meet her and reminisced eagerly about him. Nor was this the only occasion; the two women met frequently until Jane's death.[124]

The courtship between Jane and Carlyle had not gone smoothly for several reasons: Jane's mother was unwilling to lose her daughter's company, and the Welsh family considered that Carlyle was socially beneath her; economically, they were certainly correct, although their correspondence reveals an

---

[120] Thomas Carlyle to Jane Welsh, 29 July 1825, *CL3*, 357-360.

[121] Froude, *Thomas Carlyle*, vol. 1, 481, 125, in A. Dallimore, *The Life of Edward Irving: the Fore-runner of the Charismatic Movement* (Edinburgh: Banner of Truth, 1983), 53.

[122] Thomas Carlyle to Jane Welsh, 19 October 1825, *CL3*, 390.

[123] Jane Welsh to Thomas Carlyle, 25 October 1825, *CL3*, 395.

[124] H. Coghill (ed.), *Autobiography and Letters of Mrs Margaret Oliphant* (Leicester: Leicester University Press, 1974. Orig. 1899), 79-80.

intellectual parity. Nonetheless, the doctor's daughter and the farmer's son finally married in October 1826 in a small ceremony in Templand, and moved to a house in Comely Bank, Edinburgh, where they would spend the next two years.[125] There has been much speculation on the Carlyles' sexual relationship which has usually fallen on a spectrum between the view that the marriage was never actually consummated to the view that whatever sex did occur was unsatisfactory to both parties and probably ceased a few years into the marriage.[126] Certainly, they had no children, which, considering their mutual dislike of infants, would not have been seen as a loss.

Whatever frustrations may have been occurring in this area, Carlyle was, also, frustrated in the area of his work. He had published some minor works and articles, and had just completed *German Romance*, but he needed a larger focus and a long-term income.[127] He remained in Irving's shadow and, once again, drew on the preacher's support when he lobbied unsuccessfully for a position at London University. Irving gave his support despite disliking the secular nature of the university in general.[128] Acknowledging Irving's support in a letter to his brother, Carlyle admitted there was "much precious truth" in what he still described as Irving's cant, and also that he considered himself not half as good a man as Irving.[129]

At this time, Irving was dealing with the loss of his first-born by translating *Ben-Ezra* from the Spanish.[130] When this book was published, Carlyle found himself at something of a loss, contrasting the Irving of private correspondence with his published millennial views. Reflecting the preconception that all millennialists should be wild of eye and frazzled of hair, Carlyle puzzled that Irving "does not seem the least millenniary in his letters".[131] 1827 was a year of mixed fortune for Irving: still grieving the death of his son, he not only published *Ben-Ezra*, but his congregation celebrated its relocation to its new Regent Square location, yet the year ended with the death of his daughter Mary. While his public profile was still flourishing, at a personal level, Irving was, certainly, receiving the adversity which Carlyle felt would be to his advantage.

As 1828 dawned, the Carlyles were preparing for another move. Despite having made good contacts in Edinburgh, they headed to Craigenputtoch, a

---

[125] Clubbe, *Froude's Carlyle*, 200-201.

[126] Kaplan, *Carlyle*, 118-119.

[127] Carlyle completed *German Romance* the month before his marriage; it was published in January 1827.

[128] Thomas Carlyle to Margaret A. Carlyle, 26 January 1828, in C.R. Sanders (ed.), *The Collected Letters of Thomas and Jane Welsh Carlyle*, vol. 4, 1826-1828 (Durham, N.C.: Duke University Press, 1970), 310. Henceforth *CL4*. Irving supplied a "magnificent" three page recommendation. For Irving's opposition to the University, see Oliphant, *Irving*, 129 footnote.

[129] Thomas Carlyle to John A. Carlyle, 5 September 1827, *CL4*, 253.

[130] We have already considered Coleridge's marginalia to this work; in the following chapter we will consider Irving's preface from another perspective.

[131] Thomas Carlyle to David Hope, 12 December 1827, *CL4*, 295-296.

remote farmhouse in south-west Scotland owned by Jane's mother. Carlyle saw better health and frugality in the move; Jane saw no advantages at all.[132] It was to be their home for six years. In the middle of the year Carlyle heard Irving preach in Edinburgh, noting people were divided in their opinions of him, but admitting with a touch of reluctance that he thought Irving was "on the road to truth", although still perceiving a mixture of "cant and enthusiasm".[133]

Irving visited the Carlyles in their rural retreat in June 1829, staying for two days, and Carlyle wrote wistfully of the visit some months later.[134] When Irving published *The Orthodox and Catholic Doctrine of our Lord's Human Nature* in January 1830, Carlyle rose (somewhat surprisingly) to his defence. In a letter to his brother (who was staying with the Irvings at the time) he declared Irving's Christological interpretation "indubitably and palpably" correct and his opponents "utterly" wrong. He had even referred Irving's book to his mother, to whose theological opinion he deferred, and she had resoundingly endorsed the orthodoxy of Irving's teaching.[135] As someone who had been raised within the Church of Scotland, but now held substantially different views, Carlyle's perspective on Irving's Christological orthodoxy is valuable as he had little personal investment in either side of the debate. Carlyle's stand (with added support from his mother) gives credibility to Irving's claim that he was only preaching what he had "always heard" as he grew up in the Church of Scotland. It is, also, noteworthy that for all Carlyle's criticism of Irving's "vain theological speculations", he was quick to rise to Irving's defence when others attacked him theologically.

We have already noted the irony that Carlyle, no believer in prophecy, nonetheless prophesied accurately that adversity would come to Irving and he would profit by it. In another letter to his brother, Carlyle achieved this feat yet again. Beginning by saying that he had never found another man Irving's equal, he expressed the wish that the "Scotch Kirk" would expel Irving, thus freeing "his own better genius [to] lead him far away from all Apocalypses and prophetic and theologic chimeras, utterly unworthy of such a head, to see the world as it here lies visible and is, that we might fight together, for God's *true* cause, even to the death! With one such man I feel as if I could defy the Earth."[136]

Apart from his accurate prediction of Irving's eventual expulsion from the Church of Scotland, this recalls a similar image in which Coleridge also pictured himself fighting alongside Irving, although there Coleridge aligned

---

[132] Kaplan, *Carlyle*, 139; Clubbe, *Froude's Carlyle*, 227.
[133] Thomas Carlyle to John A. Carlyle, 10 June 1828, *CL4*, 382.
[134] Kaplan, *Carlyle*, 149; Thomas Carlyle to Anna D.B. Montagu, 13 November 1829, C.R. Sanders (ed.), *The Collected Letters of Thomas and Jane Welsh Carlyle*, vol. 5, Jan. 1829- Sept. 1831 (Durham, N.C.: Duke University Press, 1976), 34. Henceforth, *CL5*.
[135] Thomas Carlyle to John A. Carlyle, 1 May 1830, *CL5*, 98.
[136] Thomas Carlyle to John A. Carlyle, 21 August 1830, *CL5*, 145-146.

himself with Irving's cause; here Carlyle wanted Irving to abandon his chosen passions for Carlyle's own. Carlyle wanted to move Irving's focus from the spiritual to the "visible" world, whereas Coleridge had wanted to do almost the opposite. It is no small compliment to Irving that two of the greatest minds of nineteenth century Britain wanted him as an ally in the struggle to change and improve the world. Like Irving, Carlyle saw himself in a Romantic struggle "for God's true cause". Carlyle wanted Irving to join his cause; he could never join Irving's.

Carlyle's brother, John, struggling to establish himself as a physician in London, lived with the Irvings through the second half of 1830 and into 1831, giving him an excellent opportunity of observing the Irving household. John described Irving as the only "established" person he knew who was determined to pursue truth at all costs, and the only "fearless" man.[137] During this time, Carlyle was again facing difficulties. Jane was frequently ill and hated Craigenputtoch; the farm itself, worked by his brother, Alexander, was losing money; and Carlyle needed to produce a book that would make money. Now in his mid-thirties, he was beginning to feel disgusted with himself that the rural isolation and sacrifices had not been more productive.[138] This disillusionment produced *Sartor Resartus*, and occasioned Carlyle's first trip to London in five years. John Carlyle anticipated that his brother's reunion with Irving in London would do them both good.[139] Carlyle was optimistic of quickly finding a publisher for *Sartor* and with the resulting financial security wintering in London with Jane; in the meantime, she was to remain in Craigenputtoch.

Carlyle arrived in London in August 1831 and stayed for eight months. It had been over two years since Carlyle had seen Irving, during which time Irving and Isabella had lost another child, and the recent outbreak of charismatic gifts in Scotland was attracting the attention of Irving's congregation.[140] The Presbytery of London had moved against Irving at the beginning of 1831, and, just before Carlyle's arrival, some members of Irving's congregation had begun speaking in tongues in private. Carlyle wrote to Jane that although he could see truth revealed amongst Irving's still flourishing congregation, it was mixed with "ephemeral impurities"; yet his respect for Irving's opinion remained high.[141] A little later, when Carlyle heard about the glossolalia and belief in contemporary miracles, he described it as primarily the work of hysterical women.[142] Jane replied with amazement that Irving would

---

[137] John A. Carlyle to Thomas Carlyle, 12 February 1831, *CL5*, 234 footnote. John A. Carlyle to Thomas Carlyle, 7 July 1831, *CL5*, 295 footnote.

[138] Kaplan, *Carlyle*, 150-153.

[139] John A. Carlyle to Thomas Carlyle, 7 July 1831, *CL5*, 296 footnote.

[140] Samuel had died in July 1830. At this stage only one child, Maggie, survived.

[141] Thomas Carlyle to Jane Carlyle, 15 August 1831, *CL5*, 330; Swaim, "'Our own Periodical Pulpit': Thomas Carlyle's Sermons", 151.

[142] Thomas Carlyle to Jane Carlyle, 22 August 1831, *CL5*, 351.

associate with such "janners" (foolish talkers).[143] Naturally, Carlyle, also, expressed his frank doubts directly to Irving, whose face "thoughtfully puckered" at the divergent view, although as always the two Scots disagreed within the context of friendship.[144] Shortly before Jane joined him in London, Carlyle described Irving as "graver than usual; yet has still the old faculty of laughter". He lamented that Irving was not at the forefront of contemporary thought but "wilfully standing in the rear . . . however well he do it".[145] This was reflective of Carlyle's conviction that any effort focusing on revitalising orthodox Christianity was poorly spent.

Jane finally arrived in London on 1 October 1831 and remained there with Carlyle until March 1832, immediately enjoying better health and the wider social circle.[146] She was shocked, however, at the change in Irving in the two years since she had seen him: he had gone grey and his features were drawn.[147] Carlyle wrote to a friend that although Irving was still the best of men he was caught up in "miraculous rubbish".[148] Inevitably, the Carlyles came in contact with glossolalia when visiting the Irvings. Jane, who had recently visited a lunatic asylum, wrote to her niece that it was idyllic by comparison with what she observed in Irving's home. To her the glossolalia was "shrieking and howling in no tongue" and it distressed her that Irving seemed about to lose everything he had gained because of it.[149] Nevertheless, she remained convinced of Irving's total sincerity. Shortly afterwards, Carlyle wrote to his mother in a similar vein, describing Irving as surrounded by "a whole posse of enthusiasts, ranters and silly women", fearing that he would be ejected from his congregation, but exhorting his mother to defend Irving against any critics.[150] This exhortation was not without cause, as people from London to Annandale were claiming that Irving had gone insane (or always had been),[151] although Carlyle, himself, resolutely maintained Irving's sanity.[152] Nevertheless, Carlyle continued to warn Irving against what he seemed to regard as simultaneously a

---

[143] Jane Carlyle to Thomas Carlyle, 29 August 1831, *CL5*, 372.

[144] Thomas Carlyle to Jane Carlyle, 31 August 1831, *CL5*, 386.

[145] Thomas Carlyle to Jane Carlyle, 14 September 1831, *CL5*, 432.

[146] Kaplan, *Carlyle*, 179-180.

[147] Kaplan, *Carlyle*, 179.

[148] Thomas Carlyle to William Graham, 17 October 1831, C.R. Sanders (ed.), *The Collected Letters of Thomas and Jane Welsh Carlyle*, vol. 6, Oct. 1831-Sept. 1833 (Durham, N.C.: Duke University Press, 1977), 21-22. Henceforth *CL6*. Graham was an Annandale native turned Glasgow merchant whom Carlyle met while visiting Irving in Glasgow in 1820, Wilson, *Carlyle till marriage*, 189.

[149] Jane Carlyle to Helen Welsh, 26 October 1831, *CL6*, 35.

[150] Thomas Carlyle to Margaret A. Carlyle, 10 November 1831, *CL6*, 41.

[151] Thomas Carlyle to John A. Carlyle, 13 November 1831, *CL6*, 46; Thomas Carlyle to John A. Carlyle, 20 December 1831, *CL6*, 73; Thomas Carlyle to Jean Carlyle, 25 December 1831, *CL6*, 80.

[152] Thomas Carlyle to James Carlyle the elder, 13 December 1831, *CL6*, 65; Thomas Carlyle to Jean Carlyle, 25 December 1831, *CL6*, 80.

"scandalous delusion" and "the Devil's own work".[153] Carlyle noted that although Irving seemed to be ageing quickly, yet he remained "composed and affectionate and patient".[154]

The disparity of interests and opinions naturally led to the Carlyles and the Irvings seeing less of each other, as letters through December 1831 and January 1832 made plain.[155] Nevertheless, when news of the death of Carlyle's father reached London the Irvings paid their respects, although understandably, Carlyle was even less inclined than usual to tolerate any discussion of spiritual gifts.[156] This was the time when the trustees of Irving's church were moving against him, and Carlyle's letters explored the legalities and probable outcomes of this action.[157] Irving seemed bewildered in his thought, yet "nobly tolerant in heart", and Carlyle consistently maintained his earlier conviction that Irving would only improve through suffering, breaking through to make a greater contribution to society.[158]

Towards the end of March 1832 the Carlyles returned to Craigenputtoch where they remained for the next two years, apart from a short sojourn in Edinburgh. Carlyle revived the fantasy of a healthy rural lifestyle, jaded with a London literary scene he saw veering between the insubstantial and the materialistic.[159] Just before they left, Carlyle remonstrated with Irving about tongues. Carlyle recalled this conversation in later years in a revealing quote:

> That the '*13th of the Corinthians*,' to which he always appealed, was surely too narrow a basis for so high a tower as he was building on it; - a high lean tower, or quasi-*mast*, piece added to piece, till it soared far above all human science and experience, and flatly contradicted all that, - founded solely on a little text of *writing* in an ancient Book! No sound judgment, on such warranty, could venture on such an enterprise. Authentic 'writings' of the Most High, were they found in old Books only? They were in the stars and on the rocks, and in the brain and heart of every mortal, - *not* dubious there, to any person, as this '*13th of Corinthians*' very greatly was.[160]

Apart from the unlikelihood of Irving restricting his argument for tongues to 1 Corinthians 13, which actually says little about them, this gives insight into the nature of Carlyle's Romanticism. Truth existed, but it was not to be found in

---

[153] Thomas Carlyle to John A. Carlyle, 13 November 1831, *CL6*, 51.

[154] Thomas Carlyle to James Carlyle the elder, 13 December 1831, *CL6*, 65.

[155] E.g. Thomas Carlyle to John A. Carlyle, 10 January 1832, *CL6*, 88; Jane Carlyle to Jean Carlyle, 23 January 1832, *CL6*, 101.

[156] Thomas Carlyle to Margaret A. Carlyle, 30 January 1832, *CL6*, 111.

[157] Thomas Carlyle to John A. Carlyle, 16 February 1832, *CL6*, 126-127; Thomas Carlyle to Margaret A. Carlyle, 18 February 1832, *CL6*, 132-133; Thomas Carlyle to John A. Carlyle, 22 May 1832, *CL6*, 162.

[158] Thomas Carlyle to Margaret A. Carlyle, 18 February 1832, *CL6*, 132-133.

[159] Kaplan, *Carlyle*, 192-193.

[160] Carlyle, *Reminiscences*, 299.

appealing to external, written texts of established religion; it was only to be found through experience, be it introspective or cosmic, individual or collective. Against this, Carlyle felt, the Bible had no claim. The division on the issue of ultimate authority between the two men could not have been made any plainer.

In Craigenputtoch, once again, the Carlyles' direct contact with Irving was broken. From his rural isolation, Carlyle heard the news of Irving's ejection from his church and the large outdoor services he subsequently held,[161] and then of the group's move to Newman Street.[162] In Edinburgh at the beginning of 1833, he heard from Anna Montagu that Irving had lost a lot of weight and was very pale, but "tranquil".[163] In the middle of March 1833, Irving made his speech of defence before the presbytery of Annan. Carlyle later read a copy with a mixture of admiration and pain, believing it to reflect a "heroic temper" but distracted ideas. He fretted about Irving's future.[164] For the next few months, Carlyle made only isolated references to Irving, usually about his itinerant preaching. Back in Craigenputtoch in August, he wrote to his brother that only a prolonged rest would cure Irving, preferably in a foreign country where he would be unable to preach![165]

This residence back in Scotland had convinced Carlyle that he was now more suited to live in cities and that London was preferable to Edinburgh.[166] It had, also, become impossible for him not to notice how much Jane disliked rural isolation and associated drudgery.[167] In the middle of May 1834, Carlyle returned to London on a house-hunting expedition, with Jane to follow shortly afterwards.[168] Carlyle had only been in London a few days when in Kensington Gardens "there starts from a side-seat a black figure, and clutches my hand in both his: it is poor Edward Irving! O what a feeling! The poor friend looks like death rather than life; pale and yet flushed, a flaccid, boiled appearance; and one short peal of his old Annandale laugh went thro' me with the wofullest tone".[169]

---

[161] Thomas Carlyle to John A. Carlyle, 22 May 1832, *CL6*, 162; Thomas Carlyle to John A. Carlyle, 2 July 1832, *CL6*, 185; Thomas Carlyle to John A. Carlyle, 31 July 1832, *CL6*, 196.

[162] Thomas Carlyle to John A. Carlyle, 31 August 1832, *CL6*, 219-220; Thomas Carlyle to John A. Carlyle, 17 October 1832, *CL6*, 251.

[163] *CL6*, 313, footnote. The original letter from Anna Montagu was dated 2 January 1833.

[164] Thomas Carlyle to Margaret A. Carlyle, 26 March 1833, *CL6*, 353-354; Thomas Carlyle to John A. Carlyle, 29 March 1833, *CL6*, 363-364.

[165] Thomas Carlyle to John A. Carlyle, 27 August 1833, *CL6*, 428.

[166] Kaplan, *Carlyle*, 199-203.

[167] Clubbe, *Froude's Carlyle*, 274, 305.

[168] Kaplan, *Carlyle*, 205.

[169] Thomas Carlyle to Jane Carlyle, 17 May 1834, C.R. Sanders (ed.), *The Collected Letters of Thomas and Jane Welsh Carlyle*, vol. 7, Oct. 1833-Dec. 1834 (Durham, N.C.:

Alarmed at the change in Irving, Carlyle made several unsuccessful attempts to visit before managing to spend two hours with him. On this occasion, Irving seemed in much better health, yet almost choked, Carlyle felt, by his "delusions".[170] Jane arrived in London in June and the Carlyles took up residence in Cheyne Row, Chelsea.[171] June and July passed without the two men meeting again, and Carlyle began to suspect that Isabella was attempting to hinder his visits.[172] In early August, Carlyle once again voiced his concerns for Irving's life, and complained that the "elders" of the Newman Street church were opposing his free access to Irving.[173]

Carlyle was indignantly persistent, and in mid-August met with Irving and Isabella, both of whom had been sick. Irving was unable to rise from the sofa and Isabella did not leave them, despite her husband's request to do so. Carlyle struggled to remain civil to her. Irving managed to laugh once, precipitating a coughing-fit. Carlyle desperately wanted to see his friend in a different environment.[174] Shortly afterwards, Carlyle was heartened when Irving visited Cheyne Row and seemed to favour a period of rest in the country, and, later, when he discovered Irving had actually gone to Somerset.[175] This visit to Cheyne Row was the last occasion on which the Carlyles saw Irving.

At this time Carlyle and William Graham were both concerned about the extent to which Irving had come under control of the "elders" in this new movement, believing his future health was directly determined by the degree to which he could free himself from this control.[176] Graham felt that the reason Irving submitted to their control was a remnant of pride, mixed with self-deception, while simultaneously proclaiming Irving's genius and potential greatness.[177]

The following month, Carlyle heard with concern that Irving was in Glasgow and his consumption was worse; he feared that "the conclusion of all that wild work, will be *early death*!"[178] Carlyle believed that Irving had been

---

Duke University Press, 1977), 150-151. Henceforth, *CL7*. Also Thomas Carlyle to John A. Carlyle, 18 May 1834, *CL7*, 164.

[170] Thomas Carlyle to Jane Carlyle, 21 May 1834, *CL7*, 196.

[171] Kaplan, *Carlyle*, 207.

[172] Thomas Carlyle to John A. Carlyle, 22 July 1834, *CL7*, 246.

[173] Thomas Carlyle to William Graham, 5 August 1834, *CL7*, 255.

[174] Thomas Carlyle to John A. Carlyle, 15 August 1834, *CL7*, 269, 272-273.

[175] Thomas Carlyle to Alexander Carlyle, 28 August 1834, *CL7*, 282; Thomas Carlyle to Margaret A. Carlyle, 12 September 1834, *CL7*, 295; Thomas Carlyle to William Graham, 14 September 1834, *CL7*, 299.

[176] William Graham to Thomas Carlyle, 8 September 1834, *CL7*, 297-298; Thomas Carlyle to William Graham, 14 September 1834, *CL7*, 297-299. Graham was an Annandale native, 25 years older than Carlyle, who had prospered in the States, suffered a reversal on returning to Glasgow, and finally returned to farming in Annandale.

[177] William Graham to Thomas Carlyle, 8 September 1834, *CL7*, 297 footnote.

[178] Thomas Carlyle to Alexander Carlyle, 24 October 1834, *CL7*, 319-320; Thomas Carlyle to Margaret A. Carlyle, 25 October 1834, *CL7*, 321.

"ordered" to Glasgow by the church elders, and, although he had written an "officious" letter to Henry Drummond, he felt it was pointless to send it. Irving was declining, ignoring doctor's orders to go to a sunnier climate and continuing to preach, even though he couldn't stand.[179] When Irving died on 7 December 1834, Carlyle received the news he had been dreading. It still came as a shock and Carlyle blamed, in general terms, the madness of London, believing that it exposed Irving to influences he would have avoided had he remained in Scotland.[180] Carlyle moved to preserve Irving's reputation, attempting to evaluate contrary accounts of Irving's last days, grieved that so many seemed to regard Irving as a "quack".[181] Carlyle's journal that winter revealed more despondency than at any previous time in his life.[182] In the midst of this correspondence, Carlyle received a letter from Graham. "Could I ever forget [Irving], I were the most ungrateful, the worst of men. His friendship was worth a king's ransom; his aberrations were of the head, not of the heart; his star has disappeared from the galaxy of mighty minds. It is a mournful pleasure to dwell upon what he was. It will ever be a consolation to *you* that your friendship remained to the last, and that he *knew* it *well*."[183]

Allowing for the elegiac tone, this shows that a third party believed that Irving valued Carlyle's friendship to the end, despite their theological differences. It, also, highlights the dilemma so many have had when trying to understand Irving. Graham acknowledged Irving's sincerity: there were no problems "of the heart"; but only a few words after describing Irving's thinking as aberrant, he wrote he had a "mighty" mind! We saw in an earlier letter that Graham proclaimed Irving's genius.[184] This is another reflection of the dilemma of Irving historiography discussed in chapter three: virtually all writers have wrestled with the issue of Irving's "decline", emerging with varying and largely unsatisfactory results. As Carlyle's grief poured out in his correspondence, he became more specific about the cause of Irving's untimely death. Whereas, previously, he had blamed London as a whole, he began to see Irving's death as inevitable, the result of "his enviable fortune".[185] Here is a subtle admission, perhaps, of the envy Carlyle had felt in those early years when he had made such pointed distinctions between the popularity Irving was experiencing and "real fame".

---

[179] Thomas Carlyle to John A. Carlyle, 28 October 1834, *CL7*, 328-329; Thomas Carlyle to Margaret A. Carlyle, 20 November 1834, *CL7*, 334.
[180] Thomas Carlyle to David Hope, 19 December 1834, *CL7*, 344.
[181] Thomas Carlyle to David Hope, 24 December 1834, *CL7*, 347.
[182] Clubbe, *Froude's Carlyle* , 313-314.
[183] William Graham to Thomas Carlyle, 17 December 1834, *CL7*, 348 footnote. Emphasis original.
[184] William Graham to Thomas Carlyle, 8 September 1834, *CL7*, 297 footnote.
[185] Thomas Carlyle to William Graham, 24 December 1834, *CL7*, 350; Thomas Carlyle to Margaret A. Carlyle, 24 December 1834, *CL7*, 354.

The Carlyles both survived Irving by many years: Jane died in 1866 and Thomas in 1881. After Irving's death, Carlyle quickly ascended to the fame he had so long desired; it was almost as if two lads from Annandale could not share the London spotlight simultaneously. Long in Irving's shadow in terms of fame and breadth of acquaintance, Carlyle was working on *The French Revolution*, his breakthrough work, in the year Irving died. While his previous main work, *Sartor Resartus*, had been received well in America, it had been neglected in England. Carlyle had, in fact, come close to abandoning writing as a way of making a living; according to one source it was simply "chance" that he persevered with *The French Revolution*.[186] When this book was published in 1837, it began to establish a reputation that was only cemented further as Carlyle kept to a punishing work schedule.[187] Works on *Heroes* and *Chartism* appeared in 1841, the *Life and Letters of Oliver Cromwell* in 1845, followed in due course by his multi-volume life of Frederick the Great, which took thirteen years to complete. Along the way, Carlyle transformed into the "Sage of Chelsea" and the friendships he made included Charles Dickens, John Ruskin, Robert Browning, Alfred Lord Tennyson and William Makepeace Thackeray. Carlyle eventually gained fame the way he thought Irving should have – slowly, through persistent work. The Carlyles never seemed to appreciate the workload Irving had in combining pastoral responsibilities within a large congregation with his own significant literary output, calling him lazy due to the infrequency of his correspondence during the 1820s. Whether or not Carlyle ever noticed, another thing he and Irving had in common was their formidable Scottish work ethic.

Having examined references to Irving through the Carlyle correspondence from 1817 to 1834, we are now in a position to draw conclusions about how the Carlyles saw Irving, and to comment on the differing Romanticisms of the two men. Thomas Carlyle maintained a uniformly high regard for Irving's integrity, sincerity and intelligence throughout these years, despite disagreeing with him theologically. Carlyle tried to argue Irving out of his "delusions"; Irving tried to convert Carlyle to Christian orthodoxy: both men remained completely committed to what they believed to be true, even when the cost was high.[188] Beneath their differences, the respect remained. Jane likewise thought highly of Irving overall, when allowance is made for her often excessive language due to the loss of Irving as a suitor. In fact, the excess of her language expressed the depth of her loss, which, in turn, is an implied compliment to Irving.

We have noted, however, the frequent charges of vanity, affectation and cant that Carlyle levelled against Irving, as well as Carlyle's expectations that adversity would purge Irving of these. As the years progressed, Irving certainly

---

[186] Clubbe, *Froude's Carlyle*, 341.

[187] The positive responses to *The French Revolution* are detailed in Kaplan, *Carlyle*, 243ff.

[188] Clubbe, *Froude's Carlyle*, 327-328 shows Carlyle refusing a lucrative offer to write for the *Times*, because it would be inconsistent with his apolitical stance.

received his share of adversity, both professional and personal, but there is no indication in Carlyle's correspondence that he believed Irving's vanity and affectation had lessened. We have to ask to what degree Irving was guilty of these characteristics in the first place, or whether Carlyle possibly misunderstood Irving's position. We commented earlier that Carlyle's use of "cant" is oxymoronic where Irving is concerned, because Carlyle resolutely maintained Irving's integrity. "Affectation" carries similar connotations of insincerity. It is more than likely that Carlyle's use of these terms to describe Irving simply reflected the disparity between Carlyle's and Irving's religious positions: Carlyle's lack of sympathy for Irving's theology reduced his ability to believe that such beliefs could be held with sincerity – despite his simultaneous conviction of Irving's sincerity! Yet, Irving maintained his beliefs through both sudden fame and several reversals of fortune, right up to his death, thus, proving his integrity beyond reasonable doubt. One may disagree with Irving's theology, as Carlyle certainly did, but it is simply inaccurate to use "affectation" and "cant" which connote insincerity, to describe him. Carlyle's self-contradictions on this point indicate that despite their shared Annandale boyhood, Church of Scotland heritage, and lengthy friendship, he simply did not understand Irving's deepest motivations.

The charge of vanity probably had more substance to it. Irving always saw himself as fulfilling an important role in God's plan, and his rapid rise from obscurity to prominence in London provided ample fuel for this particular fire. In chapter four, we saw in Irving's Glasgow farewell sermon an attitude that could certainly be interpreted as vanity. Nevertheless, it is, also, important to consider the difference between the two Scots' temperaments here: while Irving's unflagging optimism for his own prospects could easily have been seen as vanity, this optimism was by no means exclusively self-focused – it comprehensively included Carlyle and almost everyone else of Irving's acquaintance. Irving did not consider himself "conceited": those who saw it in him were mistaking his attempt to shake loose from "religious or customary restraints" to venture above his "sphere" for vanity.[189] There is another factor which is probably relevant here: Carlyle's distinctive views on speech and silence. At one level, Carlyle disparaged vocal ability because true "heroes" should be so transcendent as to be barely understood by their contemporaries.[190] Elsewhere, it has been argued that for Carlyle, silence and writing were "masculine" activities, whereas speech was "feminine".[191] A. Rennick's article explores this theme through some of Carlyle's reminiscences (Southey, and Jane Carlyle) but, unfortunately, not with his reminiscence of Irving. Irving

[189] E. Irving, *For the Oracles of God, four Orations, for Judgment to come, an Argument in nine parts* (New York: S. Marks, 1825), 74.

[190] M.E. Blaine, "Carlyle's Cromwell and the virtue of the inarticulate", *Carlyle Annual*, no. 13, 1992/93, 78.

[191] A. Rennick, "Silence and Masculinity in Carlyle's *Reminiscences*", *Nineteenth Century Prose*, vol. 26, no. 2, Fall 1999, 53.

obviously wrote much (masculine) but spoke more (feminine). Carlyle's enduring affection for Irving, plus the latter's innate qualities, no doubt preserved Irving from being labelled effeminate, as Carlyle had done with Southey.[192] However, it remains highly likely that Carlyle's view of speech as essentially feminine and mundane shaped his view of preaching as an unworthy activity and fuelled the "vanity" charges against Irving.

Whether vanity or optimism and religious heroics, it is highly likely that this quality did, in fact, take a battering through the years, reflected in comments that the later Irving was less "ebullient" than previously. But there is evidence that this characteristic (whichever adjective is chosen for it) substantially remained until the end of Irving's life. In fact, as Carlyle wrote his late-life memoir of Irving, he effectively undercut his own earlier charges of vanity. Irving was, he wrote, "very sanguine; I much the reverse; - and had his consciousness of powers, and his generous ambitions and fore-castings; never ungenerous, never ignoble: only an enemy could have called him 'vain;' but perhaps an enemy could, or at least would, and occasionally did".[193] Presumably, Carlyle had not reviewed his own correspondence for some time! Carlyle went on to say that what was sometimes mistaken for vanity in Irving was simply his delight in being "loved by others", and nothing more.[194] We may choose to give more credence to the observations of the young Carlyle of the 1820s and 1830s than to the nostalgic reminiscences of the mellowed octogenarian (who had clearly forgotten his own accusations of Irving's vanity), but it is still worth noting that Carlyle, himself, reframed his view of Irving from "vain" to "sanguine". Both Irving's Romanticism and his personality led him to propose and pursue grand visions: he was guilty of hyperbole and often lacked sympathy for those who did not share his vision. He was guilty of vanity primarily in the other sense of the word – that much of what he wanted to achieve eluded him – that his dreams were substantially unfulfilled, or in vain.

Key features of Carlyle's Romanticism have emerged indirectly through this chapter so far, as we have explored his religious beliefs and seen Irving through his eyes. In fact, Carlyle and Irving are good examples of Michael Ferber's Venn diagram approach to Romanticism, as discussed in chapter one.[195] It is their differences that first become apparent, with Carlyle's view emerging as essentially secular, whereas Irving's was deeply religious. To describe two such different men as essentially "Romantic" in outlook illustrates, simultaneously, the inclusiveness of the term and the reason why, as we discussed in the first chapter, the term has frustrated so many commentators. Let us begin with their common ground – the overlapping of their Venn diagram circles, as it were.

---

[192] Rennick, "Silence and Masculinity in Carlyle's *Reminiscences*", 55.
[193] Carlyle, *Reminiscences*, 230.
[194] Carlyle, *Reminiscences*, 230.
[195] See page 17.

As we have already seen in this chapter and chapter two, both men were on a quest to change society; both valued individual and collective experience and, therefore, history; both saw certain insightful individuals – the writer or the minister – as needing to convey truth unconstrained by hierarchies and institutions; both embraced the concept of struggle and its concomitant expression, alienation; both believed in God (despite their different interpretations) and the underlying spirituality of life; both rejected materialism, Utilitarianism and mechanistic rationalism as shallow and reductionistic.[196] These elements are all on the list of thoroughly Romantic characteristics (although not all of them, of course, were shared by *all* Romantics, hence the usefulness of the Venn diagram concept) and form the area of "overlap" in the Romanticisms of Irving and Carlyle. It is fair to say that both men lived consistently and with integrity by these principles. Carlyle regularly took whatever steps were necessary to pursue his dream of literary influence, including relocating to remote farmhouses for greater productivity and refusing well-paid, but distracting, work. Likewise, Irving doggedly pursued his goal of a greater outpouring of God's Spirit in the face of criticism and opposition. Both men accepted that lack of recognition (especially in the case of Carlyle's early years) and opposition (especially in the case of Irving's last years) were a necessary part of the struggle.

What is of added interest in comparing the Romanticisms of Carlyle and Irving is their shared upbringings in the same border region of southwest Scotland. The differences in their Romantic understandings are expressive of the flexibility and diversity of Scottish Romanticism, as explored in chapter one: it is striking that two boys, very close in age and growing up in the same rural border culture, could develop such different views within the Romantic spectrum. Although Carlyle's Romanticism was essentially secular, it was formed (as was Irving's, of course) within the context of Scottish Presbyterianism and it did not completely reject all aspects of this: concepts of God and Providence remained. At least one author has examined the way in which Carlyle kept alive and transmuted the Presbyterian ideal of preaching in his own literary style, citing his relationship with Irving as one stimulus for this.[197] Carlyle's individualised religious sensibility fed back into his Romanticism: the artist, in effect, mediated his insight into the Divine, becoming a secular priest for the masses.[198] While rejecting the prophetic as it occurred within Irving's congregation, Carlyle, nonetheless, saw himself in a priestly or prophetic role as writer.[199] Carlyle's God was circumscribed by the authority of human experience, while Irving's God was, by definition, unconstrained by, and always threatened to overwhelm, the sum total of human

[196] Kaplan, *Carlyle*, 386.
[197] Swaim, "'Our own Periodical Pulpit': Thomas Carlyle's Sermons", 142-145.
[198] Kaplan, *Carlyle*, 187. We will see in chapter six that Irving saw himself in a similar mediating role as "angel" to his congregation.
[199] Kaplan, *Carlyle*, 153.

experience. Thus, though they shared numerous key Romantic values, there was a fundamental difference between them over the issue of authority. Carlyle's journey in search of an authority that could replace the Bible took him first to imaginative literature, and, then, to history itself.[200] Carlyle could neither accept the authority that Irving assigned to scripture nor his continual expectation of being overwhelmed by the Divine sublime. It was this category of Irving's thought that Carlyle designated "vain speculation". And, as we have seen, this accusation of vain speculation or simply "vanity" was frequently brought by Carlyle against Irving. Here, we have an indication of where their Romantic Venn circles did not overlap: Irving's concept of transcendence, while embracing personal struggle, allowed for and expected a significant amount of divine initiative; Carlyle's did not. For Carlyle, the focus was firmly on the individual artist/priest to search, discover and deliver illumination to the masses.

There was another significant distinction between the thought of the two men: Carlyle was elitist and Irving was egalitarian, open to the work of the Spirit amongst both men and women, and all social levels. Carlyle's universe was hierarchical, and each individual had a place within it.[201] He believed that each person contained a tension between divine forces and their opposite: only in a select few "heroes" (for example, Jesus, Shakespeare, Cromwell) would the divinity win through to accomplish great deeds; for the remainder, the most that could be hoped is that they had the discernment to recognise the greatness of others.[202] Carlyle's "ethical existentialism" was only available to the few, and while he was deeply concerned for the plight of the poor in industrialised Britain to the point of seeing revolution as a purgative for corruption, he believed egalitarianism was an illusion and forced egalitarianism led to disaster.[203] People were "infinitely unequal"; the French guillotine hadn't led to emancipation of the foolish from the authority of the wise because this was a fundamental condition of human society.[204] Carlyle's underlying intellectual elitism helps explain some of his comments surveyed in this chapter, including his distinction between popularity and fame, and his easy dismissal of the "multitudes" in Irving's church as of little account: a widespread "popularity" must by definition be of little worth precisely because it derived from the acclaim of the undiscerning majority. It, also, sheds some light on his rejection of the charismata in Irving's congregation, which must have threatened Carlyle's view of himself as a member of a non-ecclesiastical prophetic elite. Irving's vision of transcendence was an encounter with the Divine sublime that elevated God's people to a new level of unity and engagement with the Divine purposes; Carlyle's transcendence was a moment in which there was no

---

200 Swaim, "'Our own Periodical Pulpit': Thomas Carlyle's Sermons", 153.
201 Kaplan, *Carlyle*, 357.
202 Kaplan, *Carlyle*, 264-265.
203 Kaplan, *Carlyle*, 185, 325-326, 329.
204 Clubbe, *Froude's Carlyle*, 332.

"humility and love, but a spiritual elevation from whence he [could] look down, with mingled compassion and scorn, on 'the welterings of my poor fellow-creatures, still stuck in that fatal element'".[205] Irving was pursuing a Romantic theophany that was epic enough in scope to absorb and defuse the associated but discordant Romantic themes of alienation, exile and isolation. Carlyle's Romantic epiphany, on the other hand, only accentuated these discordant themes and the gulf between artist/priest/visionary and the common crowds; he was advocating a benevolent but paternalistic aristocracy.[206]

Irving and Carlyle illustrate the diversity and vitality of British Romanticism, in general, and Scottish Romanticism, in particular. Our examination of Carlyle has shed light on his views of Irving and, by way of similarity and especially contrast, further illuminated Irving's own Romanticism. Some of these contrasts, such as Irving's fuller embrace of a more egalitarian perspective and his eagerness to encounter the Divine sublime, will emerge more clearly in the following chapter.

---

[205] Willey, *Nineteenth century studies*, 116.
[206] Willey, *Nineteenth century studies*, 129.

CHAPTER 6

The "Ravished Heart": Irving's Romantic Theology

In previous chapters we established that Irving's Romantic worldview was firmly in place before he left his native Scotland. As a result, although Coleridge influenced Irving's thought, Irving's Romanticism was flourishing before his first meeting with the poet-philosopher. This chapter further examines the Romantic nature of Irving's theology, focusing on Irving's three main distinctives – his millennialism, Christology, and pro-charismata stance. Our purpose here is not to defend Irving's orthodoxy, a task that has been ably addressed by others,[1] but to look beneath the surface of his theology for inherently Romantic characteristics. At the end of chapter one, we proposed a working description of Romanticism which included: awareness of the insufficiency of reason alone and a resulting elevation of imagination and emotion; the pursuit of a transcendent sublime; a view of history as potential revelation; and an embrace of individual struggle and quest towards a noble goal that often resulted in alienation and exile. Romanticism also attempted to circumvent any authority that stood in the way of its quest for transcendence. There are several aspects of Irving's thought that show Romantic tendencies, such as his British nationalism; however, this chapter is restricted to an examination of Irving's key theological distinctives. It is important to consider the aggregate of these qualities rather than each quality in isolation: individually, each quality is not exclusively Romantic, but, in combination, they produce a clear Romantic profile.

In our first chapter, we established that in many ways, Scotland was at the forefront of Romantic thought in Europe.[2] Therefore, we will begin with a brief consideration of Irving's time in Glasgow, serving under Thomas Chalmers. As one of Scotland's largest towns, Glasgow was prominent as a cosmopolitan urban centre. An indication of the impetus of urbanisation is that for the period

---

[1] As has been seen, Irving received most opposition for his Christology. A comprehensive defence of his orthodoxy on this question can be found in Dorries, *Edward Irving's Incarnational Christology* (Fairfax, VA: Xulon Press, 2002). Other defenders of Irving's Christological orthodoxy have included: K. Barth, *Church Dogmatics* I (2) (Edinburgh: T & T Clark, 1980), 154; C. Gunton, "Two Dogmas Revisited: Edward Irving's Christology" in *Scottish Journal of Theology*, 41 (3), 1988, 359-76; C. Gunton, *The Promise of Trinitarian Theology* (Edinburgh: T & T Clark, 1991), 99f; G. McFarlane, *Christ and the Spirit: the Doctrine of the Incarnation according to Edward Irving* (Carlisle, Cumbria: Paternoster Press, 1996).

[2] See page 17.

1755-1801 the seven largest towns in Scotland experienced an average growth rate of 222%.[3] Immediately after this half century of rapid growth, Glasgow, itself, nearly tripled in size between 1800 and 1830, a period that included Irving's residence there.[4] This rapid population growth, unsurprisingly, caused overcrowding; thousands were forced into the 700 rat-infested lodging houses in the city.[5]

Glasgow became a centre of enterprise and produced a new merchant class;[6] it was not only the most commercial city in Scotland, but, also, the most evangelical.[7] In addition it was a religious melting pot, exposing Irving not only to Chalmers's "aggressive" activism with its high levels of volunteer involvement in Sunday schools, prayer meetings and charitable groups; but, also, to Catholicism and dissent.[8] Estimates of the Irish population of Glasgow in these years are as high as 32%; most of these were Roman Catholic.[9] There was, also, the grinding poverty of groups like the weavers, who had prospered before industrialisation, but by the time Irving arrived in Glasgow were poor, embittered and demonstrated a pronounced tendency to sectarianism.[10]

Chalmers's famous social experiment to end pauperism in his parish began in 1819 (the same year Irving became his assistant) and he left St John's in 1823 (the year after Irving went to London) to take a position at St Andrew's University.[11] His experiment was to administer all poor-relief programs in Glasgow from the parish, and was based on the economic theories of Thomas Malthus; critics compared it to the utopian socialism of Robert Owen.[12] Yet, despite his scheme's basis in social theory, Chalmers's ministry had its own Romantic hue. The story of his conversion appealed to the imagination and his preaching often touched the emotions of his hearers in unexpected ways, and his scheme for Glasgow was touched with a transcendentalism absent from

---

[3] T.M. Devine & J.R. Young (eds), *Eighteenth Century Scotland: New Perspectives* (East Linton: Tuckwell Press, 1999), 183.

[4] C.G. Brown, *Religion and Society in Scotland since 1707* (Edinburgh: Edinburgh University Press, 1997), 96.

[5] A. Gibb, *Glasgow: the Making of a City* (London: Croom Helm, 1983), 107.

[6] A.L. Drummond & J. Bulloch, *The Scottish Church, 1688-1843: the Age of the Moderates* (Edinburgh: The St Andrew Press, 1981), 118, 120.

[7] N.C. Landsman, "Liberty, piety and patronage: the Social Context of contested clerical calls in Eighteenth-century Glasgow" in A. Hook & R.B. Sher (eds), *The Glasgow Enlightenment* (East Linton, Scotland: Tuckwell Press, 1995), 215.

[8] Brown, *Religion and society in Scotland*, 104-105.

[9] W. Knox, *Industrial Nation: Work, Culture and Society in Scotland, 1800-present* (Edinburgh: Edinburgh University Press, 1999), 37. Knox's estimate is that half of this 32% had been born in Ireland; the other half were of Irish extraction.

[10] Brown, *Religion and Society in Scotland*, 115; Drummond & Bulloch, *The Scottish Church, 1688-1843*, 143-144.

[11] Drummond & Bulloch, *The Scottish Church, 1688-1843*, 175.

[12] S.J. Brown, *Thomas Chalmers and the Godly Commonwealth in Scotland* (Oxford: Oxford University Press), 116, 122.

Owen's socialism.[13] Hazlitt described Chalmers as pursuing "visionary reasoning" and as "a Highland seer".[14] Despite this Romantic tinge, there is little evidence that Irving's own Romanticism drew from Chalmers in any significant way, except, perhaps, to draw the conclusion that such an ambitious plan was not, in fact, ambitious enough. As Irving's responsibilities in Glasgow included intense pastoral visitation, he came face-to-face with the poverty of the Glasgow wynds far more regularly than Chalmers. There is evidence that Irving was not overly hopeful about the eventual success of Chalmers's experiment. At a point where he had visited some three hundred families within the parish, Irving wrote to his brother-in-law, "If I should report from my daily ministrations among the poorest class and the worst reported-of class of our population, I should deliver an opinion so unfavourable as it would be hardly safe for myself to deliver, lest I should be held a *radical* likewise."[15] Irving was clearly aligning himself with the more revolutionary elements within St John's parish, a stance that implies pessimism about the potential for gradual improvement, such as Chalmers envisaged. It is, therefore, likely that Irving, being presented daily with the complexity of "an industrial and competitive society", was unable to ignore the challenges which eventually overwhelmed Chalmers's plan.[16] There is every indication, then, that Irving's three years in Glasgow did not simply represent an apprenticeship under Chalmers and an increasing desire for his own ministry, but that the cosmopolitan nature of the city had a formative effect on a young man still in his twenties. The harsh reality of Glasgow's poverty may have convinced Irving that the self-seeking competitiveness of urban life was not to be routed by social and economic theory, and that the cure was far more likely to be found through a more profound Christianity that touched the heart. In Thomas Chalmers, Irving had encountered the most famous Church of Scotland evangelical of the day in the leading city of Scottish evangelicalism, but he was "unsatisfied by [Chalmers's] social ideals" and Scottish evangelicalism "failed to appeal to him. He felt that in Scotland there was too much dull formalism, timid orthodoxy, and unworthy compromise".[17]

---

[13] Brown, *Thomas Chalmers and the Godly Commonwealth*, 58, 87, 150.

[14] W. Hazlitt, *Collected Works of William Hazlitt*, vol. iv, 229 quoted in Brown, *Thomas Chalmers*, 109.

[15] Irving to Mr. Fergusson, quoted in M. Oliphant, *The Life of Edward Irving* (London: Hurst and Blackett, n.d. 5th edition), 54. Emphasis original. No date is given for this letter.

[16] Drummond & Bulloch, *The Scottish Church, 1688-1843*, 176. When Chalmers left St John's, he felt his system was flourishing, but it came to an end in 1837.

[17] A.L. Drummond, *Edward Irving and his Circle, including some consideration of the 'Tongues' Movement in the light of Modern Psychology* (London: James Clarke, 1934), 41.

It is likely that Irving's Glaswegian experience contributed to his increasing criticism of the contemporary Church he would later rail against as too pragmatic and prudent.

> This is the age of expediency, both in the Church and out of the Church, and all institutions are modelled upon the principles of expediency, and carried into effect by the rules of prudence. I remember, in this metropolis, to have heard it uttered with great applause in a public meeting, where the heads and leaders of the religious world were present, "If I were asked what was the first qualification for a missionary, I would say. Prudence; and what the second ? Prudence; and what the third? still I would answer. Prudence." I trembled while I heard, not with indignation but with horror and apprehension, what the end would be of a spirit which I have since found to be the presiding genius of our activity, the ruler of the ascendant.[18]

While this criticism was yet in the future, Irving's "Farewell Address" to the congregation at St John's, nevertheless, exhorted a more adventurous Christianity and showed some ambivalence about Chalmers's scheme. In such a setting, overt criticism would have been churlish, yet Irving, certainly, modified his congratulations to the parish on what had been achieved, by admitting that to him the plan seemed a "forlorn hope".[19] Glasgow helped convince Irving that his hunger for a revitalised Christianity could not be fully satisfied by the best efforts of contemporary evangelicalism, neither were the answers to humanity's problems to be found in the best "rational" approaches of the economists and politicians. Irving left Glasgow with first-hand evidence that confirmed his own Romantic inclinations: rationalism alone was not enough; access to the human heart was essential. Irving appeared instinctively to realise that "the inherited pieties and integrative myths seemed no longer adequate to hold civilization together".[20] This realisation was to undergird further his developing Romantic position.

Irving probably, also, extrapolated from his Glasgow experience the relative ineffectiveness of the Church of Scotland in its current form. "The Church of Scotland, inhibited by an establishment which had been intended to strengthen her, and saddled with the Westminster Confession as a doctrinal standard, could do little either to found new congregations or to enter new fields of thought."[21] These words, written by authors who were, certainly, not thorough-going Irving supporters, accurately reflect his view: later in this chapter we will see evidence that Irving saw the Westminster Confession as "inhibiting". For someone like Irving, whose earliest surviving writings indicate a determination to live an

[18] Irving, *Missionaries after the Apostolical school*, in *CW1*, 430-431.
[19] Irving, "Farewell discourse at St John's Glasgow" in *CW3*, 359-360.
[20] M.H. Abrams, *Natural Supernaturalism: Tradition and Revolution in Romantic Literature* (New York: W.W. Norton & Co., 1971), 293.
[21] Drummond & Bulloch, *The Scottish Church, 1688-1843*, 142.

adventurous life for God, the Glasgow-fuelled realisation that the Church he served was ineffective in an urban environment would have been galling. Entering "new fields of thought" and breaking through to more vital Christian living were central to Irving's thinking; therefore, the combination of Glasgow's industrial poverty, religious diversity, and the Church of Scotland's fading grip on the loyalty of the people, must have both frustrated and motivated him. Glasgow would only have intensified Irving's desire for the more adventurous and transcendent Christian vision he pursued in his later years. In sum, Irving's Glasgow experience provided an underwhelming exposure to the best that contemporary Scottish evangelicalism and rationalism could offer, and, thereby, further entrenched the Romantic worldview of his youth and stirred Romantic hopes for the future.

By the end of his time in Glasgow, therefore, Irving had already moved to a position where he was to some degree distancing himself from Church of Scotland evangelicalism. This leads to the question of whether Irving should be considered an evangelical at all, even though most writers have described Irving in this way with few qualms.[22] When Irving is held up against the "Bebbington quadrilateral" definition of an evangelical, he aligns closely with biblicism, and certainly activism, but he is less conversionist than most evangelicals, and far less crucicentric.[23] The reasons for this will emerge through this chapter, especially as we consider Irving's Christology. The aspects of Irving's theology that fail to fit neatly within an evangelical framework resonate more strongly with other strands of contemporary churchmanship: we will explore this towards the end of this chapter.

In earlier chapters we noted that contemporary scholarship has seen Irving as a Romantic figure,[24] that Coleridge and Carlyle saw him engaging in noble battle for a worthy cause;[25] another described Irving as "Herculean";[26] another

---

[22] For example, R. Brown, "Victorian Anglican Evangelicalism : the radical legacy of Edward Irving" in *Journal of Ecclesiastical History*, Vol. 58, No. 4, October 2007, 675-704; D. Bebbington, "Evangelical Christianity and Romanticism", *Crux*, March 1990, Vol. XXVI, No. 1, 10.

[23] The Bebbington definition derives from his *Evangelicalism in Modern Britain: a history from the 1730s to the 1980s* (London: Unwin Hyman, 1989), 2-3. For evidence that this has become the standard definition in the years since see T. Larsen, "The reception given *Evangelicalism in Modern Britain* since its publication in 1989" in M.A.G. Haykin & K.J. Stewart (eds), *The Emergence of Evangelicalism: Exploring Historical Continuities* (Nottingham: Apollos, 2008), 25.

[24] For example, J.J. Nantomah, *Jesus the God-man: the Doctrine of the Incarnation in Edward Irving in the Light of the Teaching of the Church Fathers and its Relevance for a Twentieth Century African Context* (University of Aberdeen, PhD thesis, 1982), 33.

[25] Pages 97, 144.

[26] G. Gilfillan, *A First Gallery of Literary Portraits* (Edinburgh: James Hogg, 1851), 132.

described him as a "Titan among Titans".[27] However complimentary these Greco-Roman allusions may be, they are less appropriate (and more grandiose) than others, equally complimentary, but more related to Irving's Scottish context. Some years after Irving's 1834 death, Horatius Bonar, fellow Scot and later Moderator of the Church of Scotland, wrote a preface to the 1850 edition of Irving's *The Last Days*. Bonar, sixteen years Irving's junior and an active participant in the Free Church of Scotland, had been profoundly affected as a youth by Irving's preaching on prophecy.[28] His preface firmly placed Irving within a Scottish Romantic context.

> Let us accept Mr Irving as the representative of a former time, and listen to him as he testifies of days gone by, and compares the sons with the fathers of the land. In the days of Wallace and Bruce, he would have wielded no second sword for Scotland in her battle for freedom; in the days of Knox, he would have taken the foremost rank by the side of him who "never feared the face of clay;" in the days of the Covenant, he would have borne aloft the standard with no feeble arm or heart; in the days of Scotland's dark defection from the truth, he would have nobly witnessed for the gospel by the side of Boston and his testifying band: and now, as one who has identified himself with every noble or holy scene in Scottish story ; as one who has been drinking from boyhood at all her ancient wells, he comes before us to give utterance to his feelings at the sight of the age on which he has fallen.[29]

Bonar saw Irving as epitomising the spirit of Scotland, having deeply and reverently absorbed its traditions. Once more, we see the image of battle associated with Irving, and Bonar saw him fighting courageously for freedom. Bonar instinctively aligned Irving with some of the most Romantic figures in Scotland's history in the context of introducing a work of eschatology. Bonar saw Irving as heir to the vigorous Protestantism of Knox and the Covenanters, as well as the heroism of Wallace and Bruce. We have already noted, in various ways, that Irving believed living an adventurous life for God was the highest possible calling; Bonar was obviously convinced that Irving had lived up to his own high standards. Bonar's observations ground Irving firmly in the Romantic tradition and emphasise the Scottish elements: we see here the Romantic themes of quest/battle; an organic view of history and nationalism; and a prophetic transcendence. The comparison with Knox surfaced again with one

---

[27] George Gilfillan quoted in R. Cochrane, *Teachers and Preachers of Recent Times* (Edinburgh: W.P. Nimmo, Hay, & Mitchell, 1886), 187. Original reference not given.
[28] J.S. Andrews, "Horatius Bonar", in N. Cameron (ed.), *Dictionary of Scottish Church History and Theology* (Downer's Grove, Ill: IVP, 1993), 84. This was Irving's preaching in Edinburgh in the late 1820s.
[29] H. Bonar, preface to E. Irving, *The Last Days: a Discourse of the evil character of these our times: proving them to be the 'Perilous Times' of the 'Last Days'* (London: James Nisbet, 1850), xx-xxi.

contemporary who wrote of Irving that "his pulpit became a throne of power, reminding you of what Knox's was in Edinburgh in the sixteenth century. Not since that lion-hearted man of God had thundered to nobles and maids of honour, to senators and queens, had any preacher in Britain such an audience to command and such power to command it as Irving."[30] The following description of Irving's preaching captured some of his central concerns.

> The sermon is upon the days of the Puritans and the Covenanters, and his blood boils as he describes the earnest spirit of their times. He fights over again the battles of Drumclog and Bothwell; he paints the dark muirlands, whither the woman of the Church retired for a season to be nourished with blood; and you seem to be listening to that wild eloquence which pealed through the wilderness and shook the throne of Charles II.[31]

Here, we see Irving's concern for the church, his native land, his invocation to his contemporaries to elevate their spiritual passion to that of nobler days, and his obvious conviction that preaching should be both poetic and dramatic. Irving, also, prized that part of his Calvinist heritage that tended to eschew existing authority structures and erastian compromise. In both his own writings and the eyes of his contemporaries, Irving not only had a thoroughly Romantic and distinctively Scottish worldview; he personified it.

In chapter four, we drew from Irving's farewell address to St John's Glasgow to demonstrate his early Romanticism. In *Oracles*, Irving's first work written since his 1822 arrival in London, we see his frustration with what he considered to be the current lack of engagement of Christians with God's voice in scripture.

> Who feels the sublime dignity there is in a saying fresh descended from the porch of heaven? Who feels the awful weight there is in the least iota that hath dropped from the lips of God? Who feels the thrilling fear or trembling hope there is in words whereon the eternal destinies of himself do hang? Who feels the swelling tide of gratitude within his breast, for redemption and salvation coming, instead of flat despair and everlasting retribution? Finally, who, in perusing the word of God, is captivated through all his faculties, and transported through all his emotions, and through all his energies of action wound up?[32]

This flurry of rhetorical questions contains obvious Romantic motifs: here is the desire to encounter the Divine sublime, which is simultaneously thrilling

---

[30] George Gilfillan quoted in R. Cochrane, *Teachers and Preachers*, 184. Original reference not given.

[31] Cochrane, *Teachers and Preachers*, 188. Original reference not given.

[32] E. Irving, *For the Oracles of God, four Orations, for Judgment to come, an Argument in nine parts* (New York: S. Marks, 1825), 15.

and terrifying; the conviction that emotion and experience should be at the core of Christian life (emphasised by the repetition of "feel"); and that the result should be a revelatory transformation of the believer for action. It is worth noting that this passage was only a few pages into the book: these are not conclusions that Irving debated at length, but convictions that he saw as so axiomatic that they needed no defence; they were part of the already well-developed Romanticism he brought with him to London. While Irving's implied answer to each of his rhetorical questions was "very few", his optimism that all his readers should *want* to feel this way was unbounded. Later in the same work, Irving indicated that he was no enemy of reason. "That our religion doth not denounce the rational or intellectual man, but addeth thereto the spiritual man, and that the latter flourishes the more nobly under the fostering hand of the former."[33] In the preface to the third edition of this work, Irving extolled his literary and theological models from the sixteenth and seventeenth centuries adding, "Their books were to me like a concert of every sweet instrument of the soul, and heart, and strength, and mind. They seemed to think, and feel, and imagine, and reason, all at once; and the result is, to take the whole man captive in the chains of sweetest persuasion."[34] Irving found in these earlier writers a holistic approach he felt had been largely lost to the Utilitarianism of his own day. Reason was essential, but never sufficient without the feelings and the imagination: it was a standard Romantic position.

Oracles was published at the beginning of 1823, before Irving's first meeting with Coleridge, thereby, excluding any personal Coleridgean influence.[35] There is little evidence that Irving was familiar with Coleridge's writing at this date.[36] The *Farewell Address* and *Oracles* gave voice to a Romanticism that was already deeply lodged in Irving in Scotland, but was heightened, no doubt, by his sudden translation to the wider London stage. It was from within the context of this deeply Romantic vision of the Christian life that Edward Irving's theology would develop, both fruitfully and controversially, from the mid-1820s until his death in 1834. Chapter seven will focus on the crises in Irving's ministerial career so here, although we will begin with a consideration of Irving's millennialism, we will concentrate more on the two distinctives that precipitated the later crises, that is, Irving's Christology and his embrace of the charismata.

---

[33] E. Irving, *For Judgment to come*, 287.

[34] Irving, *Oracles*, xvi.

[35] While I have been unable to ascertain the exact month of first publication, both Oliphant, *Irving*, 83 and A. Dallimore, *The Life of Edward Irving: the Fore-runner of the Charismatic Movement* (Edinburgh: Banner of Truth, 1983), 39, indicate it was at the beginning of the year, and Irving first met Coleridge in July.

[36] In a conversation about poetry at Basil Montagu's in May 1823, Irving praised Wordsworth's poetry, but did not mention Coleridge. T. Sadler (ed.), *Diary, Reminiscences, and Correspondence of Henry Crabb Robinson*, vol. 2 (London: Macmillan & Co, 1869), 253.

It is worth noting at the beginning that millennialism and Romanticism were comfortable co-travellers. In chapter two, we saw that the holding of millennial views (secular or religious) was no idiosyncrasy in the Romantic age. This extended easily into the Christian context with examples readily to hand from evangelicalism and Irving's native Scotland.[37] In fact, one writer has pointed out that in England, as early as the seventeenth century, these views attained a certain "respectability" that they lacked elsewhere, and that this respectability continued at least until the end of the eighteenth century.[38] The age of the French Revolution and Napoleon (often seen as a revivified Rome) also motivated many to expect the end of the existing world order through divine, social, or revolutionary means, with the hope of a new golden age to follow.[39] Inherently teleological, millennialism led Irving to apply a "more developmental and progressive interpretation" to church life and history, in line with the Romantic view of history as organic.[40] After the French Revolution, Romantics tended to withdraw from violence and political agitation to pursue inner (r)evolution, a transformation that could be achieved organically through imagination and the inner life.[41] For Romantic pre-millennialists like Irving, a certain view of history naturally followed: it was the vehicle through which God pursued his purposes and the study of history was following God's footsteps towards the End. Romanticism, like millennialism, focused on process, struggle, and dynamic movement towards transcendent goals. The themes of noble struggle, visionary goals, and radical transformation of individuals and/or society united Romantics and millennialists against the mundane forces of Utilitarianism, materialism and expediency. In our first chapter we noted Bebbington's comment that expectations of the Second

---

[37] As an example, G.T. Noel was an evangelical who took a premillennial stance and also believed Christ would return in the 1860s. G.T. Noel, *A Brief Inquiry into the Prospects of the Church of Christ in connexion with the Second Advent of our Lord Jesus Christ* (London, 1828), 34-35, 240-252, quoted in P. Meldrum, *Conscience and Compromise: Forgotten Evangelicals of Nineteenth-century Scotland* (Carlisle: Paternoster, 2006), 145. See, also, the example of the Buchanites in J. Soderstrom, "Escaping the common lot: a Buchanite perspective of the Millennium" in R.N. Swanson (ed.), *The Use and Abuse of Time in Christian History* (Woodbridge, Suffolk: Ecclesiastic History Society, 2002), 243-254 and G. Carter, *Anglican Evangelicals: Protestant Secessions from the via media, c.1800-1850* (Oxford: Oxford University Press, 2001), 190-192 for premillennialism amongst Anglican evangelicals.

[38] C. Garrett, *Respectable Folly: Millenarians and the French Revolution in France and England* (Baltimore: Johns Hopkins University Press, 1975), 121-122, 125-143, 145. See, also, J. Symonds, *Thomas Brown and the Angels: a study in Enthusiasm* (London: Hutchinson & Co., 1961), 13-47

[39] For additional context to English millennialism of the period, see C.D.A. Leighton, "Antichrist's revolution: some Anglican Apocalypticists in the age of the French wars", *Journal of Religious History*, xxiv, 2, June 2000, 125-142; Oliver, *Prophets and Millennialists*, 26.

[40] McFarlane, *Christ and the Spirit*, 75.

[41] Abrams, *Natural Supernaturalism*, 65-66.

Advent became "a symptom of Romanticism".[42] While it was possible for one to have been a Romantic without demonstrating millennialist tendencies, it was impossible to have been a millennialist in this period without demonstrating Romantic characteristics.

Millennialism painted in broad strokes and pondered the fate of nations, and Irving had particular views of the role of Britain (as will be seen below) in his eschatology. Yet, despite his overall respect for Britain and its place in God's purposes, Irving was concerned that Scottish identity be preserved at all costs and not diluted. As a recent article has noted, Irving idealised an homogenised Scotland into a Presbyterian nation blessed by God with certain attributes and consequent responsibilities; in order to facilitate this view, he blended folklore, myth and church history to serve his purposes. Scotland was an elect country within an elect nation.[43] The national identity of Scotland had been forged in and through the Reformation, which Irving did not see as linked to one particular date, but extending forwards from the activities of John Knox through the struggles of the Covenanters, and, also, backwards to the medieval Celtic church.[44] Here, Irving, clearly, demonstrated the Romantic view of history as both revelatory and organic.

Irving's millennialism became a matter of public record before his Christology gained public attention and before he had a great interest in charismatic gifts. In chapter three, we noted that several interpreters emphasised the influence of Hatley Frere on Irving's millennialism, implying that he was the cause of it.[45] However, Irving's millennial interests existed before his meeting with Frere in early 1825. Evidence for this is to be found in 1823 in *Oracles*, where after a dramatic depiction of the life to come, Irving held forth the "expectation of heaven" as a vial of transformation:[46] he encouraged his readers to imagine the *eschaton* to revitalise their religious passion. Here, Irving was offering believers Romantic transcendence via eschatology. As Irving began the second part of this book, "For judgment to come", he clearly indicated that he felt the church had erred in basing its appeals to people on reason alone: he was not going to abandon reason but in addition appeal to imagination and the affections.[47] This is a classic Romantic response to the insufficiency of reason alone. Later in the same work, he argued that "the rewards of eternity" were an effective stimulus to Christian

---

[42] Page 10. Bebbington, *Evangelicalism in modern Britain*, 85.

[43] L. Upton, "'Our Mother and our Country': the Integration of Religious and National Identity in the thought of Edward Irving (1792-1834)" in R. Pope (ed.), *Religion and National Identity: Wales and Scotland c. 1700-2000* (Cardiff: University of Wales Press, 2001), 253-257.

[44] L. Upton, 'Our Mother and our Country', 248-250.

[45] Page 64. For an example, see Dallimore, *Irving*, 58-59.

[46] *Oracles*, 75-76, 78.

[47] *For Judgment to Come*, 87-88.

"enthusiasm" to pursue holiness, succeeding where all else may fail.[48] Indeed, Irving believed that his age needed a revival of the apostolic emphasis on the proximity of the Second Coming.[49] He, also, offered a lengthy description of the wonders of life in the millennial age.[50] So Irving's millennialism was, at least, loosely in place and serving a Romantic purpose before his first meeting with Frere. Nevertheless, there is no doubt that Frere had a significant influence, and Irving's first major publication after their meeting both elaborated on this theme and acknowledged Frere's input.[51]

Oliver has argued that Irving became a millennialist "by the corpse of his infant son".[52] Irving's millennialism, however, pre-dated his son's October 1825 death. As we have just seen, the second part of Irving's 1823 publication was already moving in this direction and this interest was strengthened as a result of his *early* 1825 meeting with Hatley Frere.[53] Although Irving's first major work on the topic wasn't published until the year after his son's death, it was an extension of ideas already preached to the Continental Missionary Association in the spring of 1825.[54] *Contra* Oliver, the death of his first-born child deepened Irving's millennialism but it didn't instigate it.

Irving's first full publication on eschatological issues was in 1826: *Babylon and Infidelity Foredoomed of God: a Discourse on the Prophecies of Daniel and the Apocalypse which relate to these latter times, and until the Second Advent.*[55] Unsurprisingly, the French Revolution and Napoleon loomed large in Irving's interpretive scheme: he interpreted the 1260 days/years of Revelation 12 beginning with the decrees of Justinian in the mid-sixth century and ending at the beginning of the French Revolution.[56] Like many Protestants of his day, Irving believed the papal power was Satan's "master-piece"; fewer were bold

[48] *For Judgment to Come*, 166.
[49] *For Judgment to Come*, 242-244
[50] *For Judgment to Come*, 288-293
[51] Irving's *Babylon and Infidelity Foredoomed of God: a Discourse on the Prophecies of Daniel and the Apocalypse, which relate to these latter times, and until the Second Advent* first appeared as a two-volume edition in 1826. We will be quoting from the single volume edition of 1828.
[52] W.H. Oliver, *Prophets and Millennialists: the uses of Biblical Prophecy in England from the 1790s to the 1840s* (Auckland: Auckland University Press, 1978), 100-101. The son referred to is the first-born child, Edward Jr.
[53] E. Irving, *Oracles of God, four Orations, for Judgment to come, an Argument in nine parts* (London: T. Hamilton, 1823).
[54] E. Irving, *Babylon and Infidelity Foredoomed of God: a Discourse on the Prophecies of Daniel and the Apocalypse, which relate to these latter times, and until the Second Advent* (Glasgow: Chalmers & Collins, 1826); Oliphant, *Irving*, 106; Drummond, *Irving and his Circle*, 129.
[55] We will be referring to the second edition, published in 1828 by Chalmers and Collins in Glasgow. Another 1828 edition issued in Philadelphia was a 118 page condensation.
[56] Irving, *Babylon and Infidelity Foredoomed of God*, 96.

enough to estimate, as Irving did, the date of Christ's return around 1867-8.[57] Nevertheless, although Irving proposed this date, there is every indication that he was not rigid about it. Less than three years after giving the 1867-8 date for Christ's return, Irving wrote that it was best "not to prognosticate concerning time and place", and indicated that there could be numerous more generations before Christ's return.[58] However, Islam was about to come to an end, and Britain represented the 144,000 virgins of Revelation 14 because it was the only nation whose Churches retained biblical purity.[59] As Irving freely acknowledged, most of his interpretation was not original; he was indebted to Frere.[60]

Despite this debt, Irving's own motivations and concerns can be clearly seen in this volume. Irving argued that God revealed things to his people through prophecy "to reward the faith of his servants, to refresh the drooping spirit of his Church" so that men "might both know and feel, that the destinies of men and of kingdoms are in the hand of the Lord".[61] To Irving, prophecy was not simply about gazing idly at the future, nor was it a cheap and sensational entertainment; it had a transformational goal in the present to renew and revitalise the Church and to inspire confidence in God's overarching care, regardless of immediate circumstances. To encounter prophecy was to encounter, and be transformed by, the Divine sublime. This was not the work of rational "knowing" alone; it was, also, necessary to "feel" the conviction and weight of these issues. In Irving's hands, prophecy and millennialism became Romantic pastoral-care tools. Yet, it was, also, more complex than this, for although there were times of refreshment in these vistas which would eventually result in Christ's "reign of righteousness and peace", nevertheless all nations would experience "the terrible day of wrath".[62] The theophany to come contained both joy and awe-ful fear. The Second Coming was the greatest possible encounter with the Divine sublime because it was global and permanent. In the meantime, the contemplation and expectation of this event was supposed to trigger enough moments of epiphany in believers' lives to effect lasting transformation.

The year after *Babylon* appeared, Irving published his translation of *Ben-Ezra*, with his own lengthy preface. This work (which we have examined through Coleridge's marginalia in chapter four) was, also, eschatological in nature. Intriguingly, for his later embrace of the charismata, and several years

---

[57] For the surrounding anti-Catholic climate see J. Wolffe, *The Protestant Crusade in Great Britain, 1829-1860* (Oxford: Clarendon Press, 1991), 1-29; Irving, *Babylon and Infidelity Foredoomed of God*, 126, 141.

[58] G. Carlyle (ed.), *The Prophetical Works of Edward Irving*, vol. 1, (London: Alexander Strahan, 1867), x, 79.

[59] Irving, *Babylon and Infidelity Foredoomed of God*, 446, 512-513.

[60] Irving, *Babylon and Infidelity Foredoomed of God*, iii, 268 footnote.

[61] Irving, *Babylon and Infidelity Foredoomed of God*, 20, 21.

[62] Irving, *Babylon and Infidelity Foredoomed of God*, 550, 565.

before the initial charismatic events in Scotland, Irving predicted that the *parousia* would be preceded by a "latter rain" spiritual outpouring including "mighty and miraculous signs".[63] Thus, Irving's millennialism helped set a context for a subsequent favourable interpretation of the charismata, while the eventual arrival of the charismata naturally fed back into and intensified his millennialism.

In his preface to *Ben-Ezra*, Irving pictured the church as struggling faithfully to testify to righteousness throughout history, enduring suffering on the journey.[64] This highlighted another important Romantic theme: history was both organic and a potential source of revelation. This can be clearly seen in Irving's 1831 exposition of the book of Revelation in which he saw the seven churches as representing not only physical churches of the first century but, also, different ages of the church throughout history.[65] A sensitive reading of Revelation not only gave insight into the past ages, but, also, glimpses of the future; however, history was an essential extra lens to accompany the scriptural text. History was the stage upon which the drama played out, and although Irving's organic view of history can be clearly seen in his writing on the Apocalypse, it is, also, evident in most of his other writings.[66]

In Irving's thought, the church, itself, was cast as a Romantic hero, facing overwhelming physical and spiritual odds in an epic quest through the centuries. When the church faltered in this quest, Irving offered a diagnosis.

> And let me tell the church, that, because the resurrection of the saints at Christ's coming, and their reign with him, are so seldom set before the church, it cometh to pass that we have such shrinking from posts of danger, such fencing and fitting out of our missionaries, such shrieking out if any evil befall them, instead of that carelessness to answer the matter, that utter indifference to the fire, that rushing to marytrdom, [sic] and committing ourselves to all moral wilds and savage wildernesses, which characterised the first ages of the church.[67]

In neglecting the *parousia* and the saints' millennial reign with Christ, the church had alienated itself from a major source of courageous faith. Romanticism oozes from these lines as warrior missionaries charge into battle in a spiritual and physical wilderness in the service of a higher and greater

[63] Irving, preface to *Ben-ezra*, vol. 1, v.
[64] Irving, preface to *Ben-ezra*, vol. 1, x.
[65] The 1831 work was reprinted as G. Carlyle (ed.), *The Prophetical Works of Edward Irving*, 2 vols. (London: Alexander Strahan, 1867, 1870). For examples of Irving's view of history, cf. vol. 1, 654; vol. 2, 131, 656-671.
[66] For example, when Irving defended his Christology and the charismata, he, inevitably, invoked historical arguments, not simply as isolated illustrations, but in a narrative and organic way.
[67] Irving, preface to *Ben-ezra*, lix.

cause. There is no doubt that Irving applied these thoughts to himself, as, grieving and angered by the death of his young son, he pictured himself in a personal battle against Satan.[68] In doing so, he graphically demonstrated his belief that the *eschaton* should inform all aspects of life's struggles. Our current lives can neither be properly understood nor endured except from the perspective of the millennium. But Irving's concept of endurance was never qualified by the adjective "stoic"; he consistently thought of endurance in terms of warfare.

This *Ben-Ezra* passage, also, dovetailed with Irving's controversial spurning of prudence in his earlier address to the London Missionary Society, referred to in chapter two.

> [In the eleventh chapter of Hebrews] faith is there defined [as] the substance of things hoped for, the evidence of things not seen, whereas *prudence* or *expediency* is the substance of things present, the evidence of things seen. So that faith and prudence are opposite poles in the soul, the one attracting to it all things spiritual and divine, the other all things sensual and earthy.... This evil bent of prudence to become the death of all ideal and invisible things, whether poetry, sentiment, heroism, disinterestedness, or faith, it is the great prerogative of religious faith to withstand, because religious faith is the only form of the *ideal* which hath the assurance from heaven of a present blessing and an everlasting reward.[69]

Far from seeing prudence as a virtue, as did many of his contemporary churchmen, Irving identified it with sensuality and evil, in opposition to faith. The inbuilt caution of the majority was never going to be the catalyst to a vibrant Christianity: prudence was never a pathway to transcendence. Later in the work he portrayed God as emptying missionaries of their dependence on "human strength and prudence", as a necessary pre-requisite for filling them "with the Spirit of wisdom and truth".[70] Prudence threatened pneumatology. Irving's ideal missionaries were to head out with minimal care for security and provision, with Matthew 10:5-42 acting as permanent guidelines. As Bebbington has pointed out, Irving's stance challenged existing missiological understandings and left an enduring legacy through the nineteenth century.[71] Anticipating the charge of presumption, Irving neatly reversed it, arguing that prudence itself was presumption, if it attempted to set aside the instructions of Christ and rely on natural resources.

---

[68] Irving, preface to *Ben-ezra*, clxxii-clxxiii.

[69] E. Irving, *For Missionaries after the Apostolical School: a Series of Orations, in four parts* (London: Hamilton, Adams & Co, 1825. Orig. 1824), xv-xvi. Emphases original.

[70] Irving, *For Missionaries after the Apostolical School*, 27.

[71] D.W. Bebbington, *The Dominance of Evangelicalism: the Age of Spurgeon and Moody* (Downers Grove, Ill: Intervarsity Press, 2005), 185.

> Therefore, let no man nor body of men, no Christian nor society of Christians, nor the whole visible Church, in their presumption, dare to say, these instructions of Christ to the messengers of the kingdom are now inapplicable, are Utopian, are extreme, are to be cautiously interpreted, and prudently carried into effect. For if these be cast aside, I, for one, see not upon what scriptural basis a Missionary Society resteth.[72]

Irving not only objected to the presumption of prudence in matters of earthly resources, but, also, saw presumption wherever missionaries were subject to earthly direction: "It is a presumption hardly short of Papal, to command them. They are not Missionaries when they are commanded. They are creatures of the power that commandeth them."[73] The underlying common denominator in these two areas, and the cause of Irving's anti-prudence polemic, was that in both cases an earthly mediator is established in God's place: human resources and human guidance replaced God's provision and divine guidance. In the context of the rapidly approaching Second Coming, human mediators were not only bordering on the blasphemous, they were, also, a complete waste of time. In addition, Irving believed this stance overlooked the full range of available spiritual resources. Why wait for a message from a distant committee when direct contact with the divine was possible? When contact with the sublime is within reach, why bother with bureaucracy? Immanence was not a new concept in Christian theology, but for Irving it was less a subject for quiet contemplation than, perhaps paradoxically, a means to transcendence. Here, we have another example where Irving was eager to side-step existing authority structures in order to encounter the Divine.

There was another problem with prudence: for those about to do battle, it was often a synonym for cowardice. Irving's missionaries were not contemplatives, but warriors, and for warriors prudence was an oft-dispensed-with quality.

> When the Missionaries, the forlorn hope of our warfare, issue from the gate of our camp, let us cheer them with songs of ancient chivalry, with examples of ancient victory; let the daughter of Zion brace the heart of her warlike sons, with her heaven-derived minstrelsy; that they may go forth in the spirit of the mighty men of old, and scale the steep which frowneth upon flesh and blood, and plant the good standard of the faith upon the loftiest battlement of the enemy's strongest hold,—which strong and lofty though it be, is not more strong than the strength of our God, nor more lofty than the flights of our faith;—which strong and lofty though it be, is permitted thus high to rise and thus sternly to frown, only that it may prove the good temper of the warrior's soul, and prove before the high witnesses of the contest, how humanity in the weakest of Christ's servants, is stronger than death and the grave, than

[72] Irving, *For Missionaries after the Apostolical School*, 78-79.
[73] Irving, *For Missionaries after the Apostolical School*, 102.

> earth and hell, and can triumph over them, and lead them captives, as did the great founder and everlasting captain of the Missionary work.[74]

What gave Irving the confidence to encourage missionaries to hurl themselves with such careless bravado against the spiritual and physical circumstances opposing them? It was the inferences he drew for our humanity, via his Christology. If "humanity in the weakest of Christ's servants, is stronger than death and the grave, than earth and hell, and can triumph over them", it is so only because Christ embraced humanity in the fullest sense, and in doing so, defeated all enemies. Christ's victory ensures our victory and careless bravado is, thereby, not only justified, it is the natural and expected response of the faithful. When Christ has won such a victory, prudence has no place; it is tantamount to denying Christ's victory. With the present age sandwiched between the victory of Christ and his triumphal return, contemplation of the millennium invoked Romantic transcendence and a courageous church.

From 1830 onwards, Irving's millennialist thought found its most frequent expression in the pages of *The Morning Watch* journal. Mark Patterson's thesis on this journal and the Albury circle drew attention to the natural compatibility between the existing Romantic worldview and the premillennialism developing within this group.[75] Patterson noted that in the synergy between Romanticism and premillennialism the former provided the favourable conditions for the latter.[76] The Albury circle combined its impressive collective resources of finances (especially Henry Drummond's), energy and theological acumen to develop and publish their premillennial eschatology. Their sense of the importance of premillennialism grew in direct proportion to their growing confidence about the truth of the doctrine. Eschatology increasingly informed ecclesiology as the group became convinced that theirs was to be the *parousia* generation. Time was short; the message was urgent; people needed to listen: polemics were never far away. Patterson's description of "the Albury Circle [as] a product of its age and thus a theology shaped by romanticism's love for grand, all-inclusive systems, the enlightenment's rational methodology and their own subjective polemic"[77] gives supporting evidence that the Irving/Albury premillennialism was a profoundly Romantic product.

This brief survey has traced Irving's premillennialism from its general form of the early 1820s, through the influence of Frere and Irving's own publications on the subject between 1826 and 1830, to the Albury circle/*Morning Watch* period of 1830-1833. Irving's Romanticism pre-existed his millennialism.

---

[74] Irving, *For Missionaries after the Apostolical School*, 111-112.

[75] M. Patterson, "Designing the Last Days: Edward Irving, the Albury Circle, and the Theology of the Morning Watch" (PhD thesis, King's College, London, 2001), vol. 1, 34.

[76] Patterson, "Designing the Last Days", vol. 1, 30-34. This section is notable for its succinct insights into Romanticism as a whole.

[77] Patterson, "Designing the Last Days", vol. 1, 113.

Premillennialism did not make Irving a Romantic; Irving's entrenched Romanticism facilitated his acceptance of premillennialism. However, Irving's premillennialist enthusiasms did not precipitate any great controversy in his ministerial career, probably because (as we have seen in chapters one and three) millennialism was already an established expression of the Romantic spirit. This was, certainly, not the case for Irving's Christology, the next of his theological distinctives to appear.

Irving's incarnational Christology represented a departure from the atonement-centred preaching of the Evangelicals and was, itself, a Romantic expression.[78] Commentators on Irving's Christology have noted that he consciously strived to avoid the opposite errors of seeing Christ as simply a particularly holy man, and docetism.[79] Irving was able to identify undeveloped elements within the Protestant theology of his day and use patristics to highlight them.[80] In doing so, he initiated criticism from those who were gravitating towards one or other of those positions. In chapter two, we noted that Irving's Christology first began to arouse controversy following his 1828 publication of the three-volume *Sermons, Lectures and Occasional Discourses*.[81] However, Dorries has argued that Irving's Christology was essentially in place from the earliest examples of his preaching that have survived to us, although Grass believes that this is straining the evidence.[82] In any case, the substance of these three volumes lay in sermons he had preached during 1825, sermons that had caused no disruption in his congregation whatsoever. In the preface to the first volume, Irving stated his doctrine succinctly.

> The point at issue is simply this; Whether Christ's flesh had the grace of sinlessness and incorruption from its proper nature, or from the indwelling of the Holy Ghost. I say the latter. I assert, that in its proper nature it was as the flesh of his mother, but, by virtue of the Holy Ghost's quickening and inhabiting of it, it was preserved sinless and incorruptible.[83]

Irving's concern was to claim that Christ had assumed humanity in its full and normal sense, that is, the fallen humanity experienced by each one of us. If Christ's humanity was *not* the same as ours, there were numerous problems.

---

[78] P. Meldrum, *Conscience and Compromise: Forgotten Evangelicals of Nineteenth-century Scotland* (Carlisle: Paternoster, 2006), 134.
[79] For example, McFarlane, *Christ and the Spirit*, 70.
[80] McFarlane, *Christ and the Spirit*, 179-180.
[81] Page 30.
[82] *Edward Irving's Incarnational Christology*, 73ff, T. Grass, *The Lord's Watchman: Edward Irving*, (Milton Keynes: Paternoster, 2011), 175.
[83] E. Irving, *Sermons, Lectures and Occasional Discourses*, 3 vols, (London: R.B. Seeley & W. Burnside, 1828), vol. 1, v.

> And the measure of the potency of sin, and of its evil in one man, in any man, in all men, in the region of humanity, is the degree unto which it humbled and reduced one of the persons of the eternal Godhead. I wonder what men mean who will not look at this, and be astonied: it passeth comprehension, it passeth utterance. Holy men are lost in the adoration of it; angels desire to look into it; sinners are saved by it; and none but infidels and heretics withstand it. It is very painful indeed to me, but nothing new, as you can testify, to witness the obstinacy and perverseness with which men contend against this truth, that Christ came in the likeness of sinful flesh, to condemn sin in the flesh.[84]

Here we begin to see what is at stake for Irving in his doctrine of the Incarnation, in his passionate defence of Christ's sinlessness, and his simultaneous claim that Christ assumed fallen human nature. To argue otherwise, he claimed, was to move towards heresy. Both the seriousness of sin and the magnitude of Christ's humility are emphasised here as truths to which the appropriate response is doxology, not opposition. Elsewhere, Irving would more explicitly challenge the church to return to Chalcedonian Christology with its affirmation of the true humanity of Christ.[85]

> What mean they by their ignorant gainsaying? Is it not the thing which is to be done in you and me, sooner or later, by God, that we should be sanctified and redeemed, this very flesh of ours, by the indwelling and empowering of the Holy Ghost? If there be something so shocking in the Holy Ghost's abiding in sinful flesh, let those that think it so shocking do without it, if they can, and go down into the pit for ever. Whether is it more honourable unto God, that he should recover his creature, or lose his creature? And if sinful flesh is the thing to be sanctified and possessed of the Godhead, shall not Christ in this also have the pre-eminence? or shall it be done in us, without being first done in him?[86]

Christ's role as mediator was at stake: an incarnation that only embraced a "fake" humanity could not result in a genuine salvation, based on the Cappadocian assumption that what has not been assumed has not been redeemed. A God who was so appalled by fallen humanity that he could not embrace it could hardly be expected to save humanity. And, by implication, if Christ did not bear our humanity in its current state, then our humanity was not raised with him and we have no grounds to hope for a future resurrection. In

---

[84] Irving, *Sermons, Lectures and Occasional Discourses*, vol. 1, cxlii (140). This volume has unorthodox pagination due to a late insertion.

[85] Dorries has argued that one of Irving's great achievements was to make one of the fullest explorations of the implications of the Cappadocian position on Christ's humanity. *Edward Irving's Incarnational Christology*, 178.

[86] Irving, *Sermons, Lectures, and Occasional Discourses*, vol. 1, cxlii (140)-cxliii (140).

which case, sanctification is hardly viable if Christ's "humanity" was an exalted form unavailable to us (for example, Adam's prelapsarian nature): if Christ himself couldn't live a holy life having assumed fallen human nature, then, clearly, we have no hope of doing so. In this case, the door would be wide open to antinomianism.

> But whence this abhorrence? Is it dishonourable to vanquish sin? Doth the man become a serpent who graspeth the serpent in his gripe, and crusheth him? Do I become a devil, by wrestling with the devil and overcoming him? And doth Christ become sinful, by coming into flesh like this of mine, extirpating its sin, arresting its corruption, and attaining for it honour and glory for ever? Idle talk! They know not whether they drive. They are making void the humanity of Christ, and destroying his mediation, as virtually as if they denied his Divinity. A mediator is not of one: how truly he is consubstantial with God, so truly is he consubstantial with me, or he cannot be mediator between me and God. The Days-man must be able to lay his hand upon us both.[87]

Irving believed he was fighting not only for Christian orthodoxy but also for issues with profound pastoral implications. For example, if Christ had not fully identified with human nature *as we experience it*, this posed serious problems in a number of areas, including salvation, sanctification and resurrection: if God had not assumed fallen human nature, could he save, sanctify and resurrect it?[88] As a pastor, Irving was convinced that his understanding of the incarnation was an essential foundation for the spiritual lives of his congregation.

These features of Irving's Christology have been explored in much greater depth by works focusing specifically on this area. It is worth noting that due to the opposition he faced over this doctrine, Irving was often writing from a defensive position. Our interest – the Romantic nature of Irving's Christology – emerges much more clearly when its characteristics are stated positively, rather than in terms of what he was reacting against.

Irving's insistence that the incarnation involved God assuming full and fallen humanity was a bold assertion of divine intimacy and immanence.[89] His Christology magnified the problem of sin and Christ's kenosis (God had to assume *fallen* human nature to address the problem), simultaneously exalted the worth of humanity in God's eyes (God was prepared to endure such an incarnation to redeem us), and, also, pointed towards important implications for

---

[87] Irving, *Sermons, Lectures, and Occasional Discourses*, vol. 1, cxliii (140).

[88] See, also, E. Irving, *Christ's Holiness in Flesh, the Form, Fountain Head, and Assurance to us of Holiness in Flesh. In three parts* (Edinburgh: John Lindsay & co, 1831), 158.

[89] Hopkins argues that the encounter between theology and Romanticism often produced immanental offspring. M. Hopkins, *Nonconformity's Romantic Generation: Evangelical and Liberal Theologies in Victorian England* (Carlisle: Paternoster, 2004), 3.

the individual Christian (which we will explore later in this chapter when we consider Irving's view of the charismata). To Irving, the incarnation was a profoundly Romantic expression and the ultimate encounter with the divine sublime: the transcendent becoming mundane; deity becoming fully human; spirit becoming flesh in a flurry of paradox that was virtually overwhelming. No longer evanescent and elusive, God had become accessible.

Earlier in this chapter we noted that in Irving's pre-millennial epic, the church played the role of corporate Romantic hero, battling Satanic forces until the return of the King. It soon becomes clear that in Irving's Christology, Christ, himself, was the Romantic hero *par excellence*. The frequent Romantic themes of alienation and exile form one example of this.[90] For Irving, Christ in his incarnation experienced both. Irving portrayed Christ as misunderstood, misinterpreted, persecuted and deserted by virtually everyone he knew, including friends, family and those who had been blessed through his supernatural ministry. Irving described Christ as "deserted" during his Gethsemane experience, and experiencing "spiritual desertion" from God on Calvary.[91] This pain of this alienation was, of course, raised to a much higher level because Christ remained personally sinless and focused on the selfless goal of reconciling humanity with God. Christ, also, knew exile, both in the mundane sense of his childhood flight to Egypt,[92] and the much more profound sense of his exile from heaven. Not only had the eternal God taken on human flesh, but in order to do so authentically it was necessary that he empty himself of divine attributes. Irving gloried in this kenotic element of his Christology. "Blessed! ever blessed Son! who thus made himself of no reputation, emptied himself of his own inexhaustible fulness, and yielded himself to his Father, like clay in the hand of the potter."[93] Many individuals throughout history have experienced exile and alienation, but never to such a degree: the incarnation represented an exile of cosmic proportions as deity was exiled into humanity and eternity was exiled into time.

These themes of alienation and exile lead directly into the concept of Romantic struggle. Unsurprisingly, Irving saw Christ engaged in a continuous and multi-faceted struggle during his incarnation. One example of this struggle was with temptation. Arguing vigorously against the idea that Christ ever actually sinned, Irving believed that when faced with temptations, Christ "gave them no inlet, he went not to seek them, he gave them no quarter, but with power Divine rejected and repulsed them all; and so, from his conception unto his resurrection, his whole life was a series of active triumphings over sin in the flesh, Satan in the world, and spiritual wickednesses in high places".[94] Calvary,

---

[90] R. Sayre & M. Löwy, "Romanticism and Capitalism" in M. Ferber, (ed.), *A Companion to European Romanticism* (Oxford: Blackwell, 2005), 435.
[91] Irving, *Sermons, Lectures, and Occasional Discourses*, vol. 1, 180-181.
[92] Matthew 2:13ff.
[93] Irving, *Sermons, Lectures, and Occasional Discourses*, vol. 1, xlviii (140)-xlix (140).
[94] Irving, *Sermons, Lectures, and Occasional Discourses*, vol. 1, vii.

then, was the ultimate triumph in a sequence of life-long struggle and triumph. The incarnation was pre-eminently a time of struggle, not of glory.

> The time was not come for manifesting it gloriously, because the heat of battle was then going forward, when the warrior is all soiled with sweat, and dust, and blood. He was wrestling with sin, in sin's own obscure dwelling-place; against the powers of darkness, in their dark abode: he was overcoming sin in the flesh. And therefore was it that he appeared not in the glorious raiment of a conqueror, or in the full majesty of a possessor, as he shall appear when he cometh the second time.[95]

The metaphor of battle which has already been prominent in this chapter recurs. Clearly, the antithesis of Gnostic dualism, Irving described this metaphysical struggle in the most physical of terms. In Irving's thought, it was impossible to overstate the importance of what Christ had achieved through his incarnation and death, and he, regularly, described this in the language of Romanticism, elevating the theme of noble struggle against the odds to achieve a worthy goal to a cosmic level.

> First, His struggle with, and victory over, Satan and the evil angels;—secondly, over sin in human nature;—and, thirdly, over that confederacy of wickedness into which these two great co-operating causes of evil have wrought the world of wicked men. ...It was therefore no small work to take off the eclipse which the Almighty had thus permitted to come upon the face of his glory, and to re-establish that almightiness of power which seemed to hang in doubt, and plant the stability of all things upon a new basis, by redeeming and recovering the lost world, and making it more glorious than ever; while the evil powers, which had dared to peep and to mutter against him, and to stir up strife anew, should be utterly undone, and left in everlasting passiveness of suffering and miserable abjectness. And as the end to be accomplished was truly very great, yea, the greatest possible (creation being nothing so great a work as the redemption of creation against all power and might), so the labour and travail which had to be undergone for its accomplishment was proportionably great, yea, I may say, stupendously, inconceivably great. Into the mystery of which travail of the Son of Man to accomplish the same, I would inquire, that we may be a little able to measure the greatness of the achievement, by the greatness of the endurance in compassing it.[96]

The redemption accomplished by Christ eclipsed the creation itself, because it was achieved against opposition: in the Romantic view, great goals required a proportionate level of struggle and risk. Irving grasped for superlatives and,

---

[95] Irving, *Sermons, Lectures, and Occasional Discourses*, vol. 1, xiv (140).
[96] Irving, *Sermons, Lectures, and Occasional Discourses*, vol. 1, 157-158.

having settled for "stupendously, inconceivably great", in a quintessentially Romantic act he launched into an attempt to describe the indescribable. The Saviour had achieved something beyond comprehension and human vocabulary, but it remained an act of worship (and a Romantic quest) to attempt to understand and explain it. The natural Romantic response to overwhelming sublimity was prostration, praise and poetry combined with the awareness that such worship was simultaneously essential and inadequate.

It is passages like the one quoted above that have led some critics of Irving to allege that he was placing too little emphasis on Calvary and too much elsewhere.[97] I believe this is another instance where Irving's Romanticism informed his Christology. Irving was naturally drawn to those aspects of Christ's ministry involving active combat against the world, the flesh and the devil. This extended up to and included Gethsemane, but from the time of Christ's arrest, through his trial, scourging and crucifixion, his demeanour was essentially passive and resigned. Once dead, Christ, paradoxically, became more active, and Irving more interested.

> But if they would open their ears to instruction, then might they be taught that sin is the condition of an apostate creature, the form of a rebellious will, the very being of an enemy of God and of godliness. To make the evil of which to cease, to destroy its eternal activity against God, was the cause of our Lord's humiliation in the body and descent into hell. By which powerful and perilous ministry he did overcome and vanquish the enemy, and hath him and his dominions in his power, whenever it shall please the Father to allow him to enter in to possess them.[98]

Having withstood the worst that sin could throw at him in life to the point of an agonising and undeserved death, Christ had now taken the battle into hell, itself, as a necessary extension of his ministry. Whether Irving regarded Christ as still at "peril" at this point is ambiguous; this could be taken more generally as referring to his entire incarnational ministry. The Romantic theme of the noble struggle was very diluted if not accompanied by an element of risk. What is clear from Irving's writing is that Christ, the ultimate Romantic hero, had risked much and gained all. The breadth of the canvas on which he was painting meant that Irving's focus was far broader than the individualistic salvation emphasised in much of evangelicalism: he saw it as all-encompassing, "disseminated throughout creation".[99]

Irving's thoroughly Romantic Christology provided a logical bridge to his later acceptance of the charismata in two ways: through his theological anthropology and his pneumatology. Earlier, we noted Irving's assertion that,

---

[97] For example, Dallimore, *Irving*, 80-82.

[98] Irving, *Sermons, Lectures, and Occasional Discourses*, vol. 1, 132.

[99] C.E. Gunton, *The Actuality of Atonement: a Study of Metaphor, Rationality and the Christian Tradition* (Edinburgh: T & T Clark, 2004), 137.

although Christ assumed sinful human nature, he remained free of sin through the indwelling Holy Spirit.[100] This raises the obvious question: to what degree can the rest of the human race achieve this? After all, Christ fully identified with our humanity and believers are, also, indwelt by the Holy Spirit. The exploration of this issue raised powerful and heady vistas which motivated Irving throughout his ministry.

We have seen that Irving encouraged missionaries to embark on Romantic quests and in his *Farewell Address* to St John's Glasgow, he encouraged preachers to "court danger in a noble cause . . . launch fearlessly into the wide and open deep . . . explore all they can reach . . . [to] risk much, [and] discover much".[101] Ministers, like missionaries, were supposed to eschew safe, placid waters for the true rewards lay elsewhere. But, how did Irving apply this to those without a full-time Christian vocation?

In chapter four, we saw that Coleridge pictured himself as fighting alongside Irving in the cause of spiritual truth; in chapter five, Carlyle, also, wanted to fight alongside Irving, but only in Carlyle-approved ventures.[102] Whom did Irving want as his battle-companions?

> Now, if ye will receive these things which we have heard, and in your hearts believe them, ye must seek earnestly of the Father, that he would send forth his Spirit into your hearts, and anoint you with his power, as heretofore he anointed the man Jesus of Nazareth, that you also may go about doing good, and destroy the works of the devil. For though no one but the Son of God can discharge that ministry which brought life and immortality to those who were through the fear of death all their life time subject to bondage, yet *every one* who, like him, would condemn sin in the flesh, and obtain the victory over death and the grave, must walk in his footsteps, and in the same strength prevail over the enemy of souls and all his evil angels. But without the Holy Spirit ye can as little stir in this warfare, as without Christ ye could have known that such a warfare was to be undertaken, or such a victory to be achieved.[103]

This was not written just for missionaries or ordained ministers, but for "every one". Irving simply wanted everyone enlisted in a battle of such cosmic significance, and issued an egalitarian call to spiritual warfare. It could, certainly, be argued that Irving's idealism had produced an over-realised eschatology, but it was a theological response resulting from experience that encompassed both the poverty of the Glasgow weavers and the wealth of London. Irving's conviction that contemporary evangelicalism was inadequate

---

[100] Irving, *Sermons, Lectures, and Occasional Discourses*, vol. 1, v.
[101] *CW3*, (London: Alexander Strahan, 1865), 350.
[102] Page 144.
[103] Irving, preface to *Ben-ezra,* clxxxiv. My emphasis.

to meet the complexities of industrialised urban life was met by his greater conviction in the ability of a transcendent God to revolutionise daily life.

This passage from Irving's preface to the eschatological work *Ben-Ezra* highlights the intimate connections between Irving's Christology, pneumatology and millennialism. Christ's victory through the power of the Holy Spirit opened the way for all Christians to conquer in their own ongoing spiritual warfare: as for the Master, so for the servants.[104] This message became much more urgent, of course, because of the last days. Christ's work and the indwelling of the Holy Spirit were the keys in Edward Irving's strategy to enlist absolutely every willing believer for active duty in the greatest conceivable Romantic epic – the quest to faithfully complete the church's earthly mission culminating in the triumph of the Second Coming and the millennial kingdom.

Christ's post-baptismal victory over temptation in the wilderness was the prelude to his ministry of power: as for the Master, so for the servants. The church could not afford to neglect any of the divine weapons placed at its disposal, but, to Irving, this was exactly what it had been doing, in neglecting (or denying) that Christ assumed full humanity, and the resulting pneumatological implications. The church had been aiming too low and achieving even less. In taking this stand, Irving was again demonstrating typical Romantic willingness to bypass inherited authority systems in the name of transcendence, in this case, the established clergy-laity divide.

It is significant that Irving's *Ben-Ezra* preface was published in 1827, the year before his *Sermons* put the spotlight on his Christology. It is, therefore, obvious that before experiencing the heat of controversy, Irving was already pursuing the implications of his Christology and pneumatology and, quite consciously, opening a significant space for the ministry of the laity. Also, obvious is that by this date, the context was set for Irving's later acceptance of the charismata amongst the laity.

In the early stages of his London ministry, Irving held the traditional Church of Scotland cessationist stance on spiritual gifts: "the miracles of God have ceased," he wrote on the first page of *Oracles*.[105] Yet, even his cessationism was interpreted through Romantic eyes: it was precisely because of the absence of supernatural spiritual gifts that what "the sense can no longer behold, the heart, ravished with his [God's] word, must feel".[106] Regardless of the availability of the miraculous, Irving would settle for nothing less than a Christianity of the ravished heart; he was amazed that others were prepared to do so.

---

[104] As Strachan has noted, the reception of the Holy Spirit in his fullness was "the necessary inference and corollary" of the belief that Christ has assumed fallen humanity in its fullness. G. Strachan, *The Pentecostal Theology of Edward Irving* (London: Dartman, Longman & Todd, 1973), 89.

[105] Irving, *Oracles*, 13.

[106] Irving, *Oracles*, 19.

Irving's thoughts on the charismata progressed through several stages. In January 1825 he was still firmly cessationist.[107] By mid-1827 Irving was preaching that he couldn't see any scriptural reason why the gifts *couldn't* still operate.[108] By 1828 he had employed A.J. (Sandy) Scott to be his assistant in London.[109] Scott firmly believed that the full range of charismatic gifts remained available to the church if sufficient faith were present.[110] The difference between the positions of the two men was the issue of imminence: Scott believed the gifts were immediately available in response to faith, whereas, despite finding Scott's arguments persuasive, Irving remained at the position that the gifts would be restored at the Second Advent.[111]

It is usually assumed that the next stage in Irving's transition to acceptance of the charismata was news of the outpouring amongst the Macdonald and Campbell families in the Gare Loch region of Scotland. This view is strengthened by comments made by Irving, himself, in a magazine article published in early 1832.[112] However, this was published after Irving's full acceptance of the charismata within his own congregation in the previous October.[113] Some more obscure evidence suggests that other factors were at work. Although the first incidence of glossolalia in Scotland occurred in mid-April 1830, and Irving was, certainly, intrigued by the reports during that summer, the London investigating party (described in chapter two) did not arrive in Scotland until the end of August.[114]

The following quote is from an unpublished letter from Irving to Henry Drummond, dated 7 July 1830. It was, therefore, written at a time when Irving was aware of the initial Scottish charismata, but some seven weeks before the London investigating party set out. The immediate context is that Irving and Isabella had just suffered the loss of their fourth child. Describing himself as "stunned by the unexpected blow which it pleased the Father to give to what I had thought was my faith in him," Irving goes on to state that although he and Isabella had found a place of peace in their loss, he was disturbed by the fact that God had not granted the healing for which so many were praying. He proceeded to discuss the spiritual gifts of 1 Corinthians 12.

---

[107] Irving, *For Missionaries after the Apostolical School*, xxii-xxiii.
[108] Irving preached this soon after moving into the Regent Square Church in May, 1827. E. Irving, "Homilies on baptism" in *CW*, vol. 2 (London: Alexander Strahan & co., 1864), 276.
[109] Page 31.
[110] Drummond, *Edward Irving and his Circle*, 138.
[111] Oliphant, *Irving*, 275.
[112] E. Irving, "Facts connected with recent manifestations of spiritual gifts", *Fraser's Magazine*, January, 1832.
[113] Chapter 2, page 35.
[114] Strachan, *Pentecostal Theology*, 71. The time delay between the initial Scottish glossolalia and its London appearance was approximately one year.

> we find that the gift of miracles was connected with certain persons in the church who were not apostles but distinct from them. This proves that this gift and the office for which it was the qualification were not limited to the person of the apostles nor to the apostles' time, but belonged to the church as much as pastors and teachers and governments do . . . If so, then see the conclusion which we come to, that though the prayers of the church may be most faithful & fervent for healings and miracles and other works of the Holy Spirit which testify to the power of Christ and his presence in his Church, the answer is such (that?) cannot be obtained because there are no persons who are set apart to minister the gift which the Church has besought & which God waiteth to bestow.[115]

Here we see Irving, the grief-stricken father, wrestling with his faith and the agony of unanswered prayer. Not only did Irving's personal faith pale in the face of his four-fold tragedy, he doubted the very existence of a church that counted in God's eyes: but it could not end there. We have seen that Irving's Romantic conception of ministry enthusiastically embraced struggle, opposition and pain; he had now experienced a strong draught of this. This pain was meaningless, though, unless a prize lay on the other side, and for such pain the prize must be great indeed. The prize Irving determined on here was nothing less than restoration of the charismata to the laity. Earlier, we saw that Oliver's argument that the fundamental motivation for Irving's millennialism was the death of his first child was overstated;[116] here, we see that the pain of burying *four* of his children was a factor in moving Edward Irving further towards the charismata. Pending the favourable report from the investigating group some weeks later, the existence of the Scottish charismata merely gave potential circumstantial support for Irving's rising theological conviction, forged in the heat of his grief. In this letter, Irving did not refer to the Scottish manifestations in any way, but argued from scripture, reason and his own experience. This is further evidence that Irving was no credulous follower of the experiences of other people: in his grief, it would have been understandable if he had desperately grasped at the hope implicit in the Scottish manifestations; that he did not is testimony both to his strength of character and his intellectual integrity.

It is important, however, not to overemphasise the impact of Irving's grief on his theology. It did not cause his theology to undergo a fundamental change: essentially, he followed through the logical implications of what was already there; the grief simply added to his determination. What is important for our purposes is that when he was placed under great pressure (the death of a fourth child), Irving's default position was to intensify his expectations within his

[115] This letter is C/9/5, held in the Duke of Northumberland's archives, Alnwick Castle. Used by permission.

[116] Chapter 3, page 55 Oliver, *Prophets and millennialists*, 24. Oliver was referring to the death of Irving's first-born, Edward Jr., who died in October 1825.

Romantic worldview: the prize had to be proportional to the pain and overwhelming tragedy could expect to draw on transcendent resources.

An important theme of Irving's theology, which we have seen arising through all the imagery of warfare, is *Christus Victor*. Christ, the ultimate Romantic hero, faced the unimaginable as a man, filled with the Holy Spirit. Christ was completely victorious over everything that Satan could throw at him, including death. After ransacking hell, itself, Christ ascended to make intercession for his church. It was Irving's conviction that like its Master, the church was not supposed merely to exist in a state of contemplative sanctification, but to move in the power of the Holy Spirit into continuing spiritual warfare. While occasional defeats were to be expected, scripture was clear that the church would, eventually, be victorious. Irving had seen too much death in his home, despite fervent corporate prayer. As a grieving father and a compassionate pastor, not to mention a Romantic activist, he had to wrestle with the resulting theological problems; the letter to Drummond shows this struggle and his growing conviction that the answer was the renewal of the charismata.

If the church and individual Christians were losing too many battles, the problem was neither with Christ nor the Holy Spirit, but the church's ignorance of the full range of available spiritual artillery. The church was failing both God and its people and in delineating this failure, Irving reflected the frequently-noted Romantic tenet that "the inherited pieties and integrative myths [were] no longer adequate".[117] To Irving, neither the Church of Scotland, specifically, nor evangelicalism, generally, was living out its full spiritual heritage. To accede to the demands of institutions that were manifestly failing was to dishonour God; their authority could not be unquestioningly accepted. In this, Irving clearly demonstrated the Romantic trait of willingly bypassing existing authority structures in pursuit of transcendence. Irving had already made it clear that he felt part of the reason for the relatively moribund state of the church was its neglect of Christ's fully human incarnation as well as his second coming and millennial reign. Irving was about to add the charismata to complete a Romantic trilogy of doctrine, the restoration of which would revivify the ailing church.

Before we continue exploring Irving's relationship with the charismata, it is appropriate to make an excursus at this point to examine Irving's position, relative to other theological trends of his day. Earlier in this chapter, we noted that Irving did not fit neatly into Bebbington's standard definition of an evangelical: he was neither especially conversionist, nor crucicentric. Our subsequent examination of Irving's Christology has given further substance to this observation. Intriguingly, Irving's thought in several areas resonated strongly with the High Church tradition in Anglicanism, from which Tractarianism emerged in 1833. Like Irving, the Tractarians looked back on the

[117] Irving made many comments in this regard; for instance, in his farewell address to the St John's congregation, *CW3*, 351-352; Abrams, *Natural Supernaturalism*, 293.

eighteenth century as a sterile period for the church, glorified the patristic period and read church history romantically.[118] In keeping with the Romantic view of history, Irving and the Tractarians both saw history as an important and authoritative interpreter of scripture. In addition, with respect to the sacrament of baptism, Irving's views contained elements of the High Church tradition and earlier Reformed teaching, rather than contemporary evangelical thought. Evangelicals in Irving's day tended to view the sacraments as merely "signs", rather than "effectual means of grace".[119] Irving made his disagreement with this evangelical view very plain: in the fly leaves of his *Homilies on Baptism* he quoted the *Confession of Scotch Reformers*, "We utterly condemn the vanity of those who affirm the Sacraments to be nothing but naked and bare signs."[120] Elsewhere, Irving referred to the "the infidelity of evangelicalism, which denies any gift of God either in the work of Christ, or in the sacraments, or any where, until we experience it to be within ourselves".[121] Experiential religion was important to Irving, but it was not the arbiter of the objective work of God. Although some of his critics have alleged that Irving's teaching could barely be distinguished from the High Church doctrine of baptismal regeneration, his view was actually in the middle of the spectrum.[122] He believed that the Spirit was at work during baptism, but not that everyone baptised was saved: God's elect were regenerated at baptism, others were not.[123] "There is an imputed righteousness of Christ, and there is an indwelling righteousness of the Holy Ghost: the former of which we have in consequence of faith while yet unbaptized; the latter of which we have in consequence of the covenant we have entered into by baptism."[124] Irving saw baptism through a Romantic filter: baptism was another avenue through which the individual had access to the

---

[118] P.B. Nockles, *The Oxford Movement in Context: Anglican High Churchmanship, 1760-1857* (Cambridge: Cambridge University Press, 1994), 4, 6, 104.

[119] Nockles, *The Oxford Movement in Context,* 228.

[120] Irving repeated this quote later in the work. E. Irving, "Homilies on baptism" in *CW*, vol. 2 (London: Alexander Strahan & Co., 1864). The quote in the fly leaf is actually page 245 in this edition, although the page is not numbered; the later quote is on 345. While Henry Drummond expressed similar views in the same year Irving's "Homilies" were first published (1828), cf. H. Drummond, *A Defence of the Students of Prophecy*, 57-58, quoted in G. Carter, *Anglican Evangelicals: Protestant Secessions from the via media, c. 1800-1850* (Oxford: Oxford University Press, 2001), 170, Irving had expressed similar views in 1827, in his ordination charge to McLean, cf. *CW*, volume 1, 532.

[121] E. Irving, *The Confessions of Faith and the Books of Discipline of the Church of Scotland, of date anterior to the Westminster Confession. To which are prefixed a historical view of the Church of Scotland from the earliest period to the time of the Reformation, and a historical preface, with remarks* (London: Baldwin and Cradock, 1831), xcix .

[122] For example, Oliphant, *Irving*, 111; Dallimore, *Irving*, 178.

[123] For a detailed discussion of how Irving drew from both Hooker and Calvin, see Grass, *Lord's Watchman*, 128.

[124] E. Irving, "Homilies on baptism" in *CW2*, 273.

Divine; it was a rite of initiation that represented not just a role-play identification of the believer with Christ's death and resurrection – it actually unleashed an experience of transformation by the Holy Spirit. Evangelical teaching was woefully reductionist by comparison, and Irving's blunt critique of it is another indication that he can only be labelled "evangelical" with a number of disclaimers, with the possible result that the label ceases to be useful in Irving's case.

Irving, also, differed from some sections within evangelicalism in his views of the eucharist. Amongst Baptists and Congregationalists, for instance, the eucharist was often seen only as a reflection on Christ's sacrifice and a "badge" of denominational loyalty.[125] Irving aligned more closely with the alternative High Church Anglican view and earlier Reformed traditions which had a "higher" view of the sacraments than the Zwinglian commemorative understanding often seen in nineteenth century evangelicalism.[126] In the context of discussing the Lord's Supper, Irving once again favourably referenced the *Confession of Scotch Reformers* to criticise the prevailing view of the sacraments as "naked and bare signs" as "base and heretical" and having "alarming influence".[127] "For ordinances are not barren things without fruit, neither are they idle things without usefulness," Irving wrote, before claiming that the work of the Holy Spirit through the eucharist would bring understanding of the Scriptures, wisdom and discretion, courage, skill and love. He, also, returned to a theme we have seen elsewhere: the value of immediate access to the Divine and the avoidance of mediators. "In every other ordinance there interveneth between you and the Head of the Church another person, in baptism, both your father and the minister; in preaching, the preacher; but in the Lord's supper there interveneth no one. It is the nearest approach unto the great Head of the Church. Every Christian transacteth for himself with his living and risen Head."[128]

It flew in the face of Irving's understanding of God's economy for sacraments to exist only as superficial signs. Irving's conviction was that this was a dominant view in the evangelicalism of his day, and it alarmed him. Other scholars, while acknowledging that Irving's view was shared by many, have contended against it. Horton Davies has claimed that Anglican evangelicals actually restored the sacraments to their central place in worship, and was "a communicating as well as a commemorating and covenanting ordinance".[129] In commenting on evangelicalism's "rather impoverished" ecclesiology, Hylson-Smith nevertheless notes that their emphasis on the

---

[125] H. Davies, *Worship and Theology in England: from Watts and Wesley to Martineau, 1690-1900* (Grand Rapids, MI: Eerdmans, 1996), 134.
[126] Nockles, *The Oxford Movement in Context*, 235-236. Nockles is citing here a mid-nineteenth century Tractarian view which aligns closely with Irving's.
[127] Irving, "Homilies on the Lord's Supper" in *CW2*, 590.
[128] Irving, "Homilies on the Lord's Supper" in *CW2*, 517.
[129] Davies, *Worship and Theology in England*, 223, 225.

eucharist was often "forceful".[130] Irving's Scottish background, no doubt, contributed to his view of the sacraments: he was aware that there was a "sensual" element to the Scottish celebration of the eucharist: word alone was not sufficient.[131] Irving's view of the sacraments in contemporary evangelicalism may have been narrow, but he approached the sacraments as he approached virtually all theological topics, with the conviction that God was busy invading and transforming the mundane with the transcendent. Communion represented the "nearest approach" to Christ. Irving's fundamentally Romantic conviction explains why he stood aloof from evangelicalism and aligned more with High Church thought on baptism and the Lord's Supper. Evangelicalism had been sullied with pragmatism and the Utilitarianism of the day, so it could not be wholeheartedly embraced. Irving's opinions and actions showed that he was convinced that no one denomination or theological party had a monopoly on truth; as a corollary, it was mandatory for those in search of truth to cross these "party lines". Such an approach could only be appreciated by those who were prepared, like Irving, to elevate the pursuit of truth above denominational loyalties. Irving's various theological enthusiasms and alignments cannot be explained (as some have alleged) by an inherent credulity or malleability: the most consistent and coherent explanation is his underlying Romanticism.[132]

Returning to Irving's relationship with the charismata, after the favourable report from the committee investigating the Scottish manifestations, groups began praying in private homes in London for a similar outpouring. These groups appear not to have been instigated by Irving, although they had his support.[133] 1831 saw the arrival of the charismata in Irving's London

---

[130] K. Hylson-Smith, *Evangelicals in the Church of England 1734-1984* (Edinburgh: T & T Clark, 1988), 106.

[131] M. Todd, *The Culture of Protestantism in Early Modern Scotland* (New Haven: Yale University Press, 2002), 85.

[132] We examined the credulity claims in chapter 3.

[133] Strachan, *Pentecostal Theology*, 87. The relationship between Irving and the Scottish charismata is more complex than it first appears. It may initially appear coincidental that the charismata appeared first in Scotland, and, then, later, in the Scottish-born Irving's London congregation, but there was a direct link. Before the manifestations began, Sandy Scott (Irving's assistant whose influence on Irving's thought has already been noted) shared his pro-charismatic views with Mary Campbell in Gareloch during the autumn of 1829 (E. Irving, "Facts connected with recent manifestations of spiritual gifts," *Fraser's Magazine*, January 1832, 756, quoted in Strachan, *Pentecostal Theology*, 64). Scott's arguments were based on a distinction between regeneration and baptism with the Holy Spirit from the book of Acts. Mary was not persuaded at the time, but her mind changed in December, not because of Scott's arguments or further study of Acts, but through reading John 14-16 in the light of Irving's Christology. In January 1830, she wrote excitedly to Irving about her discoveries (Irving, "Facts connected with recent manifestations of spiritual gifts," *Fraser's Magazine*, 756, quoted in Strachan, *Pentecostal Theology*, 64-65). In the following months, Mary Campbell and those in her circle experienced healings, glossolalia and prophecy. It is, therefore, incorrect to follow

congregation, and, towards the end of the year, the publication of *The Day of Pentecost*. Irving's views in this book demonstrated that he was now completely opposed to his early cessationism. Irving's Christology overflowed into his pneumatology as Christ's identification with fallen humanity and his ministry as a Spirit-baptised human was seen to have direct implications for all believers. The church *currently* possessed "superhuman powers", which were "but glimpses of the glory which is yet to be revealed".[134] An encounter with the Divine sublime was freely available for all, but if so, what would refusal to participate mean?

> If, then, we would see the baptism of the Holy Ghost laid out at large, and embodied in a various and busy life, we must look at the ministry of Jesus; and be assured, that all which he spake and all which he did, up to the measure of infallibility in the one, and raising the dead in the other, the baptism with the Holy Ghost doth enable and require the church to perform. It is not blasphemy, but it is duty, to believe and assert that the believer is called upon to walk in the footsteps of Jesus in all respects, speaking at all times as he spake, and working as he also wrought. "These signs shall follow them that believe: In my name shall they cast out devils; they shall speak with new tongues; they shall take up serpents; and if they drink any deadly thing it shall not hurt them; they shall lay hands on the sick, and they shall recover" (Mark xvi. 17, 18). What a shame and what a crime it is, then, that the church of the believers should be found in the state in which it is; speaking all different opinions, exercising no infallible discernment of truth, and putting forth no signs whatever—in one word, making Jesus a liar, and counting it glorious to do so! I am ashamed, verily I am confounded, on account of our sin; and will open my mouth in confession and lamentation,

---

Dallimore and Hair in crediting Scott with winning Mary over to the charismata, and the eventual manifestations themselves for overriding Irving's remaining reservations, Dallimore, *Irving*, 102ff; J. Hair, *Regent Square: Eighty years of a London Congregation* (London: James Nisbet & Co., 1899), 102. It is more accurate to acknowledge the influence of Irving's Christology and pneumatology in initiating the manifestations through Mary Campbell. Both Mary and Irving were looking death in the face: Mary was, personally, close to death and Irving had seen four of his children die. In their extremity, they demanded answers of their theology and their God. If God had not shunned incarnation in fallen humanity, and the Holy Spirit had not shunned believers since, then was there a limit to what God might do through Spirit-energised believers? At opposite ends of the United Kingdom, Mary Campbell and Irving were, simultaneously, following the implications of Irving's theology, motivated by the proximity of death. The possibilities of individual theophanies opened up as they struggled to infuse the mundane with the sublime, to call fire from heaven, and to access a wider range of spiritual resources for the ongoing battle: they were partners in a Romantic quest.

[134] E. Irving, *The Day of Pentecost or the Baptism with the Holy Ghost. A treatise in three parts* (London: Baldwin and Cradock, 1831), 76.

> until the Lord shall have taken away this our reproach, and made us to cease to be a reproach unto Christ.[135]

Irving had now not only embraced Scott's position on the availability of the charismata, he had moved beyond it. The refusal to embrace the supernatural gifts of the Spirit was not simply a dereliction of duty, but a sinful denial of the words and instructions of Christ. Irving was convinced that the answers to many of the church's problems, including the crises of sickness and premature death which had touched his family so personally, lay in appropriation of the Spirit's power. Transcendent power was available; the sublime was at hand; but as we have seen, the Romantic context demanded struggle. Just as the descent of the Spirit on Christ at the Jordan precipitated him into a ministry of spiritual conflict, so, too, for his followers. Christ "must not only see us out of the narrow straits into which we had brought ourselves, but also navigate before us the open seas, through which we must win our way to our eternal safety and rest".[136] However, the charismata brought no quick and easy solutions, only a new range of armaments for intensified warfare, although Irving had no doubt as to which way the battle would end.

> Which circumstances being put together do exhibit to us a perfect example of the virtue of spiritual baptism;—man holy in his soul and in his flesh; man overcoming and expelling the devil and his angels; man redeeming the creatures from their thraldrom of cruelty and death ; man waited on and served by the angels: in one word, man supreme, both over the natural and the spiritual; the former to redeem, the latter to judge and separate, all evil angels to condemn, all good angels to sustain and to be served by. To the redemption of the natural, which the Son by incarnation procureth, is added the rule and government of the spiritual, which the Father by inhabitation conferreth. Therefore we conclude, that one baptized with the Holy Ghost is set for the command of good angels, for the judgment of evil ones; seeing that from this time forth legions of angels waited the bidding of the Son of Man, and legions of devils fled howling at his command. And the same powers of "casting out devils in his name," of "discerning of spirits," still appertaineth to those who believe, upon whom also the angels attend as "ministering spirits sent forth to minister to them which shall be heirs of salvation".[137]

Once again, Irving was painting in epic and cosmic strokes. The reality of *Christus Victor* needed to be continuously demonstrated by Christ's servants, themselves the lords and judges of angels.

---

[135] Irving, *The Day of Pentecost*, 83-84.
[136] Irving, *Day of Pentecost*, 85.
[137] Irving, *The Day of Pentecost*, 91-92.

If Irving's Christology painted Christ as the Romantic hero *par excellence*, and his millennialism painted the church as a corporate Romantic hero ushering in the times of the end, then it was completely consistent that his embrace of the charismata should extend the concept to individuals with an egalitarian flourish; after all, in chapter one, we noted that Hazlitt recognised that egalitarianism was one of the features of the "spirit of the age".[138] Acknowledging that all things are grounded in Christ, Irving wrote, "Nevertheless, as the power in the Head is supernatural, so is the power in *all and every one* of the members of the like superhuman kind: and baptism with the Holy Ghost doth bring us into that superhuman sphere and region, to act the part therein which the great Lord and Master may deem to be most meet; 'the Spirit dividing to *every one* according to his will'."[139] As Christ identified with our humanity, so we are identified with his exaltation; in the Spirit, humanity was now "superhuman", with the mission to continually demonstrate Christ's victory against the world, the flesh and the devil until his return. We have seen that encounter with the Divine sublime was often a goal of Romanticism, but that was usually perceived as an individual goal and Edward Irving was never satisfied with individual pursuits: Irving did not "paint" miniatures, but Biblical epics like his contemporary, William Blake. Irving portrayed individual encounter with the Divine sublime as a readily accessible goal that, in turn, quickly became the means of affecting the church and, then, the surrounding world. Earlier in this chapter (and in chapter two), we noted Irving encouraging missionaries and ministers to be adventurers for God when he still held an essentially cessationist position. Back then, expediency, prudence and Utilitarianism were synonyms for a timorous lack of faith; now, with the charismata on board, these terms bordered on the blasphemous.

At roughly the same time as *The Day of Pentecost*, Irving developed these thoughts further in a two-part article, "On the gifts of the Holy Ghost, commonly called supernatural".[140] Early in the article, Irving stated that the purpose of the supernatural gifts of the Holy Spirit was "to construct for God a place to dwell in".[141] Irving developed the concept of the church as Christ's body, "the container of the manifested God … the actor of His works, and the utterer of His wisdom".[142] The church was, in its own way, an incarnation; as Christ had identified with us in our complete fallenness, so now the church was called to identify with, and model, the glory of the risen Christ, including supernatural acts of power.

---

[138] Page 3. W. Hazlitt, *The Spirit of the Age* (Oxford: Woodstock Books, 1989), 233, 236.
[139] Irving, *Day of Pentecost*, 101. Emphases mine.
[140] *The Morning Watch*, Vol. II (1830) and Vol. III (1831). Reprinted in *CW5*, 509-561.
[141] Irving, "On the gifts of the Holy Ghost", *CW5*, 510.
[142] Irving, "On the gifts of the Holy Ghost", *CW5*, 518.

> We are wedded to the risen body of Christ: we are risen with Him from the dead, and should seek the things that are above, where our life is hid with Christ in God. Forasmuch, then, as we are the children of the heavenly man, we should exhibit the form and feature and power and acts of the heavenly man, of the Son of God, of Him in whom dwelleth the fullness of the Godhead bodily. ...We, then, as His children, begotten from above into His heavenly image, ought to put forth, in order to prove our sonship, some features of the supernatural, not only in the way of a holy will triumphant over the law of sin, and a word triumphant over the law of falsehood, but of a mighty power triumphing over the law of sickness, infirmity, and death: in one word, we should put forth a first-fruits of that power which He Himself will put forth in the day of His appearing.[143]

The word "power" appears three times in this short passage, as does the language of obligation: "ought" and "should". Irving's Christology and pneumatology convinced him that the church's identification with the risen Christ *required* resurrection power to be manifest through believers. Although at the close of the work, Irving wrote that believers should not be "disheartened" if they do not receive such supernatural manifestations,[144] here, he was making such manifestations a test of "sonship". Irving's lofty view of the role of individual believers fed back into an exalted ecclesiology. This was nowhere more evident than in the following passage at the end of the work.

> That the true reason why the gift of tongues hath ceased to be in the Church is, the exaltation of the natural methods of teaching above, or into copartnery with, the teaching of the Holy Ghost, the meanness of our idea, and the weakness of our faith, concerning the oneness of Christ glorified, with His Church on earth: the unworthiness of our doctrine concerning the person and office of the Holy Ghost, *to knit up the believer into complete oneness with Christ, every thread and filament of our mortal humanity with His humanity, immortal and glorious; to bring down into the Church a complete Christ, and keep Him there, ever filling her bosom, and working in her members...*[145]

The church, itself, was to become, like its Master, a Romantic theophany to the surrounding world, suffusing the mundane with the transcendent, overwhelming demonic opposition and the blinkered reductionism of prudence, Utilitarianism, and the idols of human reason with readily available supernatural weaponry. Earlier in this chapter, we noted that Christ's incarnation was "pre-eminently a time of struggle, not of glory"; the role of the

---

[143] Irving, "On the gifts of the Holy Ghost", *CW5*, 523-524.
[144] Irving, "On the gifts of the Holy Ghost", *CW5*, 559.
[145] Irving, "On the gifts of the Holy Ghost", *CW5*, 560. My emphasis.

church, while still involving struggle, was, primarily, and supernaturally, to incarnate the glory of the risen Christ until his return.

Abrams wrote that a key aspect of all Romantic thought was that it "set as the goal for mankind the reachievement of a unity which has been earned by unceasing effort and which is, in Blake's term, an 'organized' unity, an equilibrium of opponent forces which preserves all the products and powers of intellection and culture".[146] Irving manifestly attempted to do this, proposing unities: between fallen humanity and a transcendent God in his incarnational theology; between a world wracked with social trauma and violence and a religion of the heart that would deal with these issues at a profound, rather than programmatic, level; between a powerless church and the resurrection power of Christ manifested through spiritual gifts; between a directionless church and the motivation of a millennial *telos* which would be the consummation of all things. Irving's approach to all the social, theological and ecclesiological issues of his day was immersed in, permeated by, and filtered through his underlying Romanticism.

By no later than 1831, Irving's views on the millennium, Christology and the charismata neatly dovetailed into a sophisticated, internally coherent and mutually reinforcing theological system through which he interpreted both the events of his own life and the world around him. As we have now seen, Irving's thought in each of these three areas was thoroughly Romantic, with the themes of quest/struggle; alienation and exile; an organic and revelatory view of history; and a pursuit of transcendence to supplement the insufficiencies of reason prominent throughout, all supplemented by a willingness to move beyond the restrictions of existing authority structures. Irving's native Scottish Romanticism, combined with his willingness to be theologically innovative in the glare of London fame, arguably meant that he demonstrated the nexus of Romanticism and theology more than anyone else in Britain in the first third of the nineteenth century. Anyone reacting against Irving's doctrines was, therefore, indirectly, but significantly reacting against his entrenched Romanticism, whether they realised it or not.

From 1831 onwards, if any one of these three areas came under doubt, it would have required of Irving nothing less than a wholesale re-evaluation of his theological position. With his native Scottish Romanticism transplanted to London, Irving had infused his inherited Church of Scotland theology with a thoroughly Romantic spirit, while vigorously arguing that he remained true to its traditions. He was convinced that he had discovered significant answers both to the profound suffering of individuals and the destiny of the church, itself. Although there were many millennialists in Irving's time, a few with innovative Christologies, and a very small number who were open to the charismata, Irving was unique in combining all three into a consistent theological package. While Irving's specific theological innovations have been noted and discussed by scholars, the comprehensive nature of his unique role in Romanticising the

[146] Abrams, *Natural Supernaturalism*, 260. Abrams was referring to William Blake.

theology of early nineteenth century Britain has not been fully appreciated. Yet, as we shall see in the next chapter, in developing his integrated Romantic theology, Irving had, unwittingly, sown the seeds of his own ministerial decline.

CHAPTER 7

Romantic Theology in Crisis

In our previous chapter, we established that Irving's three main theological distinctives – his millennialism, Christology and pro-charismata stance – were so comprehensively Romantic that anyone reacting against them was, consciously or otherwise, reacting to some degree against Irving's Romanticism. However, Irving faced two more crises in his ministerial career: his ejection from the Regent Square congregation and his final relegation within the Newman Street Church. The facts surrounding these two events have been well established elsewhere; our purpose here is to focus on the role that Romanticism played in these two dramas from the closing years of Irving's life.

As we saw in chapter one, a striving towards infinity combined with willingness and determination to leap into the unknown were *de rigueur* for Romantics.[1] We, also, noted that anti-authoritarianism was a natural feature of Romantics, coming as an almost inevitable response to the opposition they regularly faced for their implacable boundary-leaping.[2] Put another way, insistence on self-determination and intransigence towards authority structures should be expected as Romantic character-traits; they were certainly two of Irving's characteristics.

> A liberty, a self-mastery, an independence upon the opinions of others, and a mind ever conscious of a right intention, come instead of artifice, and cunning, and plodding adherence to customary rules. And this self-guidance is hindered from degenerating into self-conceit, or self-willedness, by the constant superiority of the law of God, which is, as it were, the telescope through which conscience looks upon the world of duty.[3]

Irving showed awareness that there were dangers here, but, nevertheless, independence, self-mastery and self-guidance were advocated with the optimistic view that as long as these were deferential to scripture, all would be well. Here, clearly visible behind a veil of scriptural authority, was the Romantic tendency to promote the self as the locus of authority and freedom, above the strictures of custom and contrary voices. For those following such a

---

[1] Page 18. I. Berlin, *The Roots of Romanticism* (Princeton: Princeton University Press, 1999), 14, 106.

[2] Pages 18. Berlin, *The Roots of Romanticism,* 36, 77, 119.

[3] E. Irving, *For the Oracles of God, four Orations, for Judgment to Come, an Argument in nine parts* (New York: S. Marks, 1825), 170. This was not in the original 1823 edition.

charter the only possible response to the procrustean opinions of others was resistance. In Irving's case, the intransigence that he demonstrated in his dealings with the London Presbytery and others (and the intransigence we will shortly see him showing to the Regent Square Trustees) should not be seen as simply common stubbornness or unrelenting rigidity: Irving was capable of changing his mind and accepting new ideas. We have previously noted Irving's change from cessationism to eventual acceptance of the charismata over a period of years; another example was his enthusiasm for the views of the Jesuit Lacunza's *Ben-Ezra*, and his willingness to see some parts of the Apocrypha as inspired, despite his own entrenched anti-Catholicism.[4] When these examples and others are considered, it becomes clear that Irving was flexible and open to ideas that harmonised with his Romantic ideals; he was intransigent with ideas that did not.

From October 1830, private prayer meetings were held in London for the purpose of seeking the same charismatic manifestations that had been experienced in Scotland.[5] When these prayers were apparently answered six months later and as the charismata increasingly manifested amongst the Regent Square members during 1831, Irving acted against the advice of his Trustees in allowing the gifts to operate in the prayer meetings.[6] In Irving's eyes, the Trustees were resisting God's gracious response to the fervent prayers of his people.

Later, concerned lest he was restraining the work of the Spirit, Irving, eventually, allowed the charismata to be exercised in the public worship services and opinions were immediately divided on the issue. One body of opinion aligned with that of Thomas Carlyle as seen in chapter five, that the tongues and prophecy were simply expressions of hysteria.[7] Others held for their complete genuineness and essential role in the church services; a third view was cautiously welcoming, wanting to watch how things developed.[8] Irving, himself, put restraints in place, including the requirement that he had some awareness of the spiritual standing of those operating in the gifts.[9] Church

[4] This refers to 2 Esdras 11-12. Irving, *Babylon and Infidelity Foredoomed of God*, quoted in T. Grass, *The Lord's Watchman: Edward Irving* (Milton Keynes: Paternoster, 2011), 151-154. Irving had previously strongly opposed distribution of Bibles containing the Apocrypha.

[5] Irving, himself, didn't play a significant role in these prayer meetings, which were occurring in several different congregations. A.L. Drummond, *Edward Irving and his Circle, including some consideration of the 'Tongues' Movement in the light of Modern Psychology* (London: James Clarke, 1934), 152.

[6] Grass, *The Lord's Watchman*, 231.

[7] Page 145. Another contemporary observer, Rev. Edward Bickersteth, visited Irving's congregation and concluded the tongues were "a delusion" and left "depressed", T.R. Birks, *Memoir of the Rev. Edward Bickersteth*, vol. 2 (London: Seeleys, 1852), 27.

[8] An example of this was William Hamilton, Drummond, *Edward Irving and his Circle*, 208.

[9] Grass, *Lord's Watchman*, 231.

attendance at Regent Square soared towards the end of 1831, as did the deepening rift over the charismata. At one end of the spectrum was the "excited and almost riotous crowd"; at the other, the "sober Scotch remnant [looking] on severely, with suspicion and fear".[10] For our purposes, the essential point is that Irving's anti-authoritarianism led him to reject the Trustees' "plodding adherence to customary rules"; rules which seemed to him so obviously opposed to the work of the Spirit.

Some of the Trustees were deeply concerned about these developments and, in mid-November, Irving met with them. Correspondence at the time indicated Irving's unwillingness to compromise on this issue.[11] Therefore, when the Trustees offered Irving a compromise - to prohibit the charismata on the Sabbath, but to proceed at other services as he pleased - he could not accept it: he could not compromise without a comprehensive retraction of his whole theological position.

> But there is something deeper still, than this oneness of reason and lordship of reason resident in Christ, proved by these gifts of tongues – namely, That a person is something more than that community of reason which he doth occupy as the tenant of him whose name is The Logos, or the Reason . . . Doth not this prove that all forms of the reason within, which speech expresseth outwardly, may be inactive – as if it were dead, 'fruitless,' and barren – and yet the spirit itself be receiving great edification from God, through means which are wholly independent of intelligence? Indeed, to deny this, is to deny the possibility of *direct communication between God and the soul* otherwise than by speech or books which address us through the reason; it is to set aside the subject of spiritual gifts altogether: and methinks it takes away that personality from a man, by means of which it is that he informs, awakens, and occupies the gift of reason. The gift of tongues brings all speculation upon this subject to an end, and presents us with the fact, the experiment which decides the matter, by showing us the reason void, and the spirit yet filled with edification.[12]

To attempt to restrict the gifts of the Spirit was to undermine the indwelling of the Spirit, the unmediated action of God in the human heart and the ongoing divine enfleshment in believers. Irving was determined to maintain the viability and availability of this direct and transformational access to the divine sublime.[13] Why would the servants of God seek to restrain the Spirit of God?

---

[10] M. Oliphant, *The Life of Edward Irving* (London: Hurst and Blackett, n.d. 5th edition), 324, 322.

[11] Irving to William Hamilton, 21 November 1831, cited in Oliphant, *Irving*, 333.

[12] E. Irving, *The Nature and Use of the Gift of Tongues as stated in the Scriptures* (Greenock: R.B.Lusk, 1829), 7-8. My emphasis.

[13] Irving, "On the gifts of the Holy Ghost" in *CW5*, 558. Originally printed in *The Morning Watch*, volumes II & III of 1830 and 1831 respectively.

Irving was being asked to compromise his core Romantic ideals and in being intransigent on the issue, he was being completely consistent with Romanticism's attitude to authority and acceptance of opposition and struggle.[14]

The Trustees moved with reluctance: they had staunchly defended Irving against the London Presbytery only the year before when he had been accused of heresy; now, they were moving against him themselves on issues that were apparently less theologically weighty – no heresy charge was involved. This leads us to examine the true nature of the Trustees' objection: what was so important to them that they were prepared to eventually seek Irving's removal from ministerial office? While some writers have simply alleged that the Trustees were objecting to the charismata, can they have been objecting to the charismata *per se*, when they were prepared to allow them in all services except on Sundays? The Church of Scotland had a long tradition of cessationism, so it would have been completely logical for them to maintain this as their standard, which would naturally have led to them viewing the manifestations as either delusional or demonic. In this case, they would hardly have been prepared to allow the manifestations to continue in *any* meeting of the Church, yet the compromise they offered Irving only excluded Sundays. The manifestations were the *catalyst* for the Trustees' move against Irving, but their actions imply a wider concern.

In a letter urging the Trustees to reconsider, Irving highlighted issues that reflected Romantic themes.

> I beseech you to search your hearts, and examine how much of this complaint ariseth from a desire to do your duty as trustees, how much from dislike and opposition to the work, from the influence of the popular stream, and the fear of the popular odium, from your own pride of heart and unwillingness to examine anything new, from the love of being at ease in Zion[15]

The charismata represented the transcendent and the transcendent was, by definition, radically new. Therefore, opposition to the new, in this context, equated to opposition to transcendence. The desire to pursue what was popular, comfortable and familiar was anathema to Romantics: better a divine chaos than a stultifying tedium. Irving, clearly, saw the Trustees pursuing the latter, preferring safe and known paths to the adventurous life in the Spirit Irving had been declaring and pursuing since the beginning of his ministry.[16] Immediately

---

[14] Hair was one nineteenth century commentator who thought this compromise would have succeeded, J. Hair, *Regent Square: Eighty Years of a London Congregation* (London: James Nisbet & Co., 1899), 113.

[15] Oliphant, *Irving*, 354. Oliphant lists this letter as undated, but Grass gives the date as 17 March 1832; the letter is in private hands.

[16] See chapter 4, page 81.

before the above quote, Irving declared that he "would not by a mountain of opposition be daunted from acknowledging the work [of the charismata] and walking by the counsel of [my] God".[17] Irving, clearly, demonstrated the Romantic tenets of willingly accepting opposition to the point of martyrdom in the service of a lofty ideal and valuing the inherent nobility of minority views.[18]

There is something else important here. Irving evaluated motives, including his own and those of the Trustees, but what he rarely, if ever, demonstrated, was the ability to critically evaluate his own *perceptions* on the core aspects of his Romantic vision. Intellectually, Irving was certainly capable of doing this, and he critiqued his own perception in other areas, but not where his core Romantic values were concerned: they were axiomatic. Undoubtedly, one of the contributing factors was that Irving defaulted to the standard Romantic hermeneutic of opposition: everything new, heroic and visionary would be opposed by authorities who were, characteristically, old, cowardly and blind. Opposition was more a confirmation that you were doing something right than possible evidence that you were doing something wrong; the greater the opposition, the greater the confirmation. We see evidence of this in Irving's attitude to the "mountain of opposition" mentioned above, but we have, also, seen this at numerous points in Irving's writings. At no point did the opposition of the Trustees cause Irving seriously to doubt the direction he was taking: he, simply, saw it as a choice between listening to opposition or listening to the counsel of God (which of course was no choice at all).

The other reason Irving didn't critically evaluate his own perceptions was that he knew his own motives. In the same letter to the Trustees, Irving proclaimed his purity of motive and his sincerity (without, however, appreciating that the Trustees' sincerity could equal his own), and this is something that has never seriously been doubted by Irving scholarship.[19] Irving seemed to equate sincerity of motive with authenticity of vision: because he had no qualms about his personal sincerity, he had no doubts, whatsoever, about the authenticity of his vision. This stance, which seems ingenuous, was, also, completely consistent with Romantic themes. We have, previously, noted Irving's frustration with human "mediators" - be they synods or missions committees - as pallid substitutes for the immediacy of individual guidance by the Spirit. This aligns with the Romantic frustration with structure and authority. Consider the following general description of Romantic activity from Isaiah Berlin: "You create values, you create goals, you create ends, and in the end you create your own vision of the universe . . . There is no copying, there is no adaptation, there is no learning of the rules, there is no external check, there is no structure which you must understand and adapt yourself to before you can proceed."[20] Irving may have argued that he was not "creating", but simply

[17] Oliphant, *Irving*, 354.
[18] Berlin, *The Roots of Romanticism,* 9.
[19] Oliphant, *Irving*, 354.
[20] Berlin, *The Roots of Romanticism,* 119.

"receiving" God's vision, and that he was always subject to the "external check" of scripture, and in one sense this is true. Nevertheless, in essence, this quote is a good overall description of Irving's mode of action because scripture, while "external" in one sense, is always internally understood, appropriated and applied.

While the Protestant tradition regularly maintained the rights of individuals to read and interpret scripture according to their own consciences, it, also, usually maintained that this potentially unbounded individualism needed to be placed in the context of dialogue within a believing community. Therefore, Irving was placed between two possibilities in tension: should he see contrasting views as an invitation to potentially fruitful dialectic, or should they be resisted as opposition? Of course, it was possible to begin with the former, and end, if necessary, with the latter. The real question was whether Irving was open to serious questioning of his core Romantic values, and the answer is he was not. Irving had his own vision of what the Church should be like, one he knew was not shared by many of his contemporaries; therefore, contrasting views were more likely to be seen by him to be obstacles than opportunities.

When Irving, finally, came to trial, the formal charges brought against him were as follows:

> First. – That the Rev. Edward Irving has suffered and permitted, and still allows, the public services of the church in the worship of God, on the Sabbath and other days, to be interrupted by persons not being either ministers or licentiates of the Church of Scotland.
> Second. – That the said Rev. Edward Irving has suffered and permitted, and still allows, the public services of the said church, in the worship of God, to be interrupted by persons not being either members or seatholders of the said church.
> Third. – That the said Rev. E. Irving has suffered and permitted, and also publicly encourages, females to speak in the same church, and to interrupt and disturb the public worship of God in the church on Sabbath and other days.
> Fourth. – That the said Rev. E. Irving hath suffered and permitted, and also publicly encourages, other individuals, members of the said church, to interrupt and disturb the public worship of God in the church on Sabbath and other days.
> Fifth. – That the said Rev. E. Irving, for the purpose of encouraging and exciting the said interruptions, has appointed times when a suspension of the usual worship in the said church takes place, for said persons to exercise the supposed gifts with which they profess to be endowed.[21]

The word "interrupt" occurs in each of the five charges, and, clearly, forms a major part of the Trustees' objection to what was taking place. However, the

[21] Oliphant, *Irving*, 355-356. Oliphant refers to these charges as "anti-climactic."

fact that Irving "appointed times" in the service for the exercise of the charismata indicated that these were not interruptions *per se*, but rather departures from the normal worship routine. So, it appears that the central objection of the Trustees (at least, in terms of what they were prepared to present formally) was two-fold: to Irving's role in circumventing existing Church of Scotland polity, and the egalitarianism undergirding this. Oliphant has noted that while Irving's innovations broke "no ecclesiastical law", they were "yet thoroughly contrary to the character and essence of Presbyterian worship".[22] Romanticism prioritised the individual quest for transcendence above existing authority structures; it was implicitly egalitarian and anti-authoritarian. The Trustees' formal charges against Irving were essentially faithful Presbyterian reactions against his embodiment of these key Romantic characteristics.

Earlier, we noted that an egalitarian pneumatology was a vital component of the Romantic epic that was Edward Irving's worldview.[23] Irving was completely convinced that God's plan for the Church involved a pouring out of the Spirit on all believers, both men and women. In his eyes, the Trustees' argument was blasphemously opposing the purposes of God in the world by denying the work of the Spirit in the Church.[24] From Irving's perspective, an impartial investigating committee had evaluated the Scottish manifestations favourably, believers had prayed for six months for the manifestations to appear in London and when this had occurred, Irving had subjected them to his own evaluation. Why would the Trustees oppose the work of the Spirit? Irving believed he had already effectively answered the Trustees' objections in print, by referring both to scripture and to earlier periods of the history of the Church in Scotland.[25] Facing deposition, Irving, predictably, held to his convictions on the charismata, defending his position from both scripture and history.[26] Irving argued that there should be no objection to women speaking in tongues or prophesying if the Holy Spirit chose to speak through them; the Presbytery, certainly, wasn't in a position to judge because they had never heard the utterances.[27] Those speaking in the services were not "unauthorised" because he had authorised them.[28] Here, we see an implicit tension between the

---

[22] Oliphant, *Irving*, 365.

[23] Chapter 6, page 192.

[24] Irving, undated letter to the Trustees in Oliphant, *Irving*, 365.

[25] E. Irving, *The Confessions of Faith and the Books of Discipline of the Church of Scotland, of date anterior to the Westminster Confession. To which are prefixed a historical view of the Church of Scotland from the earliest time to the time of the Reformation, and a historical preface, with remarks* (London: Baldwin and Cradock, 1831).

[26] Grass, *Lord's Watchman*, 254.

[27] Grass, *Lord's Watchman*, 254.

[28] *The Trial of the Rev. Edward Irving, M.A. before the London Presbytery; containing the whole of the evidence; exact copies of the documents; verbatim report of the speeches and opinions of the Presbyters, &c.; being the only authentic and complete*

authority of the minister pitted against the authority of the presbytery, which soon becomes explicit. Irving had no patience with anything, including tradition, that stopped people accessing the power that God was providing. As F.D. Maurice perceptively remarked some years after Irving's death, in a comment that captures the heart of Irving's Romantic thought: "[Irving] awakened people from their tacit idolatry of systems, to the sense of a living Power amidst as well as above them."[29] In taking such a stand, however, Irving was fully aware that he was inciting the wrath of those who prioritised system above an immanental Romantic theology; he embraced the "oppositional hermeneutic" of Romanticism rather than exploring dialectical possibilities.

Irving's theme of abolishing mediation between individuals and God, also, surfaced during his trial, especially when the individual concerned was the minister (or angel) of the church. "No authority," he proclaimed, "comes between the angel of the church and Christ. See you in the seven epistles of Christ to the angels, if it tells them to go up to any synod of general assembly? . . . I will say, to my younger brethren sitting around me, that it is not sound doctrine which teacheth that the Presbytery or General Assembly, or any men, or bishops, or popes, interveneth or interposeth between the minister of a church and Christ."[30] This was a bold declaration for a new style of church government, arguing on the one hand for congregational independence, but placing the congregation firmly under the control of the minister: it was a hybrid of congregational and episcopalian government in which the local minister was the bishop.[31] It would be difficult to imagine a more forthright declaration of Irving's discomfort within the Church of Scotland yoke, and it was driven by his Romantic chafing against authority and insistence on unmediated access to divine power. Was the Church of Scotland deposing Irving or was Irving rejecting the Church of Scotland? It appears that both took place.

There was one last formal flourish of support for the embattled Irving: a petition from within his congregation acknowledged God's blessing on Irving's ministry, claimed that he had always operated within the norms of the Church of Scotland (notwithstanding his now open disdain for Presbyterianism), and that less than five per cent of the congregation supported the action the Trustees took against Irving.[32] Significantly, this same group was not unanimously in favour of the charismata; they simply wanted a less heavy-handed approach to working through the issues. The petition had little effect: the presbytery found

---

record of the proceedings, taken in short-hand by W. Harding. (London: W. Harding, 1832), 67.

[29] H.N. Pym, *Memories of Old Friends. Being extracts from the journals and letters of Caroline Fox of Penjerrick, Cornwall, from 1835 to 1871* (Philadelphia: J.B. Lippincott & Co, 1882), 261. Maurice made this remark on May 26, 1849.

[30] *The Trial of the Rev. Edward Irving, M.A. before the London presbytery*, 41.

[31] As we shall see, Irving later makes this more explicit.

[32] Grass, *Lord's Watchman*, 259.

Irving "unfit" to remain minister of the church, and, shortly afterwards, the Trustees locked him out of the building. Irving's journey with the Church of Scotland, the London Presbytery and the Regent Square church had effectively come to an end, and his entrenched Romanticism had been a significant factor (if not the most significant single factor) in precipitating the crisis, provoking the Trustees' response, and shaping Irving's own uncompromising stand.

At this point, Irving had been living in the midst of crisis (centring on one aspect or another of his Romantic theology) for four years. Alongside the tragic loss of his infant children, Irving had experienced public opposition from various quarters, including church officials and close friends. It could be argued that Carlyle was right when he predicted that adversity would bring out the best in Irving: the crisis, certainly, stimulated a fertile period in Irving's theology and the years 1828-1832 produced the majority of his published works. There is, also, no doubt, from the material we have already examined, that Irving, himself, embraced the various struggles he was experiencing: struggle was not simply an irritation; it was an essential motif woven through his extensive Romantic tapestry. If there were no struggle, there could be no expectation of a worthwhile goal to be achieved; the greater the struggle, the greater the goal must be.

As the last-minute petition had claimed, Irving retained substantial support amongst his congregation, and at the beginning of May 1832 about eight hundred people followed him to the next location in Gray's Inn Road (supplemented by outdoor services), and a few months later to Newman Street.[33] The separation that Irving had contemplated had become a reality, but what would now arise from the ashes of Irving's relationship with the Church of Scotland? Irving had, clearly, indicated he wanted a church in which all the charismatic gifts were welcomed and the roles of prophets and apostles were formally recognised.[34] Yet, we need to note one important fact: despite his advocacy of the charismata and his involvement in complex situations discerning the validity of the gifts, at no stage did Irving, himself, speak in tongues, interpret or prophesy (in the charismatic sense of the term).[35] Although he had written, "there is not any believer in the Lord Jesus Christ who ought not to desire and to pray for, and who may not expect, the gift of tongues for his

[33] Oliphant, *Irving*, 369; A. Dallimore, *The Life of Edward Irving: the Fore-runner of the Charismatic Movement* (Edinburgh: Banner of Truth, 1983), 146. According to Oliphant, *Irving*, 369, "multitudes" attended Irving's outdoor sermons in Britannia Fields and Islington Green.

[34] This last point will be explored more fully below.

[35] There was, certainly, a prophetic edge to Irving's preaching and writing, and he prophesied in the sense of predicting Christ's return and the restoration of Palestine to the Jews, however, he didn't speak "under the power" of the Holy Spirit in the way the "gifted persons" in his church did.

own spiritual edification",[36] Irving was never to have this experience himself. This was to be a vital factor in the final ministerial crisis of Irving's life.

The fledgling church formally began meeting at the Newman Street premises in October 1832.[37] The charismatic gifts were in evidence from the first service and the liberation of lay ministry was, also, seen in other ways as up to forty men from within the church preached in the streets.[38] While the new church was establishing itself, Irving's final drama with the Church of Scotland was being played out. The London Presbytery had written to the General Assembly, which, after investigating Irving's activities, instructed the Presbytery of Annan to proceed against Irving.[39] The March 1833 trial has been detailed elsewhere and the result on both sides was fairly predictable: Irving was found guilty of heresy and he defended himself vigorously and at length.[40] His new status as local-boy-turned-heretic didn't appear to lessen his popularity: his open-air preaching in Annandale gathered crowds of more than 1,500.[41]

Irving was committed to the Romantic concept of immediate access to the divine, supplemented by the discernment of the angel/minister and not dictated by forces external to the congregation. Yet, this raised an uncomfortable question that was, certainly, in the minds of the "gifted ones": how could someone like Irving, who did not personally manifest any of the charismatic gifts, possibly be qualified to exercise authority and discernment over those who did? In fact, it could be argued from Irving's own writings that *any* sort of mediator, including the angel/minister, should be disavowed.

> That because this gift of tongues and prophesying, which is its fruit, are the constant demonstrations of God dwelling in a man, and teaching him all spiritual things by the Holy Ghost, without help of any third thing or third party, to the great undervaluing and entire disannulling of the powers of natural reason and speech as a fountain-head of divine instruction: therefore they must ever be fatal to the pride of intellect, to the prudence and wisdom of the world, to the scheming, counselling, and wise dealing of the natural man; to all mere philosophers, theologians, poets, sages, and wits of every name; yea, makes war upon them, brings them to nought[42]

---

[36] E. Irving, "On the Gifts of the Holy Ghost, commonly called supernatural" in *CW5*, 559.
[37] Grass, *Lord's Watchman*, 269.
[38] Grass, *Lord's Watchman*, 271. This was a short-lived development, soon constrained by the apostles.
[39] Grass, *Lord's Watchman*, 271.
[40] Grass, *Lord's Watchman*, 271. They were proceeding on the basis of the earlier heresy charge.
[41] Oliphant, *Irving*, 391; Grass, *Lord's Watchman*, 274.
[42] Irving, "On the Gifts of the Holy Ghost, commonly called super–natural", in *CW5*, 558.

Although we have seen numerous previous contexts in which Irving does not disparage reason, we see here that if pushed to choose between "natural reason" and the perceived inspiration of the Holy Spirit, Irving sides with the latter; the Romantic vision of "constant demonstrations" of God continuing to take on human flesh being too precious to refuse. Yet, Irving's own logic in this passage would allow the angel/minister to be cast in the role of the unnecessary "third party", for, surely, his previously-quoted insistence on his ministerial prerogative to "authorise" such manifestations could, itself, be seen as a prudent and prideful intellectualism at "war" against the things of God, particularly if such a minister were not one of the "gifted"? This was a difficult tightrope for Irving to walk: on the one hand, he did not believe that those operating in the charismata were infallible as he had explicitly stated that the gifts were open to misuse; on the other hand, as the following quote shows, Irving staked out a place of privilege for the charismata.[43]

> In the incarnation, Christ's identity with the fallen man was shown, yet without sin: in the church, Christ's identity with God is shown, the power and glory of God in him are exhibited, that all men might believe in his name. This gift of tongues is the crowning act of all. None of the old prophets had it, Christ had it not; it belongs to the dispensation of the Holy Ghost proceeding from the risen Christ: it is the proclamation that man is enthroned in heaven, that man is the dwelling-place of God, that all creation, if they would know God, must give ear to man's tongue, and know the compass of reason.[44]

Once again, Irving was painting on a cosmic and Romantic canvas: glossolalia is the tangible demonstration of Christ's resurrection, ascension and glorification; as a resurrected man lives and rules in heaven, so heaven lives in the mortal bodies of those who identify with Christ's resurrection; divinity was accessible. Irving's use of the phrase "the compass of reason" was exquisite, because the ambiguity of the genitive cuts both ways. He was using it, of course, to indicate the classic Romantic position that reason has limits, a fact he believed to be amply demonstrated by the phenomenon of glossolalia; he was not using it in the sense of reason being a compass, that is, an indicator of true direction. The above quote demonstrates that the charismatically gifted in the congregation were in an exalted role, and it was through them that the new order was to be instituted. At the same time as he was exalting the concept of minister/bishop, Irving was, also, exalting the widest possible distribution of the charismata. Irving could have had no idea when he wrote the above lines in

---

[43] E. Irving, *The Day of Pentecost or the Baptism with the Holy Ghost. A treatise in three parts* (London: Baldwin and Cradock, 1831), 114.

[44] E. Irving, *The Nature and Use of the Gift of Tongues as stated in the Scriptures* (Greenock: R.B.Lusk, 1829) 11-12.

1829 just how this line of thinking would contribute to the final ministerial crisis of his career.

From early in his career, Irving had used the terms "apostle" and "apostolic" in two distinct ways. For instance, in his mid-1820s sermon on the parable of the sower, he lamented the decline from the Reformation to the present "inferior evangelical spirit" and longed for the perfection of the "apostolic spirit".[45] Yet in the 1825 preface to *Missionaries*, he was, also, claiming perpetuity for the apostolic office itself.

> Those five offices mentioned by the apostle in the Epistle to the Ephesians, "apostles, prophets, evangelists, pastors, and teachers," are not offices for a time but for all times, denoting the five great divisions of duty necessary for the prosperity of the Church; "apostles," those sent out to preach the gospel unto the people who know it not[46]

While at this point, Irving was emphasising the apostolic nature of the missionary vocation, he was obviously arguing for the perpetual validity of the apostolic office, however it be conceived. From, at least, shortly after the gifts manifested in London in mid-1831, Irving and those around him had been expecting and praying for a restoration of the office of the apostle. They saw this as necessary because of the "low state of the Church" and because Christ had appointed these offices for edification.[47] Clearly, then, there was a growing expectation that the ministry of any future apostles would not, necessarily, be limited to unreached people groups. Later that year, Irving argued for the perpetual nature of the apostolic office to the Trustees.[48]

The restoration occurred, at least to their satisfaction, at a prayer meeting in November 1832 when Drummond prophesied that Cardale was to be an apostle.[49] Intriguingly, Irving was not excited at this development and the following day he warned the people not to exalt unduly Cardale or any man, reminding them that the Church, itself, was apostolic. It was a speech that led one writer to claim that "Irving had clearly not yet realised the implication of Cardale's call – that a new authority, superior to his own as pastor, had

---

[45] Irving, *CW1*, 301. Initially published in his three-volume *Sermons* of 1828, but obviously preached earlier.

[46] Irving, *CW1*, 433.

[47] Oliphant, *Irving*, 318, referring to a letter that appears to date from about July 1831.

[48] Irving to the Trustees of Regent Square, dated 22 November 1831, quoted in Oliphant, *Irving*, 335. Despite this, as Grass indicates, it appears that "The restoration of the apostleship had not been anticipated by Irving", *Lord's Watchman*, 280.

[49] C. Flegg, *"Gathered under Apostles": a study of the Catholic Apostolic Church* (Oxford: Clarendon Press, 1992), 58-59. It is important to note that Drummond had not formally joined Irving's church, but remained Anglican up until this point, G. Carter, *Anglican Evangelicals: Protestant Secessions from the via media, c. 1800-1850* (Oxford: Oxford University Press, 2001), 186-187.

appeared in the Church".[50] On the other hand, it was possible that Irving *had* clearly realised the implication of Cardale's call for his own role as pastor, and this was the reason he was expressing reservation. There is obvious paradox here: one minute Irving was praying for an apostle, but the moment one was called he retreated from this position, and attempted to dilute his own previous emphasis on apostles as individuals, opting for the more general "apostolic spirit" concept. Irving's non-participation in the charismata had excluded him from one sphere of worship and authority; the appointment of Cardale as apostle raised an additional range of issues surrounding structure and authority. Irving, while praying for the restoration of the apostolic office, had clearly not thought through all the implications.

It was on Irving's return from Scotland to London in late March 1833 that events at Newman Street took a complex turn, which has been variously interpreted. An interpretation that began with Oliphant is that the "gifted" at Newman Street were attempting to override Irving's ministerial authority.[51] On Irving's return from Annan, she commented, "he was received, not with extraordinary honours as a martyr, but with an immediate interdict, in 'the power,' forbidding him to exercise any priestly function, to administer sacraments, or to assume anything out of the province of a deacon, the lowest office in the newly-formed church".[52] Although this interpretation was further emphasised sixty years later by A.L. Drummond, there were other voices arguing that Irving had not been manipulated out of power.[53] Grass is the most recent author to explore this issue in detail. Essentially, he maintains, the leaders at Newman Street pointed out that the Church of Scotland had removed Irving's ministerial authority, which was within their rights to do as they had granted it in the first place; on his return to London he was, essentially, unordained. Therefore, they did not consider he should take a leading role in the sacraments.[54]

Cardale, the apostle in question in the above prohibition, was quick to object to Oliphant's published allegations, and she included his objection in a footnote to later editions. Cardale pointed out that Irving acquiesced in this decision and that he, subsequently, received "apostolical ordination".[55] The time delay between the "interdict" and the "apostolical ordination" was short – from 31 March to 5 April – and, although this period of less than a week may seem

---

[50] R.A. Davenport, *Albury Apostles* (London: United Writers, 1970), 93.

[51] This was, also, Thomas Carlyle's interpretation, but his views were not published until after Oliphant's.

[52] Oliphant, *Irving*, 397.

[53] Drummond, *Edward Irving and his Circle,* 272. A similar view is held by E. Miller, *The History and Doctrines of Irvingism or of the so-called Catholic and Apostolic Church*, vol. 1, (London: C. Kegan Paul & Co., 1878), 82, 96, 130. For example, C.K. Paul, *Biographical Sketches* (London: Kegan Paul, Trench & Co., 1883), 29-30.

[54] Grass, *Lord's Watchman*, 276-277.

[55] Oliphant, *Irving*, 396-397 footnotes. Grass has pointed out that there is no indication that Irving felt humiliated by this, *Lord's Watchman*, 277.

insignificant, the implications are not. If the apostle ordained the angel, didn't the apostle have greater authority than the angel?[56] The question of authority had now firmly been raised in a public and tangible way in the embryonic church.

Earlier in this chapter, we noted that Irving's Romantic theology led to a hybrid ecclesiology, blending and placing in tension congregational and episcopalian features: on the one hand, he was freeing the laity to an extent the Trustees had rejected; on the other, he was seeing his own power as episcopal. This tension became centrally important in Irving's final ministerial crisis.

> I maintain, therefore, that a church with its minister, one or more ...its elders and its deacons, is complete within itself for all purposes whatsoever, either of self-preservation or of propagation: and that the Presbytery, mentioned in Scripture, and in our Books of Discipline, consisted of the eldership of such a church, and I do feel in this respect perfect liberty, acting as the head of the eldership of a church, to do all the acts to which a bishop in the Church of England or a Presbytery in the Church of Scotland feel themselves to be competent. Moreover, I feel assured that it is the duty of every church so to act.[57]

It is likely that these words would have contributed to the discomfort and fear of the Trustees as they moved against Irving, yet they did not refer to them when accusing Irving of breaking with Church of Scotland polity; had they done so, it would have greatly strengthened their case. To modern eyes, Irving's words appear to be simply an attempt to grasp greater power, but there is much more to it than this. Irving was bringing together those features which he believed would best equip the church to fulfil God's purposes. Firstly, he jettisoned external hierarchies of bishoprics and synods and proclaimed the self-sufficiency of each local congregation; secondly, he assigned complete leadership to the local minister. This is thoroughly consistent with the Romantic impatience with external authority structures, and the corresponding tendency to internalise authority. This was not just how Irving wanted his own church to operate; as the last sentence of the above quote makes clear, this is how he thought *every* church should be constituted.

This localising of spiritual authority recalls Irving's address to the London Missionary Society years before, when he boldly proclaimed the freedom of missionaries to obey the leading of the Spirit, unfettered by the commands of

---

[56] Tragically, although Irving believed that the restoration of the charismatic gifts and apostolic offices would instigate victory over sickness, he lost another infant, Ebenezer, in this month of April 1833, despite the presence of the charismatically gifted and an apostle.

[57] E. Irving, *The Confessions of Faith and the Books of Discipline of the Church of Scotland, of date anterior to the Westminster Confession*, cxxii-cxxiii.

distant mission societies.[58] Seen in this context, Irving's redefinition of Presbyterian polity makes perfect sense: on both occasions, he was objecting to the mediation of distant bodies in the work of the Spirit; on both occasions he was arguing that God's faithful *in situ* are the best able to make the appropriate decisions; on both occasions his implication was that the intervention of remote authorities was more likely to hinder than assist God's work. The passage of the years and the experience of conflict enabled Irving to translate his initial observation about the mission field into the context of the Church of Scotland. Why settle for hierarchical mediation when immanent inspiration is available? To do so would surely have been to spurn the gracious gift of God's Spirit. This removal of intermediaries between God and individual believers and the optimistic view of the possibilities when a revelatory God encounters receptive servants was intrinsically Romantic. However, Irving was not completely egalitarian: the minister remained in control; but the situation was further complicated by the arrival of apostles as alternative authority figures.

It will be necessary to explore this final crisis of Irving's life in some detail because it became a cul-de-sac into which he was propelled by Romantic convictions: anti-authoritarianism and the quest for a transcendent sublime, and the way in which these convictions were to be embodied within the new church structure. As we have seen, Irving's anti-authoritarianism led him to eschew synods and general assemblies in favour of autonomous congregations led by minister/bishops. Obviously, in his own congregation he saw himself fulfilling this role. Irving's acceptance of the charismata and his conviction that the apostolic office would, eventually, be restored were expressions of his thirst for transcendence in the Church of his day.[59] It is the tension between the roles of apostle and angel that has given rise to the interpretation that the leaders of the nascent Catholic Apostolic Church manipulated Irving into a position of powerlessness. Yet, such an interpretation is not necessary to explain this tension and the events that followed from it. In 1831, Irving had written to the Trustees of Regent Square his understanding of authority in worship.

> Now, my dear brethren, it is well known to you, that, by the word of God, and by the rules of all well-ordered churches, and by the trust-deed of our church in particular, it lies with the angel or minister of the church to order in all things connected with the public worship and service of God. For this duty I am responsible to the great Head of the Church, and have felt the burden of it upon my conscience for many weeks past; but consulting for the feelings of others, I have held back from doing that which I felt to be my duty, and most profitable for the great edification of the church of Christ, over which the Lord hath set me[60]

---

[58] See chapter 2, page 28.

[59] See page 199 above.

[60] *The Trial of the Rev. Edward Irving, M.A. before the London presbytery*, 4.

Irving, clearly, understood it to be his role as minister/angel to order all aspects of public worship in the church. Of course, it could be argued that Irving wrote the above when he was minister at Regent Square; now he was within the Newman Street congregation his ties were broken with both Regent Square and the Church of Scotland. However, the passage cannot be so easily set aside, because Irving's understanding went beyond the immediate context of the trust-deed of Regent Square through "the rules of all well-ordered churches" to "the word of God". Irving was convinced that the angel/minister had authority over all aspects of public worship, including who could, or could not, exercise the charismata. He described the ability to authorise the charismata as the "plenary right" of the angel/minister.[61] Yet, now, we have seen that the authorisation of the first apostle came through the charismata, and there were sources in Irving's own writings that asserted the authority of the apostle over the angel, if this were not already implied in Irving's acceptance of ordination at Cardale's hands.[62]

When writing an exposition of Revelation, Irving wrote, "The order of revelation is not from the angels to the apostles, and thence to the Church; but from the apostles to the Church, and thence to the angels."[63] Elsewhere, Irving explicitly described the vocation of apostle as a "higher calling" than that of angel/pastor.[64] It was a clear model for Irving's own subordination to the apostles. Yet, the relationship between the two roles was complex, which is nowhere better revealed than in a reply from Irving to Alan Ker, who had questioned his understanding of apostleship.[65]

> The angel of the Church is over the apostle, and the apostle is over the angel of the Church . . . Now, doth Jesus write His epistles to the apostles of the Churches, or to the angels of the Churches? But by whom writeth He them? Is it not by an apostle? So receive I, through an apostle, my instructions; and having received them, the apostle himself is the first man that must bow to them, and I will take good care that he doth so, lest he should exalt himself to the seat of our common Master, who alone is complete within Himself.[66]

---

[61] *The Trial of the Rev. Edward Irving, M.A. before the London presbytery,* 67.

[62] Carter, incorrectly, states that Irving, himself, became an apostle, cf. Carter, *Anglican Evangelicals*, 164.

[63] G. Carlyle (ed.), *The Prophetical Works of Edward Irving* (London: Alexander Strahan, 1867), vol.1, 30. This was originally published in four volumes as *Exposition of the Book of Revelation, in a series of lectures* (London: Baldwin and Cradock, 1831).

[64] Irving, *The Confessions of Faith and the Books of Discipline*, cxlv.

[65] Oliphant gives little information on Ker, other than he was from Greenock and had been bed-ridden for a long time. The letter that follows does not appear in Oliphant's one-volume 5th edition, which has been used elsewhere in this thesis.

[66] Irving to Alan Ker, 30 April 1833 in Oliphant, *Irving*, vol. 2, (London: Hurst & Blackett, 1862), 334.

The locus of authority here is inherently problematic: it would take a preternatural degree of sanctity for such an arrangement to work in practice. So, we need look no further than Irving's own writings for potential conflict and confusion about the understanding of the respective roles, privileges and authority of angels and apostles.

Drummond became an apostle in September 1833, less than a year after Cardale.[67] If Irving was hoping for the same transition from angel to apostle, it was not to be. From the calling of the first apostle at the end of 1832 (and despite Irving's sentiments as quoted in the letter to Ker) it became obvious that the balance of power within the Newman Street congregation was shifting away from Irving. The power now rested with the apostles, Cardale and Drummond, and the prophet, Taplin, whose previous occupations, respectively, were lawyer, wealthy member of Parliament, and schoolmaster.[68] In one sense, this was expressive of Irving's egalitarian ministerial emphasis, but it is noteworthy that, whatever their other gifts and abilities, none of these men, singly or combined, possessed a fraction of Irving's theological training and extensive pastoral experience. As has been noted, Irving had achieved ecclesiological independence (from the Church of Scotland) only to find himself relegated to a secondary role in the emerging organisation that was so largely (initially) his own creation.[69] The eventual outcome of this tension has been succinctly described by Flegg: "For the remainder of his life, Irving was required to accept apostolic rule and to be guided by the words of the prophets."[70] The final months of Irving's life demonstrate alternate periods of acceptance and chafing against this new order. What is clear, though, is that Irving's own Romantic theology was the main contributing factor to this scenario. In the quest for transcendence and a desire to shed ossified structures, Irving had, simultaneously, elevated the authority of the charismata, the authority of the apostles, and his own authority as angel-bishop without adequately working through how they related to each other.

1834 was a year of generally declining health for Irving, culminating with his death in Glasgow in December. During these final months, various friends, especially Thomas Carlyle, struggled to get Irving to move to a warmer climate for health reasons, or at least away from the demands of London. There was a sense of alarm at Irving's decline, along with various attributions of blame.

Early in 1834, Irving made a trip to Scotland from which he returned very ill.[71] On his return to London another incident occurred which highlighted the

---

[67] Flegg notes the circularity in this: Drummond had prophetically called Cardale to the apostolate; now Cardale was calling Drummond to the same role, having earlier appointed him as angel over the Albury congregation. Flegg, *"Gathered under Apostles"*, 64, 63.

[68] Flegg, *"Gathered under Apostles"*, 64.

[69] Grass, *Lord's Watchman*, 280-283.

[70] Flegg, *"Gathered under Apostles"*, 60.

[71] Oliphant, *Irving*, 407.

tension between apostolic and angelic authority. It occurred during the absence of Cardale and Drummond, who had, themselves, gone to Scotland to follow up Irving's visit.[72] Taplin spoke prophetically, nominating several people to the role of evangelist and Irving affirmed this in his role as angel. As soon as the two apostles heard of this development, however, they wrote rebuking both Taplin and Irving.[73] Offended, Taplin left the church for some months; Irving, caught in the cross-fire of prophetic and apostolic authority, wrestled with the issue, and ultimately confessed his error.[74] Irving's view that his role as angel included the right to sanction prophetic utterances was, clearly, being contravened by the apostles themselves. Would Irving's anti-authoritarianism assert itself against this nascent structure that had so clearly come about because of his own visionary Romantic agenda, yet was simultaneously relegating him to a lesser role and promoting other visionaries?

In the middle months of the year, Irving kept a low profile, presumably attempting to recuperate; he and his family were now living in the Newman Street Church premises. Carlyle was alarmed, believing his attempts to visit Irving were often opposed either by the Newman Street leaders or Isabella.[75] In September, William Graham, a friend of Carlyle, wrote to him expressing anger at the relationship between Irving and the church leaders, breaking off when he had run out of insults. "These daringly presumptuous men called Elders are become his imperious taskmasters; he is sunk under their proud control; he is now their 'thral' [sic] instead of being the Angel of the Church, its Prophet, Lawgiver and director; he is the degraded slave of these bloated, inflated, deceiving, self-deceived, &c., &c."[76] Back in Scotland himself, Graham was urging Carlyle's intervention. Carlyle's replies were mournful and resigned; faint optimism barely covered his sense that Irving's death was near. Irving's "old Annandale heartiness" could be perceived occasionally, Carlyle wrote, but he had aged ten years and had difficulty breathing. Carlyle was delighted when he heard that Irving had actually left London, hoping it was for a milder climate.[77] Later news, however, indicated that as Irving progressed through Wales, his health deteriorated and Carlyle began "to fear it is in sad truth almost over with him".[78]

There has been some disagreement about Irving's last trip to Scotland which ended in his death in Glasgow: was it his own desire to go, or was he following

---

[72] Oliphant, *Irving*, 407.
[73] Oliphant, *Irving*, 407.
[74] Dallimore, *Irving*, 163; Oliphant, *Irving*, 407.
[75] Thomas Carlyle to John A. Carlyle, 15 August 1834, in C.R. Sanders (ed.), *The Collected Letters of Thomas and Jane Welsh Carlyle,* Vol. 7: October 1833 – December 1834 (Durham, N.C.: Duke University Press, 1977), 269-273. Henceforth *CL7*.
[76] William Graham to Thomas Carlyle, 8 September 1834 in *CL7*, 297 footnote. Graham was from Ecclefechan and knew both Carlyle and Irving.
[77] Thomas Carlyle to William Graham, 14 September 1834 in *CL7*, 297.
[78] Thomas Carlyle to John A. Carlyle, 28 October 1834, in *CL7*, 328.

the apostles' orders? The options have been comprehensively surveyed by Irving's latest biographer, who concluded that Irving was responsible for the decision, responding to a much earlier prophecy that he had a great work to do in Scotland.[79]

In these last few months of Irving's life, the tension between his role and authority as angel and that of the apostles continued to be a central issue. Irving was wrestling with a conflict that was essentially of his own making. In April he wrote to Henry Drummond, "Besides this I do well know that it pertaineth to an angel fully accomplished of the Holy Ghost for his office to minister and to rule and to discern in a fourfold measure, apostolical, prophetical evangelical & pastoral, whereby he is enabled consciously to apprehend and with discernment to obey every thing spoken by the Lord through this fourfold headship in the house."[80] The angel was to both rule and obey, and Irving reserved the right to exercise discernment as to what he was to obey; clearly, he was attempting to retain the right to reject prophetic and apostolic utterances as he saw fit. Less than a month later, in one of his last letters to Drummond, Irving claimed that he had been unfairly judged in some issues where the parameters had not been clearly enough established by the apostles.[81] Irving wrote that he often felt he had been "hardly dealt with", and that some of Drummond's words had been like "drawn swords", rather than edifying; but Irving, also, wrote that he was aware of "great disorder in my spirit"; he felt guilty of pride and rebellion and had "need of being humbled to the dust".[82] In context, these comments express the tension that existed between the authority claims of apostle and minister. Irving was in a sad position: he had seen the fledgling Newman Street Church as the vehicle of freedom through which he would, finally, fulfil his Romantic agenda, but he now had less freedom than during his years in Regent Square.

The Newman Street Church would not have come into existence had it not been for Irving's determined stance on allowing the charismata in public worship at Regent Square. From the earliest days of the charismata in Regent Square in 1831, Irving's consistent stance had been that his role as angel/minister encompassed the authority to determine who could, or could not, speak "under the power", and, also, to rule as to whether those utterances were according to the word of God. Cardale, Drummond, Taplin and all the other "gifted ones" had been raised up within that theological understanding; yet, as time passed, it seems they moved increasingly outside this concept of "angelic authority".[83] It is difficult not to suspect that this development occurred at least

[79] Grass, *Lord's Watchman*, 289-291.

[80] Letter dated 7 April 1834, C/9/37 in the Alnwick collection. Used by permission.

[81] Letter dated 1 May 1834, C/9/38 in the Alnwick collection. Used by permission.

[82] Letter dated 1 May 1834, C/9/38 in the Alnwick collection. Used by permission.

[83] Although Irving was moving in his writings towards congregational autonomy, there was an obvious tension looming with the parallel concept of apostolic authority.

partly because Irving, himself, never spoke in tongues or prophesied.[84] Just as we saw that the tension between the roles of apostle and angel arose from within Irving's own writings, here, likewise, Irving's own writings implied that, as one not evidencing the charismata, he was destined for a secondary role. Infusing the mundane with the transcendent and by-passing overly rigid authority structures had been at the core of Irving's Romantic vision, but now the vision that had come had brought its own increasing authority structure which by-passed the original visionary.

Irving taught that every believer could expect the gift of tongues, adding that they should not be disheartened if they did not receive it.[85] Yet, we can hardly doubt that "disheartened" would be a mild description of how Irving, himself, would have felt at his own lack of charismatic experience, in the light of his lofty aspirations. This, after all, was the man whose overriding ambition had been to bring a higher form of Christianity to nineteenth century Britain, who taught that the gifts of the Holy Spirit were given "to construct for God a place to dwell in", and that believers ought to "prove" their sonship and Christ's resurrection power through supernatural signs.[86] If the gift of tongues and prophesying brought all other wisdom "to nought", then where did that leave Irving in the eyes of the apostles and prophets?[87] By implication, in failing to demonstrate the charismatic gifts in his own life, Irving, himself, was failing to live out the standard he had proclaimed as freely available. And, if God was overlooking him, with all his ministerial training, experience, and fervent desire for spiritual adventure, and bestowing these gifts on others, what did it say about his own standing in God's eyes? In the last few months of his life, Edward Irving wrestled with this devastating gulf between his Romantic expectations and the reality of his circumstances.

It seems that Irving did not fully discern that the root cause of the tension between his authority as angel and the authority of the apostles, as well as his increasing isolation as one "ungifted" among the "gifted", lay within his own writings. When this tension was added to the struggle of the fledgling church to form its own identity and was filtered through some powerful personalities, it is no surprise that friction resulted. It is possible, of course, that this tension might have been creatively resolved had Irving lived longer. On the other hand, if Irving had survived beyond 1834 and remained "ungifted", he may have

---

[84] Dorries has argued that Irving wouldn't have committed himself so strongly to tongues if he had never had the experience personally, D.W. Dorries, "Edward Irving and the 'Standing Sign'" in G.B. McGee (ed,), *Initial Evidence: Historical and Biblical Perspectives on the Pentecostal Doctrine of Spirit Baptism* (Peabody, Mass: Hendrickson, 1991), 53. However, as Dorries supplies no evidence, this appears to be merely wishful sentimentality on his part.

[85] Irving, "On the Gifts of the Holy Ghost, commonly called supernatural", *CW5*, 559. This first appeared in two parts, in *The Morning Watch*, Vol. II of 1830 and Vol. III of 1831.

[86] Irving, "On the Gifts of the Holy Ghost", 510, 523-524.

[87] Irving, "On the Gifts of the Holy Ghost", 558.

continued to chafe against the harsh reality that his lofty hopes were not fulfilled; we must leave this dilemma for speculation. What we can conclude is that by championing a pneumatology with a privileged place for charismata that he did not evidence himself, Irving unwittingly paved the way for his own relegation to a secondary role. In his attempt to bring heaven down to earth and to encourage the church to accept its role as the ongoing incarnation of resurrection power in God's cosmic drama, Irving instigated a new model for the church. Yet, this new model simultaneously attempted to empower the laity through the charismata, create minister-bishops and place all under apostles. The inevitable tensions in this unusual ecclesiological hybrid that derived from his Romanticism precipitated Edward Irving into the terminal ministerial crisis of his career.

We have now surveyed the ministerial crises that formed so much a part of Edward Irving's final years. Irving could not compromise in the Christological crisis with the London Presbytery and the Church of Scotland because he saw their stance as heretical; nor could he compromise his position on the charismata which indirectly led (via the Trustees' policy objections) to his ejection from Regent Square. In both cases, far too much was at stake: Irving felt his own stance was biblically, theologically and historically coherent, and that of his opponents was not; his stance furthered God's purposes, his opponents' did not. The final crisis with the Newman Street leaders resulted, partly, from the apostle/angel authority dilemma and, partly, from Irving's privileging of the charismata, to his own cost. Irving proved quite capable of withstanding the authority of the Church of Scotland in all its forms: the London Presbytery, the parish of Annan, and the Regent Square Trustees. Irving believed his intransigence was justified because he was pursuing his Romantic agenda in full sincerity. Yet, in the conflict with the Newman Street leaders, Irving ultimately acquiesced to their authority. This was because the Newman Street Church, created largely by Irving's own actions, was, also, the vehicle through which he expected to see his Romantic hopes fulfilled. At this stage of Irving's life, he had staked everything on the Newman Street Church – there was, simply, nowhere else to turn, even when he was caught in the crossfire of competing authority claims.

It is apparent that the theological "lightning rods" in Irving's ministerial crises were intrinsically and comprehensively Romantic. As we saw in chapter six, Irving's Christology and pro-charismata views were both infused with an egalitarianism that was in tension with his Presbyterian context. Yet, Irving was, simultaneously and paradoxically, developing a model of minister-as-bishop. Irving's anti-authoritarianism mixed with his uncritical faith in his own perceptions in key areas meant that he was confidently intransigent where his core Romantic values were concerned. Had Irving defended these issues with less vigour, some of these crises could have been averted. He could, for instance, have accepted the initial offer of the Regent Square Trustees simply to keep the charismata out of the Sunday services. But this seemed to him too much like trying to quash the work of the Spirit. Edward Irving was attempting to defend his Romantic theology in the midst of battle at several levels, and we have seen that battle was a metaphor Irving, himself, was comfortable with, and others readily applied to him.

Edward Irving attracted opposition because he rapidly and comprehensively processed Christian theology through the filter of a Romantic worldview and presented this to Britain in the 1820s and early 1830s. He was at the forefront of this by some years. In this sense, it can be said that in their opposition to Irving, the London Presbytery, the Church of Scotland and the Trustees of Regent Square were actually opposing Romanticism. With the benefit of hindsight, it is easy to see that Irving's emphases on spiritual gifts, immanence, increasing congregational autonomy and unmediated access to the Holy Spirit would have been threatening to these bodies. Permeating all these controversies labelled as contentious or heretical was Irving's underlying Romanticism. In the case of the crisis with the Newman Street leaders, Irving was ultimately constrained by his own Romantic theology of the charismata and, especially, the inherent tensions in his own writings between the relative authority of apostle and angel. As one who had spent most of his adult life trying to reach beyond the restrictions of existing church authority structures to grasp a transcendent future, and was forced to spend so much of his later years defending his views, it is, perhaps, understandable that Irving didn't spend the time to systematically work through the apostle-angel contradictions; Cardale's apostleship seemed to catch Irving unawares. Irving's theology, elsewhere, was coherent, but on this point it was confused, and the apostle-angel nexus became the final crisis of his career.

Conclusion

In examining the historiography of Edward Irving in chapter three, we saw that one of the persistent questions being asked was why his career ended in the way that it did. One minute his pulpit oratory was taking London by storm, then came accusations of heresy, rejection by ecclesiastical authorities, and an early death. What was the reason for the apparent reversal of fortune in a career that showed such promise? In trying to address this question, numerous answers have been proposed over the years: Irving was a fanatic; he was credulous; he lacked theological aptitude; he was deluded; he was manipulated by others. As we have seen, these explanations do not hold up under detailed examination.

We have argued that the main key to understanding Irving's ministerial career – both its achievements and its reversals – was his underlying Romanticism. While numerous writers have indicated (usually, briefly) a link between Irving and Romanticism, the breadth and depth of the impact of this major cultural shift on his ministry have seldom been fully appreciated. Irving's Romanticism shaped his worldview, his preaching, his theological distinctives, and his lofty vision of what could be achieved both through his own personal ministry and through the wider Church. The opposition and eventual deposition that Irving faced through his career within the Church of Scotland, followed by the tensions and his eventual relegation within the Newman Street church, were, likewise, ultimately triggered by his comprehensive Romanticism and his unwillingness to compromise on those values. Irving's life was consistent with his theology, embracing and expressing the Romantic *zeitgeist* of self-sacrificial struggle and alienation for a noble cause; a hunger for the mundane to be infused with the transcendent; an organic and teleological view of history; and impatience with Utilitarianism, prudence and restrictive authority structures.

Irving's native Scottish Romanticism developed further through his experiences in Glasgow and London. Although Irving had the friendship and respect of men like Coleridge and Carlyle, he was never cowed by them. Despite being much closer in age and upbringing to Carlyle, Irving had a greater theological affinity with Coleridge. The Sage of Highgate and the Sage of Chelsea, both intellectual giants of Romanticism, tended either to be adored or avoided; Irving defaulted to neither position, but was open to their input (Irving always listened to Carlyle, even on religious matters, even if they never agreed) without allowing it to swamp his own views. The influence Coleridge (or anyone else) had on him was always kept (despite Irving's dedicatory paean to Coleridge) within the confines of his own Romantic vision. On the other hand, it has been demonstrated that Irving's influence on Coleridge was far greater than has been previously recognised.

Often described as an evangelical, Irving's Romantic agenda led him to stand critically aloof from several key aspects of evangelicalism, noticeably its conversionism and crucicentrism, and the way in which he felt it had capitulated to the gods of prudence and utility; he had no interest in aligning with church "parties". Adjectives like "evangelical" or "Presbyterian" can only be used lightly of Irving before immediately being qualified. Irving's Romanticism led him not only to criticise contemporary Church of Scotland evangelicalism, but, also, to appreciate High Church Anglican and older Reformed traditions and even, on occasion, Catholic writers (*Ben-Ezra*): although steeped in a standard Protestant anti-Catholic polemic, Irving was, nevertheless, able to accept these writings by a Jesuit that called attention to the millennial vista. Confusing as these various alignments must have been to many of his contemporaries, Irving, thereby, demonstrated the core Romantic tenet that truth is not constrained by any one system, and that those in pursuit of transcendence must seek it beyond the established boundaries of inherited formulas. Long before controversy arose, Irving was quite conscious of the fact that he would move beyond accepted Church of Scotland parameters into uncharted territory, and that he would face opposition. On the verge of beginning his London ministry, Irving wrote, "There is a sea of troubles, for my notions of a clergyman's office are not common, nor likely to be in everything approved. There is a restlessness in my mind after a state of life less customary, more enterprising, more heroical . . . certainly more apostolical . . . In truth I am an adventurer on ground untried."[1] The later years of Irving's life, certainly, proved the accuracy of this early insight. The "sea of troubles" reflects Hamlet's quandary, and Irving's response was, certainly, to "take arms" and enter battle.[2]

The popularity of his preaching gave Edward Irving the opportunity to present his thoughts to a large audience. In seizing this opportunity in the early 1820s, he was at the forefront of integrating Christian theology within a Romantic worldview in Britain and, unsurprisingly, both acclaim and controversy ensued. Other Christian leaders and movements would soon pursue their own Romantic theologies and become more widely known, but Irving was in the front line.[3] The nexus between Romanticism and religion is one that

---

[1] Irving in an 1822 letter to one of the Caledonian Church office bearers (apparently Andrew Robertson), quoted in J. Hair, *Regent Square: Eighty Years of a London Congregation* (London: James Nisbet & Co., 1899), 34.

[2] The beginning lines of Act 3 of Shakespeare's *Hamlet* are
"To be or not to be – that is the question:
Whether 'tis nobler in the mind to suffer
The slings and arrows of outrageous fortune,
Or to take arms against a sea of troubles
And, by opposing, end them."

[3] The Oxford Movement is the best-known of these. One observer said, "Newmanism would never be the success it is if it hadn't been for that flood of Irvingism." Benjamin Wills Newton in *The Diary of Alfred C. Fry*, 234, quoted in G. Carter, *Anglican Evangelicals: Protestant Secessions from the via media, c. 1800-1850* (Oxford: Oxford University Press, 2001), 194.

deserves much further study, both historically and sociologically. In a lecture given more than forty years ago, Isaiah Berlin made a strong claim for the influence of Romanticism.

> The importance of romanticism is that it is the largest recent movement to transform the lives and the thought of the Western world. It seems to me to be the greatest single shift in the consciousness of the West that has occurred, and all the other shifts which have occurred in the course of the nineteenth and twentieth centuries appear to me in comparison less important, and at any rate deeply influenced by it.[4]

Berlin's statement highlights that the influence of Romanticism (and its descendants) is not sufficiently appreciated in society, generally, or in the Church, specifically. Romanticism has both enriched and challenged the Church, and continues to do so; the trajectory of Edward Irving's career is one powerful demonstration of this.

The battle to remove the taint of heresy from Irving's name was fought during the last few decades of the twentieth century. A corollary of that effort was that a new generation began to appreciate his theological acumen, especially his Christology and pneumatology; certainly, his works contain a more capable and reflective theology of the Holy Spirit than any that was written during the first fifty years of the twentieth century Pentecostal movement. The Pentecostal movement has, understandably, embraced Irving as an ancestor, but Pentecostal historians tend to regard Irving as having no direct influence on the Pentecostalism of the twentieth century; this view tends to overlook the ongoing practice of the charismata in the Catholic Apostolic Church, which continued into the early twentieth century. This is, certainly, a promising area for further research.

However, labels such as "proto-Pentecostal" or "millennialist", though they are appropriate enough to use of Irving in context, ultimately diminish the comprehensive nature of his thought and his hopes. His thought ranged widely across theology and history (and to a lesser extent, politics) so to choose one label from *within* this spectrum of interests is to risk distortion. We need to stand back, as it were, from the pixels in order to see the wider perspective. Therefore, we return, in closing, to the issue of taxonomy addressed in our first chapter, where we noted that some scholars were so frustrated by the mercurial nature of Romanticism that they wanted to abandon the term. Our journey with Edward Irving has, as a by-product, shown once again the usefulness of the term: only Romanticism is capacious enough to coherently accommodate all of Irving's theological passions. Only his underlying Romanticism is able to comprehensively explain Irving's alignments and separations, why he flexed on some issues and stubbornly refused to budge on others.

---

[4] I. Berlin, *The Roots of Romanticism* (Princeton: Princeton University Press, 1999), 1-2. The original lecture was given in 1965.

In all of this, Edward Irving was not merely the protagonist of a Romantic theology; he personally *became* a Romantic metaphor. Reardon has written, "Your true romantic hero is an exile, a wanderer on the face of the earth. He has no real place in society, and society in truth alienates him."[5] This was, certainly, Irving's experience. It is appropriate, here, to revisit a passage quoted in an earlier chapter:

> Some there are blessed with such weak passions and strong reason as to steer without foreign help; but though such may be found to succeed, instead of being admired for their noble independence by the crowd who cling to ancient and present customs, they will generally be stigmatized as self-conceited, or persecuted as innovators, so that disturbance from without, if not from within, shall invade every one who, shaking loose of religious or customary restraints, adventures for himself.
>
> Yet such adventurers should all men become. What to us are the established rules of life, that they should blindly overrule us? Must we be bound in thraldom, to fill and do no more than fill, the narrow bounds of the condition we are born into? Is there nought noble, nought heroical, to be undertaken and achieved? Must the budding desires of our youthful nature be held in check by the narrow prescriptions of an age and an authority we despise; and the labour of a life end in nothing but contemptible drudgery, to keep our tabernacle in being? - Adventurers above your sphere I would have you all to become; brave designs, not antiquated customs, should move your life. A path heroical you should trace out, and follow to glory and immortality.[6]

While this was from Irving's first major publication, he wholeheartedly followed his own advice in the remaining eleven years of his life. It was a Romantic declaration that embraced opposition and "persecution". Of course, like most Romantics, Irving could have changed his situation at any time. Romantic heroes are not usually forced into exile and alienation; their own principles or quests drive them there, far from comfort and acclaim. As we have seen, Irving found rapid fame and acclaim on his arrival in London, yet he was on a quest that took him through rejection and alienation. It could have ended at any time with a compromise or two, but, then, choosing compromise over principle, comfort over a transcendent goal, was something hard-core Romantics (for example, Irving's contemporaries, the poets, Byron and Shelley) would never do. Irving, therefore, not only presented early nineteenth century Britain with a Romantic theology, he lived his life as something of a Romantic hero, refusing to compromise, believing for greater things until the

---

[5] B.M.G. Reardon, "Religion and the Romantic movement" in *Theology*, vol. lxxvi , no. 638 (August 1973), 408

[6] E. Irving, *For the Oracles of God, four Orations, for Judgment to come, an Argument in nine parts* (New York: S. Marks, 1825), 74.

end. The crises that Edward Irving faced arose directly from his own Romanticism; his integrity throughout each crisis is one reason why men, such as Coleridge and Carlyle, admired him so much; his intransigence on his central principles was based on an unwavering faith in the veracity of his own vision. The early death of such a man in the midst of exalted, but unfulfilled, hopes is sadly, a fittingly tragic end to a Romantic tale.

Bibliography

Manuscript sources

Alnwick: The Drummond papers in Alnwick castle contain letters from Irving to Henry Drummond.

Waddington collection: Barbara Waddington's comprehensive collection of electronic scans of Irving's letters held in various archives and private hands will shortly be published.

Works by Irving, Coleridge & Carlyle

Beer, J. ed. *The Collected Works of Samuel Taylor Coleridge: Aids to Reflection*. London: Routledge, 1993.

Carlyle, G. *The Collected Writings of Edward Irving*. 5 vols. London: Alexander Strahan, 1864-5.

———. ed. *The Prophetical Works of Edward Irving*. 2 vols. London: Alexander Strahan, 1867-70.

Carlyle, T. *On Heroes, Hero-worship, and the Heroic in History*. New York: Wiley & Putnam, 1846.

———. *Reminiscences*. London: J M Dent, 1972 Orig. 1881.

Coburn, K. and M. Christensen, eds. *The Notebooks of Samuel Taylor Coleridge*. London: Routledge, 1990.

Coleridge, E.H. ed. *The Poems of Samuel Taylor Coleridge*. London: Oxford University Press, 1960.

Coleridge, H.N. ed. *The Literary Remains of Samuel Taylor Coleridge*. Vol. 3. London: William Pickering, 1838.

Coleridge, S.T., *On the Constitution of Church and State*. London, 1830.

Colmer, J. ed. *On the Constitution of the Church and State, The Collected Works of Samuel Taylor Coleridge*. London: Routledge & Kegan Paul, 1976.

Griggs, E.L. ed. *The Collected Letters of Samuel Taylor Coleridge*. Vol. v. Oxford: Clarendon, 1971.

Irving, E. *Babylon and Infidelity Foredoomed of God: a Discourse on the Prophecies of Daniel and the Apocalypse, which relate to these latter times*. 2nd ed. Philadelphia: Church Missionary House, 1828.

———. *The Coming of Messiah in Glory and Majesty, by Juan Josafat Ben-Ezra, a converted Jew: translated from the Spanish, with a preliminary discourse, by the Rev. Edward Irving*. 2 vols. London: L.B.Seeley & Son, 1827.

———. *The Confessions of Faith and the Books of Discipline of the Church of Scotland, of date anterior to the Westminster Confession. To which are prefixed a historical view of the Church of Scotland from the earliest period to the time of the Reformation, and a historial preface, with remarks*. London: Baldwin & Cradock, 1831.

———. *The Day of Pentecost or the Baptism with the Holy Ghost. A treatise in three parts*. London: Baldwin & Cradock, 1831.

———. *Exposition of the Book of Revelation, in a series of lectures*. 4 vols. London: Baldwin & Cradock, 1831.

———. *Farewell Discourse to the Congregation and Parish of St. John's, Glasgow*. Glasgow: Chalmers & Collins, 1822.

———. *For Missionaries after the Apostolical School: a series of Orations, in four parts*. London: Hamilton, Adams & Co., 1825.

———. *For the Oracles of God, four Orations, for Judgment to come, an Argument in nine parts*. New York: S. Marks, 1825.

———. "Introductory essay." In *The Life of Bernard Gilpin*, edited by W. Gilpin. Glasgow: William Collins, 1830.

———. *The Last Days: a Discourse on the evil character of these our times: proving them to be the 'Perilous Times' of the 'Last Days'*. London: James Nisbet, 1850.

———. *A Letter to the King, on the repeal of the Test and Corporation Laws, as it affects our Christian Monarchy*. London: James Nisbet, 1828.

———. *The Nature and Use of the Gift of Tongues as stated in the Scriptures*. Greenock: R.B.Lusk, 1829.

———. *The Orthodox and Catholic Doctrine of our Lord's Human Nature*. London: Baldwin & Cradock, 1830.

———. *Sermons, Lectures, and Occasional Discourses*. 3 vols. London: R.B. Seeley & W. Burnside, 1828.

Jackson, H.J. and G. Whalley, eds. *The Collected Works of Samuel Taylor Coleridge, Marginalia,* volume III. London: Routledge, 1992.

Whalley, G. ed. *Marginalia*. 5 vols. Vol. 1, *The Collected Works of Samuel Taylor Coleridge*. London: Routledge & Kegan Paul Ltd, 1980.

Woodring, C. ed. *Table Talk*. Vol. 1. London: Routledge, 1990.

Secondary sources

Abrams, M.H. *Natural Supernaturalism: Tradition and Revolution in Romantic Literature*. New York: Norton, 1971.

Allan, G. "A Theory of Millenialism: the Irvingite movement as an illustration." *British Journal of Sociology* 25, no. 3 (1974): 296-311.

Allen, D. "A Belated Bouquet: a tribute to Edward Irving (1792-1834)." *Expository Times* 103, August (1992): 328-331.

———. "Regent Square revisited: Edward Irving - precursor of the Pentecostal movement." *Journal of the European Pentecostal Theological Association* 17 (1997): 49-58.

———. "The significance of Edward Irving (1792-1834)." *Paraclete* 22 Fall (1988): 18-21.

Andrews, J.S. "Horatius Bonar." In *Dictionary of Scottish Church History and Theology*, edited by N. Cameron. Downers Grove, Ill: IVP, 1993.

Andrews, W.W. "Edward Irving." *The New Englander* 1863.

———. "Martin Luther and Edward Irving: their work and testimony compared." *The Hartford (U.S.) Daily Times*, 29 December 1883.

Anon. "A biographical sketch of Edward Irving." *Methodist Review* 31 (1849): 109-118.

Anon. *A Brief Statement of the Proceedings of the London Presbytery in communion with the established Church of Scotland in the case of the Rev. Edward Irving, and of a book, written by him, and entitled "The Orthodox and Catholic doctrine of our Lord's Human Nature"*. London: Basil Steuart, 1831.

Anson, P.F. "A Liturgical Backwater." *Orate Fratres* 22, no. 2 (1947): 62-66.

Armour, R.W. and R.F. Howes. *Coleridge the Talker*. New York & London: Johnson Reprint Corporation, 1969.

Ashton, R. *The Life of Samuel Taylor Coleridge: a Critical Biography*. Oxford: Blackwell Publishers, 1996.

———. *Thomas and Jane Carlyle: Portrait of a Marriage*. London: Chatto & Windus, 2002.

Badcock, G.D. "Christ and the Spirit: the Doctrine of the Incarnation according to Edward Irving." *Studies in World Christianity* 3, no. 2 (1997): 267-268.

Barth, J. R. *Coleridge and Christian Doctrine*. New York: Fordham University Press, 1987.

———. ed. *The Fountain Light: studies in Romanticism and Religion*. New York: Fordham University Press, 2002.

———. *Romanticism and Transcendence: Wordsworth, Coleridge, and the Religious Imagination*. Columbia: University of Missouri Press, 2003.

———. "Wordsworth's 'Immortality Ode' and Hopkins' 'The Leaden Echo and the Golden Echo': in pursuit of transcendence." In *The Fountain Light: studies in Romanticism and Religion: in honor of John L. Mahoney*, edited by J.R. Barth. New York: Fordham University Press, 2002.

Baxter, R. *Narrative of Facts, characterising the Supernatural Manifestations, in members of Mr. Irving's congregation, and other individuals, in England and Scotland, and in the writer himself*. London, 1833.

Bebbington, D.W. *The Dominance of Evangelicalism: the age of Spurgeon and Moody*. Downers Grove, Ill: Intervarsity Press, 2005.

———. "Evangelical Christianity and Romanticism." *Crux* 26, no. 1 (1990): 9-15.

———. *Evangelicalism in Modern Britain: a history from the 1730s to the 1980s*. London: Unwin Hyman, 1989.

———. "Romantic Apocalypses." In *Romanticism and Millenarianism*, edited by T. Fulford. New York: Palgrave, 2002.

Bellhouse, G.T. "Edward Irving." *The Regent Square Magazine*, December 1934.

Berlin, I. *The Roots of Romanticism*. Princeton: Princeton University Press, 1999.

———. *Political Ideas in the Romantic Age: their rise and influence on Modern Thought*. London: Chatto & Windus, 2006.

Berry, C.J. *Social Theory of the Scottish Enlightenment*. Edinburgh: Edinburgh University Press, 1997.

Berry, W.G. *Scotland's Struggles for Religious Liberty*. London: National Council of Evangelical Free Churches, 1904.

Billington, A., A. Lane, and M. Turner. *Mission and Meaning: essays presented to Peter Cotterell*. Carlisle: Paternoster Press, 1995.

Birks, T.R., ed. *Memoir of the Rev. Edward Bickersteth, late Rector of Watton, Herts.* 2 vols. Vol. 2. London: Seeleys, 1852.

Blaikie, W.G. *A Memoir of David Brown*. London, 1898.

Blaine, M.E. "Carlyle's Cromwell and the Virtue of the Inarticulate." *Carlyle Annual* 13 (1992): 77-88.

Bloom, H., ed. *Romanticism and Consciousness: essays in criticism*. New York: W.W. Norton & Co., 1970.

Boulger, J.D. *Coleridge as Religious Thinker*. New Haven: Yale University Press, 1961.

Brough, J.C.S. "Edward Irving, one hundred years after." *The Presbyterian Messenger* (1934).

———. "Regent Square and Edward Irving." In *The Centenary of Edward Irving*. London, 1927.

Brown, C.G. "Religion and Social Change." In *People and Society in Scotland, 1760-1830*, edited by T.M. Devine and R. Mitchison. Edinburgh: John Donald Publishers, 1988.

———. *Religion and Society in Scotland since 1707*. Edinburgh: Edinburgh University Press, 1997.

Brown, M. "Romanticism and Enlightenment." In *The Cambridge Companion to British Romanticism*, edited by S. Curran. Cambridge: Cambridge University Press, 1993.

Brown, R. "Victorian Anglican Evangelicalism: the radical legacy of Edward Irving." *Journal of Ecclesiastical History* 58, no. 4 (2007): 675-704.

Brown, S.J. *The National Churches of England, Ireland and Scotland, 1801-46*. Oxford: Oxford University Press, 2001.

———. *Thomas Chalmers and the Godly Commonwealth in Scotland*. Oxford: Oxford University Press, 1982.

Burdon, C. *The Apocalypse in England: Revelation Unravelling, 1700-1834*. Basingstoke, Hampshire: Palgrave Macmillan, 1997.

Burwick, F. "Coleridge and De Quincey on Miracles." In *The Fountain Light: studies in Romanticism and Religion: in honor of John L. Mahoney*, edited by J.R. Barth. New York Fordham University Press, 2002.

Butler, P. "Irvingism as an Analogue of the Oxford Movement." *Church History* 6, no. 2 (1937): 101-112.

Cage, R.A., ed. *The Working Class in Glasgow, 1750-1914*. London: Croom Helm, 1987.

Calder, G.J. "Carlyle and Irving's 'London circle': some unpublished letters by Thomas Carlyle and Mrs. Edward Strachey." *Proceedings of the Modern Language Association* 69, no. 5 (1954): 1135-1149.

Cameron, G.G. *The Scots Kirk in London*. Oxford: Becket Publications, 1979.

Campbell, D., ed. *Memorials of John McLeod Campbell*. London: Macmillan & Co, 1877.

Campbell, J.D. *Samuel Taylor Coleridge: a narrative of the events of his life*. London: Macmillan and Co., 1894.

Cardale, J.B. "On the Extraordinary Manifestations in Port-Glasgow." *The Morning Watch* (1830).

Carlyle, C.B. "Fanaticism in the Church of England." *Methodist Quarterly Review* 35, no. 1 (1892): 49-62.

Carruthers, G., and A. Rawes, eds. *English Romanticism and the Celtic world*. Cambridge: Cambridge University Press, 2003.

Carter, G. *Anglican Evangelicals: Protestant Secessions from the via media, c. 1800-1850*. Oxford: Oxford University Press, 2001.

Chambers, D. "Doctrinal attitudes in the Church of Scotland in the pre-disruption era: the age of John McLeod Campbell and Edward Irving." *Journal of Religious History [Australia]* 8 (1974): 159-182.

Chandler, J. "History." In *An Oxford Companion to the Romantic Age: British culture 1776-1832*, edited by I. McCalman. Oxford: Oxford University Press, 1999.

Cheyne, A.C. *The Transforming of the Kirk: Victorian Scotland's Religious Revolution*. Edinburgh: The Saint Andrew Press, 1983.

Christenson, L. "Pentecostalism's Forgotten Forerunner." In *Aspects of Pentecostal-Charismatic Origins*, edited by V. Synan, 15-37. Plainfield, New Jersey: Logos International, 1975.

Clark, J.C.D. *English Society 1660-1832*. 2nd ed. Cambridge: Cambridge University Press, 2000.

Clubbe, J., ed. *Froude's Life of Carlyle*. London: John Murray, 1979.

Clubbe, J., and E.J. Lovell. *English Romanticism: the grounds of belief*. DeKalb, Ill: Northern Illinois University Press, 1983.

Cochrane, R. *Teachers and Preachers of recent times*. Edinburgh: W.P. Nimmo, Hay & Mitchell, 1886.

Coghill, H., ed. *Autobiography and Letters of Mrs Margaret Oliphant*. Leicester: Leicester University Press, 1974.

Craig, C. "Coleridge, Hume and the chains of the Romantic Imagination." In *Scotland and the Borders of Romanticism*, edited by L. Davis, I. Duncan and J. Sorensen. Cambridge: Cambridge University Press, 2004.

Crisp, O.D. *Divinity and Humanity*. Cambridge: Cambridge University Press, 2007.

Curran, S., ed. *The Cambridge Companion to British Romanticism*. Cambridge: Cambridge University Press, 1993.

Curry, D. "The life of Edward Irving." *Methodist Review* 45 (1863): 5-29.

Dallimore, A. *The Life of Edward Irving: the Fore-runner of the Charismatic Movement*. Edinburgh: Banner of Truth, 1983.

Davenport, R.A. *Albury Apostles: the story of the body known as the Catholic Apostolic Church*. London: United Writers, 1970.

Davie, M. "Christ and the Spirit: the Doctrine of the Incarnation according to Edward Irving." *European Journal of Theology* 8, no. 1 (1999): 106-107.

Davies, P.E. "An Examination of the views of Edward Irving concerning the Person and Work of Jesus Christ." New College, 1928.

Davies, H., *Worship and Theology in England: from Watts and Wesley to Martineau, 1690-1900.* Grand Rapids, MI: Eerdman's, 1996.

Davis, L., I. Duncan, and J. Sorensen, eds. *Scotland and the Borders of Romanticism*. Cambridge: Cambridge University Press, 2004.

De Matos, A.S. "Edward Irving: Precursor do Movimento Carismatico na igreja Reformada." *Fides-Reformata* 1 (1996): 5-12.

de Quincey, T. *Literary Reminiscences from the Autobiography of an English opium-eater*. Vol. 2. Boston: Ticknor, Reed, and Fields, 1854.

Devine, T.M., and R. Mitchison, eds. *People and Society in Scotland, 1760-1830*. Vol. 1. Edinburgh: John Donald, 1988.

Devine, T.M., and J.R. Young, eds. *Eighteenth Century Scotland: New Perspectives*. East Linton: Tuckwell Press, 1999.

Dixon, L.E. "Have the 'Jewels of the Church' been found again: the Irving-Darby debate on Miraculous Gifts." *Evangelical Journal* 5, no. 2 (1987): 78-92.

Dorries, D.W. "Edward Irving and the 'Standing Sign' of Spirit Baptism." In *Initial Evidence: Historical and Biblical Perspectives on the Pentecostal Doctrine of Spirit Baptism*, edited by G.B. McGee. Peabody, MASS: Hendrickson Publishers, 1991.

———. "Edward Irving: the Forgotten Giant." *Evangelical Quarterly* 59, no. 2 (1987): 183-185.

———. *Edward Irving's Incarnational Christology*: Xulon Press, 2002.

———. "Nineteenth century British Christological Controversy, centring upon Edward Irving's Doctrine of Christ's Human Nature." PhD, University of Aberdeen, 1987.

Drummond, A.L. *Edward Irving and his Circle*. Cambridge: James Clarke, 1934.

———. "Edward Irving and the Gift of Tongues: an Historical and Psychological study." PhD, New College, 1930.

———. "Edward Irving, rise and fall of a Prophet, martyrdom by mistake." *The Times*, 7 December 1934.

Drummond, A.L., and J. Bulloch. *The Scottish Church, 1688-1843: the Age of the Moderates*. Edinburgh: The Saint Andrew Press, 1973.

Drummond, H., ed. *Dialogues on Prophecy*. Vol. 1-3. London, 1827-29.

Dunton, H. "Millennial hopes and fears: Great Britain, 1780-1960." *Andrews University Seminary Studies* 37, no. 2 (1999): 179-208.

Dyer, A.S. "The Irvingites, or the Catholic Apostolic Church" In *Sketches of English Nonconformity*: Mowbray, 1904.

Edwards, D.L. *Christian England: from the 18th century to the First World War*. Vol. 3. London: Collins, 1985.

Elliott, P. "Edward Irving's hybrid: towards a nineteenth-century apostolic and Presbyterian Pentecostalism." In the forthcoming (provisionally titled) *Religious Leadership* (Brill, 2012)

______ "Nineteenth century Australian charismata: Edward Irving's legacy." In *Pneuma* Volume 34, no. 1 (2012)

Erskine, T. *The Brazen Serpent, or Life Coming through Death*. Edinburgh, 1831.

———. *Letters*. Edited by W. Hanna. Edinburgh, 1878.

———. *On the Gifts of the Holy Spirit*. Greenock, 1830.

Ferber, M., ed. *A Companion to European Romanticism*. Oxford: Blackwell Publishing, 2005.

Findlater, J. "The Propaganda of Futurism." *Evangelical Quarterly* 9, no. 2 (1937): 169-179.

Fitzpatrick, M. "Enlightenment." In *An Oxford Companion to the Romantic Age: British Culture 1776-1832*, edited by I. McCalman. Oxford: Oxford University Press, 1999.

Flegg, C.G. *"Gathered under Apostles": a study of the Catholic Apostolic Church*. Oxford: Clarendon Press, 1992.

Flikkema, B. *Edward Irving: a bibliography*. Appingedam, Netherlands, 1997.

Froude, J.A. *Thomas Carlyle: a History of the First Forty Years of his Life, 1795-1835*. 2 vols. Vol. 1. London: Longmans, Green, & Co., 1882.

Fruman, N. *Coleridge, the Damaged Archangel*. London: Allen & Unwin, 1972.

Fulford, T., ed. *Romanticism and Millenarianism*. New York: Palgrave, 2002.

Garnett, J., and C. Matthew, eds. *Revival and Religion since 1700: essays for John Walsh*. London: Hambledon, 1993.

Garrett, C. *Respectable Folly: Millenarians and the French Revolution in France and England*. Baltimore, ML: John Hopkins University Press, 1975.

Gibb, A. *Glasgow: The Making of a City*. London: Croom Helm, 1983.

Gilfillan, G. *A First Gallery of Literary Portraits*. Edinburgh: James Hogg, 1851.

Gilley, S. "Edward Irving: Prophet of the Millennium." In *Revival and Religion since 1700: essays for John Walsh*, edited by J. Garnett and C. Matthew, 95-110. London: Hambledon, 1993.

Gould, B. "Irving, Carlyle and the Apostolic Church in Birmingham." *Journal of the Presbyterian Historical Society of England* 14, no. 5 (1972): 201-205.

Gouldstone, T.M. *The Rise and Decline of Anglican Idealism in the Nineteenth Century*. Basingstoke, Hampshire: Palgrave Macmillan, 2005.

Graham, W. "Edward Irving and James Hamilton." *United Presbyterian Magazine* (1879).

Grass, T. *The Lord's Watchman: Edward Irving*. Milton Keynes: Paternoster, 2011.

———. "'The Taming of the Prophets': Bringing Prophecy under Control in the Catholic Apostolic Church." *Journal of the European Pentecostal Theological Association* xvi (1996).

Green, G. *Imagining God: Theology and the Religious Imagination*. Grand Rapids, MI: Eerdmans, 1998.

Gribben, C. *The Puritan Millennium: Literature and Theology, 1550-1682*. Milton Keynes: Paternoster, 2008.

Gunton, C.E. *The Actuality of Atonement: a study of Metaphor, Rationality and the Christian Tradition*. Edinburgh: T & T Clark, 2004.

———. *The One, the Three and the Many: God, Creation and the Culture of Modernity*. Cambridge: Cambridge University Press, 1993.

———. *The Promise of Trinitarian Theology*. Edinburgh: T & T Clark, 2004.

———. "The Triune God and the Freedom of the Creature." In *Karl Barth: Centenary Essays*, edited by S.W. Sykes. Cambridge: Cambridge University Press, 1989.

———. "Two dogmas revisited: Edward Irving's Christology." *Scottish Journal of Theology* 41, no. 3 (1988): 359-376.

Haakonsen, K. "Scottish Enlightenment." In *An Oxford Companion to the Romantic Age: British Culture 1776-1832*, edited by I. McCalman. Oxford: Oxford University Press, 1999.

Hair, J. *Regent Square: Eighty Years of a London Congregation*. London: James Nisbet & Co., 1899.

Hanna, W., ed. *Memoirs of Thomas Chalmers*. 2 vols. Edinburgh: Thomas Constable, 1854.

Hanson, L. and E. Hanson. *Necessary Evil: the Life of Jane Welsh Carlyle*. London: Constable, 1952.

Harding, W. *The Trial of the Rev. Edward Irving, M.A., before the London Presbytery; containing the whole of the evidence: exact copies of the documents; verbatim report of the speeches and opinions of the Presbyters, etc; being the only authentic and complete record of the proceedings taken in short-hand.* London: W. Harding, 1832.

Harrison, J.F.C. *Robert Owen and the Owenites in Britain and America: the quest for the new moral world*. London: Routledge & Kegan Paul, 1969.

———. *The Second Coming: Popular Millenarianism 1780-1850*. London: Routledge & Kegan Paul, 1979.

Haykin, M.A.G., and K.J. Stewart, eds. *The Emergence of Evangelicalism: Exploring Historical Continuities*. Nottingham: Apollos, 2008.

Hazlitt, W. *The Spirit of the Age*. Oxford: Woodstock Books, 1989.

Heady, C. "'The Last and Perilous times of the Gentile Dispensation': Edward Irving's *The Last Days* and the conversion of the Jewish conversion trope." *Prose Studies* 25, no. 3 (2002): 41-57.

Heffer, S. *Moral Desperado: a Life of Thomas Carlyle*. London: Weidenfeld and Nicolson, 1995.

Hilton, B. *The Age of Atonement: the Influence of Evangelicalism on Social and Economic Thought, 1785-1865*. Oxford: Clarendon Press, 1988.

———. *A Mad, Bad, and Dangerous People?: England, 1783-1846*. Oxford: Oxford University Press, 2006.

Hogan, T. "The Religion of Thomas Carlyle." In *Reinventing Christianity: Nineteenth century contexts*, edited by L. Woodhead, 149-162. Aldershot: Ashgate, 2001.

Hole, R. *Pulpits, Politics, and Public Order in England, 1760-1832*. Cambridge: Cambridge University Press, 1989.

Holmes, R. *Coleridge: Darker Reflections*. London: Harper Perennial, 2005.

Hook, A., and R.B. Sher, eds. *The Glasgow Enlightenment*. East Linton, Scotland: Tuckwell Press, 1995.

Hopkins, M. *Nonconformity's Romantic Generation: Evangelical and Liberal Theologies in Victorian England*. Carlisle: Paternoster Press, 2004.

Hopps, G. and J. Stabler, eds. *Romanticism and Religion from William Cowper to Wallace Stevens*. Aldershot: Ashgate, 2006.

House, H. *Coleridge: the Clark Lectures 1951-52*. London: Rupert Hart-Davis, 1967.

Houston, R.A., and I.D. Whyte, eds. *Scottish Society 1500-1800*. Cambridge: Cambridge University Press, 1989.

Hulme, T.E. *Speculations: Essays on Humanism and the Philosophy of Art*. London: Routledge & Kegan Paul, 1971.

Hunt, S. ed. *Christian Millenarianism: from the Early Church to Waco*. London: Hurst & Company, 2001.

Hylson-Smith, K. *Evangelicals in the Church of England, 1734-1984*. Edinburgh: T & T Clark, 1989.

Jasper, D. *The Sacred and Secular Canon in Romanticism: Preserving the Sacred Truths*. London: Macmillan Press, 1999.

Jay, E., *Mrs Oliphant: a Fiction to Herself. A Literary Life.* Oxford: Clarendon Press, 1995.

Jones, T.E. *The Broad Church: a Biography of a Movement*. Lanham, Maryland: Lexington Books, 2003.

Jones, W. *A Biographical Sketch of Rev. Edward Irving, A.M.* London: Bennett, 1835.

Kaplan, F. *Thomas Carlyle: a Biography*. Cambridge: Cambridge University Press, 1983.

Kearsley, R. "Christ and the Spirit: the Doctrine of the Incarnation according to Edward Irving." *Scottish Bulletin of Evangelical Theology* 20, no. 1 (2002): 109-110.

King, N. *The Romantics: English Literature in its Historical, Cultural and Social Contexts*. London: Evans Brothers, 2003.

Kirby, T.A. "Carlyle and Irving." *English Literary History* 13, no. 1 (1946): 59-63.

Kitson Clark, G.S.R. "The Romantic Element: 1830-1850." In *Studies in Social History: a tribute to G.M. Trevelyan*, edited by J.H. Plumb. London, 1955.

Knox, R. *Enthusiasm: a Chapter in the History of Religion*. Oxford, 1950.
Knox, R.B. "Edward Irving." *Outlook* (1971).
Knox, W. *Industrial Nation: Work, Culture and Society in Scotland, 1800-present*. Edinburgh: Edinburgh University Press, 1999.
Landels, W. *Edward Irving*. London, 1864.
Landsman, N.C. "Liberty, Piety and Patronage: the social context of contested clerical calls in Eighteenth-century Glasgow." In *The Glasgow Enlightenment*, edited by A. Hook and R.B. Sher. East Linton, Scotland: Tuckwell Press, 1995.
Larsen, T. "The reception given *Evangelicalism in Modern Britain* since its publication in 1989." In *The Emergence of Evangelicalism: exploring historical continuities*, edited by M.A.G. Haykin and K.J. Stewart. Nottingham: Apollos, 2008.
LaValley, A.J. *Carlyle and the Idea of the Modern*: Yale, 1968.
Lee, D.Y.T. "The Humanity of Christ and the Church in the teaching of Edward Irving." PhD, Brunel, 2003.
Leighton, C.D.A. "Antichrist's revolution: some Anglican apocalypticists in the age of the French wars." *Journal of Religious History* xxiv, no. 2 (2000): 125-142.
Lenman, B. *Integration, Enlightenment, and Industrialization: Scotland 1746-1832*. London: Edward Arnold, 1981.
Lively, R.L. "Bodleian sources for the study of two Nineteenth-century Millenarian movements in Britain." *Bodleian Library Record* 13, no. 6 (1991): 491-500.
Long, A. "Christ and the Spirit: the Doctrine of the Incarnation according to Edward Irving." *Faith and Freedom* 51, Aut-Wint (1998): 170-174.
Lorimer, P. "Edward Irving, a review of *The Collected Writings of Edward Irving*." *The United Presbyterian Magazine*, no. October (1865).
Lovejoy, A.O. *Essays in the History of Ideas*. Baltimore, ML: Johns Hopkins Press, 1970.
Low, L., and A.J. Harding, eds. *Milton, the Metaphysicals, and Romanticism*. Cambridge: Cambridge University Press, 1994.
Lucas, E.V. *The Life of Charles Lamb*. Vol. 2. London: Methuen & co, 1905.
Machin, G.I.T. "Resistance to repeal of the Test and Corporation Acts, 1828." *Historical Journal* 22, March (1979): 115-139.
Mackintosh, H.R. *The Doctrine of the Person of Jesus Christ*. Edinburgh: T & T Clark, 1912.
Macleod, D. "The Doctrine of the Incarnation in Scottish Theology." *Scottish Bulletin of Evangelical Theology* 9, Spring (1991): 40-50.
Macleod, J. "Edward Irving and his Circle." *Evangelical Quarterly* 10, no. 2 (1938): 215-218.
Manwaring, R. "The Life of Edward Irving: the Fore-runner of the Charismatic Movement." *Churchman* 98, no. 1 (1984): 78.
Marrat, J. "Edward Irving." In *Northern Lights*. London, 1885.
Martin, J.S. "Martin Howy Irving: Professor, Headmaster, Public Servant." University of Melbourne, 2006.

Mayor, S.H. "The Pentecostal Theology of Edward Irving." *Expository Times* 85, April (1974): 220-221.
McCalman, I., ed. *An Oxford Companion to the Romantic Age: British Culture 1776-1832*. Oxford: Oxford University Press, 1999.
———. *Radical Underworld: Prophets, Revolutionaries and Pornographers in London, 1795-1840*. Cambridge: Cambridge University Press, 1988.
McFarlane, G. *Christ and the Spirit: the Doctrine of the Incarnation according to Edward Irving*. Carlisle: Paternoster Press, 1996.
———. "Christology and the Spirit in the teaching of Edward Irving." PhD, King's College, 1990.
———. "Edward Irving and the uniqueness of Christ." In *Mission and Meaning*, edited by A. Billington, A. Lane and M. Turner, 217-229. Carlisle: Paternoster Press, 1995.
———. *Edward Irving: the Trinitarian Face of God*. Edinburgh: St Andrew's Press, 1996.
———. "Strange news from another star: an Anthropological insight from Edward Irving." In *Persons, Divine and Human*, edited by C. Schwobel and C.E. Gunton. Edinburgh: T & T Clark, 1991.
———. "The strange tongue of a long lost Christianity: the Spirit and the Trinity." *Vox Evangelica* 22 (1992): 63-70.
McGee, G.B., ed. *Initial Evidence: Historical and Biblical Perspectives on the Pentecostal Doctrine of Spirit Baptism*. Peabody, MASS: Hendrickson Publishers, 1991.
McGowan, A.T.B. "Christ and the Spirit: the Doctrine of the Incarnation according to Edward Irving." *Evangel* 17, no. 3 (1999): 98-99.
———. "The Trinitarian Face of God." *Scottish Bulletin of Evangelical Theology* 17, Spring (1999): 55-56.
McIntosh, J.R. *Church and Theology in Enlightenment Scotland: the Popular Party, 1740-1800*. East Lothian: Tuckwell Press, 1998.
McIntyre, J. "Christ and the Spirit: the Doctrine of the Incarnation according to Edward Irving." *Expository Times* 108, August (1997): 346-347.
McKusick, J.C. "David Vallins: Coleridge and the Psychology of Romanticism: feeling and thought." *Studies in Romanticism*, no. Winter (2002).
Mee, J. "Anxieties of Enthusiasm: Coleridge, Prophecy, and Popular Politics in the 1790s." *Huntington Library Quarterly* 60, no. 1-2 (1998): 179-203.
———. *Romanticism, Enthusiasm, and Regulation: Poetics and the Policing of Culture in the Romantic Period*. Oxford: Oxford University Press, 2003.
Meldrum, P. *Conscience and Compromise: Forgotten Evangelicals of Nineteenth-century Scotland*. Carlisle: Paternoster, 2006.
Merricks, W.S. *Edward Irving: the Forgotten Giant*. East Peoria, Illinois: Scribe's Chamber Publications, 1983.
Miller, E. *The History and Doctrines of Irvingism*. London: Kegan Paul, 1878.
Miller, F. "Edward Irving and Annan." *Records of the Scottish Church History Society* 4 (1930-32): 87-92.

———. *Poems from the Carlyle country: together with papers on two of Carlyle's early friends and some fragments in prose*. Glasgow: Jackson son & Co., 1937.

Mulvihill, J. "The Reverend Edward Irving and London pulpit popularity." *Nineteenth Century* 14 (1990).

Murray, I. *The Puritan Hope: a Study in Revival and the Interpretation of Prophecy*. London: Banner of Truth, 1971.

Najarian, J. "Edward Irving (1792-1834)." In *Encyclopedia of Romanticism: Culture in Britain, 1780s-1830s*, edited by L. Dabundo. New York & London: Garland Publishing Inc., 1992.

Nantomah, J.J. "Jesus the God-man: the Doctrine of the Incarnation in Edward Irving in the light of the teaching of the Church Fathers and its relevance for a twentieth century African context." PhD, Aberdeen, 1982.

Newlands, G.M. "Christ and the Spirit: the Doctrine of the Incarnation according to Edward Irving." *Journal of Theological Studies* 49, April (1998): 473-475.

Newlyn, L., ed. *The Cambridge Companion to Coleridge*. Cambridge: Cambridge University Press, 2002.

Nicol, J. *Thomas Carlyle*. Charleston, SC: Bibliolife, 2008.

Nockles, P.B. *The Oxford Movement in Context: Anglican High Churchmanship, 1760-1857*. Cambridge: Cambridge University Press, 1994.

Norton, R. *Memoirs of James and George Macdonald of Port-Glasgow*. London, 1840.

———. *The Restoration of the Apostles and Prophets in the Catholic Apostolic Church*. London, 1861.

Oliphant, M. *The Life of Edward Irving*. 5th ed. London: Hurst & Blackett, 1862 orig.

Oliver, W.H. *Prophets and Millennialists: the uses of Biblical Prophecy in England from the 1790s to the 1840s*. Auckland: Auckland Univeristy Press, 1978.

Orchard, S.C. "English Evangelical Eschatology 1790-1850." Cambridge University, 1969.

Otto, P. "Sublime." In *An Oxford Companion to the Romantic Age: British Culture 1776-1832*, edited by I. McCalman. Oxford: Oxford University Press, 1999.

Paley, M.D. *Apocalypse and Millennium in English Romantic Poetry*. Oxford: Clarendon Press, 1999.

Patterson, M. "Designing the Last Days: Edward Irving, the Albury Circle, and the theology of The Morning Watch." PhD, King's College, 2001.

Patterson, M., and A. Walker. "'Our unspeakable comfort': Irving, Albury, and origins of the Pretribulation Rapture." *Fides et Historia* 31, Wint-Spr (1999): 66-81.

Patterson, M. & Walker, A. "'Our unspeakable comfort': Irving, Albury, and the origins of the Pre-tribulation Rapture." In *Christian*

Millenarianism: from the Early Church to Waco, edited by S. Hunt. London: Hurst & Company, 2001.

Paul, C.K. “Edward Irving.” In *Biographical Sketches*. London: Kegan Paul, Trench & Co, 1883.

Perkins, M.A. “Religious thinker.” In *The Cambridge Companion to Coleridge*, edited by L. Newlyn. Cambridge: Cambridge University Press, 2002.

Persky, J. “Retrospectives: a Dismal Romantic.” *Journal of Economic Perspectives* 4, no. 4 (1990): 165-172.

Pilkington, G. *The Unknown Tongues discovered to be English, Spanish and Latin*. London, 1831.

Plumb, J.H., ed. *Studies in Social History: a tribute to G.M. Trevelyan*. London, 1955.

Pope, R. *Religion and National Identity: Wales and Scotland c. 1700-2000*. Cardiff: University of Wales Press, 2001.

Poston, L. “Millites and Millenarians: the context of Carlyle’s *Signs of the Times*.” *Victorian Studies* 26, no. 4 (1983): 381-406.

Prickett, S. *Origins of Narrative: the Romantic Appropriation of the Bible*. Cambridge: Cambridge University Press, 1996.

———. “The Religious context.” In *The Romantics*, edited by S. Prickett. New York: Holmes & Meier, 1981.

———. *Romanticism and Religion: the Tradition of Coleridge and Wordsworth in the Victorian Church*. Cambridge: Cambridge University Press, 1976.

———, ed. *The Romantics*. New York: Holmes & Meier, 1981.

Purves, J. “The interaction of Christology and Pneumatology in the Soteriology of Edward Irving.” *Pneuma* 14, Spring (1992): 81-90.

Pym, D. *The Religious Thought of Samuel Taylor Coleridge*. Gerrards Cross: Colin Smythe, 1978.

Pym, H.N. ed. *Memories of Old Friends. Being Extracts from the Journals and Letters of Caroline Fox of Penjerrick, Cornwall, from 1835 to 1871*. Philadelphia: J.B. Lippincott & Co, 1882.

Reardon, B.M.G. *From Coleridge to Gore: a Century of Religious Thought in Britain*. Longman, 1971.

———. “Religion and the Romantic movement.” *Theology* lxxvi, no. 638 (1973): 403-416.

———. *Religion in the Age of Romanticism: studies in early Nineteenth Century Thought*. Cambridge: Cambridge University Press, 1985.

———. *Religious Thought in the Victorian Age: a Survey from Coleridge to Gore*. London: Longman, 1980.

Reid, J.K.S. “Blinded Eagle: an Introduction to the Life and Teaching of Edward Irving.” *Scottish Journal of Theology* 8, no. D (1955): 442-443.

Rennick, A. “Silence and Masculinity in Carlyle’s *Reminiscences*.” *Nineteenth Century Prose* 26, no. 2 (1999): 53-62.

Ritchie, J.E. *The London Pulpit*. London, 1854.

Robinson, H.C. *Diary, Reminiscences and Correspondence*. 2nd ed. 3 vols. London: Macmillan, 1869.

Root, J.C. *Edward Irving: Man, Preacher, Prophet*. Boston: Sherman, French & Co, 1912.

Ryan, R.M. *The Romantic Reformation: Religious Politics in English Literature, 1789-1824*. Cambridge: Cambridge University Press, 1997.

Sadler, T. ed. *Diary, Reminiscences and Correspondence of Henry Crabb Robinson*. 3 vols. Vol. 2. London: Macmillan & co, 1869.

Sandeen, E.R. *The Roots of Fundamentalism*. Chicago: University of Chicago Press, 1970.

Sanders, C.R. *Coleridge and the Broad Church Movement*. New York: Octagon Books, 1972.

Saunders, L.J., *Scottish Democracy 1815-1840: the Social and Intellectual Background.* Edinburgh: Oliver & Boyd, 1950.

Sayre, R. and M. Lowy. "Romanticism and Capitalism." In *A Companion to European Romanticism*, edited by M. Ferber. Oxford: Blackwell Publishing, 2005.

Schwobel, C.and C.E. Gunton. *Persons, Divine and Human: King's College Essays in Theological Anthropology*. Edinburgh: T & T Clark, 1991.

Shea, F.X. "Religion and the Romantic Movement." *Studies in Romanticism* ix (1970).

Sher, R.B. *Church and University in the Scottish Enlightenment: the Moderate Literati of Edinburgh*. Princeton, N.J.: Princeton University Press, 1985.

Simpson, D. "Romanticism, Criticism and Theory." In *The Cambridge Companion to British Romanticism*, edited by S. Curran. Cambridge: Cambridge University Press, 1993.

Simpson, R. *Traditions of the Covenanters; or, Gleanings among the Mountains*. Edinburgh: Gall and Inglis, n.d.

Soderstrom, J. "Escaping the common lot: a Buchanite perspective of the Millennium." In *The Use and Abuse of Time in Christian History*, edited by R.N. Swanson. Woodbridge, Suffolk: Ecclesiastical History Society, 2002.

Stafford, F. "Scottish Romanticism and Scotland in Romanticism." In *A Companion to European Romanticism*, edited by M. Ferber. Oxford: Blackwell Publishing, 2005.

Stafford, J. K. "Richard Hooker's doctrine of the Holy Spirit." University of Manitoba, 2005.

Stevenson, D. *The Covenanters: the National Covenant and Scotland.* Stirling: The Saltire Society, 1988.

Stevenson, K.W. "The Catholic Apostolic Church: its History and its Eucharist." *Studia liturgica* 13, no. 1 (1979): 21-45.

Stewart, H.L. "Carlyle's Conception of Religion." *The American Journal of Theology* 21, no. 1 (1917): 43-57.

Stewart, K.J. *Restoring the Reformation: British Evangelicalism and the Francophone 'Reveil' 1816-1849*. Milton Keynes: Paternoster, 2006.

Story, R. *Memoir of the Life of the Rev. Robert Story*. Cambridge, Macmillan, 1862.

———. *Peace in Believing: a Memoir of Isabella Campbell of Fernicarry, Rosneath, Dunbartonshire*. Greenock, 1829.

———. *St Giles Lectures, third series, Scottish divines, lecture viii*. Edinburgh, 1883.

Strachan, G. "Edward Irving and Regent Square: a Presbyterian Pentecost." *Journal of the Presbyterian Historical Society of England* 14, no. 5 (1972): 186-195.

———. *The Pentecostal Theology of Edward Irving*. London: Darton, Longman & Todd, 1973.

———. "Theological and Cultural origins of the Nineteenth century Pentecostal movement." In *Essays on Apostolic themes*, edited by P. Elbert, 144-157. Peabody, Massachusetts: Hendrickson Publishers, 1985.

Stunt, T.C.F. *From Awakening to Secession: Radical Evangelicals in Switzerland and Britain 1815-35*. Edinburgh: T & T Clark, 2000.

———. "Trying the spirits: Irvingite signs and the test of doctrine." In *Signs, Wonders, Miracles: representations of Divine power in the life of the Church*, edited by K. & Gregory Cooper, J. Woodbridge: The Boydell Press, 2005.

———. "'Trying the spirits': the case of the Gloucestershire clergyman (1831)." *Journal of Ecclesiastical History* 39, no. 1 (1988): 95-105.

Sutherland, M. "Preaching as Truth: the Religious Epistemology of Edward Irving." *Colloquium* 36, no. 1 (2004): 3-19.

Swaim, B. "'Our own Periodical Pulpit': Thomas Carlyle's Sermons." *Christianity and Literature* 52, no. 12 (2003).

Sykes, S.W., ed. *Karl Barth: Centenary Essays*. Cambridge: Cambridge University Press, 1989.

Symonds, J. *Thomas Brown and the Angels: a Study in Enthusiasm*. London: Hutchinson & Co., 1961.

Todd, M. *The Culture of Protestantism in Early Modern Scotland.* New Haven: Yale University Press, 2002.

Torrance, T.F. *The Incarnation: Ecumenical Studies in the Nicene-Constantinopolitan Creed A.D. 381*. Edinburgh: The Handsel Press Ltd, 1981.

Trench, M. ed. *Richard Chevenix Trench, Archbishop: Letters and Memorials*. 2 vols. Vol. 1. London: Kegan Paul, Trench & Co., 1888.

Tulloch, J. *Movements of Religious Thought in Britain during the Nineteenth Century*. Leicester: Leicester University Press, 1971. Orig.1885.

Upton, L. "'Our Mother and our Country': the Integration of Religious and National Identity in the Thought of Edward Irving (1792-1834)." In *Religion and National Identity: Wales and Scotland c.1700-2000*, edited by R. Pope, 242-267. Cardiff: University of Wales Press, 2001.

Van-Dyk, L. "Christ and the Spirit: the Doctrine of the Incarnation according to Edward Irving." *Calvin Theological Journal* 32, no. N (1997): 510-511.

Viereck, P. *Conservative Thinkers from John Adams to Winston Churchill*. New Brunswick: Transaction Publishers, 2006.

Walker, A. *Restoring the Kingdom*. Guildford: Eagle, 1998.

Walker, N.L. "The trials of Irving and Campbell of Row." *The British and Foreign Evangelical Review*, April (1867).

Ward, J. "Christ and the Spirit: the Doctrine of the Incarnation according to Edward Irving." *Journal of the European Pentecostal Theological Association* 20 (2000): 143-145.

Warfield, B.B. *Counterfeit Miracles*: Scribner, 1918.

Weinandy, T.G. *In the Likeness of Sinful Flesh*. London: T & T Clark, 2006.

Wendling, R.C. *Coleridge's Progress to Christianity: Experience and Authority in Religious Faith*. London: Bucknell University Press, 1996.

Whale, J. *Imagination under Pressure, 1789-1832: Aesthetics, Politics and Utility*. Cambridge: Cambridge University Press, 2000.

Whitley, H.C. *Blinded Eagle: an introduction to the life and teaching of Edward Irving*. Chicago: A.R. Allenson, 1955.

———. "Edward Irving: an interpretation of his life and theological teaching." PhD, University of Edinburgh, 1953.

Wilks, W. *Edward Irving: an Ecclesiastical and Literary Biography*. London: W. Freeman, 1854.

Willey, B. *Nineteenth century studies: Coleridge to Matthew Arnold*. London: Chatto & Windus, 1955.

Wilson, D.A. *Carlyle till Marriage (1795-1826)*. London: Kegan Paul, Trench, Trubner & Co., 1923.

Withers, C.W.J. *Urban Highlanders: Highland-Lowland migration and urban Gaelic culture, 1700-1900*. East Linton: Tuckwell Press, 1998.

Wolffe, J. *The Protestant Crusade in Great Britain, 1829-1860*. Oxford: Clarendon Press, 1991.

Woodhead, L. ed. *Reinventing Christianity: Nineteenth Century Contexts*. Aldershot: Ashgate, 2001.

Worsfold, J.E. *A History of the Charismatic Movements in New Zealand*. Bradford: Puritan Press, 1974.

Worthen, J. "In bed with Sara Hutchinson." *The Cambridge Quarterly* 28, no. 3 (1999): 232-248.

Wright, R.S. ed. *Fathers of the Kirk: some Leaders of the Church in Scotland from the Reformation to the Reunion*. London: Oxford University Press, 1960.

Author Index

Subject Index

ND - #0088 - 090625 - C0 - 229/152/13 - PB - 9781842277836 - Gloss Lamination